'Can I have a Word Boss?

They're expecting that parcel to come in on Saturday...'

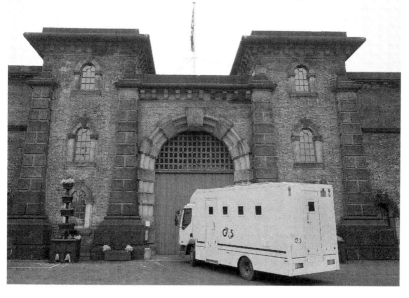

Forty Years in Her Majesty's Prison Service

Phil O'Brien

This edition published in Great Britain 2018 by

Farthings Publishing,
8 Christine House,
1 Avenue Victoria,
Scarborough YO11 2QB

http://www.farthings-publishing.com

ISBN 978-0-244-10871-7

September 2018 (f)

Dedication

This book is dedicated to my wife and family who had to live with the tensions of my job.

Acknowledgements

The contents of this book stem from memories of the many staff and prisoners with whom I have worked over many years. I would particularly like to thank all those I have mentioned in print; those whose inspiration, thoughts and support have had a direct impact which led to me writing this book. The Ministry of Justice has been made aware of this publication.

I also acknowledge 'The Who', some of whose lyrics I quote in this book.

Author's Note

Various names, nicknames, times, dates and identifying personal characteristics have been changed and some characters have been changed and some created as a composite of several people.
A Glossary explaining abbreviations used in this book appears after the Contents page.

Contents

Glossary of Terms used:

A Face, A well known criminal

AG, Assistant governor grade, used to be junior governor grade

A grand, £1000

A Peterman, A safe-breaker

A player, someone with kudos in the prisoner hierarchy

ACC, Assistant chief Constable

Blagger, armed robber

BOV, The Board of visitors, a group of local worthies who attended the establishment on a rota basis to take applications from prisoners and to ensure fair play

CAMMS, staff resources office

Canvas Cardie, Straight jacket

Cat, Category

Claret, Blood

Coke, Cocaine

C and R, Control and restraint, a legal method devised to control unruly prisoners

Controlled Unlock, No more than 4 cells at a time open, would happen following a disturbance or similar serious incident. It would ensure staff were in the majority

Demos outside the American Embassy, 70's anti-Vietnam War demos

DDG, Deputy director general

ECR, Emergency control room

ED, Evening duty

Go on his toes, Escape.

Happiness is door-shaped, Prisoners banged-up permanently.

HMYOI, Her Majesty's Youth Offender Institution

Hooch, prison brew

LBB's, Locks bolts and bars, a daily cell fabric check that landing officers had to carry out and sign for daily

Moody, false/dodgy

MDT, Mandatory drugs test

Note in the box, refers to a note placed in the mail box on the wing. Normally a confidential note to security

OSG, Operational support grade

Pad, A cell

Patrol State, All the wing locked up with an officer patrol.

PCO, Prison custody officer

Pegging, Night patrols turned a key in a lock that indicated that they were awake and at their posts during the night state

PKK, Kurdish Workers Party

PLO, Police Liaison officer, one is attached to each establishment.

Potted, Refers to prisoners throwing a pot of excrement and urine over an officer

PEO, Physical education officer

PO, Principle officer/group manager

POUT, Prison officer under training

POA, Prison Officers Association

Prison Controller, A person designated by the Ministry of Justice to oversee the contract in a Private Prison on their behalf

PSC, Prison Service College

Rick, Mistake.

R39, Solicitors letter not to be opened by staff,

Rule 10/74, known by the prisoners as a lie-down. Refers to prisoners being transferred out for 28 days when trouble was expected in which they would have been involved

RVI, Royal Victoria Hospital.

SERCS, South East Regional Crime Squad.

Shank, A home-made weapon

Snout, Tobacco

Smack, Heroin

SMT, Senior management team.

SO, Senior officer/first line manager

SO19, Firearms Unit London's Metropolitan Police Service.

SSU, Special secure unit

'Staunch,' the highest praise one prisoner can give another. Means they are totally reliable

Stretch, Prison sentence

Subsistence Allowance, a tax-free allowance that used to be paid to staff for spending over 10 hours plus outside their establishment on escort

The chaps, traditionally refers to those prisoners at the top of the hierarchy

To make one, To escape

USR, Use of staff resources

YP's, Young Prisoners.

Weed, Cannabis.

Weighed in, A jockey has to prove he/she was carrying the correct weight post race before he/she is ratified as the winner

Wembley Mob, A team of armed robbers in the 1970's who were identified by the first supergrass, Bertie Smalls.

Works Department, Responsible for maintenance in the prison

1150, a prisoner's record/file

1991

All in a Day's Work

It was after midnight. The second week of July. I was driving home through the North Yorkshire countryside when I started to shiver. I stopped the car. My fingers locked together and my knuckles turned white. I nudged open the door with my shoulder and stepped outside. Somewhere in the distance, I could hear another vehicle, but immediately around me there was only the sound of crickets and a cool night breeze. I walked up and down the road for a while, to see if I could sort myself out. Eventually, when I stopped shivering, I stood alone in the darkness and looked up towards the sky. I took a couple of breaths.

He'd arrived mid-morning, the prisoner from Scotland, on his way to the Court of Appeal. He was supposed to be lodging at Full Sutton overnight. Unfortunately, at lunchtime, one of the landing officers had unlocked his cell by mistake. The prisoner had wandered out, come upon a converted cell where another officer was censoring mail and seized the opportunity. He'd picked up a paperknife and then pushed the startled officer into a corner, before quickly using a combination of a desk, a filing cabinet and a chair to barricade the door.

'Get the fuckin' governor down here or I'll slit this bastard's throat.'

11

Summoned by the Head of Operations, I'd been briefed about the situation and put in charge of the intervention team. Training mode. Focus on the task. Compartmentalise emotions. Block out negative thoughts.

Hours had passed. I'd made periodic visits to the Command Suite for updates and to receive the intervention code word. Back to our discreet base.

'Still unpredictable. They're having trouble establishing a rapport.'

I'd had to keep the team in a constant state of readiness. Prepared to act with purpose at a moment's notice. It takes its toll.

Late in the evening, the indications had been that the perpetrator was about to take his hostage on the move. Suddenly, the tension had increased another notch. We'd braced ourselves to intervene.

Then, without warning, he'd given up.

'I'm coming out.'

Code word received. The hostage negotiators had stepped back. We'd taken over. The door had opened slowly. He'd stepped out.

'Stay there. Do exactly what I tell you. Face back with your arms raised.'

We'd disarmed him. Searched him. Removed him to the segregation unit. After a de-brief in the Command Suite, I'd taken my team to the club for a drink. We'd been joined by Pete Waugh, who may or may not have been responsible for my posting to Wakefield when he was national chairman of the POA. Pete had retired at Full Sutton, but he still lived on site. If he had been responsible for my posting, he'd got his reward tonight.

I'd included him in the round when I'd bought my group a drink.

Back out on the road. Still taking breaths. It was unusual for me. I began to ponder how I'd got here....

Part I

Prison Officer

Chapter 1 (1970)
'Welcome to the First Day of the rest of your Life'

Leeds Prison loomed dark and forbidding as I reached the top of the lane. When the gate flew open, I had handed over my introduction to the officer in a smart black uniform. I was nervous. There was an air of menace about the place and a smell of urine. One of the lads who had attended the initial test with me had said that between twenty and twenty-five percent of applicants would survive the first round, and that only twenty percent of those remaining would manage to get through to the final interview. He wasn't amongst the thirteen recruits gathered in the PO's office.

'Welcome to the first day of the rest of your life,' said the Training PO, as he swept in. He was in his late thirties, ruddy cheeked, wearing regimental insignia. 'You won't find this job easy. You'll be threatened. You'll be abused. Possibly even assaulted.'

Those were thoughts I had had last night.

'But one thing you can be sure of is that your colleagues will stand by you. If you embrace the training, both here and at the college, and if you adopt the discipline required, you'll not regret joining.'

Although I knew nothing, the adrenalin started pumping. I began to feel encouraged. As if maybe I could do it.

'Do your job correctly, you'll grow as a person.'

The Training PO went on to outline what would be expected of us during the next month. We'd be attached to various areas of the prison. We'd be given a notebook. We were told to make a note of any aspect of the job we believed to be significant. The PO would check and sign our notebooks on a regular basis.

As well as the military insignia on display, many of the staff exhibited a Forces bearing and, particularly in the presence of prisoners, addressed each other formally with the prefix Mr.

I was attached to a landing on C Wing. The officer in charge was extremely helpful. He took the time to explain how the landing functioned, and a cleaner provided me with a cup of tea. At exercise time, I was ordered to take up a position beside the alarm bell. I felt a bit self-conscious as I stood, uncertain, surveying the yard, wearing civilian clothing and a crown badge.

Although I wasn't really sure what I was looking for, I realised later that I'd been luckier than a few of my fellow recruits. During my break, I heard that some officers had been awkward and ignored the POUTs.

'It's sink or swim, mate. Find out for yourself. Nobody told me.'

After exercise, we lost five prisoners to solicitors' visits.

In the middle of the afternoon, a prisoner who was due for transfer, and who clearly had reservations about the idea, appeared to shove an escorting officer.

'Right,' says the landing officer, hitting the alarm bell. He ushered me and the cleaner into the wing office.

Within seconds, another group of officers arrived on the scene. Shiny boots, peaked caps, the caps slashed to appear more regimental.

'He's a silly boy, boss,' the cleaner mumbled. I turned around. He shook his head. 'That's Oddjob and his crew. He'll get a good hiding for assaulting a screw.'

A couple of days later, I was working in the censor's office with Mr Corrigan. Our job was to read every piece of prisoners' mail before it was distributed to the wings or posted out.

'They can't complain about the prison; describe its location, mention prison routines or name members of staff.'

Mr Corrigan was one of the old school. Twenty-five years on the job. Grey-haired, jowly and, in many ways, an intimidating presence. He did everything by the book - almost! Alert like a hawk.

'Give them an inch, they'll take a bloody mile.'

'Right, sir.'

'Right.'

Staff should be particularly aware, I learned, of anything that might constitute an escape plan.

That night, when the Training PO had finished auditing my notebook, he asked me how I'd got on with Mr C.

'Fine, sir. He's been very helpful.'

'He can be a bit of a grumpy old bugger.'

I said nothing. Not sure whether I was supposed to respond.

'There's an old lag. He goes by the name of Baggy. Everybody here knows him. One morning, a few months ago, Mr C was waiting at a bus-stop in town when Baggy pulled up and offered him a lift.'

Although I was tired, I was trying to be attentive. Trying to appear diligent. Trying to absorb knowledge.

'Anyway, without thinking, Mr C smiled and got in. They hadn't gone more than a few hundred yards, though, when he started having second thoughts.'

"'I hope this vehicle isn't hot, Baggy.'"

'Baggy kind of looks at Mr C.'

"'It's only a bit warm, Mr C. Only a bit warm.'"

I laughed.

'Stop and let me out now," he's screaming. Baggy's panicking. He can't see the problem. "Let me out of the fuckin' car.'

I'd palled up with Albert, a lad about my own age, who came from York. Albert was a mod. He had the haircut. He listened to the music and was into scooters. Whenever Albert and I were on the landing together, one of the officers always asked us if we were bachelors.

We would nod.

'You'll be going to Brixton then. That's where they send the twenty-one-year-old bachelors.'

At first, we weren't sure if it was a wind up. Later, we learned that the London prisons were invariably short of staff. With Brixton manning every Crown Court in London and Greater London, it's usually the place where there was the greatest need.

It sounded as if we might be going to Brixton.

Chapter Two
Prison Service College
Wakefield - Initial course

'Left, right, left, right, left, right.'
We're learning to march.
'Left, right, left, right, left, right.'
We were on the parade ground at the Prison Service's college, it was cold and wet.

Although I hadn't marched before, I soon got the hang of it. I started to enjoy it. One poor lad in our section really struggled. He seemed entirely uncoordinated. He couldn't organise his feet.

'Shun!'

'Bring your left leg up at ninety degrees. Stamp down. Feet in a 'V' shape'.

The training officer asked a couple of the older recruits with forces experience to take over as section leaders. Before the end of the morning, everyone got an opportunity to lead a section.

'Anyone posted to borstals or detention centres will be expected to march their charges to and from all activities.'

I could see how this might work with younger prisoners, but I wondered if we'd be expected to march adults in the same manner.

'Stand easy.'

There was rarely time to ponder things long. I would swing my hands behind my back. Top of the arse. The tension seeped out of me.

The afternoon session was self-defence. It was led by a physical education instructor from Hull, with a martial arts background. Things were fast and furious. One or two of the older recruits found the going fairly tough. My partner was a lad from Stafford. He was the same size as me. We picked up the techniques quickly. The instructor started using us to demonstrate moves.

'Remember, if forced to defend yourself, aim at the upper body. Avoid the spleen, the liver and the kidneys.'

The subject of Brixton kept resurfacing. After an early morning run through the streets of Wakefield, we were cooped up in a classroom learning about courts and escorts. Another forty-five minutes of seemingly crucial information.

'If you end up at Brixton, this'll be important.'

I coloured slightly. He was looking straight at me.

'Cuffs. Making sure the wrist's dry, attach the cuff to the prisoner and be certain it's tight enough to prevent his removal of it. If the wrist's slight, you might have to use an insert.'

He held something up. Presumably an insert. It was too small to see.

'Check the cuff a couple of times until you're super confident he won't be able to slip it.'

The Training Officer tugged at the cuff that he'd attached to his own wrist.

'If he asks to go to the toilet, or wants to warm his hands, or if he gets near any soap...'

Soap?

'...be suspicious. Be very suspicious.'

He stopped, he asked if there were any questions. Somebody coughed. Nobody asked a question.

'Courts and escorts. Crown Courts, prison officers. Magistrates' Courts, police. Somebody has to check the van before you get in with your prisoner. As the junior officer, you'll most likely be attached to the con. Make sure he sits on your inside.'

Van check. Attached to the con. My inside.

'When you're manning a dock, you're responsible for everything that happens in that area. If your prisoner's off bail, he'll surrender himself to the court usher, who'll direct him to you. You take him out of sight of the public and search him. Then you explain to him what's expected of both of you when you enter the courtroom.'

If I can remember what's expected of me. Never mind him.

'Don't forget, you're responsible for the security of the dock. As soon as the prisoner surrenders to his bail, he's in your custody. Stay alert.'

'What if he plays up?' somebody asks.

'You restrain him. But you can only remove him upon a signal from the judge. It's his court.'

'What about help?'

'An alarm in the dock. A message to the cell area.'

It sounded grand.

'What was I saying?'

'Signal from the judge.'

'Right.'

The training officer paused for a moment. He picked up a book. 'Your only real prop will be your dock book.' He held up a big, thin, hardback book. 'In here, you'll note the prisoner's name, the charge, and the plea. Once the jury have returned their verdict, you'll make a note of it and subsequently the sentence passed. If the prisoner's found not guilty, you'll release him from the dock. If he's found guilty, it depends on the decision.'

By the end of the morning, my head was a bit frazzled. But I was quite excited about the prospect of Brixton.

'Left, right, left, right, left, right.'

It was two o'clock in the morning and we were making a fair bit of noise. A police dog van has just overtaken us and screeched to a halt. The driver jumped out and walked angrily and purposefully back along the road. His dog was going mad in a cage in the van.

'What the fuck do you think you're doing?'

We thought we were marching back to the college. After classes, one of the lads had taken us to a pub he'd known. He'd promised good beer, Yorkshire prices and a lock-in. On the return trip, someone had decided it'd probably be a good idea to practise our marching. He'd formed us into a section and we'd set off up the road.

'Speak bloody one of you.'

A voice at the back of the section managed to explain our presence in the area.

'Bloody prison officers? I can still bloody well nick you. You're making a racket and we've had complaints.'

For a moment, nobody said anything more. But the police officer seemed to calm down when he realised what we were.

'That's it. No more. Get out of my bloody sight.'

We began to move.

'Quietly.'

We tried to move quietly.

'And be in no doubt. Any bloody more and I'll nick the bloody lot of you.'

Assorted mumbles. We understood. Although we were still steaming drunk.

When we reached the square, up near the college, the lad from Stafford started barking out commands. And then he marched us around for another half an hour.

By the time I got to bed, it's almost four o'clock.

Another thing impressed upon us at the training college was the importance of gate and key integrity. Although it was made clear that it would be a long time before any of us trainees made gatekeeper—in a lot of jails, we were told, it was the prerogative of only the most experienced officers - it was crucial that we understood the significance of the position.

As far as the public is concerned, the Training Officer told us, the gatekeeper was the face of Her Majesty's Prison Service. How well the gatekeeper presented himself determined how well the prison was viewed. It didn't matter if it was Mrs Smith and her eight kids, there to visit her wastrel husband, or a solicitor, or an MP, or the Archbishop of York, we had to be immaculate and we had to be professional.

As far as keys were concerned, they were kept at the gate and were issued on a personal tally basis. Each officer was given a set of keys and a numbered tally as soon as he arrived at his establishment. Apart from his truncheon, his keys were an officer's most important tool. They gave him access to gates and rooms throughout the prison, including into cells.

Keys, we learned, must be kept in a pouch, and out of sight of prisoners at all times. There are prisoners, apparently, who possessed photographic memories, and who had the capacity to form an accurate impression of a key merely by stealing a momentary glance at it.

Maintaining the integrity of keys, the Training Officer stresses, was absolutely paramount in preventing escapes.

Immaculate. Professional. Gatekeeper. Keys.

My heart skipped a beat. It was the morning after the pub visit and I was waiting in the breakfast queue. Around me, I can hear people talking about some idiots who could be heard marching up and down the parade ground in the middle of the night.

When I got into class, the escapade was still a hot topic. I searched out my mate from Stafford and a couple of the others and we decided it would be best if we kept our counsel.

Unusually, the Training PO was late for class. When he arrived, a few minutes after our impromptu meeting, it was clear he was flustered and somewhat annoyed.

'Everybody report immediately to the lecture theatre. The Chief wants to speak to you all.'

In the lecture theatre, Mr Challenger stood at the lectern, severe and impeccable in his uniform and braid. He got angrier and angrier as he described what he'll do to those trainees responsible for marching up and down the parade ground at 3am, when every sane person in the town was trying to sleep.

'They don't deserve to wear the uniform. I'll find out who was there. And their feet won't touch.'

Outside the lecture theatre, after the Chief has stormed off, leaving a stunned silence, we held another hurried meeting. We decided to split into smaller groups. Keep our heads down. Hope it blew over.

We've just had a full day's training on security and everyone seemed enthusiastic about it. Security's clearly the crux of what we do. The Training Principal Officer takes the lead again.

'Your most important task is to prevent escapes. You can help achieve this in several ways. Firstly, by making sure prisoners don't get access to any tools suitable for breaching cell walls.'

All tools are secured in cabinets. They're booked in and out by officers for legitimate use.

'Secondly, by not allowing prisoners to camouflage their activities. There must be no opportunities for the disposal of debris. Which means daily cell fabric checks: locks, bolts and bars.'

No prisoners tunnelling out with spoons. No tugging the hedges with pieces of string. No *Cool Hand Luke*.

'A prison depends for its security upon its strength in depth. The first line of security is within the institution itself. That is, within the wings, within the cells. It depends on you having intimate knowledge of the prisoners in your charge, on your knowing them so well, that you can predict what they're going to do, before they even do it. You, my lads, are the first line of defence. Ultimately, it'll be your knowledge and experience as officers, and the regular scrutinising of cells and wings, the monitoring of visits, the observation of patterns of behaviour, and all other aspects of internal intelligence, that will be the bread and butter of your working life. The reason you get out of bed in the morning.'

Apparently, the second line of defence, if anyone managed to get past me, is outside the wings, but still inside the prison. It consists of dog patrols and mechanical devices like CCTV, geophones, and other visible and audible alarm systems. Listening to the Training Officer, I felt a big responsibility. And suddenly the gravity of the occupation descended upon me. Alertness. Communication. Party control. Maintaining the roll. Everything adds up to our primary objective: security. When we got an opportunity to use the radios, I felt a bit self-conscious. The voice coming through didn't like me. There was a lot of interference. Fingers and thumbs.

We finished the session by learning how to search a prisoner and, lastly, we were taught how to carry out a systematic search of an area.

'Your fingers must check all external clothing: coats, sweaters, shirts, turtlenecks, socks, shoes. You must always run your fingers fully around the waistband of shorts, pants, trousers.'

You get used to it, I suppose.

'When you're carrying out a daily examination of locks, bolts, bars and walls, you'll not tickle them, like a bloody girl, you'll test them firmly, with a metal tool. You'll always move furniture in cells. When you're searching a prisoner's possessions, you'll remove them from any containers and thoroughly search both the item and the container. You'll question the amount of equipment in a cell if you suspect the prisoner is hoarding stuff or if you believe he might have taken property from other prisoners on the wings. As regards confidential legal documents, you won't read them, but you will flick through them to ensure nothing illicit is concealed inside.'

At the end of the day, everyone in our group agreed that this was probably the best session we'd had thus far. We couldn't wait to receive our postings. Finally get to work.

We're working on court escorts again and the Training PO keeps laughing and saying we'll be going to Brixton. 'Pay attention, you bachelors, you'll be doing a lot of courts.'

At the end of the day, we found out that the PEI has arranged a game of football against the staff from Leeds. Most of our cohort was fairly fit after all the self-defence and marching, and we thought we had a chance.

We won the game 26-0. My friend from Stafford, who was strong and direct, scored eight times, and greeted each goal as if it was the winner in the cup final. One of the lads had been playing regularly for Dover in the Southern League, a winger, tricky and very fast. From midfield, I managed to get a double hat-trick. But it was hardly a contest.

'Well done, everyone,' said the PEI at fulltime. 'But don't get carried away.'

Perhaps he was worried some of the lads might have been thinking about packing in their training and going to play for Inter Milan.

'You'll still be better off working on the wings.'

I found out later that many of the Leeds players averaged thirty hours overtime a week. No wonder they couldn't run.

We'd been told to report to the lecture theatre. From the lectern, a PO called out four names. The lads in question were told to report to the library. The rest of the group watched a film about searching.

The four lads, we learned subsequently, failed to make the grade in the weekly written assessment. Just like that, they were finished.

A couple of days later, we receive our postings. I would be working at HMDC Kirklevington, which was near Yarm, on Teesside. Albert had been posted to Aldington in Kent. Another detention centre. We laughed when we reflected upon the fact that neither of us had got Brixton despite all the 'brain-washing' we had suffered. My mate from Stafford was returning to the West Midlands.

According to my PO, Kirklevington was a junior detention centre. It catered for lads between the ages of fourteen and seventeen. Mostly from Yorkshire and the North East.

'You can expect the majority of the lads to be serving three-month sentences. They require discipline. They need control. Think about the parade ground. There'll be a lot of bloody marching for those boys to do.'

Mr Whitty, our section's assistant governor, held one-to-one meetings with the remaining trainees.

'You've performed well, Mr O'Brien.'

I smiled and told him how much I'd enjoyed it. And I let him know how much I was looking forward to starting at Kirklevington.

'When you're eligible, you should consider applying for the AG's exam.'

'Thank you, sir.'

'Don't thank me. You deserve the opportunity. The process. First, there's a written exam. If you're successful, you'll be invited back to Wakefield for a series of interviews.'

'Interviews, sir?'

'The Country House Test.'

It sounded a bit grand for a lad from Bradford.

In our last session of close-combat training, the PEI informed us that we'd had the singular privilege of being participants in his final course. He's received a posting to Hull. He was going home on promotion.

He used me and my mate from Stafford to demonstrate some of the most important things we've learned over the last couple of months. Roared on by the rest of the group, we went at it hammer and tongs. In fact, much to the amusement of the PEI, it almost culminated in a genuine tear up.

At the end of the session, we stopped and shook hands. Our training was over. We'd have a good drink together that evening before everyone packed up their kit and went their separate ways. As we made our way out of the gym, I found myself wondering how often we'd come across each other, if at all, in the years of service ahead.

Chapter Three

A Short, sharp shock

'Stand at ease, keep quiet, any talking you're on report,' I'd accompanied the cleaning officer Bobby Paton onto the parade ground with our party. He was giving the orders, it was 10 o'clock my first day proper, the trainees, as I have been instructed to call them, stood smartly at ease in a straight line.

We were subsequently joined by the Garden's party, the Works party, those on PE and the Workshop party.

All brought smartly to attention before being stood at ease, the senior officer dismissed the party officers to the staff-hut so that they could take a break. Myself and Bobby spent the next fifteen minutes patrolling the party lines to make sure nobody broke rank or spoke. The SO in his late thirties, tall, slim, stern looking, stood in the middle of the parade ground, watching and listening intently, hands clasped firmly behind his back.

I'd arrived the previous day with all my worldly goods in two suitcases. Welcomed at the gate by an auxiliary officer with a southern accent and a moustache, he took me to the PO's office and introduced me to Mr Laverack. Short and stout with a weathered complexion, I later learned that he been a mounted patrol officer at Dartmoor earlier in his career. He gave me a potted history of the Establishment.

'We've been open seven years, this building is the new-build and contains the reception cells, segregation unit, kitchen, dining hall, classrooms, visits, probation officer's office, the SO's office and the Centre office. In the back of the Centre office is night accommodation for the sleep-in officer. We use auxiliary staff to carry out night patrol duties but an officer 'sleeps-in' in order to take immediate command in case we have an incident during the night state.' He stopped for a breather before continuing, 'the majority of trainees, that's what we call them, are housed in dormitories upstairs.

The original building, where we are going now, was a former country house and you'll find it's kept all its original features. It now contains the Governor and Chief's offices, the Administration department and the boardroom. Directly opposite its entrance was the former stables, that's now our maintenance department, where the Works are situated.'

He introduced me to the Governor, Mr Williamson and to the Chief Officer 2, Mr Frost. The governor, rotund and jowly with a permanent grin; the Chief, a little taller, thinner, more formal, both welcomed me and promised a 'catch up' once I began my duties in earnest, they were on their way to a meeting.

We had then collected my cases from the gate and Mr Laverack had escorted me to the lodge, a six bedroom property situated at the entrance to the staff quarters just off the main road. 'This building had been designated as the bachelor quarters. At present you are our only bachelor so you'll be in here on your own,'

Bobby had been quick to tell me that though I was nominally on induction 'you'll be expected to get straight into it, we only have a small staff here and we have to cover for those on rest days. The emphasis is on discipline, cleanliness and progression, it's all go from unlock to lock-up for everybody. The trainees have to say "excuse me sir", every time they pass a member of staff and we march or double march them as circumstances require, you'll note the PEI's always double march them. You'll be allocated to a Dorm and will be responsible for five trainees, you will be their first port of call for anything they need. Everyone is given a blue tie on reception, you will monitor their progress and write periodic reports on your trainees. They will want to prove to you that they warrant red tie status as soon as practicable.

Their aim is to earn the maximum remission, to serve just eight weeks four days and a breakfast of their three month sentence. That means attaining that red tie;

They need to impress you but they will test you, they know you are new, it's what happens, it's all part of the game.'

As Bobby predicted I didn't have to wait long to be 'tested.' The following week I was in charge of the cleaning party, I set out the tasks for my 10 man party then periodically visited each area throughout the morning to check on the quality of the work.

Twice in less than an hour I'd found one lad missing from his work area, talking with another lad. I admonished the first time, gave him a final warning the second: 'I'm making a written note of this which I'll send to your personal officer and if I catch you not in your work area on my next round you will be placed on report.'

'Who's shagging your missis whilst you're in here I wonder?' He murmured as I turned to leave, I whipped round and got right into his face, he straightened up startled and immediately returned to his task. I didn't have to tell him again, his work ethic improved.

The following day I was pulled aside by the SO who told me the lad had complained, he asked me what had happened. After I'd outlined the scenario he advised me: 'safer to place them straight on report, no matter how tempting that is.'

I love being outdoors, after Bradford and being brought up with the smell of the Mills (dried blood on sheeps' fleeces) who can blame me? Kirklev's the countryside, I love it. The Garden's party is one of my favourite tasks, I get detailed it quite a lot, I suspect some of the older hands, who I know find it cold and a bind, have had a word with the PO, told him how much I love it.

I had up to twenty trainees on the party, all the lads wore boots and gaiters, Roly the Farm foreman would set out the task which was invariably, hoeing between rows of vegetables. My job was to walk up and down the rows making sure all carried out the task as directed and didn't escape, I loved the fresh air. I was getting to know the lads and often picked up a hoe to give a hand, I remained mindful of my prime aim to ensure no one escaped.

Sunday was Governor's Inspection; all the lads spent the morning making up their bed packs and cleaning and polishing their items of clothing. This was important in measuring their progress, most recent receptions struggled with this initially though they got help from staff and orderlies, after a month the standard was 'best Army' many were very, very impressive.

Quite a few of the lads ended up joining the Forces through our contacts with local Regiments, local recruitment officers came to observe and interview them close to discharge. They already had three of the disciplines required: they could march well in formation, they could make-up a bed-pack and keep their kit immaculate, the necessary discipline and respect for rank had been drummed into them.

My football career had taken off again I'm playing both for the prison side and for the Kirklevington village team. Bobby Paton plays for both sides, a native of Edinburgh and a Hib's supporter, he's very skilful. So good in fact that a local semi-pro side tried to poach him, they were subsequently successful and he signed for them.

The local village team was run by a wealthy farmer, he often picked us up in his Jag from work and took us to wherever we are playing, as you can appreciate this made us feel very important. However I came unstuck in a cup game at nearby Stokesley when, whilst going to head the ball, an opponent trying an overhead kick, connected with my nose. It bled most of the night, the doctor confirmed the following day that a bone in my nose had been cracked, I would need to attend hospital for them to break it and set it, I didn't go I couldn't afford the time off with still being on probation, I decided it would heal in time and that I'd always have the option of a hospital sorting it later.

On my first weekend off I found myself on a coach full of players, staff and their families on the way to Humberside to play Everthorpe Borstal in the Prison Service Cup.

The game was played at a frenetic pace, with no quarter asked nor given, they had a couple of Physical Education Officers playing who were fast and very physical if not so skilful. However they were unable to handle Bobby and as the game wore on and they tired, a couple of goals from him, a 1-2 victory made our journey worthwhile. The Everthorpe staff put on a pie and pea supper in the prison club for us all before we left, a superb introduction to the 'prison service family.'

Our two PEI's were not footballers but had a wide knowledge of fitness in general and put on a varied programme of activities for the trainees

They encouraged me to use the gym as often as I wished, including joining in the evening activities.

I thoroughly enjoyed the evening 5 aside football sessions, Gavin invariably joined in half way through the session, on the opposite side to me. His sport was weight-lifting; indeed, he was highly qualified referee and coach in this discipline, a shoulder charge from him had me bouncing off the wall bars, much to the amusement of the trainees. However, by the end of the session I was getting positive vibes from the boys, Gavin picked it up, 'this will do you a lot of good with them.' It did. Football and similar music tastes became an ice-breaker and no longer did they feel the need to 'test me.'

A couple of lads squared up to each other in the gym, they were immediately told: 'you can settle it in here with gloves under supervision. A PEI will act as referee, there will be no rounds, seconds or timekeepers, it will be stopped when it's obvious who the winner is.'

At least once a week I was detailed to take a party to clean my quarter. I used to put on some music whilst they worked, Cream being a particular favourite of us all, the sounds of Ginger Baker's drumming always upped the quality of their work I found.

At Christmas, the Chaplain would put on a carol service. He doubled as the local vicar and as well as members of the Visiting committee, some members of his congregation joined us.

All the trainees attended and sang with great gusto the fact that mince pies were served to all afterwards had no bearing on this I'm sure.

The mince pies were the best I'd ever tasted, big thick crust just as I liked them.

Tommy the cook and baker was RAF trained and though as mad as a hatter was a superb craftsman. His kitchen was immaculate, he ruled it with an iron fist but his prisoners were taught well, the quality and variety of his food was consistently of the highest standard.

He invariably put a lunch aside for me when he was making up the Governor's 'to taste,' part of every Governor's daily routine, I would eat mine out of sight in his office when the Governor had gone.

One day I attended the kitchen to pick up a trainee so that I could interview him prior to writing a progress report on him. The trainee was wiping tables in the dining room which was directly opposite the entrance to the kitchen. I knew that whoever was on this task had a duel responsibility; his other task was to warn Tommy if the Chief or the Governor were in the vicinity. Tommy was stirring a huge tureen of custard with a tab hanging out of the corner of his mouth when my trainee suddenly appeared at the kitchen entrance: 'Mr D, Mr D, Chief,' just as the figure of Mr Frost appeared. Tommy without breaking sweat or missing a stir deftly let the cigarette butt slip from his mouth into the tureen and continued to stir.

'Cup of tea chief?' 'Yes, thank you Mr D.'

I quickly left the scene with my trainee before I collapsed with laughter.

Friday tended to be discharge day when I would take a couple of trainees to Egglescliffe station in a taxi. They would be easily recognisable on the station with their regulation haircuts and brown property bags. Their goodbyes were genuine and heartfelt: 'see yer boss, I mean hope not but all the best.' I never once experienced any abuse from them as the train left the station, similar music tastes and regularly competing with them in the gym on equal terms had built a mutual respect.

The other auxiliary on the gate was a local called Tommy. In company with his sons he owned and trained a few greyhounds which he ran in nearby Stockton. It was an unregistered track, a 'flapping track.' He was aware that both Bobby Paton and I liked a punt, albeit on the horses, almost as much as we enjoyed football and was always suggesting we visit the dog track as his guest.

The first occasion we went was memorable even though not profitable. We met up with Tom who was clearly pleased to see us. 'Don't have a bet until I return, I'll speak to a few of the owners, try work out what's expected to win. Our dog Pie and Peas can't beat at least a couple of these on the time trials we've had, I won't be long.' I was to learn that Tom always named his dogs after northern food favourites.

It was a warm friendly place, full of wit, 'Could the owner of the Porshe return to the car-park as it's on fire? only joking but can the owner of the Ford Cortina BDC 469D be aware you've left your lights on,' boomed the Tannoy. A lot of laughter and backslapping but also a few sharp suited more serious looking individuals talking out the side of their mouths. I detected an undercurrent of potential skulduggery. I got the impression that plots and dodgy deals were being planned around every paint-peeling corner. The atmosphere was fabulous.

The dogs were parading; we identified Tommy's dog from its number cloth. A couple of Bookies had set up in a what appeared to be a corrugated shed close to where we were standing, a crowd started to gather behind us and edged us forward as it grew bigger and the Bookies got ready to 'price-up.'

The handlers started to put the dogs in the traps and Tommy returned. 'The feeling seems to be the 1 dog should beat the 2 dog. Ours has no chance, too inexperienced but nobody knows about the 6 dog it's a foreigner from Easington.'

As he finished a big chap in a donkey jacket burst between us and hit the nearest Bookie with a wad of notes. The Easington dog was immediately wiped off all the Boards, the traps opened and it made all to win with ease. I remember thinking it's not going to be easy winning money here unless you can get an edge, some of these are serious punters and clearly 'know the time of day.'

The Head of Education or the Tutor Organiser as his official title was then, offered to source me a car, he had links to a local garage. Nobody in my family had owned a car previously so it was with pride I handed over £300 for a four-year old mini, NUP 632D. The British School of Motoring had the unenviable task of introducing me to highways and byways.

The lads suddenly became keen to help me progress and I found that I was expected to run them into Yarm for a drink after we'd finished an evening duty, 'the practice will be really good for you, your confidence will increase.'

Around this time I was called up by the Warden (Governor) Mr Williamson to be informed that I'd passed my probation, he went on to task me with 'reviewing our use of staff resources, you clearly have potential.' Later that day I was brought down to earth when I failed my driving test. Of course, the lads had the solution, 'you need more practice. Get them L plates on again and we'll go down for a drink.'

I initially hadn't a clue how to complete my USR project but thanks to invaluable input from Jimmy Brown and Bobby Paton I finished it on time and Mr Williamson was very pleased with it. Trust two Scotsmen to know how to save money.

Jimmy was a Glaswegian, an elder-statesmen, after national service he had joined the prison service at Hollesley Bay Borstal before moving to Kirklevington when it opened. His wife was from the West Riding like myself, he occasionally invited me round for tea as well as mentoring me at work. He had a son and daughter in their mid to late teens. The son was a talented footballer and golfer and a younger daughter of about 5 years, a real bundle of energy who was taken with a popular TV advert of the time about eggs that she loved to parrot, 'e for b and Georgie Best.' She started to call me 'e for b,' would follow me to work when the sun was out and we would shout it out to each other until I reached the gate.

I passed my driving test at the second attempt and by this time I had been joined in the bachelor quarters by Bob Ambler who was awaiting allocation of a quarter when his wife and child would join him.

Bob came from Wakefield and was like myself, a racing fan, indeed a relation of his worked for the brother of the now legendary trainer Sir Henry Cecil, at his stud in Helmsley.

We were on the same shift pattern, we had finished one Wednesday lunch-time, were scheduled rest day the following day and not due back on duty till Friday at 07 00.

Tommy had given us a tip for a horse owned by a friend of his who had a Restaurant in Stockton. It was due to run in an early race at Ayr on the Thursday.

We decided to go up to watch it run and to back it on course, this would be my first long journey since passing my test.

Up late, we'd been out for a few 'snifters' the previous evening, we got away just before eleven. I remember being a bit nervous when we first hit the A1. By the time we reached Hexham I'd grown in confidence. On to Carlisle, Mennock, Sanquhar, Kirkconnell, we arrived at the course about 14 29, in just enough time to see the horse we had gone to back beaten into third place, luckily, we didn't 'get on.'

We enjoyed the remainder of the meeting even though we didn't make any money, there was a great holiday atmosphere.

Instead of coming straight back we decided to spend the evening visiting a number of bars in the town. We were a couple of miles outside Sanquhar on the return journey when I suddenly felt the passenger side of the car scraping alongside a jagged edge of rock. I brought the car to a halt, Bob was moaning, clutching his side.

'I'll make you are as comfortable as possible, hang in there I'll sprint back to that emergency phone we passed just up the road, I won't be long.' It was just after midnight.

When I got back to the car a policeman was already comforting Bob, he immediately asked me for a full explanation of what had happened.

'We are returning to North Yorkshire from Ayr races.' He looked at me sternly, 'but the races finished about 18 00 hours what were you doing till now?'

I sobered up, this wasn't going well, 'we've never been up here before so we decided to have a look around, there was a lot of people about it was a great atmosphere. As far as the accident was concerned, a lorry coming in the opposite direction temporarily blinded me.' His demeanour suggested he was sceptical about what I was saying. 'I don't know what we are going to do now we are supposed to be on duty at 0700 hours.'

He looked at me quizzically and asked, 'on duty, what do you do?'

'We are prison officers, sir.'

Bob sat up straight at this point, though still clearly in pain, he had realised where the line of questioning was leading, we didn't want to have to admit to spending most of the evening in bars.

His voice and attitude changed as soon as he realised what we were. He took us to his sub-station, gave us refreshments, offered the use of a phone so that I could contact a bemused night sleep-in officer, Jimmy Brown to inform him about the accident, 'You are where?' he bellowed down the phone, 'I take it you won't be back for your shifts?' 'That's about the strength of it Jim, sorry.' 'I'll sort it get back here safely and as soon as.'

The policemen smiled at overhearing my grovelling, 'Boss not pleased?' 'That's one way of putting it,' I replied, 'and he's from Govan.' He chuckled 'few better men to give out a bollocking I should think.'

'Look, your car might be a write-off, it doesn't look good but I'll ensure it's removed to a local garage post haste, this is their address and number.' He handed me a business card. 'My brother should be up soon, he'll be travelling into Dumfries to work, I'll get him to give you a lift.'

We took the lift and hitch-hiked from there to Darlington where we took the bus from Darlo to Yarm.

We missed our shift and our plight was the subject of much mirth from the rest of the staff. Poor old Bob was still sore I'd lost my car and I'd only just passed my test, however I will be eternally grateful to one of Dumfries and Galloway's finest.

The car was repaired finally, Eagle Star my insurance company were as sceptical about my 'explanation' as was the PC from Sanquhar, it took them four months to sanction the work; I was off the road for six months in total.

Of course, the lads insisted on testing it out as soon as I was mobile again. A trip to Middlesbrough after an evening duty, with me at the wheel, for as much Guinness as they could sink in an hour, then back via our favourite 'Chinese' in Stockton, was the order of the day.

We were about to enter Stockton on the return journey, full of chat, when suddenly the car wheels jolted. I had been half-turned answering John Coates in the back, I remember swerving to avoid some traffic lights, I became aware of cars coming in the opposite direction, flashing their headlights, suddenly a car overtook me coming to a halt a safe distance in front of me.

'That was a bit inconsiderate,' I said. 'Yes,' said John Coates as we passed the stationary car, 'you'd think a policeman would know better.'

This time the car overtook us more aggressively, blue light flashing, it stopped a cock hair in front of us.

I got out to be confronted by an apoplectic officer no older than me.

'Can you tell me why you have gone over the top of a mini-roundabout, through a set of traffic lights on red, gone the wrong way up a one-way street and then failed to stop for a police officer?'

I'm thinking, bloody hell just my luck, I was sweating. I could recollect something coming through the door about a new one-way system, traffic islands to be introduced when I was without my car. I had taken little notice of it at the time and had binned it.

I was about to explain that this was the first time I'd made this journey for some time following a crash in Scotland when I realised that this explanation might only make my current situation worse.

'I'm sorry it appears the road system has changed since I last made this journey.'

Still visibly bristling, the officer was scribbling away pointedly ignoring me.

The lads, who had remained in the car in the first instance, now started to edge closer.

'Your name, address?'

'Philip O'Brien, The Lodge, Kirklevington Grange.'

'What's that?' He was still steaming.

'It's the bachelor quarters at the DC we all work there.'

'Like our section house?'

He put his pen down, started to thaw, 'you should all know better, you lot, you're braver than me letting him,' pointing directly at me, 'drive you anywhere!'

He screwed up his first piece of paper and discarded it.

'Right,' he said, where's best for you to produce your driving documents?'

'Yarm please' I replied.

'Now I don't know where you think you were going?'

'To Stockton for a Chinky,' piped up John Coates from the back.

'Most certainly not, Stockton's had enough of you for one night, you are going to get into the car Philip, you will proceed to the end of this road until you come to something called a traffic light. If it indicates red you will watch it turn from amber to green before you proceed. About two hundred and fifty yards further on you will come to a round-a-bout. You will not go over the top of it instead you will give way to traffic coming from your right before taking a left. Now fuck off straight home and don't ever give me cause to stop you again.'

It was a subdued atmosphere until we reached Yarm and then the piss-taking began in earnest, 'stop when you reach the lights Philip, that's a good boy proceed only on green.'

Unfortunately, this wasn't the last incident involving the police and my car. I got up bleary-eyed one morning after a late night. I knew there was something wrong when I passed the place where I normally parked my car, halfway between my quarter and the prison club. It didn't immediately register what was wrong, however as

Tommy let me through gate I exclaimed in panic, 'Tom somebody has nicked my car!'

Tom took charge straight away and rang Yarm police, I supplied them with the car's details; I 'slopped' my Dorm out in a foul mood.

A couple of hours later the SO sent an officer to relieve me so I could take a call from the police. They had located my car, it had been taken by a couple of lads from Stockton who had ran out of petrol on the A1 near the York/Knaresborough turn off, a traffic patrol nearby had become suspicious of them and had taken them in to custody, they were currently being held in Knaresborough.

Yarm police were on the way down to collect them and I could go with them to collect the car if I could be relieved. They confirmed that the car was roadworthy, a bit of damage to the driver's side door lock as they had sought entry.

I was given permission to go with them and on arrival the local police were keen to let me in 'to have a word with them.' They clearly expected me to give them a 'dig,' I just balled them out, they looked terrified.

Working in Reception with Jimmy Brown was an interesting experience. When a new trainee arrived we would check his weight, height and note any distinguishing marks, his own clothes would be stored, he would be issued with prison uniform and a blue tie.

The short, sharp shock process would begin as soon as the trainee was presented by his police escort. 'Stand on that spot, do I make myself clear? Stand up straight no slouching, arms down by your side now!'

The last command delivered by one of us right into the trainee's face. Real fear was shown at this stage, it wasn't unusual for tears, I've even seen the police escort shiver.

'Good morning Mr O'Brien, good morning sir,' it was PO Laverack on his rounds.

'How would you like a month's detached duty at Brixton, they cover all the Crown Courts in London, including the Old Bailey. It will be good experience for you?'

'I'd like that very much sir.' 'Right, leave it with me. We've been asked to supply a member of staff each month for the foreseeable future, you'll be the first to go.'

A fortnight later I reported to the gate at Brixton to be booked-in and given a set of keys, I'd travelled down the previous day and found 'digs' for the duration, with an old lady who lived on her own in a terrace house just off Brixton Hill.

The Detail PO at Brixton had instructed the Gate SO to direct me to reception on arrival, I was to team up with an SO Shaw.

When I located the SO he handed me a food box, took my keys and told me 'to get straight into that pixie.'

The 'pixie' turned out to be a green van with bars on the windows, it took us about an hour to reach our court at Southend! The SO immediately took his leave of me, 'put the foodstuffs from your box in the fridge, put all the files on my desk, I'm going shopping.'

He returned within quarter of an hour with bacon, eggs, sausages, baked beans and proceeded to make a fry-up. 'Take a loaf from the rations and make some toast, loose tea from the same place and make us a brew,' I was instructed.

It was nearly ten o'clock when we sat down to eat, I'd been on duty since seven. I was starving, I've never enjoyed food as much. At the end of the meal we split the cost.

Sid Shaw was a big bluff south Yorkshireman, an ex-pit deputy with hands like shovels. When he realised I'd never been in a court before he sat me down and went through the process. My only listed case was an off bail, driving without due care and attention and no tax. He pleaded guilty, received a non-custodial sentence and I discharged him from the dock just before we broke for lunch.

However, following a walk along the front at Southend and an ice cream cornet we returned to await the 'list' for the following day.

We didn't leave the court until 18 00 hours arriving back at the prison just after 20 00 hours, apparently 'we have to get our over 10 in,' I was told.

The following day I was working on D wing, a wing within a wing with its own exercise yard. All the prisoners were category A which means that if they were to escape it would be highly dangerous for the public, the Police and for the security of the state. Many were armed robbers and were all 'on the book.' This meant that whenever they left the wing their escort carried a book which contained an up-to-date picture, space to time and date this movement, the book was then handed over to whoever was to accept responsibility for them when they reached their destination, be it visits, reception…the time and date process would be repeated.

Later on the same wing I'm monitoring the association area on D2. I did this from outside the association room door which I found strange because my view was limited. Apparently, the only time a staff member goes inside the association room is to open and close cell doors and to give out the mail. The SO said, 'that's so no member of staff is taken hostage.'

I took a call from Chief Frost from Kirklevington late afternoon to be told that AG Whitty from PSC Wakefield had been up to leave me application forms for the AG's exam.

A couple of months later, at Kirklevington, I awoke with a start, a small stone hits the window, I hear muffled voices, 'come on Phil you can't go to bed yet it's not midnight.' I open the window and see Gavin and John Coates, 'Come round the club see in the New Year with us.'

I was immediately part of a north east tradition called 'first footing.' This involved visiting every quarter and receiving a kiss, a mince pie and a drink, I was inebriated when I finally fell into bed at 04 00 hours the alarm going off to signal my early shift two and a half hours later was most unwelcome.

Quarters living led to a sense of community but little privacy. I went out a couple times with Jimmy Brown's eldest daughter Judith and it was the talk of the place. In fact, Jimmy and the rest of the family had gone away when our courtship first began. Whether anybody rang him whilst he was away I'm not sure but he was certainly informed before he'd unpacked on his return. Both him and his wife were fine about it despite the six-year age difference, it gradually petered out without any awkwardness or animosity and it certainly didn't stop the youngest following me to work whenever she spied me, with her refrain, 'e for b, e for b.'

At last I'm not rattling about on my own I've been joined in the bachelor quarters by a lad called Clive, a little older than me with a Triumph Spitfire! I've upgraded to a Ford Capri but Clive's motor is something else. Apparently, he's come from Northallerton prison some sixteen miles south of us 'under a cloud' whatever that means.

Bob Ambler offered to take the Mini off my hands but it's never been the same since the crash, he was aware of this but it's leading to a bit of tension. The lesson, don't sell a motor to a colleague if it can be avoided.

I've been out with Clive a couple of times and recently met a girl called Joan on one of these jaunts. I've seeing her now on a regular basis, she's got her own flat and is a terrific cook.

I went down to Leeds to sit the Assistant Governor's exam, it consisted of literacy, numeracy and intelligence test questions, I looked forward to getting the results.

I've done more detached duty than anyone else; the PO lets us swop if anybody doesn't fancy it, provided he is informed in advance and that it is accepted by both officers that they carry out the full range of each other's duties, so that he is not inconvenienced. Most of the lads have kids and are not keen to be away from their families for that long. Myself, Bobby Paton and John Coates were happily doing the Lion's share, Bobby and John love their overtime.

Brixton opened up a new world to me so I decided to put in for a permanent transfer. I discussed it with Joan who, as a typist has transferable skills and she said she'll join me if I get it.

Mr Laverack was at first surprised then happy when I told him of my intention. Apparently if I choose to transfer to Brixton that obviates Kirklevington's detached duty commitment and he'll get a replacement off the next POUT's course for me. I could see how it could be a bonus for him, it made his job easier but I knew Bobby and John wouldn't be happy when my move curtailed their overtime, I'd not be popular with them if I got it.

In less than a week, my transfer had been approved they wanted me to start straight away. The PO decided to let me go immediately, Kirklevington's detached duty commitment was cancelled and I finished my final shift to a chorus of 'good riddance you've stolen all our overtime. How are we going to afford that new telly, that holiday in Benidorm, Christmas presents for the kids....?' ringing in my ears. I quickly realised that the way to a prison officers' heart was through his wallet not always his stomach.

It had been an excellent introduction to the 'Service' but Brixton would offer me more responsibility more quickly because of their shortage of full-time staff, this was something I'd noticed whilst on detached duty, and that I felt was crucial to my career progression, I couldn't wait to load up all my worldly goods into my two suitcases and to fire up my Capri.

Chapter 4 (1972-1978)

Organised chaos

'Phil will you go to the gate and pick up two guys from the Canadian Embassy?'

I'd been at Brixton almost a year by then and my confidence and knowledge was increasing daily, I'd not regretted the decision to move.

I was working on Legal visits, a rest day call-in. These visits took place in a self-contained unit. When I returned with my two visitors my SO told me to restrict access to the unit whilst he accompanied the two sharp-suited Embassy guys to a solicitor's visits room. When he returned he gave me a list of prisoners, 'pick these up Phil and we'll get visits underway,' before he retired to the back office out of view, with his visitors.

When I returned with my prisoners a number of legal visitors had arrived and visits started immediately. I would periodically patrol the whole area but as legal visits must be in sight but out of hearing, to protect solicitor-client confidentiality, I didn't linger too long outside any of the rooms.

I did of course note that the room to which the SO had taken the Canadians contained Ronald St Germain. I was aware that he and his co-accused were awaiting trial for an alleged fraud on the Royal Bank of Canada, and that their trial listed for the 'Bailey,' was imminent.

I also knew that they had carried out a shares sting that had financially ruined a Tory MP called Archer.

At the end of the afternoon when I had returned all prisoners to their wings and visitors to the gate my SO brought me up-to-date.

'Apparently St Germain put out a contract on one of his co-accused. I suspect whoever accepted it then bottled it and told the authorities. Apparently his brief has Mob connections and is also involved.

Their case is listed for April and they are getting a bit jumpy.

They said St Germain and his brother Roger, who is under arrest in Canada, and someone called Jack Pullman are the main men. Pullman is 'the bagman' for Meyer Lansky, Hyman Roth in the Godfather Phil!'

I presume the room was bugged, I never asked and the information was not volunteered.

This 'firm' was the real deal. I realised immediately that the risk I was dealing with now was on another level.

Brixton prison was situated in south west London and was a remand or local prison. It's staff had responsibility for manning all the crown courts in London and greater London, indeed its remit went as far east as Southend and as far north as St Albans.

Reception each early morning and early evening resembled Piccadilly Circus at rush hour, scores of bodies passing through, prisoners getting checked, processed, cuffed-up, put onto big green buses and 'pixie' vans, both with bars on the windows, bound for court; then returning each evening. How it worked day after day, year after year with so few mistakes I haven't a clue! I'm sure the wrong person was produced at court at some time but I can't remember it happening in the six years I worked there. Organised chaos with a purpose!

I was allocated to C wing on my arrival, C4. Our day started at 07 00 hours and once the wing roll had been reconciled, the PO ordered unlock.

This was the signal for the whole landing to make for the nearest sanitary recess to slop-out.

Crowding into this area prisoners would re-fill their water jugs and empty their chamber pots. This process was complicated on my first day by the fact that a couple of the toilets were out of commission. What a stink!

The cells were roughly 7 feet by 11 feet, and inside, to the left of the door were two bunk beds. After slop-out the prisoners would clatter down 4 flights of metal stairs to collect their breakfasts. The food was placed on a metal tray and the prisoners had to tramp back upstairs to eat their food in their cells. This process was repeated at lunch-time and at tea-time.

At supper-time the evening duty officer would go around each cell with a cleaner, dispensing cocoa and a sticky bun.

Long bang-ups were interrupted by domestic and solicitors' visits, and prisoners were allowed an hours exercise each morning.

Our landing cleaners were a rum bunch, the number one was an Australian fraudster with links to the greyhound breeding industry. He took the Sporting Life each day. Another was an Iranian national with links to the Shah. He'd been over here as a student but had attempted to rob a bank in Brighton for some unknown reason, He seemed to want for nothing. Joan had joined me by this point and we were living in a flat just off West Hill in Wandsworth, Cromford road. She was born and brought up in the racing centre of Middleham in North Yorkshire and we went back often when we managed to get time off together, this became known on the landing. We would often talk racing and the number one cleaner would offer me his Sporting Life to peruse at the end of the day when we got a quiet moment. Not that there were many.

The Iranian took a call one day from one of Middleham's most colourful trainers at the time, Ken Payne, so he certainly had the 'connections.' Payne was famous for landing audacious gambles with horses with little previous form, and trained for a lot of people in show business until his operation infamously collapsed. I was told that the roads in and out of Middleham were jammed with horse boxes as owners scrambled to get their hands on their horseflesh.

We also had a Geordie pornographer, who did his work efficiently but who preferred to keep his own counsel. Not something 'Pebbles' our most colourful cleaner could ever be accused of. 'Pebbles' was a transvestite and was well known to both staff and prisoners from previous sojourns in the jail.

When Jim, my fellow landing officer of the time first introduced us, I must have blushed as she smiled coquettishly, I distinctly remember Jim admonishing her. Her modus operandi on the out was to entice the rich including MP's and senior army officers, to the Embankment with promises of carnal pleasure, then she'd give them a smack and roll them, take all their money when they got all hot and bothered.

'She can handle herself in here with these, no problem; the hassle comes if we get another on the landing then it becomes a competition for the men's attention,' Jim confided in me.

Our scheme of work was the 'V' scheme. It involved a shift with an evening duty built-in, a day when you were reserve ED but you were invariably called-in for the evening, a rest day when you were always called-in, a scheduled short day when nominally you worked until lunch-time but invariably you were extended till 17 00 hours. Thirty plus hours overtime per week, effectively a licence to print money! I'd never been so well off.

During the day there were two officers per landing, you would lose roughly half your landing to court after breakfast. The remainder of our day was taken up with unlocking prisoners for solicitors, for domestic visits and for exercise.

A senior officer and four staff manned the wing for the evening duty; you were supposed to work in two's managing two landings each but custom and practice meant as we were all wing regulars we opted to man our own landing alone.

I used to unlock a quarter of the wing at a time and let them slop out, occasionally I might have to hurry an individual up but this was rare, myself and Jim had built up a good understanding with the prisoners and they tended to comply. That said some prisoners did criticise our approach by referring to our landing as 'the rule 43' landing, inferring that we operated constant bang-up!

From 19 00 hours onwards, the landing would start filling up with returns from court and new receptions, it would be unusual if there were any spaces left on my landing by 21 00 hours.

That's not to pretend that it was always 'sweetness and light.' I was standing on the landing one morning with Jim, as our prisoners returned from exercise and he was telling me about a prisoner we'd received the previous evening: 'involved in the Parkhurst riot Phil, I checked his 1150, we'll have to watch him, I'll point him out.'

'That's him,' he pointed to a stocky individual, average height with close-cropped hair who was just passing the 2's landing making his way towards us.

As he reached the 3's a prisoner on that landing must have recognised him and called out to him, he made as if to divert to the 3's landing to answer the call.

'Bilkie get your arse up here now,' Jim shouted. Bilkie looked up, about turned and started ascending the stairs towards us.

We used to lock all the cells once exercise started and we didn't open them till it finished and prisoners were standing outside their individual cells. This was to prevent pad-thieving.

We also split the landing in half and Bilkie was housed in Jim's half in the top right-hand corner one cell from the end.

As Bilkie passed us Jim followed in his slip-stream repeating the mantra 'you're not at Parkhurst now. You're on mine and Mr O'Brien's landing and you'll do as you are told as soon as you are told.'

Bilkie kept on walking towards his cell with Jim still following him repeating the mantra.

I watched Jim and Bilkie vanish into the latter's cell.

The rest of the prisoners were now standing outside their cells. I immediately started locking-up my section, at the time keeping my eye on Bilkie's cell. After a short while when Jim didn't emerge, I became aware of prisoners in the adjoining cells peeking into Bilkie's. Something was going off. I hurried to Jim's end banging-up as I went along. It was testament to the respect and control we'd built-up that this proved easy. 'Tel, give us a hand when you've done, we could have a bit of bother at Jim's end,' I called to my fellow footballing mid-fielder Terry Joy who was working on the landing below.

I arrived at Bilkie's cell to be met by an up-turned table and chair, slopping-out equipment and eating utensils spread across the floor, Jim with his hat still on but askew, his arms around the prisoner in a bear-hug as he fended off punches to his head.

I grabbed Bilkie's arm and pulled him from the cell, TJ had joined me by this time and we took an arm each and escorted him off the landing. He stopped struggling almost immediately.

Jim followed close behind, still angry, issuing threats and kicks in the general direction of the three of us whilst occasionally wiping away blood from the base of his nose.

As we reached the 1's landing I heard the Training SO say to a group of visiting magistrates, 'this is C wing. There's an excellent relationship between prisoners and staff in here.' They looked aghast as we swept passed them.

We made our way to the segregation unit, Barry Fenton our wing SO had already forewarned them; Jim made his way to the Detail office to report sick.

We entered the unit then from seemingly nowhere a stocky PO appeared and started swinging punches. We were told to release our prisoner so that we weren't caught in the cross-fire.

I went straight to the office to place Bilkie on report, as, as first on the scene, that was my responsibility. It would be my first adjudication.

Mr Wiggington listened intently the following morning as I read out my evidence and when I'd finished Bilkie was asked to respond.

'It 'appened exactly as the officer said Governor. I'm sorry.'

'7 days CC and forfeiture of all privileges, take him away,' was the Governor's response.

Jim was likely to be absent for some considerable time, I was about to get the responsibility I'd moved south for. Though I would be detailed ad hoc staff to work the landing with me and most would be senior to me, it was custom and practice that in this situation the regular landing officer made the decisions on how the landing was run. I would be in charge.

C wing was the main remand wing, every prisoner unless they were category A would start out on our wing. Once they were committed to crown court they would be allocated to A wing if they had served a previous adult custodial sentence, or to B wing if they hadn't. B wing was considered easier to work because those on A wing were more 'jail savvy' and therefore more demanding. Our wing was chaotically busy because on average prisoners would be produced five or six times at Magistrate courts before they were committed to the crown court, they might return, they might be bailed at court or at any time during our working day. They were allowed a daily domestic visit and if we weren't unlocking for this we were unlocking for solicitors' visits.

Some prisoners were experienced and confident but for others it was their first experience of custody and their fear was palpable.

To those on their first night I always gave this advice, 'keep your head down, don't discuss or confide, you don't know who you can trust. Blend into the background and don't borrow. If you are unsure about anything come and see me I will never turn you away.'

I quickly learned that aggression and violence simmers constantly under the surface, often the product of ancient feuds, young men's quarrels. Everything could appear normal then for some reason, something would make the hair stand-up on the back of your neck, the mood, the atmosphere would change. The friendships that could exist between unreconstructed men of violence could thrive in camaraderie for a while, as long as the pecking order was strictly adhered to. When it broke down though the results could be devastating.

Others however, were 'plastic gangsters,' 'plastics' were forever boasting, noisy and always flexing their muscles, they tended to fall to pieces when challenged, and reasonable cons had no time for them.

'Can I have a word boss?'

'You need to watch that geezer in cell 15 he's been going around telling the more vulnerable somebody is going to get them, but he'll look after them for 2 ounces a week, he's a prick.'

My No 1 and others, made sure I had a complete picture of what was going on, a stable landing was in everyone's interest.

The wing No 1 was an ex -Army officer, always smartly turned out in sports jacket, cravat, cavalry twills and brogues, first to be opened up in a morning and last to lock-up, he had a stand-up desk just outside the PO's office, pride of place, always on view, he maintained the wing roll!

A visiting magistrate one day mistook him for the Governor, he was accused of property fraud.

Officers quite often critiqued the permissiveness they perceived in others more than any other quality. In a job that placed a high value on control that could make sense but watching the officer on the 1's, by far the busiest landing, I could see how levelling this charge against him was crass stupidity. I remember making this point to a detached duty officer who was working with me and who had criticised the 1's officer. 'He isn't being permissive he's being flexible, achieving his ends by engaging his prisoners in a dialogue instead of simply saying no. It's so busy down there if he wasn't doing that he'd be forever scrambling about 'putting out fires.' He needs their trust and cooperation!'

Within my first week I'd been approached by a tall athletic-looking officer from Northern Ireland to ask if I played football. When I confirmed that I did he followed this up, 'Do you fancy turning out for us on Sunday, we play all our home games at Chiswick, Civil Service grounds, the pitches are immaculate.'

'I'd love to but I'm working this weekend.'

'Don't worry about that I'll get you relieved.'

What I hadn't said was that I was a rest day call-in but I soon learned that this made no difference. I came on duty at 07 00 hours that first weekend and was working on A3 landing.

A3 was an extension of D wing, the self-contained wing for category A prisoners. Though not physically separated from the rest of A wing at this stage, it was run separately from the main wing by a senior officer and three officers. The prisoners were particularly demanding. I'd slopped and fed the prisoners, had a run in with a bank robber who proved reluctant to lock up at the appropriate time and who had said to me, 'I hope somebody's keeping your missis warm whilst you're in here,' as I secured his door. Shortly after 09 00 an officer appeared on the landing, 'away you go superstar, the Chief's sent me up to relieve you.'

I'd met Norman at the gate and we had driven over to Chiswick. Big Norm hadn't exaggerated; the pitch was like a bowling green, immaculate. I played in midfield with a lad called Terry Joy, from Bristol, but who turned out to be a Leicester City fan. He was very useful. Norman was solid at the back. After the 3-1 victory I got showered and changed and was ready to return to the prison when Norman counselled that we'd need refreshments before we returned. I got back on my landing for 15 00 hours, nobody complained they just asked how we'd got on. To cap it all I was then offered an evening duty and since it was pointed out I was being paid all the way through, even for the time I'd been away playing football, I thought why not and accepted it? I remember thinking I must have earned more today than most pros in the second and third divisions of the football league! Joan was less impressed when I got home at around 21 20 hours.

Football quickly enlarged my circle of friends and as I found throughout my working life participating in sport helped me integrate more quickly wherever I went. It was particularly important as I moved up the ranks when, as PO, then a governor grade and still representing the Establishment, or playing for outside clubs with others from my Establishment, I was something of a novelty. This didn't apply to senior PE grades who often formed the core of staff teams. I ensured that everybody knew that rank didn't count once we were on the field of play but neither did sporting friendships give anyone 'a get out jail free card' if I caught them not where they should be, or if they weren't carrying out their tasks to the standards required, when we were back on duty. Many staff lived in Quarters in the Crystal Palace and South Norwood areas and tended to be Palace fans, though I developed an interest in them which has lasted to this day, I never went to see them play. I did go one evening with Norman to watch Arsenal v Leeds United, not to follow the Yorkshire team, I am Bradford City through and through, but to marvel at Highbury, I thought it was a superb ground. Norman was there to closely observe Terry Neil, his fellow countryman and the Arsenal captain, of whom he was rightly proud. On another occasion we went to Wembley together to watch England v Northern Ireland, there wasn't too many of us in the Northern Ireland end that night, nevertheless they gave a good account of themselves, it took a lone strike from Keith Weller to win the game for the hosts. The highlight however was when a number of us from the staff team managed to get tickets for the England v Holland game, the PO let me go early straight from the 'Bailey.' England had a good side and were still playing with the confidence of 1966 World champions, however we witnessed a masterclass from the Dutch. Cruyff, Neeskins, and Johnny Rep were superb, two goals from Jan Peters ensured them victory on the night. They had introduced us to what the following day's papers called 'total football.' 'Think me, Les Hill and TJ might struggle in midfield against Cruyff and Neeskins Norman, they're a bit special?'

The Northern Irishman just smiled.

Tony and I had started at Brixton on the same day but for different reasons. He had been in the Special Forces prior to joining the Prison Service, after demob he had been working in a prison in the south midlands. Following a sit-down protest on behalf of PROP (preservation of the rights of prisoners), a prisoner had made as if to attack him as the exercise yard was being cleared. Tony chastised him but because this was in the full view of all the prisoners, he was called up by the Chief the following morning and sent to the Maze prison in Northern Ireland for a period of six months detached duty.

On his return he was posted to Brixton, a 'put up or shut up' situation. What the Chief said in those days was law, there was no such thing as grievances, health and safety, paternity leave....

When on shift together in the early days we would meet up in the officers' tea-room. We soon learned that certain people sat in certain seats on a seniority basis. Not that anybody ever asked Tone to leave 'their seat.'

We were walking through the gate after breakfast one morning following a hospital officer.

As he collected his keys a Chief Officer who was standing nearby with a staff detail board suddenly bellowed: 'You should have been here at 07 00 hours Mr L.'

'Why, what happened?' was the officer's quick riposte before vanishing into the prison.

I had exchanged my tally for my keys and straightened-up to face the Chief, just as this exchange took place. I burst out laughing; the chief went crimson before giving me a right royal bollocking, those following shuffled through, heads bowed, determined not to make eye contact with him.

The prison club was a hive of activity, a central point for a lot of staff, a place where many on detached duty spent most of their subs and more.

Friday night was card night, I played a couple of times in my early days before Joan joined me and we started to live together in Wandsworth.

The atmosphere could occasionally resemble that of a Wild West saloon, a barely repressed sense of violence in the air. I remember one evening midway through the night a nearby table being turned over and a lad on detached duty storming out. Apparently, he'd lost all his subs.

However, there was a hilarious incident just after 21 00 hours the same night when the evening duty staff joined us. A hospital officer came in but found he was behind a group about five deep barring his way to the bar. He immediately let out a cry, sank to the floor and started to convulse. Three officers directly in front of him, detached duty staff, immediately went to his aid. In a flash he was on his feet and had taken their place at the bar. Max the barman who had clearly anticipated this, had already poured his drink. A group of Brixton regulars, positioned at the side of the bar known as 'rat bags corner,' just shook their heads and chuckled.

My first twenty-week court posting was to Woodford Crown Court in Sir Winston's former constituency.

I had reported to Reception where PO McNamara gave me a list of prisoners, 'Pick these up from the wings as quick as you can.' He detailed another officer accompanying me , 'Collect the rations from the kitchen.'

We cuffed the prisoners up and got on a single-decker green bus with barred windows. I subsequently discovered that they came from the police compound at Vauxhall and that the police used them at weekends for dealing with demonstrations outside the American Embassy.

We had a 06 40 start and PO Mac would aim to have us clear of Brixton by 07 00 hours. Invariably we would make our way to Wandsworth via the South Circular to pick-up a prisoner before making our way over Vauxhall Bridge. Then it was down Westway to the Scrubs for another pick-up. Pentonville would be next on a busy day before making our way to Holloway to pick-up a female staff member if we had a female defendant listed.

We would arrive at court shortly after 09 00 hours when John Keating would start making the breakfast. Ronnie Mulholland and myself would uncuff and locate the prisoners before providing them with a cup of tea.

We would then sit-down to bacon, eggs, sausages, beans, copious slices (prison issue) toast, washed down with strong tar-like (prison issue) tea.

That first day SO Russ Scoulding told me that as the junior member of staff I would be in charge of the court at Chingford, Reg the driver would drop me there straight after breakfast and return for me at 16 00 hours.

'Chingford's a Magistrates court but sits as a Crown court as required to reduce the list at Woodford.'

As soon as I had arrived at Chingford the resident policeman Fred, came over to introduce himself, he then handed over the first defendant. I took him out of public view, searched him before explaining what would be expected of us both when the trial began.

My first case was a theft, the man pleaded guilty and with no previous convictions he received a fine, I discharged him from the dock. My next defendant failed to appear so the Judge issued a bench warrant for his arrest.

My list concluded for the day by 14 00 hours so I rang PO Mac to inform him, 'we don't need you here. The coach will be there for you at 16 00 hours.'

Back to Woodford and John Keating had prepared us a meal; meat and potato pie, carrots, cabbage, swede with apple pie and custard for 'afters.' Perfect.

I nearly fell asleep on the return journey as we wound our way through the East End, to Holloway, Pentonville, down Baker Street to pick up the Westway to Scrubs before finally making our way across Vauxhall Bridge to drop one off at Wandsworth. We arrived back at Brixton just after 20 00 hours and were off duty by 20 15 hours - we'd qualified for our 'over ten' subsistence.

On the days that Chingford didn't sit I would help out at Woodford, often with Jack in Court 1. Jack had joined Brixton from Parkhurst after the riot and had an impish sense of humour. Originally from Blackpool he called everyone 'blossom' or 'flower', he loved football and used to often travel with us to prison service cup matches as a spectator.

The 'essentials' he took into court were, his dock book, his Daily Mirror and a copy of Penthouse or Fiesta, not necessarily in that order. He was a wonderful character.

I was assisting one day when the court usher brought our defendant across to me, I took him out of sight and searched him. A tall dark-haired man, thin, but with an expanding drinker's waist-line, early forties, he'd swaggered across court in a style I found unique to London prisoners and which I'd dubbed 'the Lambeth Walk.'

The charges were read out; three counts of handling stolen goods to which a not guilty plea was entered The case was expected to last a week.

The Judge granted continuous bail and after the defendant had left the dock at the end of the first day we were approached by the officer in the case who told us, 'I don't hold out much hope. This jury is all from the East End and they never find against one of their own, I should know. I'm one of them. He's a fence and a good one. He's been constantly active without us managing to feel his collar for the last fifteen years. He did a bit of Borstal in his mid-teens but nothing since.'

This case dragged on a little longer than anticipated but when the judge finally sent the jury out he withdrew bail. They were out for a couple of hours and during this period we got talking to the defendant. He addressed Jack, 'I noticed that you are interested in the horses. What about the dogs?'

'Yes we both like a punt but generally we prefer the horses. That right Phil?'

'That's right but I went dog racing a few times up north.'

'Well gov I've got a dog we run at Walthamstow and if I go down the Mrs will keep it in training and when the price is right, it wins, it's called Blackwater two!'

With that we went back into court. 'Not guilty your honour,' said the Foreman in relation to all three charges. I noted the officer in the case mouthing a silent, 'what did I tell you?' in our direction.

As I discharged the man from the dock he said, 'don't forget what I said about the dog gov, it's gospel.'

We soon discovered that racing took place at the Stow each Tuesday, Thursday and Saturday and started backing it, a fiver each, every time it ran. We must have had at least thirty quid each without any return and we were beginning to lose faith, this coincided with our twenty weeks at Woodford coming to an end.

'What will we do Phil, you're going to Visits and I'm off to work in Reception, we won't see much of each other?'

'Been thinking the same. Time to call it quits,' was my reply.

I suppose you can predict what happened next? It won on its next four outings, at prices ranging from 11/2, 5/1, 9/2, 11/4. We would occasionally see each other from afar, Jack would just look to the heavens and bemoan our bad luck. 'I know blossom' is all he could say as I held up the paper with the results from a distance.

Visits Staff were a 0745 start and I would immediately attend A wing to be the breakfast patrol whilst the regular staff, who had started at 07 00 hours, went to the Mess. The wing number 1 Bernie Silver looked after the Occurrence book and had entered all the predictable discharges in advance. He was locked-up during the patrol state. I'd no sooner sat down when an officer would come on to the wing, 'ten for the Bailey Phil.' He went up to the landing and unlocked them himself; the prisoners would wait at the gate exit for him. He would bring me their cell cards and I would tick their names off in the Occurrence book.

'Six off to the ILS gov.'

'Two to Bow Street.'

'Four off to the RCJ gov.'

The ticking off process repeated a few more times and in no time the regular wing staff had returned and I was relieved.

I had reported then to SO Ken Haydock in visits. He told me, 'as the junior officer you will be the property officer. This is a list of what you can and cannot accept. For the remands who can wear their own clothes it will mainly be shirts/under garments and socks exchanged on a one for one basis. You will be responsible for searching both incoming and outgoing property.'

The days on visits flew by, Ken was an excellent SO, supportive and hands on. A food room was attached to Visits but was run separately. Visitors to remands were allowed to bring-in a meal plus a bottle of beer or half a bottle of wine.

We got very little trouble, occasionally a youngster who'd never had 'no' said to him might 'cut up rough' if his visit didn't last as long as he had expected. Remands were allowed a daily visit of fifteen minutes and because not many turned-up early morning those that did, got longer. Ken's idea was that we let the room fill up before knocking them off.

The fact that we were doing this was quickly noted by some of the jail savvy long-term remands who started taking their visits earlier. The afternoon sessions were always extremely busy from the off and never let-up until 16 00 hours. We did make sure everybody got at least twenty minutes but it was impossible to be as accommodating as we were in the morning because of the greater volume of visitors.

It soon became obvious to me that as a group we were getting a reputation for fairness because of the number of prisoners that started to acknowledge me when I met them in the main prison and in the grounds.

We occasionally got 'celebrity' visitors but they caused much less fuss then than I'm sure they would today, with instant news linked to social media. A QPR footballer used to visit a group of 'kiters,' credit card fraudsters. A self-effacing guy who would happily sign beer-mats for staff.

Another was a famous chat-show host, a 'housewife's favourite' who was involved with the daughter of a heavy-duty armed robber whose co-accused I'd fallen foul of.

I'd been breakfast patrol on A wing and this man had rung his bell to go to the toilet. Because of his Cat A status I had to wait for the centre PO to approve and assist. The prisoner wasn't impressed. Whenever I moved from my desk either to patrol or deal with a property application, I could feel all their eyes on me, I dread to think what he said about me to his colleagues at London Weekend Television when he returned to work.

Every day a massive guy in his early fifties and a smart blonde woman in her early thirties used to come to visit a Cat A on a murder charge. They would rush in after half-past three and we often speculated whether they ran a pub or a market stall. They were East Enders. Because they arrived so late we could only allow them the minimum time. We had speculated in the early days how many of us it would take to sort the big guy if he ever complained. Not that they ever did, in fact just the opposite, whenever any of us approached the table to terminate the visit, they would immediately comply and thank whoever had made the request. The prisoner had shot and killed a prominent East End gangster I later learned.

Friday was always a particularly busy day at court, Sections day and Judges seemed to use it to weigh off those found guilty previously but remanded for Reports. This made my breakfast patrol particularly busy.

'Twenty two off to the Old Bailey.'

'Thirteen for Inner London Phil.'

'Ten for the Royal Courts of Justice gov.'

A number of those up for sentence only, had been missed off the predicable list in the Occurrence book.

My head was spinning trying to keep up with the changes, I was relieved when the regular staff returned and I vanished to Visits, 'my day job.'

I'd been at my desk no more than five minutes when I got a phone call from the A wing SO telling me to get back over to the wing, they couldn't reconcile the roll. I must have messed up the discharges.

I made my way over with a bit of trepidation, the SO was the one I had spent the day with at Southend Crown when I was on detached duty. The secretary of the POA, ex South Yorkshire pit deputy with a reputation for blunt, robust speech, Sid, came out of his office with a frown until he recognised me then his manner softened 'look you've missed this one,' pointing to a name in the book. 'You mustn't let the escort staff rush you, they just want to get on their transport and away, that's how mistakes are made. Make them wait, the roll has to be right.'

I caught sight of Bernie Silver and his 'Maltese firm' standing within earshot expecting to witness my bollocking.

I thanked Sid, confirmed that it wouldn't be repeated and returned to Visits.

'What did he say?' They couldn't believe he'd given me such an easy ride.

'Hey that's 'cos you're a fellow Yorky, anybody else he'd have crucified.'

A couple of weeks after this incident I'd just arrived back on Visits after my breakfast patrol when the alarm bell sounded.

We were directed to the back of the Mess where an alley ran parallel to the prison wall; on the opposite side of which were some prison quarters just outside the prison compound.

There we met a large group of prisoners who had escaped with the aid of a dustbin wagon.

We were joined by staff returning from the Mess and vicious hand to hand fighting took place.

We used staves, and some prisoners and staff used dustbin lids and clothes props taken from nearby gardens. Those we managed to subdue were located on A1 landing which had been cleared to receive them. Many were bleeding profusely, and the prison regime was put on hold.

We had been told that an unknown number had got clear off the immediate area and a police helicopter was tracking them.

In the afternoon I was a member of a party under the command of a senior officer and we were patrolling the area between the gate and reception.

Mid- afternoon we got a call to attend Reception and an unmarked police car came to a halt near us.

The rear door opens and a man in his early forties with long hair gets out. The SO raises his stick when he was stopped in mid swipe by a startled cry from the driver, 'not him gov he's one of ours!'

Later the same day I was asked to escort the doctor as he examined the unsuccessful escapers on A1. Many had scalp wounds, bloody noses, broken fingers, a couple of the cells were heavily marked with congealed blood.

The doctor asked each inmate 'everything okay?' Most just groaned or mumbled through broken teeth. An exception was a seasoned bank robber named Mickey Salmon, 'Micky the fish.' He faced me and said 'we had a go gov and came unstuck, no hard feelings.'

I then opened the door of one of his co-accused, Danny Allpress with whom I'd previously had a couple of run-ins. He just looked at me and smirked.

They had all been on A3 and had taken advantage of a 'custom and practice' that involved the SO and three others coming back early from the Mess, before the wing was fully staffed, to get these prisoners out onto their enclosed exercise area. They had taken advantage of their numerical superiority, attacked the staff, taken their keys, gained access to the Compound and high-jacked a dustbin wagon they'd been observing for weeks, in a pre-planned escape attempt. Short cuts are okay until they go wrong. The prime movers were the Wembley mob, a team of bank robbers who had been grassed up by one of their own, (Bertie Smalls RIP). They were facing hefty sentences.

My written test results for the AG's exam had been sent to Kirklevington and Chief Frost rang me to tell me I had been successful, I was subsequently called to Wakefield for 'The Country House Test.' Before I went my colleagues at Brixton were at pains to tell me, 'it's a class thing they want to see if you can use a knife and fork properly, a Bradford lad like you who is used to using his fingers to eat has got no chance....'

In truth I didn't know what to expect I had little time to read the paper work sent to me, my focus was working as much overtime as possible and gaining experience at ground level. On that latter point I'd been put in charge of a five-handed prisoner escort to Harwich Magistrates a couple of days before; a team of smugglers, of which at least two were Dutch. We had no problems on the escort but a couple of days later I noted the police must have reviewed their security risk based on new information and all five were re-categorised Cat A!

The next time they went to court there was a PO in charge and a police out-rider escort! This was the kind of responsibility I'd come to Brixton to experience.

I know much more now about management assessment systems than I did then, I can remember being asked to Chair a meeting, doing written intelligence tests, psychometric testing, verbal reasoning, abstract reasoning, personality testing.

I appreciate in retrospect they were trying to determine if I had the required skills and experience, motivation and enthusiasm, personality and attitude. Putting us in situations where they hoped we would show that our personality closely matched that of the position in the organisation we were seeking to attain. They were seeking to judge if we were likely to be successful and content in that role.

I was unsuccessful on that occasion but was invited to attend again the following year. I'd agreed I would but had forgotten about it; too concerned with increasing my bank balance as we were planning to buy a cottage back up in Yorkshire strategically placed within travelling distance of a number of prisons, in the 'golden triangle' - in Estate Agent's parlance - in the York, Leeds, Harrogate areas.

I took a phone call from the Chief at the PSC asking why I hadn't confirmed whether or not I would attend, the day before the assessment was due to start. He quite rightly read me the riot act and made it clear it was a 'don't call us we'll call you' or not situation from then on as far as I was concerned. I was going to have to seek progress through the ranks.

Night duty saw a PO in charge with a senior blue collar assisting him and the next senior managing the radio links, we didn't have a fully equipped and manned Emergency Control Room in those days. The PO and his assist checked the warrants for court the following day, rumour was they would then get their heads down.

The junior staff would be on a wing, pegging, an electronic keying system for demonstrating that staff have completed the requisite patrols. My first night-time duty was on B wing. I started pegging at 22 00 hours and my last peg was at 06 00 hours. There was one pegging point on the 2's landing and another on the 4's, they were at the opposite ends of the landing to each other. I would peg at half hourly intervals. I was allowed to miss two pegs per night for meal-break purposes but they hadn't to be consecutive. This first duty was uneventful, the PO visited me at about 05 50 and he slipped me a piece of paper with a list of times he was purported to have visited me through the night. I transferred these times to my night occurrence sheet. He was on his way to take off the 'doubles' and ensure the ovens in the kitchen were fired-up for the incoming catering staff. The porridge was a priority.

I was relieved by the day staff at 07 00 hours and as soon as the roll was reconciled I went to the Roundhouse where the Chief Officer checked my pegging times.

My second night was on F wing; three of the landings housed overflow prisoners from the Hospital, prisoners on medication, the 4's housed 'star' convicted prisoners who worked in Reception and the officers' Mess.

The pegging points were on the 2's and the 4's as they were on B wing. It was a terrible night, one prisoner started banging and screaming just after 21 00 hours, I would calm him down periodically between pegs but communication was difficult because he appeared to be speaking 'in tongues.' As soon as I left he started again only this time he picked up his chair and smashed it before attacking his table, others on the wing were expressing annoyance by loudly complaining but some joined him and started breaking up their cell furniture. I alerted the PO just after midnight. He immediately attended with his assist, a hospital officer and a dog handler. The prisoner who was small but squat, fought like a lion, finally we managed to turn him over and pull his trousers down, the hospital officer administered largactil and he slept like a baby for the remainder of the shift. That intervention silenced the rest of the wing.

Saturday evening, I reported for my night duty. I was knackered as earlier in the day I'd been down at Dover Borstal playing in a prison service cup match, I'd managed to snatch an hour of shut-eye in the chair before setting out for work.

Norman, the superb captain that he was, had asked the PO to take pity and allocate me a task 'that was not too strenuous.' I had been allocated Rooms and Pads. I would be working with a Hospital officer.

The task involved being responsible for some of the most disturbed prisoners, many on heavy medication which is why the Hospital officer was in charge.

Fred welcomed me, asked me how we'd got on before taking round the evening medication, his orderly made me a coffee before banging up.

We talked awhile then Fred said 'come with me young Phil I'll take you to your bedroom.' He showed me a little room which contained a couch, pillow and counterpane. The window was covered by flowery patterned curtains that didn't quite meet in the middle.

'Right,' he said, 'we'll split the night you get your head down first.'

I awoke with a start, I was aware of light shining through a gap in the curtains, I jumped up quickly and rushed down stairs.

My heart missed a beat when I saw Fred. He was sitting down with his feet up on his desk snoring. I shook him, he came to immediately and before I could say anything, 'Great Phil. Is that the time? I'll get my head down now.'

'Fred, bloody hell how long have you been asleep, it's 05 55?' 'Christ I'll be getting relieved soon I'd better do my meds, get ready to hand over, put the last peg on Phil.'

'But Fred, how long have you been asleep?'

He was gone, before I could pursue it further the PO had entered the wing on his 'rounds,' 'everything okay?' 'Yes fine sir.' I daren't tell him any different, I put on the final peg.

Fred was getting the meds ready. I couldn't get near him and within no time a hospital officer had come in early to relieve him and he was gone!

I was left to face the Chief, I'm thinking he will check the pegging sheet and realise we both must have been asleep, I was in bits as I made my way to the Roundhouse.

'Thank you, Mr O'Brien, everything okay Phil?'

It was Mr Mac, the PO I had been with at Woodford, now acting Chief. I was awaiting a bollocking. What was this? Was he indicating that everything was okay?

'Yes, fine Chief thanks.' I exited the office quickly.

It was all round the jail when I went back on duty the following night, Fred had remained awake and pegged all night long, he had feigned sleep when he heard me scampering down the steps. He laughed at me the as I made my way past him on my way up to the wards; a task more fitting to my junior status.

There were three wards all containing murder charges. There was a table and a chair just inside each ward, with a bedside light and a pegging point directly behind. All the prisoners were Cat A's and therefore had to be checked (pegged) every fifteen minutes. The wards were considered the worst night duty and tended to be the doubtful privilege of the most junior staff. Unusually for prisons at that time, each ward had a TV at the far end which had to be switched off at 22 00 hours, lights out.

It was with trepidation that I made my way through the ranks of beds towards the TV at 22 00 hours. There was audible moans and groans, 'fucking leave it on gov it's not doing any harm,' I felt the animosity. Just before I leaned up for the controls a voice firmly said, 'fuck 'em gov - turn it off, goodnight.' The grumbling had ceased immediately, I took a quick look over at the prisoner who had spoken in support. It was the East-ender who had allegedly blown away a local 'face,' the man who used to get a visit just before the end of each session.

A friend from my teenage years, Dave Turner had come to London as nineteen-year old with a view to joining the Met when he was old enough, he was a DC on the Flying Squad when we got reacquainted.

He quickly offered to show me around, we met one evening in the King's Road, Chelsea.

Most of the pubs had door staff and a cover charge but Dave kept producing what resembled a bus pass with a guy's photo on it as well as his warrant card. It was the same script at every pub to the bouncers, 'okay if we come in and have a look around for this geezer, do you know him?'

We were let in everywhere on that basis and not charged.

The busiest place we went in, though it was four or five deep at the bar, parted like the red sea on a signal from the barman to allow us through! Two pints appeared in front of us as if by magic, I didn't pay for them neither did Dave as far as I can remember.

We ended up in a pub in Streatham just after 23 00 hours. Dave introduced me to a man standing behind the bar, his former DS on the Squad. He told me out of hearing that he was currently suspended but had a house in Windsor worth over £300,000, I found myself wondering later if that and his suspension were somehow connected. He subsequently joined us. He had an austere fine-tuned appearance, wore a decent suit which marked him out as a figure to be reckoned with. Dave had earlier mentioned the fear he engendered in 'the chaps' when they realised he was onto them. His suspension was never mentioned but it was made clear he was anticipating 'early retirement' and months of sun in Spain. My experiences earlier that evening along the King's Road made me realise how the lines between what was permissible and what was not, could be easily blurred.

We staggered out of the back door of the pub at 04 00 hours.

Joan had a variety of jobs 'temping' with a view to seeking a permanent position at the place she enjoyed the most. She worked at Leisure Arts with a cousin of Charlie George as well as at Young's Brewery, both local firms, before securing a full-time position in the Wandsworth Child Guidance Unit. Though she loved the latter she never quite came to terms with living in London. It was a case of you can take the girl out of North Yorkshire but you can't take North Yorkshire out of the girl.

The excessive hours I worked of course didn't help. I remember coming home late one evening after another double shift. I'd just got off to sleep when I was awoken by the noise of a party next door. We were living in a ground floor flat and it sounded as if the partygoers had opened their patio doors and had strayed outside. The music and chatter got louder and louder and I was getting angrier and angrier, Joan tried to calm me down and reason with me at the same time. She pointed out that someone had put a note through our door notifying us about the party and issuing us with an invitation! 'For most normal human beings this was the start of their weekend, you've actually volunteered to work again!'

This didn't help as the glasses clinked and the music seemed to get louder and louder. I was fully awake, I became aware of a neighbour on the other side to us, remonstrating with the party people, the music was momentarily turned down whilst he spoke, they had awoken the baby.

Then I heard what sounded like a punch, I jumped out of bed, 'they've fucking hit him.'

I quickly put my trousers and shirt on and rushed outside carrying my truncheon. "okay you're having a go at him and his baby how about me I'm working tomorrow and I've had enough of you as well?" I noted the man with the baby was still standing I began to wonder had he been hit?

They were all looking at me open mouthed, suddenly they all turned round and went indoors, the music was turned off. Shortly afterwards I became aware of car engines starting up and people leaving. Joan wasn't impressed, she kept her back to me for the rest of the night, I hadn't covered myself in glory!

Joan thawed out fairly quickly, helped by the fact that a couple of people in the street started to acknowledge her for the first time, most notably the wife of the man who had been holding the baby. She had given her a sweet smile and said 'hello.'

My next job was at the Central Criminal Court, the Old Bailey and one of the most important courts in the land. It would be my workplace for twenty weeks and I felt privileged to be working there. The Judge in my designated court 11, was his honour Edward Sutcliffe QC.

My first case was a four-hander, one of the defendants shared my surname, one was reputed to be of Russian aristocratic stock but was also an 'E' man. He'd been sprung from Chelmsford prison because his expertise was essential to their 'scam.' It had been a long-firm fraud.

The defendants had set about developing a decent credit history to win the trust of their suppliers. They had done this by placing numerous small orders with wholesalers and had paid promptly. Through this they had built up a good credit record. Then they placed several larger orders with those businesses with whom they had dealt. Once they had received the goods they promptly disappeared and sold them from various trading places, keeping all the money. Because of the 'E' man I had extra staff detailed to be with me for the trial's duration. Tony, who was at court on my first day, had asked the SO to put him in my court. It took most of that day to swear-in the jury.

I remember the Judge warning the jury that because of the complexity of the case it was likely to last for ten to twelve weeks, other staff commiserated with me, they felt it would be dry and boring but I found it fascinating.

Tony had another day at our court later that week but the SO had required him to work in the cells area. When we broke for lunch he was missing, we would normally eat together but I thought nothing of it presuming the SO had put him on another task or sent him on a short escort, as occasionally happened.

When I went back into court I quickly realised that the public gallery was empty, an usher was standing in front of the door to bar entrance, the jury was not in court.

Suddenly both the Defence and Prosecution counsels appeared from behind the Judges chair, followed quickly by his Honour. The Judge then addressed the Defence counsel asking him to voice the concerns he had just raised with him in chambers. Counsel described how his instructing solicitor had seen a member of the jury having lunch with a policeman in a local hostelry over the recess period. His Honour then confirmed that the prosecutor had been made aware of this. This he confirmed but he said neither he nor his instructing solicitor could shed any light on the matter. The judge then ordered that the jury be brought in so that it could be investigated.

The jury took their seats and I noticed an attractive woman in her early thirties sneak a glance at me and blush before turning away.

The judge gave a brief overview of the reason for the delay before putting the accusation to the blushing lady.

She explained that the part-uniformed man in a civilian sports jacket was in fact a prison officer. I had found myself colouring, felt that people were looking at me and I almost missed the remainder of the conversation that concluded with the acceptance that it was nobody involved in the case and that the case had not been discussed.

The public were once again admitted and the case continued. I gradually regained my composure, the lady did glance at me again mid-afternoon, blushed and quickly looked away.

As the afternoon session drew to a close, my attention was drawn to the foyer immediately outside court, Tony was standing there, I knew he wasn't waiting for me, it suddenly dawned on me what had happened. He was out of order and should have forewarned me.

Shortly before the end of the month my defendants started giving evidence. The Russian was the first to be called and was escorted to the box by a detached duty staff member who was assisting me. It was just after lunch, Budgie Burgess's meat and potato pie though delicious was weighing heavy on my stomach, the officer was sitting on a seat next to the witness box.

He had been sat there for about fifty minutes when suddenly he keeled over, he remained motionless on the floor as ushers rushed to attend to him. I went over also and helped them carry him from court.

He subsequently admitted to the PO that he had fallen asleep after Budgie's lunch, this had made him keel over. He'd then decided discretion was the better part of valour hence he pretended to have collapsed. The PO was not amused and 'barred' him from the 'Bailey' for the remainder of his detached duty tour.

Just before he started to sum up the judge took a day out to prepare. I was asked to assist Taff Hughes in an adjoining court. Alan Mackenzie was up for sentence having pleaded guilty to manslaughter. I recognised him as the man who had come to my rescue when others had being trying to intimidate me into not turning the telly off in the wards when I'd been on night duty. I was amazed when he was given the relatively light sentence of three years, and I mentioned this subsequently to Taff. 'Fair comment Phil but you haven't heard the evidence, it's been a strange case, most of the prosecution witnesses could easily have appeared for the defence. He shot a 'Teddy Machin' who was clearly not liked, particularly by the old bill.'

The E man had been a bit suspicious of me in the early days of the trial but he'd gradually accepted me; his two co-defendants had given me no cause for concern throughout the case.

They changed with the Judge's summing up, they got nervous, disagreeing with his Honour's points of law which very clearly indicated their guilt as far as they were concerned.

I remember being incredulous, they firmly believed that the goods at issue were theirs to do with as they wished. I suppose that the successful fraudster must believe that to appear credible to their 'marks!'

The jury were sent out to deliberate late morning, just after 11 00 hours, they returned with a verdict just after 16 00 hours, guilty verdicts for all on all charges.

It amused me to see the reactions of some of the jurors when the men's many antecedents were read out prior to sentencing. Receiving sentences of between 4 – 6 years imprisonment they quickly regained their composure and appeared sanguine. They were discussing appealing against the unfairness of the Judge's summing up as I led them from court to the cells area. Just before I handed them over my namesake turned to me and said, 'ditch your Guardian for the Telegraph Mr O'B; it's better for business.'

The next miscreants in my court were two old-timers, one Franny D was in custody, the other was an ex cabby called Abraham who had been on continuous bail and had a dodgy 'ticker'. I ended up holding his tablets. He didn't look well and this was a constant worry. They had been accused of shooting a Yank called 'Scotch' Jack Buggy (he had served with the US forces based in Glasgow and had stayed in Britain after the war). Buggy had served a 9-year sentence for shooting someone outside a London club, before it was alleged my old boys shot and killed him in a club in Mayfair in 1967.

A posse of retired police officers gave evidence. Indeed, Tommy Butler of Great Train Robbery fame got a mention because he had taken an interest in the original inconclusive investigation as one theory was that at the time he was shot, Buggy was trying to trace some of Roy James's money. He had befriended James in prison.

An Australian shoplifter gave evidence that he remembered that both defendants were working in the club at the time of the murder. He said he had been in the gaming room when he heard three shots, then Franny came in from another room and told everyone to go home he claimed. I had a bit of excitement when Franny's wife broke down in the witness box when describing 'being followed into my Milliners by the Flying Squad!' Franny stood up to remonstrate with the prosecutor, sitting down immediately and apologising when I rose to join him. Buggy's body had been found a month after he had disappeared, bound in bailing wire, floating off the Sussex coast. Though my defendants then looked old, frail and incapable, they had clearly been 'players' in their day. They were eventually found not guilty, clearly the correct decision on the evidence given and I remember being particularly relieved when releasing the ex- cabbie from the dock as my first aid skills had not been tested.

A3 landing had been partitioned off from the rest of A wing in the aftermath of the escape. Sid Shaw had been involved in its reorganisation and its regime had been tightened-up considerably. It was now a wing within a wing with its own discrete entrance. It held a group from North London accused of a number of gangland killings. The Press had called them Legal and General after a TV advert of the time. Sid used to have them lining up at their doors with their trays before being allowed to move down to the servery in single file. They couldn't look any less menacing, I remember thinking, if only the Press could see them now.

I was down the 'Bailey' for a day during the early part of their trial and the prosecutor, during his opening speech, had accused them of some misdemeanour in relation to the case whilst they were on the wing. One of their number got to his feet in protest, then turned to me 'what? with Sid Shaw in charge, do me a favour. Impossible! tell him gov!

Joan had never settled in London so we decided to buy a cottage back up in Yorkshire, I would go for promotion to senior officer, we'd get married and seek a posting back 'home.'

We gave up the lease on the flat and I went to lodge with Kenny Maude and his girlfriend Pat. Kenny was from Halifax originally so we had West Yorkshire in common, he also loved his football. In his early forties he rarely made the starting eleven but he could be relied on to always turn-up just in case, a superb character. He'd joined the Army very young and had a long Forces career before pitching-up at Brixton. He was popularly known as the richest man in Brixton as to say he was careful with his money was an understatement.

I remember going back to Pat's at breakfast time one day and I found Ken engrossed in an old copy of the News of the World. It was all about Jeremy Thorpe and the shooting of a dog called Rinka by a pilot called Gino Newton. The dog had belonged to a Norman Scott who claimed to have had a sexual relationship with Thorpe.

I pointed out to Ken that this was ancient news, 'I actually processed Newton a couple of months ago when working in Reception. This happened ages ago, you'd know that if you weren't so tight, bought a paper regularly, kept up with the news.'

'This Scott chap Phil, he was Jeremy's bit of bufti.'

I couldn't wait to see the likes of Terry Joy and Terry Lock to tell them what the richest man in Brixton had said.

I had taken the senior officers' written exam and had been successful so I subsequently attended Head Office for a final part of the process, the interview. I had prepared carefully; my priorities had changed. The Board members went through my career to date, asked me some management questions about staff motivation and it seemed to go well.

I was subsequently called-up by the Chief to be told I'd been successful. My next task was to compile a list of reasons why I should be transferred back up to Yorkshire. We'd got married by this time and we were expectant parents. The Chief made it clear that he would welcome it if I opted for an in-situ posting, which was flattering but a non-starter as far as Joan was concerned.

My old pal Albert had joined me at Brixton also by this time, like me he had developed a passion for the place whilst on detached duty and had decided to transfer up to London. He had also been successful on the promotion board but had opted for an in-situ posting, we were both now acting-up on a regular basis and I used to cover his night duties in D wing control room, by doing this I could maximise my time off on a weekend when travelling up to the cottage we'd bought midway between Wetherby and York.

I was acting SO on D wing one day, going through the depositions for a little 'firm' which had been 'captured' tooled-up in a van outside the Bank of Cyprus in Seven Sisters. The police clearly had had advance warning and had had the place staked out. According to the depositions one of the robbers had claimed, 'I was only waiting to cash a cheque gov,' as he sat in the van with a 'sawn-off' on his knee. One of the robbers was a nemesis of mine from a previous time on remand, Mickey Ishmael, he'd complained about me putting his light on during the night-state when I'd been carrying out Cat A checks and we'd had a bit of conflict with each other on a couple of occasions subsequently. His co-accused George Davies had been released early from his last sentence after a high-profile campaign against his conviction which had included digging-up the cricket pitch at Headingley before a test match. Ishmael had struggled to be civil when I handed him his depositions sometime later.

Thirteen months after being placed on the senior officers' list I received the offer of a posting to Wakefield. Even though Wetherby Borstal, Thorpe Arch Remand Centre and Thorpe Arch Open prison were all much closer to where I would be living than Wakefield, I could see the advantages in career progression terms of working in a Cat A Dispersal and main lifer centre. Promotion to first line management was an added bonus, so I accepted the offer and I couldn't wait to start.

Chapter 5 (1978-1984)
First Line Management

I had been checking invoices in the Canteen office when the alarm bell sounded. I rushed in to the Centre.

'Divvy shop Phil,' shouted the Centre PO.

My team of four had joined me from the Canteen shop opposite.

When we had arrived at the workshop we were met with a tremendous racket, an IRA prisoner was attacking the machinery with an iron bar, I identified him as the current O/C of the paramilitary group; the previous incumbent of this position had starved himself to death in the prison in 1976. The rest of the prisoners tended to be older and less physically able and their two instructors, were sheltering in an office. A prisoner from the south who had come with a bad reputation of violence against both prisoners and staff, but who had settled down, stood guard at the office door.

We drew our staves and quickly subdued the miscreant and as we were taking him to the segregation unit, another alarm bell sounded quickly followed by yet another.

We deposited our prisoner and answered the next bell in the Tent shop. When we arrived there two IRA prisoners had climbed on to the work-bench and were threatening us with scissors. The shop staff had moved all the other prisoners away from the incident area and were observing the action silently, offering no support to the IRA.

I gave them a cursory glance which told me many of them were frightened so I was confident they wouldn't join-in or offer any support.

I had moved closer to the bench seeking to engage the IRA in conversation, they had moved closer towards me, still issuing threats and waving the scissors in my face. Suddenly from close behind me someone wielded a stave which took one of the prisoners out! The other, distracted by his companion falling from the bench, was easily subdued.

Wakefield had been designated a dispersal prison after the Mountbatten and Radzinowicz Reports of 1966. It held prisoners in the highest security group serving long sentences, 365 were serving life and the rest were serving 5 years and over when I arrived. It was also a main lifer centre. At that time it was the largest dispersal prison, holding 710 in the main prison and 12 in the pre-release hostel. The latter was situated just outside the prison wall, adjacent to the gate and was run by a principal officer. The living accommodation was made up of large Victorian wings each holding up to 175 prisoners.

On my first day in my new rank I had been met at the gate by Dave Hall, a childhood friend and an officer at Wakefield. He had taken me to meet the training SO but before handing me over to him asked him if I could be spared on the Thursday of that week to travel to Nottingham for a prison service cup-tie. The SO agreed as long as I would act as a 'Hostage Taker' for a Negotiator's course he had arranged for my second week.

The SO then gave me a tour of the prison including the workshops, Engineering VTC, the Machine shop, Textiles 1, 2 and 3, the Laundry, Plasterers CIT, Painters CIT, the Braille unit, Tailor's VTC, the Works department, the Education department, the Gardens....

The following week I'd been told to turn-up in loose-fitting clothes so I dressed in track-suit bottoms and a T shirt. The SO had met me on the car-park and had 'smuggled' me into a room at the back of the Hostel which was being used for the exercise.

I was given sundry bottles of drinking water and a metal bar, I was then left for half an hour to get into character. My brief was to be an anti-social personality, someone who had been frustrated his whole life who lets his resentment boil-up inside before cracking.

I was aware that in a hostage situation if you can control the communication you can control the outcome.

The training SO told me towards the end of the week that he'd been pleased with the way it had gone, that I'd tested some highly regarded staff to the limit. The fact that I was 'an unknown' with a put-on cockney accent had thrown them. He decided at the penultimate session that he wanted me to create a situation where it was necessary for a physical intervention to take place. The team was led by a squat Scotsman who removed me with ease using one hand, in his other hand he carried a shield. I'd met Ian McCaul, ex SAS. He would come to my rescue in unusual circumstances many years later.

I was allocated temporarily to B wing where my cleaning officers were Bob Benge and Dave Kilvington, both extremely experienced with excellent interpersonal

93

skills. All our prisoners wore blue jeans and a jacket - prison blues. Rush hour was at meal-times and at the end of work periods.

Association took place each evening between 1800 hours and 2000hours. Prisoners could opt to stay in their cells alone during this period but their cell would be locked or they could associate with each other. On the ground floor were two TVs, one tuned to BBC, the other to ITV. Some chose to sit at tables playing chess or cards, there was also pool and table-tennis facilities. All the prisoners worked, many in the Tent shop sewing '10 stitches to the inch boss,' I was told. They had a quota to fulfil 'in order to earn my maximum wage boss, 76p a week!' The wages were credited to their canteen accounts. They were paid each Tuesday when they could buy personal hygiene items, soap, shampoo, tobacco, papers and matches only. This was a time when everybody smoked and drugs had not entered the system. Wednesday was when the canteen remained open all day for general sales. Thursday was the day we received receptions from Liverpool who had access to the canteen; prisoners already at Wakefield could use the canteen to transfer money into their prison savings account each Thursday.

The kitchen was on B1 so meal-times were our noisiest time. Prisoners from all the wings would tramp down to B1 to pick up their meals, the ebb and flow was controlled from the Centre by a PO and his officer assist.

All those in workshops would also pass through B wing as part of the line-route system to work. I used to position myself on the 2's to ensure people kept moving whilst my cleaning officer checked the cells to make sure that all those who should go to work, had done so. I remember standing by our wing notice board one day and an officer from D wing passed by on his way to a workshop. He acknowledged me before letting out an angry expletive, 'Kilvington the bastard.' I followed his eyes to the notice board which said: Today's quiz word is --- with what I presumed was the answer.

I could see the officer's Daily Express peeping out of his stick pocket. I remember thinking he'll have to concentrate on monitoring the prisoners today. My cleaning officer was very talented, he'd collected all my applications, cleared the cells, allocated cleaning tasks to his prisoner party as well as working out the Daily Express quiz word and had published it, all before 08 30!

I was standing on B2 shortly after I'd arrived watching movement to work when a familiar face wearing E man yellow stripes passed me sporting a smirk, escorted by an officer called Dave Pratt. About half an hour later Dave came to tell me that the prisoner Danny Allpress had alleged that I'd beaten him up at Brixton and he confirmed that he'd alerted the chief. Sometime later I was called up by the chief who put the allegation to me. I told him about the escape attempt, the hand-to-hand fighting in the back lane, the commandeering of the dustbin wagon to aid the escape. I confirmed that I had no contact with Allpress on that day other than when I was escorting the doctor on A1. I admitted that prior to the incident I'd had a couple of verbal spats with him, but that I'd never laid hands on him and he'd never complained about me before. Allpress was transferred to a prison in the south the following day which was exactly what he wanted.

Chief officer 1 George Challenger would carry out periodic staff parades, stick and whistle parades. He would proudly inspect his troops, the smile temporarily removed from his face one day when he came to a member of the Works dressed in a brightly coloured pullover!

When I returned to the wing after the parade, I remember hearing a lot of shouting and threats from a cell on the 4's. George Morgan was screaming at a young officer call Barry. Morgan had already served a long sentence for murder at Wakefield, had been subsequently discharged but had killed again. He was extremely strong and dangerous. It was clear he needed to be relocated to the segregation unit, I knew that if he decided to fight it would be a long journey. These were the risks I was weighing-up in my mind before briefing my intervention force. Suddenly it went quiet, young Barry came to stand beside me having wisely left the landing. Morgan then came into view escorted by Norman Chicken, an officer in his middle fifties waiting to retire. Although from the north east originally he'd been at Wakefield since it was a 'house of correction,' or so the joke went. 'One off to the segregation unit SO,' said Norman as he passed by. Bob Benge seeing the look of horror on my face quickly countered, 'don't worry Phil he thinks the world of Norman, he's known him on both his sentences, he came looking for him as soon as he came back, he'd never hurt him.'

Nevertheless, I informed the ECR and they covered the journey visually, having arranged dog handler support. Morgan was successfully relocated without further incident.

The following day I was in position on the 2's when the prisoners were returning through my wing via line-route from work. They would make their way to the Centre before dispersing via the radial system to their respective wings. The position I'd taken up gave me the best overall view both of my landings and the movement. Bob Benge my cleaning officer was on his rounds unlocking our cells in anticipation of our prisoners' return from work.

After a while my eyes had been drawn to the 1's, old Norman was sitting on a chair distributing the mail and I noticed somebody who thought he was 'a player' trying to push in front of a couple of older, inoffensive prisoners. Norman quickly rebuked him and sent him to the back of the queue. I remember thinking 'that's what being a proper prisoner officer is about but can you teach it? is it innate? does it come with experience?

I had an A and E man on the landing, he was 21 but looked about 15. He was serving 16 life sentences for possession of arms and explosives, conspiracy to murder, conspiracy to cause explosions and the murder of 2 soldiers in Belfast. He was a fanatic, only 17 when he shot the soldiers; he never made an application, wanted nothing from the system was escorted everywhere. He was later to test my leadership skills when I attended a serious incident in which he was involved in his workshop.

Conversely, I was working a rest day call-in on A wing a couple of months later when I had a 'blow-up' with a man called Maguire who was serving a sentence in relation to the Guildford pub bombing. He had recently arrived and I was explaining the process for IRA visits. He took great exception to me referring to him as an IRA man, highly unusual I remember thinking at the time, but I started to notice that other IRA prisoners barely acknowledged him and he certainly kept his distance from them.

This was my first experience of dealing with paramilitary prisoners serving sentences, the Old Bailey bombings had taken place whilst I was at Brixton and the Price sisters were held in D wing, looked after by female staff on detached duty from Holloway but I'd had only minimal contact with them. I now found myself looking after one of the male Old Bailey bombers, as well as a man convicted of trying to blow-up the Central Telephone Exchange in Coventry, another who shot and killed a train driver in London whilst on a bombing mission, others serving time for conspiracy to cause explosions and arson. They had their own command structure and lived by the mantra 'nor meekly serve my time.' Though they worked, used the canteen, accepted visits, they avoided relationships with staff and most other prisoners. They were escorted separately everywhere by the Security team.

Wakefield housed a number of sex offenders, a large contingent of lifer inmates, many of whom were domestic murderers. They tended to be more compliant than the populations of the other dispersal prisons. We certainly suffered fewer disturbances than them. The IRA could not expect to get the support for their disruptive activities that they might be able to rely on in other dispersals.

Periodically they would make incendiary devices and one day we suffered a series of fires. I was told subsequently that it had been meant to be a diversion for an escape attempt. We managed to put out the fires before too much damage had been done. Interestingly, the IRA contingent had been joined in this by Franklin Davies who was serving 18 years for his part in the Spaghetti House siege. The IRA did have a tendency to take-up 'a black cause', whether they were asked for support or not. On this occasion they were all dispersed to other jails for 28 days subject to rule 10/74.

When they'd returned I quickly noticed the dynamic within the group started to change. They had been joined by a prisoner who had shot and killed a Senator in Ireland but who had escaped from Portlaoise prison after his sentence to life. He had come to Britain and had been arrested in a flat in Liverpool where police had discovered gelignite, guns, as well as a list of the addresses of British Cabinet ministers. A 'source' told me that he was senior in the Organisation to the previous O/C and he was making his presence felt. One of the 'volunteers' had exhibited homosexual tendencies which had not been challenged by the rest of the IRA up to this point - but this was about to change.

He'd been called to a meeting with the new O/C and we noted when he came out he was ashen-faced, he 'banged-up' straight away. I noticed that the other IRA then started to ignore him, things remained tense for a while between him and them and he started remaining close to staff members, at least staying within our sight, whenever he was unlocked.

Conversely the previous O/C became noticeably quieter. My newly developed 'source' told me 'he's been told to stop seeking constant confrontations with staff until he is ordered to by the new main man boss. However, a few of us are not happy with the way (name deleted) has been treated; he earned a lot of respect at

Hull in the riot, he got involved, took his beating and bang-up afterwards and never complained, Puff or not he's got some arsehole.' Little did I know then that my relationship with this 'source' was to last off and on till the end of my career.

On our night for 'the film' we would unlock at 1755, five minutes before everyone else, we would escort our prisoners to a classroom in the Education block set aside for this purpose.

Graham Cowley was the projectionist, I would be seated near him at the back of the classroom, on a chair perched precariously on a desk so that I had an overview of the whole room. Two alarm bells, one at either side of the room, were covered by two officers, as precariously perched as I was! Health and safety had not yet been invented. I remember being down there one evening, when we were about forty minutes into the film; a faction about the Manson Family. Graham had stopped to put a new reel on, the film started again and the credits came on. Clearly the wrong reel had been put on first. Graham looked across at me, I indicated for him to carry on, it was too late to start again and only one prisoner queried it when I got back to the wing so we must have been the only ones that noticed the rick.

Later that week I was a rest day call-in working in the segregation unit. The PO in charge of the unit was Pete Waugh who was also National Chair of the POA. Dave Hall worked with him in Segregation and he had told me that Pete had mentioned before I arrived that 'a Bradford lad' on the SO's list was looking for a posting north. He mentioned my name, asked if Dave knew me, Pete was apparently close to someone in Posting section. Dave had confirmed that we had known each other since Nursery school, and that he'd followed my career at Brixton through a close friend he'd made at Leyhill whilst on his Initial course. The friend had been subsequently posted to Brixton. Apparently, Pete immediately got in touch with his contact and I received my posting within days of this conversation.

Pete however was in London on Union business this day and I was standing in for him in the Adjudication room. The charge was; 'anyway offends against good order and discipline'. This was a general catch-all charge used and occasionally abused by staff.

The reporting officer, ex Forces, was very precise, two cleaners had been jointly charged and had pleaded not guilty. The officer read out his evidence which in essence amounted to an attempt to perform an indecent act together.

The prisoners countered that the officer had made a mistake, that it had been their tea-break. They had gone back to the cell of one to collect his cup. 'The cell door had been left on the latch by the cleaning officer and as I opened it governor, a gust of wind clanged it shut behind us, we'd been joking about football, he blamed me for the door slamming and playfully pushed me onto the bed just as the reporting officer arrived on the scene. It was an accident, nothing untoward was going on we were horsing about.'

The governor turned to the officer who immediately countered in his guttural Scot's accent, 'when I entered the cell governor, Jones was laid on the bed face down and Williams was stood over him, his trousers were down by his ankles and his penis was erect.'

A quick embarrassed change of plea by given by both prisoners. I had to rescue a young escorting officer by sending him out of the room whilst I took his place. He was red-faced, cheeks puffed-out - he looked ready to burst....into giggles.

I later congratulated the officer on the succinct way he had presented his evidence.

Nevertheless, I did notice that at that time there was generally a more understanding attitude to homosexuality in prison than there was on the 'out.' It wasn't uncommon for prisoners to form relationships with each other that were generally regarded as 'marriages.' The prisoner who was standing by the door of the Divvy shop, protecting the elderly Instructors and his fellow-prisoners when the IRA was trying to destroy it, was involved in one of these relationships. Indeed, officers who knew him better than me were convinced this was the main reason for his better behaviour/more pro staff attitude. You couldn't afford to be complacent however, homosexual quarrels would occasionally break-out, one might try to 'pinch' the boyfriend of another or a couple could be split-up by a prison transfer. I noticed that a number who embraced the homosexual culture in prison would be essentially straight on the 'out.' I would watch them with their wife and kids in the visits room. They would do it discretely, not wishing to be stigmatised – keeping their distance from homosexual company during the day and never discussing what they did at night in the showers.

Mr Challenger called me up one day to inform me I would be going next into the Emergency Control Room,

I'd barely been in the jail for six months at this stage and I was still getting used to the prison's geography, I did wonder if this was a good idea but I kept my counsel. The Chief followed this up by suggesting I take-over as the relief canteen SO, 'it will be good for your career....' Bob Benge said later when I'd arrived back on the wing and told him, 'take care with it Phil, it can be a poisoned chalice, I know somebody else has been offered it and he turned it down, I wouldn't be surprised if he put you up, somebody's clearly told George you can count!'

As well as being a superb officer Bob proved an exceptionally nice man. I must have seemed a bit out of place when I'd first arrived. My previous experience of working with YP's at 100 miles an hour and then the frantic chaos of Brixton had not prepared me for the way time moves more slowly in a long-term prison.

He watched me charge around sorting out all my applications before 08 30 one morning before closing the office door and asking politely if he could have a word. 'Phil, I don't wish to be insulting but you'll find,' he placed the prisoner location book which contained individual sentence lengths between us, 'how long's he doing?' 'Life,' I answered, 'and him?' '25, where's this going Bob?'

He replied, 'They have plenty of time, you will find they won't expect the answer today like they might in a local prison, we have more time to research queries here and prisoners appreciate that.' He was right. Nobody came looking for an answer at lunch-time and I gradually adapted to the pace of life.

We worked a three shift system in the Emergency Control Room, 06 00 – 1400, 1400 – 2200 and 2200 – 0600.

We had a bank of cameras to scrutinise and telephones to man, we had a dedicated number for emergencies and a direct line to the police which we tested daily.

I had an experienced group of officers to assist me, who did a six month stint whilst the SO's did twelve months. The officers' movement was phased so that I only lost one officer every six weeks. An excellent system that allowed for continuity and made it easier to introduce the replacement without sacrificing the quality of the output. My job was to have an overview of everything that was happening in the establishment, to take charge initially when a serious incident occurred until a Senior Governor grade attended the ECR to take charge. I was soon to be tested.

I was on the early shift, weekend duty. It had been a quiet morning, exercise had been cancelled due to inclement weather so prisoner movement had been non-existent up to that point. We had carried out regular radio checks with the patrols to ensure they remained alert but apart from that it was a case of camera-watching for the staff, and perusal of the racing section of the papers for me.

At about half past eleven the centre door opened. 'What's happening?' 'It can't be anything serious,' I answered my own question, 'nobody's rung us.' 'I wouldn't be so sure Phil, that's Maudsley,' said John Galloway. With that the phones started ringing and we were straight into command mode for dealing with multiple murders in custody. We informed the Dog patrols to cover Maudsley's movement to the segregation unit, informed the gate to prepare quick access and egress for the Emergency Services, I informed and briefed the Governor. The team worked like a well-oiled machine, completing their tasks as per laid-down procedures and keeping me up-to-date. We were soon joined by the Governor Brian Emes and a senior police officer and the next two hours went by in a flash. The prison was now a crime scene, Robert John Maudsley had stabbed and garrotted one prisoner and hid him under his bed. He had then cracked the skull of another with a make-shift dagger smashing his head against the wall.

As a postscript to the incident the governor sent us a note congratulating the team on the quality of the response. It was a nice touch which was very much appreciated. He wasn't the only one impressed, I was in awe of how quickly and effectively my team had swung into action after such a quiet first part of the shift.

My time in the ECR was interspersed with cover in the canteen when the in-post SO was on leave.

I can vividly remember coming back from my first 'shop' at Brooks the Wholesalers of Barnsley. At the gate, Woody a former canteen officer piped up, 'Phil, the Auditors are here.' We used to get the majority of our goods from Brooks; batteries, tea, sugar, toiletries. The tobacco order was supplied from a shop near the prison. We would purchase fruit with cash from an unofficial float, from a man who appeared from the shadows, or so it seemed, from a shed on the same site as Brooks.

We would arrive back around lunch-time when everyone was locked-up and I could bring the van right up to the centre doors to unload it. I remember ringing Brian the on-leave in-post SO a little nervously: 'Brian, the auditors are here what do I tell about the cash float in the back?' 'Tell them it's your tea-boat,' was the not particularly helpful answer. I spent the rest of my lunch-break checking the till rolls for my morning's shop, the VAT items before presenting all the paperwork for the morning's transactions to the Finance EO.

Two external auditors turned-up mid-week to do a full stock-check and found everything to their satisfaction, I'd passed my first test.

Les Frost had joined my ECR team and as he used to work for the Timeform organisation in Halifax, racing formbook specialists, here was someone I could discuss racing with, he was a welcome addition, an excellent officer as well I hasten to add. His sister was still working for Timeform and managed to supply us with complimentary editions of their famous Blackbook, the ultimate form guide. It used to amuse my team when, after watching me spend a couple of hours devouring the Blackbook and when they asked me what I intended backing that day I would tell them, 'there's nothing I fancy.'

I must have been three quarters of the way through my ECR stint when the Chief called me up to inform me that we were about to receive an officer from Hull on detached duty. He would be giving evidence in a forthcoming trial involving a number of staff from that prison who had allegedly beaten-up prisoners after a riot at the jail in 1976. 'He's a young officer and looking at the 6 ECR teams I think yours will best integrate him.' I remember thinking bloody hell - that's all I need.

The team were a bit disgruntled at first when I put the proposition to them and we discussed how we would play it. As the astute Mr Challenger had surmised however, they were too professional to put staff and prisoners at risk by refusing to work with him.

Craig joined us and was quickly fully integrated, carrying out all allocated tasks. I had put him in charge of the radio fairly early to test his acceptance with the dog patrols. A couple of handlers ignored him; a risk, something I had to deal with immediately.

I went to see the in-charge dog patrols as soon as I could get a relief, identified the dangers of ignoring the radio, explained that we were complying with the Chief's request, he hadn't given his evidence yet, when and if he did, things might change but that wouldn't be our decision to make. The dogs worked in perfect harmony with us from then on.

Craig was an okay lad from Bradford, a few years younger than me and though he used to live close to the gasworks where my dad worked for many years, and I realised I'd often played football near his house on Bradford Rover's pitch although we'd never met before.

The fateful day arrived, Craig had been absent all week giving his evidence, he was due back in the ECR for our Saturday late shift, there was a lot of anger about.

Seven Hull staff had been found guilty and had received non-custodial sentences but had lost their jobs. It had filtered through that the PEI from my officers' training course was amongst them. Indeed it came out during the trial that he'd taken the lead when governor grades had either lost control or 'gone walkabout.' He would have been easily identifiable to prisoners. The anger amongst our staff was palpable, people expected action from the POA, Craig was now persona non grata.

I had come on duty at 13 00 hours, there was tension in the air, a couple of senior officers had met me at the gate to commiserate, I knew it would be a long shift. When I arrived in the ECR, the deputy governor Alan Rawson was already there, we exchanged pleasantries if you could call it that. Within minutes Craig joined me followed almost immediately by Pete Waugh and another POA committee member, Colin Slater.

Pete addressed me directly, 'Will you vacate the ECR as per the POA directive?' I turned to my team and asked them to follow me. We all went down to the governor's office, Pete Waugh led the way. Brian Eames asked me to state my reasons for the action I'd taken. I waited for what I thought might be my punishment, would I be sent off duty, suspended?

Mr Eames turned to Pete Waugh and asked him what he anticipated would happen next.

Pete told him we would be redeployed in the prison. Craig and the Dep remained in the ECR but as they couldn't provide the safe cover required, visits were cancelled and we operated a restricted regime. A few from the south who were expecting visits, smashed-up and we relocated them to segregation. We operated a controlled unlock at tea-time to feed. The remainder of the shift passed off without further incident, I was physically and mentally drained when I got home.

The following day I was back working in the ECR, Craig had gone sick, the day passed quietly. I remember thinking there would be a price I would probably have to pay for my actions but that I might have to wait till I was eligible to apply for a PO's board to find out what it was.

Craig never returned, there was a couple of articles in the local papers about his alleged mistreatment but this gradually fizzled out.

Shortly before I took up my new post in the canteen I learned that 8 of Hull's rioters led by Ronald St Germain, had successfully challenged the prison service's disciplinary system and won. Not satisfied with ruining the MP Archer he'd been responsible for a change in prison law in relation to the Board of Visitors and adjudications.

When accepting the Chief's request to take over in the canteen he'd made it clear that I would have his complete support and that I could select my staff and organise my working hours to best suit the smooth-running of the canteen.

I picked 8 officers to work with me from a healthy number of applications and I was happy with the balance. I had selected one officer who had never been given a fixed post before even though he'd been at the prison for about 7 years. The rest of the team nicknamed him the head-banger. He was fearless on and off the rugby field apparently. I could see he was a bit highly strung but he was clearly an intelligent lad. Most managers would agree that it can be good to have a team of contrasts but of course if you have a hothead amongst the group you've got to be prepared to clean-up after him.

Myself and 4 officers would go to Brookes the Wholesalers each Monday morning, I would split the lists of items required between us. The heaviest items were large packs of sugar, I used to rib a couple of the staff mercilessly as they struggled to lift items the Barnsley lasses at the check-outs handled with ease. These girls were strong and tough, it wasn't just a rumour.

Wednesday was the day we opened all day for general sales. I vividly recall one Wednesday working at one end of the canteen with Eric Creed. Dave Wigley and Tony Ellis were working at the other end. Eric had a heart of gold and was extremely strong. You only had to mention that your car engine was sounding funny and he would be out on the carpark stripping it down for you during his lunch-break.

He also had a word or three for anybody and everybody, he didn't discriminate; in fact he rarely shut up. Some staff found this annoying but the prisoners loved it. We paid the prisoners in cash but the highest denomination initially was ten pence. We would put the cash in a large heavy drawer which we would constantly have to open and shut to take cash and give change but equally importantly, to prevent theft as we turned to pick-up goods from the shelves behind us.

As the night progressed and the drawer became heavier, I struggled with it whilst Eric with his superior strength seemed to just clip it whilst he 'yattered' to prisoners, and it flew shut. I noticed Dave and Tony looking over and laughing as Eric once more narrowly missed trapping my fingers, oblivious to the near miss as he continued to rabbit!

The first task each Friday would be to do a mini-stock check in preparation for the EO finance coming down later to do his mini stock check, he would carry out a full stock check monthly. Cigarette papers came in packs of 100 we'd been doing it long enough to be able to work out roughly how many we would sell therefore how many packs to split before sales began. I remember walking into the canteen one Friday half-way through my 2 year stint and being met with the sight of scores of open cigarette packs to count! 'Dave, who the fuck has opened all these?' 'The head-banger,' was Dave Wigley's quick retort. 'Well why didn't you stop him?' 'We couldn't honest Phil, he was on a roll, gone, in his own little world.'

Each Friday afternoon before they went off duty workshop staff would bring the prisoners' pay books to my office on the centre. I would check all the entries and reconcile the totals. I would already have my canteen sales figure for the week as part of the morning stock check process. The difference between the 2 figures would be what I would hand over to the Finance EO or collect from him before I paid the prisoners the following Tuesday.

Knowledge of the two figures and consideration of the savings transactions each Thursday gave me a good idea of the amounts still held by prisoners and I used to ring Mel Blenkin the security PO to up-date him. This would be money the chaps would use on betting, snout and hooch. We knew who the bookies and brewers were and Mel would plan his searches around this information.

Thursday morning was a favourite shift for my staff. I would make-up lists and they would go out special order shopping without me. They went in pairs to collect permitted supplements from Boots and for items required by Asian inmates for cooking, items we didn't stock routinely. Normally they would grab the lists and be gone, eager to be free. This particular morning Ollie Cole and Alan Barrow were hanging about the exit, Graham Cowley was grinning, his partner big Jim Wheatley was clearly uncomfortable. Jim was a Londoner, tall good-looking and single, he was also my jogging partner. 'Okay, what's up?' 'It's Jim boss he's barred from Boots,' piped up Graham. 'He's what?' I exclaimed. 'He's dumped one of the lasses in there he's been seeing and threats have been issued,' Graham continued.

'Jimbo what are you doing to me?' I said. Silence from Jim, giggles from the rest.

'Okay, Jim, Graham you two go collect the Asian order, Ollie and Alan can go to Boots but in future big man keep your private life separate from our business.'

I mentioned earlier that we knew who the bookies and brewers were and as we realised that though we could never stamp it out completely we would control it by monitoring it closely and not letting it get out of hand. For example, the bookies would 'ban', not accept bets from a debtor, it would be a blanket ban across the board. This would be done on the basis that if anyone used force over an unpaid bet, we would close them down, segregate them before relocating them to another prison at the other end of the country. It worked! I might add this happened decades before the licenced betting fraternity showed a modicum of care for gamblers on the 'out,' with their mantra, 'once the fun stops stop! Both my prisoner orderlies were interested in racing. Indeed one used to take the weekly Handicap book, which he would offer me to read during a break, whilst the other was in for robbing a Bookmaker's which ended with a fatality. They would often join in conversations I would have about racing with Tony Ellis and Dave Wigley who also liked a bet. We had a couple of unwritten rules, no betting slips were ever produced in front of me and prisoners never used my first name. I would allow the prisoners and officers to call each other by their first names in the privacy of our office.

We would often go back to visit Joan's family in Middleham and to walk the moor. Her dad, who had died when she was in her early teens, had worked for a number of trainers and because of him she still had a lot of contacts within the sport. On a recent visit someone who had worked for local trainer Neville Crump had told us that they expected the trainer's horse Salkeld to go very close in the Grand National. As Captain Crump was already a National-winning trainer this was crucial information. The first opportunity I got I imparted the tip to my team in the privacy of our office, our orderlies of course overheard and we all 'lumped on.'

Suffice to say Salkeld only got to the first fence in the race! I was met with long-faces from my punting staff and my two orderlies when I went in to work on the following Monday and I wasn't too happy I hasten to add as I'd done a nice few quid myself.

However, it's a manager's responsibility to raise staff morale, 'just look at it as one of those things! At least he expended no energy, he's still very fit and he'll be off for his life in the Scottish National in a couple of weeks, I've been told to keep the faith and that's what I advise you to do'.

Neville Crump didn't let us down a second time the horse won the Scottish National at a nice double figure price, staff and orderlies all smiles again. The 'bookie' I suspected my orderlies used, remarked to me as I served him in the canteen, 'I laid a lot of it off with Edgy, naming the 'main' bookie, 'so I haven't done too bad.' Edge in fact had suffered a double whammy. My source had told me the previous week that Edge had made so much money recently that he was to hand a large sum over to his wife on visits so that she could go on holiday to Spain. I had informed the security PO who had searched him and confiscated 500 notes! We would intervene of course when they got too big for their boots and if we suspected staff had been corrupted. How did he come about the notes? The answer was a member of staff changed his 10p pieces for them. They came in over a period of days in a heavy sports bag, the exchange rate £1 for the staff member for every 60p changed. His name was also given to the security PO.

When all the rest of the inmates were locked-up on a Wednesday lunch-time I would stay back with one member of staff and pay the National R43 inmates. These were prisoners who because of the nature of their crimes had to be kept separate from the mainstream population.

Two of these prisoners stood out because they couldn't look or sound more different. Stefan Kisco with his squeaky voice had been convicted of the murder of a school girl and was universally despised by both staff and prisoners. Thomas Bradshaw was a contract killer who it had been alleged had been paid by Ronnie Knight to kill a man called Zomparelli. The latter, in the eyes of the Knight family had received too lenient a sentence for the fatal stabbing of David Knight, Ronnie's brother. He was on the unit because he was considered a 'supergrass.' After I'd been promoted and moved on, and DNA evidence became established, it was proved that Kisco could not have committed the crime of which he had been convicted and he was released after many years of incarceration.

Quite often after I'd paid and shopped the R43's and the prison was locked-up, the security PO would bring one of his 'sources' to me and we would reward him with some snout, matches and papers from what my predecessor had called 'my tea-boat.' We'd renamed it the chief's float. I would reward my own 'source' from the same float and when we met up again many years later at Frankland we would often reminisce about those times.

Towards the end of a quiet Thursday evening I was balancing a savings card at one end of the canteen. At the other end a couple of recent new receptions from Liverpool were purchasing items. Suddenly I heard a shout, I looked over and saw that 'the headbanger' had vaulted the counter and was holding a reception by the throat with his feet off the ground!

'What the fuck's going on?'

'He's tried to pay with this boss,' blustered an incredulous 'headbanger,' holding up a fifty pence piece.

'Boss, I got it at Liverpool earlier today, they've just started issuing them,' countered the terrified recent reception. A quick phone call confirmed this and order was restored. I remember thinking it's a pity our inter-prison communications weren't better.

Though I reported directly to the Chief, a governor grade Peter Earnshaw had overall responsibility for the canteen. He would visit periodically and to ensure good governance, inspected all the books. He was supportive and during the period of our stewardship we averaged a profit of 10.11% on sales. I was required to make a profit, 11% was the guide-line, not that 'the chaps' always appreciated this, 'why can't you lower some of the prices boss?' The profit was transferred at the end of each financial year to the common fund. It provided for recreation items like snooker and table tennis tables for prisoners. We were able to demonstrate that complaints about the canteen had been reduced by 80% and we had been successfully subject to external audit.

The week before I finished my canteen tour of duty I was joined by the Chief 1 designate of a new dispersal prison to be imminently opened in Durham, Mr Sayers. He was spending a week acclimatising to long-term conditions and researching best practice. As Mr Challenger was dropping him off he had asked me to 'come to my office before you go off duty.'

'I've got some bad news for you Mr O'Brien. You haven't been granted a promotion board. I can't understand it as you've done so well in every task we've given you and your annual staff reports confirm that I'm sure.'

The truth was we both knew that this was payback time for walking out of the ECR, but we left it unsaid. 'Thanks Chief I'll be back for another go next year or whenever, they won't get rid of me that easily.'

'That's the spirit son, take care.'

In truth it wasn't unexpected, I'd come across people who had been officers for years at both Kirklevington and Brixton who were consistently excellent in my experience, and when I'd asked others in a position to know, why they hadn't been promoted I would be told, 'Don't know Phil, there's a black mark on his record of service clearly, he might have fallen out with a PO, Chief or a Governor somewhere, but I know what you mean. I'd go on an escort with him anytime, work with him anywhere. You know you can trust him, he'll back you up.'

A more transparent staff reporting system had largely negated this situation before I retired.

The Chief continued to show his faith in me and I was next selected to work in the Detail office. Eddie Smith was the PO initially and he was excellent. The officer, an old pal from the canteen, Barry Thornton, also worked in there. Barry's job was to put all the staff's predictable shifts on the Detail board so that the PO could add overtime as necessary. My job was too check, total and reconcile all overtime worked before submitting it to the Chief for his approval. This would clearly be good experience for me once I'd done my 'penance' and advanced. I was beginning to realise that the further you progress the more important the management of budgets/numbers becomes.

Dick H was the Chief's clerk and he would come up to the office each day to collect my completed USR forms. Dick liked a bet but he also liked a pie and a pint in the club at lunch-time. He was aware that I held a credit betting account with Tote Bookmakers.

'Phil, I won't have time to go up town at lunch-time do you mind putting one on for me?'

I rang them in a couple of times then I started to lay them myself, much to the amusement of Dave Wigley who had replaced Barry Thornton over time and PO Eric Robson who had replaced Eddie Smith.

Dick had no idea that the others knew about our 'little arrangement'. They would watch him pick up the USR's and surreptitiously slip me his list of horses and money. Dick's bet was a yankee, a four horse accumulator, which, if all the horses won would mean a sizable pay-out for me.

Dave and Eric would spend the afternoon awaiting my demise as we listened to the racing results on the radio. Dick rarely backed favourites and favoured 'co-incidence bets.' He would favour horses with names like, Dusky Dick or Dick's Delight. I must have winced, broke out in a cold sweat a couple of times, when the likes of Dick's Delight came in second, beaten a short head at 33/1, my obvious discomfort a cause of much mirth in the office. Dave said to me one day, 'I hope he cops and bankrupts.'

I served my 'penance' and was granted a PO's board the following year. I prepared for it diligently. There were going to be no mistakes.

However, when I went in for the interview I noticed that one of the panel had been the Deputy Governor at Wakefield for a short time when I had been in the canteen. He'd been a betting man and we'd actually discussed in the past, whether it would be possible to make serious money for the common fund if I was allowed to run 'a book' from the canteen, he brought this up as soon as I sat down.

In truth it wasn't a question I was anticipating or necessarily wanted to answer but I explained that I would ensure no prisoner got into debt because I wouldn't give credit and yes money could be made to improve facilities but we would have to expect a negative press, problems with the tax authorities and the British Bookmakers Authority.

I then went on to explain how operating the canteen with good governance allowed us to make a small but regular amount for the common fund, built-up trust between the staff that ran it and prisoners when it was ran consistently fairly and that as a manager who had an overview I was in a position to keep the Security PO informed on who held the money and how it was being used. Crucial information that informed his security strategy. How it had informed his strategy for dealing with the specific threat posed by paramilitary prisoners, the Dep was nodding animatedly in agreement at this which increased my confidence.

I was out in no time and it seemed to go well.

A few weeks later I heard that I'd been successful, I'd made PO. My old pal Barry Thornton rang to congratulate me, he had been promoted to SO a couple of months prior and was in-post at a Youth Custody Centre in the North East, Castington. More importantly he told me that they were in the process of building a new unit and would need another PO.

Barry was aware of our ambition to buy a plot of land in order to build our own house. 'Plots are a lot cheaper than around York and Wetherby boss and more plentiful.' I had become well known at Wakefield for going around Mr Persimmon's and Mr Wimpey's show houses and purloining their plans on my weekend off, with the house-build project in view.

I had a discussion with Joan and she agreed it was worth a punt, helped by the fact that she was in the early stages of compiling her family tree and she had discovered branches in Northumberland. 'It'll give me time to research some graveyards/parish registers whilst you're at work.'

I set about compiling a submission as to why I should be posted to Castington. This was subsequently endorsed by the current Deputy Governor Peter Atherton and he actually sought me out to congratulate me on the quality of the submission which was a nice touch which I very much appreciated. Within a month I'd been offered the post and I couldn't wait to start, Barry had told me that I would be one of a small group of PO's who were senior managers and who had a fair amount of autonomy, 'more than you'd get in a bigger jail Phil.' Exactly what I needed to further progress my career.

During my last shift at Wakefield we were involved in a lock-down search for a gun. I would traditionally meet the chief prior to leaving the prison for the final time and I was looking forward to that. Mr Challenger had been consistently supportive since I'd arrived, I never mentioned the fact that I was one of those at the training school that he'd threatened to sack after we'd kept everybody awake marching up and down the parade ground, of course, but I would have liked to have shown my appreciation for how well he'd encouraged me.

However, the search dragged on and my meeting was cancelled as finding the gun was the priority so we weren't dismissed until after 21 00 hours. A few fond farewells but no drink in the club! In truth we were all knackered and just wanted to get home. So that was Dispersals for you, unpredictable and high-risk.

Chapter Six (1984-1991)

Group Manager

'We've a hostage situation upstairs boss.' 'Okay Willie, you're trained. You'll be number 1 negotiator, I'll sort you some back-ups, establish a rapport and I'll brief the governor and the Chief.' Willie Shaw was an experienced landing officer with excellent interpersonal skills, he got immediately 'into role mode.'

Negotiators work in pairs but only one will be operating at any one time. This is a strategy to prevent the negotiator falling-in into the black hole of the perpetrator's crazy world. I quickly ensured Willie had back-up and the process continued.

The negotiators were skilfully using stalling tactics, no matter what the perpetrator requested, no matter how small, 'Sorry I can't give you that, I'll have to ask the boss.' The negotiator can't make executive decisions. Convincing perpetrators that the obvious is in fact false is a skill all good negotiators need and Willie Shaw had it in spades!

'Look, no one's going to judge you for coming out, it takes a brave man to walk out that door. Your friends would respect you.'

Willie was skilfully controlling the dialogue, delivering his lines in a calm but authoritative voice, assertive, firm but non-confrontational, clearly controlling the dialogue. I was hopeful it would be over soon and it was, within the hour.

Both prisoners were located in the segregation unit. We quickly discovered that the more passive of the two prisoners had 'agreed' to be taken hostage to help the perpetrator get a transfer back home to the West Midlands. This didn't happen and both spent some time segregated, pondering the wisdom or otherwise of their actions. Young prisoners could be impulsive and rarely consider in advance what might be the consequences of their actions, something I was to witness often in my first few weeks as a wing PO.

HMYOI Castington shared a site with HMP Acklington, a category C prison. Both establishments occupied a former airfield in Northumberland about seven miles south of Alnwick. Castington was a male youth custody centre holding long-term inmates between the ages of 17-21. The accommodation was single cell and the prison offered full and part-time education programmes, vocational courses in construction, painting and decorating, motor mechanics, general laundry, catering and gardening.

I took over from John Nichol as the PO on B wing, when John moved to Security. My wing SO's were Tom Naughton and Ben Slater; both came highly recommended. Tom was a Brummie, ex Royal Navy, Ben was a Geordie, an ex -miner. My cleaning officers were both ex Army, Mickey Thomas and Bertie Ashurst, both had held rank in the Forces, were used to handling young men and they had established an excellent rapport with our YP's. I quickly felt blessed but what they and the prisoners thought of me in the first few weeks is open to question.

We used to operate a minor report system. A minor report was used when it was felt that though a prisoner had transgressed and it had to be dealt with officially, it was deemed that the transgression didn't warrant a Governor's adjudication.

I would hold the disciplinary in my office. The officer would read out the charge, I would ask the prisoner to make his plea, guilty or not guilty, give both the officer and the prisoner time to explain, respond to what each said, before deciding guilt or otherwise. The penalties I could hand out following a finding of guilt tended to be a period of 'bang-up' (no association) or fines.

I remember flying out of the office one day to confront a prisoner when I heard him behaving the same way towards a member of staff as he had when I'd dealt with him on a 'minor' the previous day! Tom Naughton pointed out to me sensitively sometime later in the privacy of my office, that it was nothing personal, 'a lot of YP's have a short attention span boss, you'll get used to it, it's the difference between handling adults and young prisoners.'

Tom had dealt with youngsters at his previous establishment, Onley and had a superb rapport with them.

I used to lodge with a couple in Acklington village, they had been supplying short-term accommodation to staff since the early 70's when the first prison on-site, Acklington opened.

The man of the house 'Curly' was the Steward of Togsten working mans' club. Leaving the house early one morning I tripped over one of his shoes near the gate! I remember thinking, it must have been a good night in the club last night!

Curly took me along there one evening and introduced to their oldest member, an eighty-year old ex-miner. Later, out of hearing, he told me that earlier in the year he had arranged a club outing to Vaux's brewery in Sunderland. The old miner had got to the club early to claim a good seat on the bus and was very excited. 'He'd already had about seven pints when the bus came and, of course, we had a couple of cans or three on the way doon. Suffice to say Phil, he was so drunk when we arrived at the brewery that we had to carry him in!' The security staff on the gate couldn't believe it. They said they had seen a few carried out after the tour but that this was the first time they'd seen someone carried in! He slept all the way home.'

Returning from a lunch-time session in the gym one day I was met by a clearly distressed landing officer: "Can you come upstairs Sir? I've found a body!"

He'd shredded one of his sheets, braided the strips and made a cord. After climbing onto his bed he had tied the cord to the bars of the cell window, made a noose of the other end which he had pulled tight around his neck before stepping out into space...

The officer was in bits. He'd spoken to the lad as he banged him up at lunch-time, he'd appeared okay, he'd given landing staff no clues that there was anything wrong. I sent the officer off duty having de-briefed him, taken his statement, and sealed the cell.

I learned over the years that often a number of warning signs preceded a self-inflicted death in custody, and that often mood and demeanour proved unreliable indicators of risk. They appeared reasonably happy just before death however warning signs included:

food refusal
refusing to work
refusing medication
agitated behaviour
smashing property
becoming quiet and withdrawn

This lad had exhibited none of the above and his relationships in and out of prison had shown no signs of disruption. It took two or three days for the gloom to lift, but as far as I was able to determine no prisoner had had prior knowledge; and there was certainly no blaming of staff by prisoners as occasionally happened at other establishments.

My time at Castington coincided with an upsurge in football-related violence and the extra unit was quickly filled up with 'firms' from Newcastle, Sunderland, Middlesbrough, Leeds, Manchester and Liverpool. We quickly identified the risks to good order and control associated with this and came up with an inter-agency plan to deal with it.

The psychology department led by Cynthia McDougal and selected officers, devised an innovative course to mitigate the potential for violence. Mickey Thomas, one of my cleaning officers played a leading role. It involved written exercises and role play and it proved very successful. Not only did it improve relationships between prisoners and staff but it also encouraged respect between agencies, proved they could better serve the needs of prisoners and protect the public by working together, rather than in isolation. It wasn't always sweetness and light but what trouble there was from time-to-time was never football related.

As a prisoner, the first thing you need to be able to do in prison is to develop the ability to distinguish friend from foe, to differentiate the harmless from potential danger. It's this ability to 'profile' that can keep a prisoner safe. There is a tendency for them to stick up for their own, but the first aim of the course was to convince them that any 'beefs' they might have with each other outside, were suspended while inside. The second part was to come up with more constructive ways of filling time. The education department was excellent, well used and was housed in a specially constructed unit. It had a number of first class vocational training courses that were always fully subscribed.

We had a super gym, playing fields and even a squash court! The PE department was well-staffed and was run by a forward-looking Lancastrian, (obviously as a Yorkshireman I had trouble getting my head round this), called Jim Clow. Jim and his talented staff would attempt to put on a varied set of activities for officers who wanted to get fit during the lunch-break. Most of us would play 5 aside football till the cows came home. However, I remember turning up one lunch-time and PEI Jimmy Hughes introducing us to the game of shinty!

Jimmy was originally from Govan, nevertheless, despite the accent he explained the rules in great detail and with clarity.

The game commenced and all went well for about two minutes until Bob Russell who worked in the Admin department and who was one of the most decent and civilised people you could wish to meet off the field of play, changed once on it. He was a talented footballing centre-half and extremely competitive. When he tackled you, he left his mark!

A couple of body-checks, shinty's raised, sticks clashing and even the man from Govan proved that though you can take the man out of the place, you can't take Govan out of the man, he waded in, shinty raised. A halt was called to proceedings before World War 3 broke out. It was back to more sedate 5 five-a-side football for quite a significant period following this incident.

An officer called Neil off C wing asked if I played rugby. He played for Blyth, a local rugby union team. I had played a bit of league but was a novice when it came to Union rules. He convinced me to turn out for the 2nds or 3rds I can't remember which and I was accompanied by Martin Dajoux, an excellent young officer who went on to become a PEI, and an ex RSM, Bertie Ashcroft, both from my wing. Bertie was one of those annoying people who doesn't look the part before kick-off, cig-in-the-gob, bandages on the knee, scruffy shorts but supremely talented once the first ball is kicked.

I was put on the wing and Neil explained the rudiments of the game and off we went. I thoroughly enjoyed the experience and even scored a try. In the clubhouse after the game I was informed that custom and practice dictated that anyone who scored a try on their maiden outing had to buy a bucket of beer! As you can imagine this is not what a Yorkshireman wants to hear so I did a quick risk assessment. This involved making a note of how far it was to the exit and what was between me and it; five large ugly men, I paid-up with a grimace rather than a smile. I did turn out for them a few more times before returning to football, ending-up playing wing forward or flanker. This position gave me more freedom than playing on the wing and I felt, and was much more involved.

The success of the football hooliganism course received national coverage and featured on the BBC news. We had tested it out with a football game between the staff team and participants in the course; I played in the game, it went well and snippets of it featured in the news-feature I seem to remember.

We then decided to test it further by having a game of rugby; staff versus prisoners.

I'd moved to take over in security by this time and when it became known that I would be playing rumours abounded that a couple of ounces had been put up for whoever crocked the Security PO! This wasn't personal - it was just business. It's a tradition in prisons to hate Security, they stop all the 'fun,' it's part of the game.

In the event, the game started and the man from Govan and his team-mate from Ashington Rugby club, a 'ringer' who shared my surname, came flying in tandem to complete the first tackle, all but putting the kid carrying the ball into the next field. A bit of pushing and shoving ensued as both sides came together, hand bags at ten paces, huffing, puffing and posturing, before the game restarted.

From that moment on until the final whistle no quarter was given by either side but it was one of the best and fairest games I was ever involved in. There were cheers from the side-lines whenever I was caught and 'downed.' It was nevertheless humbling at the end to receive heart-felt thanks and congratulations from some of the hardest of the lads. I remember thinking we're making progress, we must be doing something right.

Shortly after I'd arrived Dave Faulke the Training PO had offered me a Personal Ability and Leadership Course (PALS), as he was unable to attend as he had only recently taken-up his new post.

It was based at HMYOI Deerbolt in Barnard Castle. On arrival we received a brief from PO Brian Edwards who told us we would be put through a couple of exercises locally before spending time under canvas 'up on the Pennines.'

Within quarter of an hour a group of fourteen of us from prisons and regional offices across the whole of the northern region were speeding towards Barnard Castle in a mini-bus, armed with a map each of the town with the brief to make for the Auction Mart post haste as soon as we were dropped off! We would be timed!

I'd been studying my map carefully; it transpired that none of us knew the geography of the area. I was one of the last to be ordered from the bus and had had time to identify some large structures near the Mart. I set off at a fast trot, and arrived at the Mart within six minutes. We all arrived at our destination, a number panting, within ten minutes of each other. I remember we were all standing around in small groups talking animatedly to each other when suddenly a police car screamed to halt close to us and a women wearing a head-scarf got out closely followed by two male officers.

'That's him,' she shouted pointing at one of our group, 'He stole my bag!' We stood open-mouthed as one of our group was led away!

Once we had recovered we gathered round for a quick conflab, identified where the Police Station was and decided to go up there mob-handed to plead our group member's case.

It gradually dawned on us that this was part of the programme, an early test for the group.

The desk sergeant played his part superbly and didn't make it easy for us to formulate our arguments. Brian reappeared after about fifteen minutes to break it up and we all returned to Deerbolt for a debrief.

Brian then informed us that once again we would be dropped in town in pairs, each pair was giving a small 'float' from which we would be expected to buy provisions suitable for eating while camping.

Later that evening it was pitch-black and we found ourselves inside the perimeter of a local army barracks, light sweaters under field jackets and trousers, combat boots; our task is to take possession of a piece of raised cloth, blowing in the wind in the distance but guarded by an armed army patrol, I remember thinking 'this is something else!'

The following day, late autumn, we were up in the Pennines where it was bracing to say the least. We were given grid references and armed with compasses we took it in turns to lead the group towards identified points. Late afternoon Brian called a couple of us across and told us we would pitch tents here for the night, that our 'meal' had been buried, he gave us a grid reference of where we would find it. Our task then was to go back to the group to brief them.

We quickly uncovered a couple of rabbits, potatoes, carrots and a cabbage. One of our number, an SO at

Liverpool who lived in a small-holding near Preston, was soon expertly skinning the rabbit, the tents were erected, we got a fire going, and myself and a girl from area office went in search of kindle. When we returned a gorgeous-smelling rabbit stew was almost ready to eat.

The following day, high-up in Pennines one of Brian's assists, a fellow PO from Deerbolt, was explaining about the topography and history of the area and about the war-plane debris to be found. He clearly knew his stuff and he made it come alive. It was fascinating.

Later in the day as the mist and rain closed in we were split into two groups I was put in charge of one. It was made clear we were now in competition, we would make our way as quickly as possible towards a given grid reference, but that it was the group effort that would be rewarded, it was not about the individual. I had an ex-Royal Navy Scot, who, though a bit of a character, was a tad overweight, I also had two girls from area office on the group. The groups were evenly matched, though my Scot's friend struggled and the girls helped me see him through. They were superb, showed real team spirit and a will to win, as our team eventually did. Our final destination, Tan Hill, England's highest sited pub!

Brian called two of us over to give the next brief.

'Pitch your tents in that field over there, we'll be here for the night. Now we have arranged with the pub landlord that from 19 00 hours we, or rather you, will run the place, providing refreshments and entertainment. Go back to the groups, tell them what's required, arrange who's doing what and be ready to go on time!

Initially, nobody wanted to provide the entertainment but everybody wanted to run the bar.

By 21 00 the restaurant was full, those providing refreshments were like old hands and the SO smallholder from Liverpool had just finished a brilliant ten minute monologue to rapturous applause. Yours truly had given a rendition of Cliff's 'bachelor boy' to a more muted response. Our ex Royal Navy Scot was doing requests by the end of the night. He had a superb voice and repertoire and might have struggled on the enforced march but he was the star of the show that night, encore after encore; a superb talent unearthed.

We returned to base the following day for an end of course meal and individual feedback from the facilitators. We had learned how to receive, interpret and impart instructions, how to brief a group clearly, how to take the lead when required. We had learned the importance of considering individual needs, how to recognise the strengths and weaknesses of others and to take this into consideration so that everyone is able to contribute to their optimum.

Brian and his team were extremely flattering about my contribution and I couldn't have been happier with their appraisal. One of the most worthwhile and well-organised courses I ever attended.

I had been to view a plot of land for sale in a small coastal town called Alnmouth shortly after I arrived in the area. It was a decent plot, about a third of an acre but it didn't have the sea-view we craved.

A couple of weeks later we viewed another decent sized plot of about a third of an acre in an historic and beautiful coastal village called Warkworth. It was a bright, clear day and it had a view of the river Coquet meeting the North Sea, I could see the lighthouse in the distance, we had to have it. The vendor was looking for offers in the region of £20,000. We got it for £19,200, and the next thing was to find someone to build it.

Six months in a cramped flat in Amble where the kids attended school was the price we had to pay for the future benefit of our own place, which would have plenty of space and a view to die for.

We got a local builder to tender using our plans and using conventional materials, as well as two kit-build firms, Begus and Clanwood Homes. We settled for a conventional build on the grounds of cost.

The build was relatively trouble-free though our plans did make the front-page of The Alnwick Advertiser one weekend when a number on site complained about us 'putting a house amongst a lot of bungalows!' Actually, there was already another house on-site; nonetheless it was an inauspicious start with what were to be our new neighbours. It lead to John Nichol who had become my champion, mentor and critic in equal measure to declare: 'hooligans coming-up from Yorkshire trampling all over our rules and regulations, destroying our countryside.....'

We were soon settled and I could progress my career.

By January 1987 the prison population stood at 46,350 some 2,600 more than the year before. It had risen to 49,100 by March of that year, close to capacity, with many housed miles away from homes and families. The total for England and Wales became 51,029 by July

1987 with an 'overflow' of 648 being held in Police cells, a significant cost to the Prison budget.

Prison officers, including me, had thrived on a tradition of excessive overtime which cost a fortune and was fundamentally inefficient. The POA leadership exploited the difficulties of the service in order to buttress their position and in some areas reduced prison governors to subservience. The management of the service was reluctant to confront the union. Industrial action could and had put prisons at risk and had brought about what management most feared: disorder, a break-down of security, and, escapes.

In April 1988 the Home Office was negotiating pay and conditions with the POA. The average earnings of a prisoner officer were £15,000 (of which 30% was overtime). Nevertheless, some staff began to take industrial action. On 29 April prison officers at Gloucester refused to obey the Governor's orders. The Home Secretary directed that there would be no further negotiations until normal working had resumed. The prisoners took advantage of this situation, which they were following on their radios, and started a disturbance. Copycat riots broke out at several prisons including ours.

Indeed, during a general smash-up when I attended my old wing (I had moved to security by this time) a lad called Hunter, who had a history of climbing onto rooves at previous Establishments to shower staff with debris, proudly pointed out: 'I've done every window apart from those in your old office Mr O'B,' as if he expected me to thank him!

He quickly determined my mood by the look on my face.

'If you go, I'll come down for Mr Ashurst and Mr Thomas.'

By May 1987 the Home Secretary had reached an agreement with the POA which led to Fresh Start. The essence of this was to recruit new staff and do away with the system where the average prisoner officer worked sixteen hours overtime per week. It was estimated that it would save 15% of what was previously spent on prisons.

Our local committee held a packed meeting to outline the Fresh Start proposals. If accepted, the PO rank would earn £17,500 for a 49 hour week. With the overtime I worked I was on track to earn £26,000 that year. It was to mean a considerable drop in income for me!

When Fresh Start was put to the vote locally and nationally it was accepted by the membership. The only dissenters at Castington were myself and one of my SO's, Robbie Kirk, Robbie was sitting next to me when the vote was taken. I don't remember him doing much overtime so maybe he just followed my example. Mr Nichol had the last word on the matter: 'You are Zapata the original Mexican overtime bandit and Robbie's into Foster and Allan, need I say more? Two nutters!'

We were on the 'losing' side; staff voted overwhelmingly for a higher salary, excessive hours were to be a thing of the past, shifts were to be more 'family-friendly,' they refused to be a slave to the job like my generation had been and in the end, I reluctantly had to accept that they were right. It did, however reinforce the notion that the only way now to maintain or preferably enhance my living standards, was by attaining promotion.

As usual John Nichol left me a first-class fit-for-purpose Security department. he kept a close eye on me and the fact that he used to relieve me each day for lunch-break, helped him do this.

Fresh Start had extended my role. I was also the Orderly officer which meant carrying a radio throughout the day so that I was first response to any incident, hence my need for a relief.

Francis Masserick, a scouser with a sense of humour, had been the Dep when I first arrived but he had been succeeded by a northern Irishman called Ivor Woods. He became Head of Custody in Fresh Start terms and I reported directly to him. Ivor also had humour but was much more hands on than Francis had been; he wanted to understand the minutiae; little did I know then that our relationship would last throughout our respective careers.

I had inherited an ultra-violet device from John Nichol and had decided to use it to catch a bully whom wing staff believed was 'taxing,' (taking) canteen items from more vulnerable prisoners. In conjunction with canteen staff I had 'marked' up items the victim had ordered, unbeknown to him.

I nicked the perpetrator when I had reason to believe he had the items he wasn't authorised to have in his possession. I produced the evidence at the adjudication to the perpetrator's amazement. He spent some time segregated before I transferred him out.

This 'first' encouraged staff to furnish me with more and more information crucial to minimising bullying and maintaining order and control. They could demonstrate to prisoners the 'good' that could come from giving information. It unearthed a latent talent amongst some staff for gathering intelligence, and I quickly had to develop a card index system for storing it.

Some of the information was so sensitive that staff would ask me to see the 'source.' Searching officers would bring the prisoner to a discreet empty office off the main drag. He would be left with me whilst they went for a coffee, I never kept them any longer than they would normally be away for a cell-search. Ivor soon found my 'secret location' and I often spotted him looking in as he passed. He was clearly interested and pleased to see it happening but he never compromised it.

With the introduction of Fresh Start we found that we had to carry-out the same tasks with less staff. Ivor had asked me to devise a safe and secure line-route system to facilitate prisoner movement to work.

Some of the staff, including a number of my PO peers were sure it would cause mayhem, 'prisoners will assault each other Phil!'

The reality of the situation was we couldn't have it both ways. If we escorted individually with less staff we'd be getting people to work at the time you would normally be bringing them back in for lunch! My staff and I manned the route covering alarm bells along the way, we soon had it up and running smoothly and it speeded up movement to work without incident. It was soon accepted to be a much more efficient system than the one operated previously.

I liked to visit all my areas of responsibility each day and I built-in time to visit the workshop and wing patrols, gate, and reception, twice a day, I would attend the visits room each afternoon. Apparently this hadn't been done much in the past and was resented, particularly by some workshop officers.

They had given me the nickname chopper and did unflattering drawings of me in the Occurrence book, I was too intrusive! God only knows what they were getting up to before I started. Ivor heard and gave me his total support, John Nichol always had my back on all matters relating to security, order and control; that was the true measure of the man.

The Head of Custody usually dropped by my office at lunch-time for a debrief. He turned up one day but I'd already been relieved by John Nichol and I'd shot off down the gym.

'I was making your excuses to Ivor, Phil, when your security SO Mr Harrison entered the office and said: 'I've something Phil must see as soon as he comes back. Shall I leave it in his in-tray or put it on top of his Sporting Life?'

Of course John couldn't wait to give me Ivor's answer.

'If he needs to see it as straight away you'd better put it on top of his Sporting Life!'

'Give that Harrison a clip Phil, he did that on purpose, he's from Consett, dodgy people from up there.'

John found it difficult to resist winding me up and of course, my occasional impetuosity helped him no end in this endeavour.

I learned an important lesson around this time, I had made a boob with an annual staff report. The officer had done very well in his first year on our group and I'd marked him accordingly. Latterly his performance dipped but as he correctly pointed out I'd never warned him nor given him time to improve.

I immediately carried out a review on how to manage underperformance:

- Act early. Don't let the situation escalate until it becomes chronic;
- Gather information to understand what people are doing wrong (and what they are doing right);
- Talk with them one to one. Get straight to the point with a clear outline of the issue and specific feedback on their performance;
- Allow them time to respond;
- Together, come up with ideas for tackling underperformance;
- Decide on a course of action, starting with a key issue;
- Follow up to review progress and give further guidance.

I got Joan to type this up for me, put it in card-form for guidance, I was never caught-out again, an important part of the management learning curve.

Information from the wings started flowing in to me thick and fast so I began teaching the officers responsible, how to spot potential sources, this was something that I didn't remember being taught in any detail during our Initial training but it was a skill I'd started to think about and develop at both Brixton and Wakefield.

I'd realised that a potential source might be somebody who held a grudge, wished to work towards a transfer or sentence reduction, be tempted by material reward or might just want a quiet life that a bully made impossible. I told them that when setting up a meeting to always assume that someone was watching, and always to look the potential 'source' full in the eyes but keep moving on.

Each wing ran an officers' tea-boat,' the cleaning officer would normally accept responsibility for it. He would bring money to the gate each week for milk purchased and my staff would hand it over to the milkman on their behalf. I was told that some of this money was going missing and this had led to a poisonous atmosphere between my staff in the gate and wing staff. I then discovered that money from the visits float couldn't be reconciled; another area my group were responsible for. This money came from items of food and drink sold to visitors and would also be kept in the gate overnight. I had my suspicions and I was determined to resolve the situation as a matter of extreme urgency.

On my next weekend on I received a phone call from our police liaison officer. A complaint of sexual abuse had been made against one of our officers by his daughter. The schoolgirl had a Saturday job and had told her boss who had informed the Police.

Our PLO was already aware of my suspicions about this man and was about to join colleagues searching his house. 'Is there anything particular you feel he might have Phil?'

'Well John Nichol had 'lost' a micro light, a torch and a pair of cuffs he used for training purposes when he was doing this job and I know he suspected that this bloke had taken them, he was on the group, he had access.' I also mentioned the missing milk and visits money.

A short time later he called me back, they'd located John's missing items, he denied taking the money, he was charged with theft of prison property and sexual activity with a minor.

I informed the Governor, Chief and Prison Service HQ before liaising with the Admin department the following day to draw up documents for his suspension.

I spent the next few months travelling to and from Bedlington Magistrates Court for his remand hearings, he was on constant bail throughout this process.

In the end the Magistrates decided not to proceed with the sexual assault charge as they felt there was not enough evidence.

I was dismayed then to be told that the Police didn't intend proceeding with the theft charge on the basis that 'it was minor not worth the cost to the public purse'!

I was outraged and went to Ivor to plead our case with the prosecuting authorities. I pointed out that his personal record showed that he had been suspected of embezzling prison club funds at his previous Establishment, again he had had access. That rather than dealing with it he was allowed an expenses paid move to Castington, that there were governance issues for us managers, and that staff were watching closely how we were dealing with this... just because another Establishment 'bottled' dealing with him we shouldn't.....' To his great credit Ivor intervened successfully and the theft case was sent to Newcastle Crown Court for trial. By the time it came to court I had already moved to pastures new on promotion.

I finished at lunch-time one Friday and I wasn't due back on duty until the Tuesday of the following week. I received a phone call mid-afternoon from Colin Baker who was standing in for me, he told me two prisoners had escaped from the Workshop. Deep depression.

After speaking to Ivor I immediately set to work on an escape prevention pack; there wasn't going to be much leisure time that weekend.

Ivor had expressed concern about the relatively large number of new staff straight from the school that we'd recently received for the new units: 'they're not as streetwise as most staff.'

That was true but only experience cures that. I had found them keen to please and learn and it certainly hadn't been any of this group who resented my workshop patrols when I'd started on Security. It started me wondering why Workshop staff had been so uncomfortable about my checks; what were they trying to conceal and should I have done my rounds randomly being less predictable?

My subsequent inquiries determined that no staff member had entered into a conspiracy to aid the escape. However there was evidence that other prisoners in the shop knew it was going to take place and had helped it succeed by deliberately diverting the attention of staff, both on the day and whilst it was at the planning stage.

It was probable that at least one, if not both of the prisoners, entered the roof space to do a recce of the proposed escape route on a couple of occasions before the day of the escape and that they took into the shop and secreted items that would be needed to aid their escape.

I had all this at the front of my mind as I developed the training package.

I had agreed the approach with the 'big man from Strabane' as we'd taken to referring to Ivor in private, and both he and John Nichol attended the first course to give it their seal of approval and support.

My aim was to twofold: to educate staff about the methods prisoners use to 'condition' them, and secondly, to show them how to spot the tell-tale signs that prisoners are planning an escape.

In relation to the first point I demonstrated that prisoners planning an escape would seek to discourage staff from entering an area they have been working on for escape purposes.

I showed how they would do this by picking on, therefore picking off, the most resilient member of staff. They might use spite, bile or create a threatening atmosphere. Alternatively, they might seek to build-up relationships with individual officers with the aim of getting them to vary the laid-down routine. All tried and trusted methods that had worked successfully at other places in the past. I gave examples of this; the most prominent being the mass-escape from the Maze prison in Northern Ireland in 1983 which was still fresh in the memory.

We discussed the factors that might cause someone to contemplate escape: breakdown in a family relationship, 'dear John,' boredom and loneliness. We agreed the need to be aware of mood changes.

The training sought to show how a potential escaper will analyse the structure in which he is housed and will make a plan to defeat it. This he will be accomplish by checking the floors, the walls, the ceilings, plumbing and electrical fittings. He will study staff routines, paying particular attention to staff working in the grounds. Bricks are one of the easiest materials to break through. All brick walls get their strength from their bond. If the prisoner can break the bond he can break the wall. I demonstrated that the simplest method of doing this is to select the position from where he wishes to exit. Then by starting in the middle, he can remove all the mortar from around a single brick. He will do this by continually scraping away at the mortar with a make-shift chisel. It might take him a few days as he can usually only work on it when the Establishment is in a patrol state. Once he has removed the first brick the bond is effectively broken, he may have to remove several more before the rest are loose enough to remove by hand.

At the end of each session, the prisoner will need to collect all the powdered mortar scraped from between the bricks and wet it with water or urine so that he can re-use the mortar to cover up the work he has already done, adding a bit of soap to aid the rebinding process. This is in order to prevent any staff noticing what he has been up to. He will further obscure this work by putting his bed, table, or some other object up against the area in which he has been working. The training sought to reinforce the necessity of the traditional, daily locks, bolts and bars check, making it crystal clear why this must never become merely a perfunctory task.

Our prison was surrounded by a mesh fence and the whole area was patrolled by staff, the fence was a secondary perimeter barrier for escape purposes.

Clearly it wasn't much use breaking out of your cell if you become stuck in the grounds. The patrols will pick you up. Our escapees had taken on the secondary fence barrier and beaten it!

The fence was made of weaving metal links; I set out to show that cutting the links in a set pattern reduced the number of cuts that had to be made and therefore shortened the time it would take to escape. On the other hand I pointed out that, solid mesh metal fences could be climbed using a home-made claw grip. I sought to demonstrate that these could be easily made if you had the capacity to heat a 6" nail and drill it through a 4" length of broom handle. Much easier to do in a larger prison like Wakefield with its Welding shop than at Castington, but not impossible. Our escapees had shown a level of skill and cunning, as well as an ability to condition staff. These were skills fundamental to any escape and risks I had to counter. It took me three months to put all staff, including Governors through the course. It proved time well spent.

I found myself giving a variation of this course over the next forty years, particularly where I hooked-up again with 'the big man from Strabane.' He would frequently remind staff 'there are no new ways to escape, they're all variations of things that have been tried before and our complacency helps facilitate them.'

Six months later I applied for and was granted a promotion board. If successful I would be leaving the uniformed ranks after two decades to join the junior governor grade rank, G5.

The big day arrived and I got the 10 19 train from Newcastle to Kings Cross.

One of the board members was Francis Masserick who had been the Deputy Governor at Castington when

I was first posted there, he knew the prison and its geography extremely well. He had clearly briefed the other board members about the prison and about the escape. Not unreasonably, many of the questions asked concerned this with particular emphasis being put on how I'd managed the aftermath.

I explained about the training package and confirmed that all staff had been put through it. And how I now regularly took a snapshot of a activities. How we tested our systems regularly by doing contingency exercises. How we had got staff to recognise that since Fresh Start we had to do more to best serve and protect the public, but with less.

I acknowledged that I'd upset staff in the past by my 'managing by walking about' but now they'd started to accept change and that by linking it to priorities like security, control and the safety of staff and prisoners they had better appreciated the need for it. I could produce indicators that demonstrated that the way we worked now was more effective; there were fewer assaults; we were finding more on searches. Both staff and prisoners were volunteering more intelligence; incidents of bullying had reduced significantly. We'd got all staff to accept that security was everybody's responsibility, not just the preserve of those working in the security department. How Ivor had encouraged me to be the high profile champion of necessary change.

I was tired on the train going back up to Northumberland but I was satisfied that I'd done my best. The board had seemed happy with my answers and extremely interested in the detail. They had been fair, so what more could I ask? I was fast asleep by the time we pulled into Newcastle and the guard had to give me a tug.

Within a month I heard that I was to be placed on the promotion list and was invited to apply for advertised vacancies. Joan was keen to return to Yorkshire and Full Sutton prison near York, was desperate for staff. Following some high-profile incidents of disorder, staff of all ranks had proved reluctant to move there. It was a no-brainer - or was it?

'You'll be the one with no brains Phil if you go there. Looks like the cons are running it. It's dangerous!'

I decided to bite the bullet and express an interest anyway, I was immediately offered a place which I accepted. I took up my new role as a junior governor grade on the 1 April 1991. I hoped the date wasn't an omen. However, many staff at Castington were sure it was and made sure I knew it!

PART 2

Governor Grade (1991-1995)

Chapter 7

Governor Grade (1991-1995)

A Baptism of Fire!

I had barely got my key in the lock when a prisoner who had his back to me, (he had been peering up the corridor, waiting for an escort to the gym), saw me and moved quickly into my face issuing threats. 'Who the fuck do you think you are, we'll fucking break you if you think you can come down here and bring your own rules?'

He was jabbing his finger right in my face, the ferocity of his verbal assault was such that I didn't immediately notice that he had been joined by two other prisoners, they stood silently but menacingly at either side of him. Nobody came to stand with me!

'I haven't seen my old man in twenty years and you fucked me off and when I get down there there's a black geezer off another wing using it.'

'Look I was carrying out instructions, I was told that the special room facility had been withdrawn because it had been abused. If another governor allowed it to be used he wasn't following orders.'

This only seemed to inflame him further, I was sure he was going to strike me, I began to shiver, perspire, his fellow inmates remained at his side mute, looked straight ahead, arms down by their side. No staff came out to assist me though I thought both the Censor's office and the Detail office, which were nearby, were manned. We were in sight and hearing of the Cleaning officers' office.

I remember thinking that part of his strategy must have been to prove to staff that I was helpless and there to be abused therefore I wasn't worthy of support. If I was right it had worked!

Then it began to dawn on me and I started to question. I'd got twenty years in, the decision I'd taken was done in good faith, I'd never been left isolated like this before, this isn't right.

My confidence and composure started to return slowly; I'm began to think 'fuck this'.

He must have noticed the change and he started to goad me.

'Okay you want to have a go?'

He was still jabbing his finger at me but he'd moved back a bit.

I must admit I'd gone through the fear barrier at this point and was close to letting one go.

'I don't know who you think you are or why you've been sent down here but we run this wing and that won't change.' With that he wheeled round in unison with his 'bodyguards' and was gone.

I secured the wing gate after them, entered my office and collapsed into my chair. Welcome to D wing Phil!

Full Sutton was a purpose-built, maximum security prison for men in category A or B. It opened in 1987 and was sited about eleven miles east of the city of York in open countryside, in the village of Full Sutton, near the town of Pocklington. It did not accept prisoners serving less than four years nor those who had less than twelve months to serve.

My first day at Full Sutton went okay but the place was very tense; it was clear that the prisoners had the upper hand. It was immediately obvious that they had got used to by-passing uniform staff and demanding instant access to the duty governor. It was clear I would need operational cool when carrying out this task.

I was in charge of a wing that had been recently vacated by Iraqis living in this country, who had been detained for the duration of the Gulf war.

We were planning for an intake of National R43 inmates; these would include sex offenders, high-level police informants (supergrasses) and a number who for various other reasons, drug debts, feuds with others in the prison, would be deemed vulnerable if placed on normal location.

The second day I had to travel by train to Newcastle Crown Court for the trial of officer Bithel.

I gave my evidence under the gaze of Ivor, a member of the POA committee and John Nichol, who was once again working in Security. The officer was subsequently found guilty and received a non-custodial sentence, he did of course lose his job. The judge released me from court as soon as I had given my evidence and I returned immediately to Full Sutton.

I heard later that as I was leaving the witness box the 'big man from Strabane' turned to John Nichol to comment on how well he thought I'd done.

'Yes Governor but would you buy a used car from him?' Mr Nichol always liked to have the last word where I was concerned!

Duty governor on my first weekend-on it had been constant hassle, at lunch-time I had a food refusal on one of the wings, potatoes too lumpy! There were indications that these were organised to disrupt, wings appeared to take it in turns and the complaints occasionally, but not always had merit.

Later that afternoon I got a call to attend the segregation unit, I was briefed by a tall recently promoted senior officer who had come to us from Leeds. A high-profile prisoner subject to Notice to Staff 10/74, a 'lie-down,' was running around the exercise yard, creating havoc. On my arrival, he clambered part way up the wire mesh and refused to come down. The senior officer, who to his credit had spent some considerable time trying to reason with the clown before calling me, was now all but spent. I instructed the ECR to inform the duty BOV member and asked them to arrange for a C and R team to join me. I went to the yard to try to reason with the idiot but urged on by the rest in segregation he wasn't for listening to me.

Twenty minutes later we'd forcibly removed him back to his cell and put him into one of those 'canvas cardies' that do up at the back. I was making my way back to the senior officer's office; he was briefing the recently arrived BOV member; when suddenly, he collapsed and started to hyper-ventilate. We needed an ambulance for him, he never returned to work at Full Sutton.

The following day didn't start well when an idiot ran into the back of me at a junction in Easingwold, on my way to work. I was duty governor again, covering for a colleague who had gone sick with stress. It was a horrendous day. Food protests at lunch and tea on different wings, we were now sure they were planned in advance and coordinated. One prisoner stabbed another during the evening on their way back from the gym; there was 'claret' all the way up the main corridor, I didn't get home till midnight!

After a couple of months we received our prisoners. PO Alan Close and a couple of very talented Senior Officers had worked-up the systems it has to be said with only minimal input from me, I always seemed to be away fighting fires, metaphorical and physical, in other areas of the prison

The majority of our prisoners were much less demanding than those on normal location. However we did have one, a Londoner, who was much more street-wise than the rest and who had reputedly been an informant for one of Scotland Yard's most famous or infamous detectives, depending on which crime correspondent you chose to listen to. Two books on him were subsequently written with contrasting views on his honesty.

The prisoner was a heavy-duty successful criminal involved with drugs and money laundering on an international scale. In time I was to discover that many organised criminals were also confidential informants for one set of cops or other. That the drug business was a business of informants. Partners, friends, brothers, it made me wonder if there were any 'staunch' people left. It was a multibillion pound business in which it is understood everyone was grassing everyone else.

The prisoner was a pain in the arse, a shit, wanted all the attention at the expense of other prisoners, I know he held an equally high opinion of me. My PO told me one day that he had nicknamed me 'the Pawnbroker' on the basis that whenever he asked me to do anything I always said 'leave it with me!'

The Governor, Mr Staples was determined to get a grip of the prisoners and asked me to set-up a Working Party to look into the possible use of one of our wings, F wing as a means of providing the main prison with help in dealing with recalcitrant prisoners. I had a principal officer, two senior officers, a psychologist, and two officers, one a POA committee member, to assist me.

I enjoyed chairing the Working Party, we met five times before submitting our report.

We knew if our recommendations were approved they would have to be introduced using existing resources and would have to complement existing work within the establishment.

We had sought to find ways that would provide the Governor with elements of control to deal with destructive, subversive inmates, that would be seen to be effective. We recognised that though segregation removes most of the opportunities for disruptive behaviour it does nothing to help a prisoner resolve the problems which may lie at the root of his failure to cope with normal prison life. We acknowledged that the most dangerous prisoners would require long-term segregation and would need to be regularly assessed to discover what degree of freedom and association they could safely accept. We submitted our recommendations on the basis that in the fairly open regime of a long-term adult prison this must be consistent with staff having complete confidence in the ability of the system to support and maintain control. I was pleased to hear that both the

Governor and the Unions were in agreement with our suggestions and were keen to see them implemented as soon as possible. A serious incident on one of the wings was soon to hasten the need for these changes as well as leading to a new challenge for me.

The Governor rang me at home one day whilst I was on a rest day. There had been a serious incident on D wing earlier in which the duty governor and a PO had been threatened with scissors before much of the wing had been destroyed by rioting inmates. Someone with experience would be required to take over immediately in the aftermath, to regain order and he felt I best fitted the bill and it would be where I would be working on my return to duty.

Clearly I'd 'talked the talk' whilst chairing the working party, it was now time to show I could 'walk the walk.' Bloody 'ell!

The events that led to the incident started on visits the previous day. Staff observed a prisoner accept and try to conceal a parcel which they believed contained drugs. They intervened as he attempted to plug it. A melee ensued before the prisoner was removed to the segregation unit.

The prisoner had been a prominent member of PROP (preservation of the rights of prisoners) and was therefore well-known with a following. Just before lock-up at tea-time a rumour went round the prison that he had been beaten-up. His friend, a man named Peters, demanded to see him. The duty governor attended the wing and refused the request on the basis that he had just seen the prisoner in the segregation unit as part of his duty tour and that he could confirm that he hadn't been assaulted and indeed he just told him that he had no complaints.

This failed to satisfy Peters who demanded loudly that he be allowed to go check for himself. A number of other prisoners immediately sought to support him, including an IRA faction and some younger hangers-on. An IRA prisoner began slashing at the governor and a PO with a pair of scissors, the younger prisoners started damaging and destroying wing fabric and contents. In terms of the whole wing it was less than fifty per cent that got actively involved. Nevertheless a number of young staff, having never experienced this type of violence previously, vacated the wing in fear.

At this point a number of London gangsters, including two from bitterly opposing families on 'the out,' perhaps fearing either serious injury or even the deaths of the duty governor and the PO, no doubt also to protect themselves in the aftermath, and to demonstrate that they weren't involved, removed the two staff to the relative safety of the PO's office and stood guard at the door. C and R teams subsequently restored order. This was the febrile atmosphere I was about to be sent into to change! My second meeting with Peters is described at the beginning of this chapter.

My first day on the wing there was still a bit of tension about, the IRA faction and a number of others identified in the disorder had been relocated elsewhere in the system, Peters remained because despite him voicing the demands that pre-empted the disturbance he'd not involved himself in the violence, indeed he'd banged himself up when it got out of hand.

He had come to see me on application on my first day.

'Any chance of a private visit with my old man gov, my parents split when I was six, the old man emigrated to Australia, he's back now but this will be the first time we've met since I was a kid...'

When a prisoner needed privacy, for example, if there had been a death in the family, discussions when a marriage was breaking down, permission had been given to use a private room that used to double as a legal visits room. It was sited just away from the main visits area and was therefore discreet. Unfortunately the privilege had been abused, couples having sex in it, just prior to the disturbance. It was a privilege withdrawn in its immediate aftermath.

I informed Peters of this, refused to support the application and he had stormed out of my office not best pleased. He was furious when he went into visits and found a prisoner from another wing using it! This led to the incident described at the beginning of this chapter.

I patrolled the wing daily and I was extremely concerned that the first couple times I did it I found all the officers were in the wing office rather than patrolling, they did come out onto the landing to be fair and I stayed awhile to chat with them. I knew I would have to keep this up, the body language of some of the prisoners told me this was new to them as well and a minority clearly didn't like it and made their feelings clear, 'you lost gov, didn't they give you an office?'

A couple of days later I'm about to start my rounds, it was mid-morning. Arriving on a spur I found the search team surrounded by prisoners who clearly objected to the process. I intervened and remained there until the search had been completed. This was intimidation pure and simple, an attempt to prevent officers carrying out a legitimate task, I knew then it was going to be a slog.

I remember one of the lads that had acted as Peter's bodyguard when he was threatening me, coming to see me to make an application shortly after the incident. His application was legitimate and I approved it. However, I noted that he was the Laundry orderly which should have meant he behaved more responsibly and not have got involved. I made a mental note to deal with him when the opportunity arose. The other little shit that had stood with him was discharged soon after; he was only doing a 5 but clearly thought he was a gangster or a 20 year bank robber! I made a mental note if he returned he'd be mine. He was from Halifax.

I spent a couple of weeks without a PO as mine had been detailed to non-frontline duties for a spell, post-incident.

Within a couple of weeks I got a new PO, Anna posted in on promotion from Holloway. She made an immediate impact. She was excellent on process, particularly sentence planning and this became part of our approach to re-establish staff control. Another was a prisoners' consultative committee, which I would 'chair' although a prisoner called Downer clearly felt this should have been his role! I'm afraid though that although Anna was quickly accepted and a breath of fresh air, a significant minority still wanted to fight me!

Anna liaised with prisoners' home probation officers, a team-based approach. We championed offender engagement in sentence planning. We identified protective supportive factors e.g a prisoner's family as well as other significant relationships to aid the transition from offender to ex-offender. From my point of view, it was part of the counter-conditioning process, we had to re-establish the primacy of the prison system. Easier said than done when your wing contains the rumoured chief-of-staff of the IRA who was so important to the Organisation that the police had foiled a plot to free him by helicopter when he was on remand at Brixton. Leading figures in both the Kray and Richardson 'firms.' A Turkish Cypriot 'firm' of armed robbers and drug importers, who if you believed the national Press, had made enough money to clear the national debt....

Ivor had joined as the Deputy Governor on promotion and though he accepted that an open regime was normal in a long-term establishment. He maintained, 'that doesn't mean prisoners can do exactly as they wish from day-to-day.' He firmly believed that the regime should offer a range of constructive activities as well as the opportunity of association. That all should work! This came as a shock to the system to many of the white mature, notorious prisoners, the organised London criminals. They had been used to getting up when they pleased, at their leisure. Their power had enabled them to condition staff to allow them to live a life of comparative freedom. Some of those employed as cleaners received full pay for doing nothing, the work was being done by other prisoners on their behalf. Ivor had jumped on this straight away:
'Wings are selecting their own cleaners direct when these decisions should pass through a Labour Board

with a significant input from the Security Department. Nobody will ring up again and state that an inmate will not volunteer for off-wing work but is happy to be a cleaner. There's been a tendency over the years for officers to take the line of least resistance in response to demands from prisoners and look where it's got us, disturbances, bullying, it stops now from next Monday everybody works or attends education!'

Ivor had been brought in to support the Governor in establishing stability and though I know he respected the sentence planning work we were carrying out, particularly Anna's contribution, (he mentored her and she was promoted to the governor grades within a couple of years) he left me in no doubt that my principal tasks were to promote security, control and justice.

Security referred to my obligation to prevent prisoners escaping. Control dealt with my obligation to prevent prisoners from being disruptive. Justice was about treating prisoners with fairness and humanity. For these basic requirements to be met there are two basic rules. They are:
a) Sufficient attention has to be paid to each of the requirements.
b) They must be kept in balance.

Quite soon prisoners started seeing the benefits of joining in the sentence planning process and modifying their behaviour. Both solicitors and home probation officers started extolling the reports submitted by Anna and the personal officers and when people started being re-categorised and progress could be measured, attitudes started to change.

I remember one prisoner coming to see me one day: 'Boss all of a sudden our parole reports are going in on time, people are getting re-categorised quicker. Why didn't this happen before?'

'Because when staff are fighting fires all day long, and dealing with disruption, everything gets put back.'

However, I had to chuckle one day when a south London robber came to see me on application, the brother-in-law of a well- known sit-com actress. The request was appropriate and I granted it, but as he was leaving the office he turned back to me and said: 'you realise that there will be trouble on Monday if you start that 'going to work' nonsense!' The chaps still liked to think they had the final say.

I went in early, I'd got up at 05 00hours, on the first day of 'the all must work rule.' In the event everything passed off peacefully. We'd introduced the proposed changes through the prisoner/staff consultative committee and though there was a bit of anger expressed by the prisoners in the first instance, we'd given them a month to get used to the idea prior to implementation.

Things began to gradually improve on all fronts though as if to prove the adage 'one swallow doesn't make a summer,' Anna put her bag down somewhere and forgot about it momentarily when she was dealing with a query, somebody scooped it up and made off with it!

I had just given the order to bang-up so that we could search the whole wing, when it was returned fully intact. I remember thinking, we'll get there in the end.

Things continued to settle, the vast majority of prisoners were either working or attending full-time education, the joint leader of the alleged south London torture gang was excelling at Art. I noticed him and a few others had gone through the Chaplain and declared themselves Muslim. I queried the sudden conversion with him one evening whilst I was on my 'rounds.'

'It's for the food gov especially the curry.'

The IRA Chief of Staff Brian Keenan, a confirmed agnostic Communist who he was playing Bridge with him, merely smiled.

However I had an extremely intelligent former university-educated chemistry student who had more degrees than good sense. He had been a lone-wolf operator, a one-man angry brigade. He had been convicted of making and sending bombs to selected members of the elite.

I pulled him off education at the request of a distraught teacher. He was asking questions that you would have to be an Oxbridge professor to answer. He was hogging the attention, hell-bent on disrupting the class and humiliating the teacher.

I removed him and put him in a workshop, I was determined to teach the prat a trade! Our paths were to cross on a number of occasions in the future after he'd caused the fall-out with the Home Secretary of the day and his Prisons' Minister and cost the Head of the Prison Service his job.

A new cook and baker was posted-in and the quality of the food improved, complaints about it were less frequent but I remember a lifer clown from Sunderland coming into see me one day to complain about and show me his weird diet, one I'd never heard of! He caught me on a bad day or at least that's how I justified it to myself later. Half way through his rant, I stopped him, picked up my cheese sandwich and said: 'what about me, I've had fucking cheese all week?' Without thinking I launched it at his head. He couldn't believe it, whipped round and left the office never to return. Not very senior-managerial on reflection!

The threat of industrial action to do with continuing niggles over the implementation of Fresh Start seemed ever present. We were sent on stand-by to lodge overnight at a police college near Lancaster with a view to deployment at HMP Liverpool if uniform staff walked out. Thankfully it came to nothing and we returned home the following day. Crossing a picket-line was still foreign to me, even though I'd resigned from the POA and joined the Prison Governors' Association by this time. Throughout our long service together Ivor continued to chide me over my Labour Party sympathies and my red tie! He'd started at Castington by calling me Tony Blair! He knew how to hurt, I was firmly in Gordon Brown's corner.

I received a call one afternoon from a GP in Glasgow who tried to convince me that one of our chaps up there on home leave, was too ill to return. When I was less than enthusiastic I felt him panicking, his voice cracked, he was virtually pleading, to my mind he was being put under pressure. I suspected that my jolly Glasgow bank robber was on his shoulder. I made it clear I wasn't going to negotiate and that if my man didn't return by the time required to fulfil his release terms I would report him as an absconder to Glasgow's 'finest.' He returned on time. It was the 'chap' who had 'returned' Anna's bag. I'm sure that the fact that he was awaiting this period of home leave at the time was purely coincidental and that he was just being 'a good citizen.'

He was an interesting individual, tall, muscular and very intelligent. Not connected to any particular group but respected by all. He'd done the best part of a twenty year sentence. After a couple of years causing mischief he'd settled down and applied himself through the Open University before attaining a first class degree in Sociology. The discipline required to achieve so highly had also helped him progress through the prison system and he was now a category C prisoner awaiting re-allocation to a less secure prison.

I got the opportunity to move him when I received a call from the duty governor of a cat C prison, Lindholme.

They were desperate to get rid of a little Columbian drugs mule who had moved there from one of our vulnerable prisoner wings but the Prison Department then panicked, having second thoughts about putting foreign prisoners in lower category jails and rescinded the decision. They demanded he be returned to the High Security Estate immediately. He spoke little English but knew enough to realise relative freedom was being snatched away and he'd spent all day weeping and they clearly couldn't handle it. We agreed a 'swap' for my Glasgow man, I knew there was no way he would cry, however I do remember thinking I can't be sure he won't set them off!

Sure enough about a fortnight later the same governor rang me up trying to return my Glasgow man. I pointed out that he was a cat C prisoner and that they would require grounds to re-cat him to B before I could even think of accepting him. I knew he was too clever to give them grounds to do that. The problem was they felt intimidated by him, which I understood, but at the same time he was being paid the same as me and I had to handle him and another hundred plus of a similar ilk. My man was 'playing them' I knew he'd soon settle, cat D open conditions and full time attendance for his 'Masters' at a red-brick university was his aim and I didn't doubt he'd make it. You can take the boy out of Easterhouse but sometimes it takes a little longer for Easterhouse to leave the boy.

When I'd left my previous wing I'd been replaced by an ex Healthcare PO from Lindholme and as far as I could tell he'd done an excellent job. He'd stopped me on a couple of occasions to commiserate about the aggravation on my new wing. He told me that he'd only accepted the posting at Full Sutton because 'they let me have your wing!' He clearly felt guilty, what a turn-up! I admired his honesty and felt no resentment, I believe in fate and had no doubt it would work out.

My mate Alan Brown who had been at Full Sutton for almost a year when I arrived, and who had responsibility for Personnel and Training, had advised me to apply for a business administration course. The course, which Alan was already attending, was run from PSC Wakefield in conjunction with tutors from Leeds Metropolitan University.

I applied and was accepted for the course to start in the new academic year. A number of people had dropped out at the end of the Alan's first year so our year combined with Alan's and we 'freshers' were expected to catch-up.

The 'freshers' included a lad from Rotherham who had started as a POUT with me at Leeds, this was the first time we'd seen each other since our Initial course. He worked at that time at a Women's prison in the south and used to travel up and down by train with my friend Keith Saunders who worked at the 'Scrubs'.

I remember Keith telling me about one return journey they made: 'couldn't believe it Phil, I'd just ordered us coffees and was thinking of buying a kit kat when he took hold of my arm and said have one of these producing from a carrier bag more biscuits than Tesco's and Sainsbury's combined could muster! I couldn't believe it!' He'd clearly raided the Staff College stores of which there was one on each landing to allow domestic staff to replenish each room after cleaning them. To call him 'a character' didn't do him justice and this wasn't the last surprise he had in store for us.

As well as tightening-up the regime the Governor John Staples and Ivor were keen to bring staff of all grades and disciplines together and when approving my training had tasked me with finding a way of accomplishing this. The conditioning process prisoners had used so successfully, splitting uniform staff and governor grades, had also been used to set wing staff against civilian staff by putting pressure on them over the 'late' arrival of things like private cash which would take time to process. This was something prisoners refused to consider.

So for part of my Business Administration Diploma I'd been given a budget by the Governor to establish a team-building course. I'd found a converted barn to live, cook and sleep in, we had Malham Cove and the

Yorkshire Dales on the doorstep and a pub less than a mile away.

With the help of the PE Departments at both Full Sutton and Castington , I'd devised a series of exercises on the lines of my PALS course at Deerbolt.

It proved such a success in a short space of time that the national Chairman of the POA, Brian Caton rang me up to see if we could accommodate a member of staff on long-term sick due to stress, as a way to help him regain his confidence and fit him to return to work. I was only too pleased to get the call. I liaised with Brian and we arranged it. The officer returned to work on a phased basis post the course.

This formed just a part of my dissertation which was about how best to attract and retain Staff, about how to win today while positioning yourself for success in tomorrow's market place. In effect, anticipating greater competition from the private sector. How to anticipate and steer change in this newly more competitive environment. Little did I know then that within eighteen months I'd be part of the first public sector team selected to compete against a number of private sector organisations for the right to re-open a prison that had been mothballed a couple of years previously.

We would occasionally have individual seminars with our nominated tutors. The biscuit plunderer had been sitting in his tutor's office one day when she was called away for an urgent consultation with her manager.

He noticed a list of questions on her table, took a copy of one and to our utter amazement produced it in front of a couple of us later that evening over a game of snooker.

To say we were well prepared for the following days exam is an understatement!

Back to Full Sutton, and despite the improved atmosphere and more compliant prisoner population, the threat of violence was always bubbling under the surface.

I received a call from the Head of Ops early one afternoon and was told to get an intervention team together.

A prisoner from Scotland who was on his way to face further charges in the south and was lodging with us overnight, had taken a member of staff hostage. He'd been unlocked after lunch by mistake, wandered along the landing, passed a room in which an officer was censoring mail using a paperknife. The prisoner had seized the opportunity and the knife and taken the officer hostage, when we interrogated his file we discovered he had previous for hostage-taking!

The negotiation process had continued into the late evening. I had been summoned to the Command Suite on a number of occasions to receive progress reports and to agree the intervention password with Mr Staples, the incident commander. My team had no breaks.

We had to remain out of sight of the negotiators in case that put them off their task. Our roles were diametrically opposed, they were seeking to build-up a rapport with the perpetrator, a peaceful resolution, whilst we would only be deployed once it had been decided by Gold Command that there was no chance of this happening and that the hostage was in imminent danger. We would then intervene using force and we were kitted-up accordingly.

168

My role was to lead the assault eventually but in the meantime to keep the team in a state of readiness to act swiftly and decisively at a moments notice. Not easy as the negotiations drag on. I was lucky to have an excellent squad, totally professional, they kept themselves in a state of readiness, mind cold, blocking out negative thoughts, not panicking, compartmentalising their emotions, focused on the task.

Late in the evening, the indications were that the perpetrator was about to take the hostage on the move. 'Freemason,' I received the agreed intervention code word, we sought to intervene, but the perpetrator immediately gave up. I administered his surrender and we removed him to the segregation unit before attending the Command Suite for a debrief.

We continued making progress with prisoner participation in the rehabilitation programme particularly in relation to sentence planning.

However one weekend I came on duty to be met by Cathy James, the governor in-charge. She told me that my nemesis Downer had taken offence at something I'd written in a report on him and was threatening 'to do me!' He'd received a synopsis of the report from his solicitor. Cathy confirmed that she had informed the ECR and had made contingency plans to support me should it be necessary. I could feel the eyes of everyone in the Control Room on me as I made my way, with some trepidation, along the corridor to my wing. It was a High Noon feeling.

The cleaning officers acknowledged me as I entered the wing but looked nervous. Poor bastards I remember thinking, they have enough to put up with without me adding to their woes.

Nothing for it, meet whatever comes head-on, I decided to start with a tour of the wing. By this time, I suspect there was an early warning system for staff to alert them to my presence, I rarely found them in offices when I 'toured.'

I dealt with a few queries from prisoners and staff, there was no sign of my nemesis. I had been back in my office for about fifteen minutes, when there was a knock on the door which opened before I could react and in strode Brian Keenan. Then followed the strangest conversation I can recall. He wasn't making an application but as the most senior IRA man he wasn't interested in sentence planning or reports, he would have nothing to do with this system and I knew from my experience of them at Wakefield, it was a waste of time trying to engage them in this.

I remember being extremely wary at first as we talked in general terms about the prison and politics, nothing controversial, he never touched on Irish politics. He did somewhat surprise me when he mentioned that the site on which the prison stood had been the Pocklington aerodrome and that his father had served here with the RAF during the last war! We must have spoken for about fifteen minutes when we came to a natural pause, he courteously got up and left. Strange, feeling me out but why?

Before I'd time to re-assess further in strode a recently showered Downer, just back from the gym. He sat down before being asked and proceeded to tell me that I was out of order with the remarks I had made about him in his Cat A review report before validating what I'd written about him by telling me: 'if I'd seen you yesterday I'd have done you, but I'm cool with it now, I've no time for you, you're a two-faced fit-up merchant!'

He slammed the door as he left.

What do I do, nick him? I can recall thinking There was clearly a threat issued but everything that happened in my first couple of weeks on the wing carried a threat. We are now seeing some progress, albeit slowly, with prisoners working, attending education, getting involved in the sentence planning process. Prisoners in the Cat A estate will always pose the biggest threat, that's why they are Cat A's! The estate is small and caters for those doing the longest sentences, you can't pick and choose who you will accept and who you will swerve, you have to deal with them all at some time if you spend any time in the system, because they move around.

If the chief enforcer for the Krays and the joint leader of the alleged South London torture gang; supposed bitter gangland rivals on the 'out'; can put this aside, as they clearly could in prison, I could forgive Downer....well maybe not but I never seriously considered nicking him. We'd continue to clash, but it didn't appear to be affecting my relationship with any other major 'players,' including his brothers-in-law the Arifs who appeared to accept that if me and him continued to 'front-up' that was our business.

I hadn't forgotten the errant laundry man and when Mr Staples decided to make C wing a dedicated Lifer wing I called him up and told him I was relocating him there, he almost broke-down and cried as he pleaded to stay!

Peters? A changed man. We spoke often, he got involved straight away with the sentence planning process and made Cat C. Indeed, I was walking through nearby Stamford Bridge one lunch-time and a car pulled-up alongside me:' how's it going governor, I've got my Cat D now and I'm working out, it was Peters!' Prison can and does work when you have accepted processes and assessments of risk in play and most importantly, you deliver!

Anna was still working her magic and when my old friend Alan Brown took the opportunity to return to his home establishment, Frankland, I was asked by the Governor to replace him in Training and Personnel. Anna was given the promotion her efforts deserved and she took over from me on D wing.

I was asked to meet with the Head of Ops one evening before he went off duty, I would be in-charge for the evening period. He briefed me to expect a prisoner that Northern Irish Special Branch would be lodging with us overnight. I was to locate him in a discrete area of the prison, establish a rapport with him, discuss our IRA prisoners with him to establish the pecking order. He was a tall but slight figure in his middle forties, I was to see and hear him speak often in the media in the years that followed, as peace-process talks progressed. I went through the list; most he knew but just confirmed the intelligence we already had on them and acknowledged those in the SSU as particularly dangerous which confirmed that we had them correctly located.

He went pale and got very nervous when I mentioned Brian Keenan, he was clearly the one!

One of my new tasks was to liaise with the unions on the Governor's behalf on an ad hoc basis. I attended a meeting in the early days in my new role with the POA

172

chairman. He was a South Yorkshireman who despite supporting his members with a passion, was openly appreciative of the work Ivor had done in relation to re-establishing the authority of staff and making the prison a safer working environment. I undoubtedly enjoyed a favourable relationship with rank and file staff because of my relationship with Ivor. However, this particularly convivial meeting took place in the club. It was after 22 00 hours, the beer was still flowing, my opposite number was ready to discuss all matters late into the early hours and this became obvious...However when all was said and done he could then waddle away to his quarter two minutes away while I had an hour's journey ahead of me and I still hadn't had my tea! I determined these meetings would have a limited agenda from then on and would be time-bound.

I also had responsibility for media relations and John Staples introduced me to the Editor of the York Evening Press. The governor was keen to find a way of providing the public with positive news of the prison following years of negative headlines in relation to fires and disorder. It was agreed that I would supply a weekly column for the paper with the heading: Full Sutton News. In effect I would write to all Departments to find out what they were doing, deciding what would make good copy. I would then compile my column and submit it to the Governor who edited it before it was forwarded to the Evening Press. In the early days the Paper would send us a supply of free copy which we made available to the wings. Like us all, the prisoners took great delight seeing their accomplishments recognised in print.

John Staples had made it clear that though my role was essentially to give the establishment a better profile he didn't expect me to do just 'puff pieces.' I had reported hooch and weapons finds in my column and a Japanese Radio Station had picked it up via Reuters. They ended up interviewing me one morning early, they were mainly interested in 'hooch,' what it was, how it was made!

Though I was subsequently nominated for a Butler Trust award for my work in this area my TV and Radio interviews didn't impress my peers nor my family who insisted that despite my many years living away from the City, 'you've never lost that Bradford accent.'

I received a call one evening on my weekend off from Governor in charge Gerry Hendry: 'There's a riot at Stockton prison Phil, as you live not too far from there I've despatched a C and R team, can you meet them?'

I met my team in the gym, ensured they were kitted-up and ready to go before making my way to the Command Suite for a briefing

There, to my surprise I was met by Stockton's Governor Mr Alan Rawson: 'hello Mr O'Brien I haven't seen you since you walked out of the Control Room at Wakefield.' There was no answer to that, in truth I'd forgotten about it, it had never been mentioned since I left Wakefield, Ivor had never given the impression he knew about it though as my line-manager at Castington he would have access to my personal file.

'What was that about,' asked Brian Edwards, a fellow Commander and the facilitator of that superb PALS course I had attended at Deerbolt? Back home for 05 00 hours, all sorted, no staff injuries.

Shortly after this incident the fact that I'd walked-out of the Control Room at Wakefield became a talking point back at my home station. Somebody could have overheard my exchange with the Governor at Stockton and told a friend at our prison, I never found out why it suddenly came up. There were however a number of ex Hull staff at Full Sutton including at least two Governor grades, including Ron Barrett, Head of Operations. There appeared to be a definite split on how my action was viewed between those who had come-up through the ranks and the accelerated promotion grades, the latter viewing me less favourably. Cathy James mentioned it to me in passing one day and I detected disapproval. I could respect that, she'd been supportive throughout my time there and we shared a love of the Waterboys, swopped tapes discussed their music, it didn't negatively impact on our relationship longer-term.

I was duty governor, it had been a quiet day, when I was called to the Governor's office at about 17 00 hours. Ron Barrett was there and between them they briefed me to expect a High Risk Category A escort from Frankland prison. Ron explained that there had been an incident at Frankland involving this prisoner and a mobile phone, things were sketchy but they wanted rid of the prisoner post-haste. He was a major Turkish drug-dealer and a member of the PKK. Under no circumstances was he to be allowed access to a phone when he arrived. Ron needed more time to assess the situation when he had all the facts, he could have been planning an escape with outside help. I was instructed to locate him in the SSU.

The Special Secure Unit had a bad mix. It contained two IRA men who had shot a PC and a Special Constable on the A64. The senior of the IRA men, as well as escaping from inside a Belfast prison, was responsible for the death of the highest ranking SAS officer to die in the Troubles, following a shoot-out when he was on the run.

It also held two high-ranking Mafioso, including one who was suspected of killing the banker Roberto Calvi who had been found suspended from Blackfriar's bridge.

It also held one of the Gartree helicopter escapers, he had a serious lip problem, he never shut up. I toured all the wings during the early part of the evening, briefing the senior officers and I tasked one with control and restraints experience to have a couple of teams standing by to assist me in the SSU at lock-up, should I need them.

I attended the SSU last to test the temperature and to brief the senior officer. He told me that the Mafia weren't out on association, he thought there had been a disagreement between them and the IRA! The SO did express concern about me banning the new reception from using the phone. I returned to my office to await the escort's arrival.

About fifteen minutes before lock-up the traffic on my radio informed me that the new prisoner was on his way to the SSU. Sure enough about five minutes later I got a call from the unit's senior officer. The Turk had asked to use the phone, my instructions had been relayed to him and he'd gone straight out on the yard to discuss it with the IRA, who were now refusing to come in for lock-up.

I immediately rang Dave Gant, the governor in charge for the weekend, and briefed him, agreed a course of action, before attending the SSU and going straight onto the yard.

The Turk and the Gartree crank were straight over to find out why I'd banned use of the phone for the new arrival. I explained that those were my instructions and that he could seek an explanation tomorrow and ask for a review. The senior IRA man said nothing but was listening intently. There was a bit of spleen from a couple of hangers-on: 'this has never happened before, you're making up the rules as you go on...' Suddenly there was a noise behind me and the first of two C&R teams arrived. I motioned them to the office before my gaze returned to those on the yard. They all looked towards the senior IRA man. He was clearly pulling the strings.

The Turk approached me speaking softly: 'I have no wish to cause trouble what's going to happen now?'

'Well no matter what some might think I'm not acting off my own bat, the governor in charge knows what's happening and has approved my course of action. I will ask everyone to leave the yard and if they don't I will have to forcibly remove them. I can't leave people of their security category outside any longer.'

They all moved away to the centre of the yard for a quick discussion before coming in. The Turk nodded to me as he passed, the senior IRA man looked at my name-badge as he on his way in, enquiring of his co-accused: 'a cousin of yours?'

I quickly de-briefed my teams and up-dated Dave Gant. Late home, supper burnt again!

I started looking for my next challenge and noticed that a bid team was being formed to compete with the private sector for the right to re-open a prison in Rochdale that had been moth-balled some years previously. Applications to join the team were being sought so I applied, hoping that my management course and previous experience might make me a suitable candidate.

Within a few weeks I received a call from Peter Earnshaw who was to head-up the Public Sector team. He had been my line-manager at Wakefield when I'd run the canteen. He offered me a position which I accepted.

So my time at Full Sutton came to an abrupt halt, support for the Bid Team was a priority for the Service and I was to be released to join it as a matter of urgency.

It had certainly been a character-building experience in spite of the fact that I'd got two decades of service in before going there. I left with a tremendous respect for front-line officers, particularly those new to the Service; it was a tough first posting.

On my last day a steady stream of people came to my office to say their goodbyes. It was particularly gratifying to see Pete Cartwright, a POA committee member who I'd worked closely with on a number of staff discipline and welfare issues. Pete had also been a crucial member of the Working Party I had chaired. I'd learned a fair bit in my first governor role but I needed more experience before I was fit for the next grade. It was time to go and seek it!

Chapter 8 (1995)
A Brave New World?

We are in Rochdale's 'place to be seen' (if that's not a contradiction in terms); our Hotel's receptionist had 'marked our card!'

I was giving a debut outing to my red jacket purchased in Mark's and Spencer's in St Albans whilst I'd being visiting my sister in Harpenden earlier in the year.

I thought it was a good fit, though I'd already suffered mild chiding about it when we had met up in our Hotel's foyer, and this reached a crescendo when we had entered the bar 'of the place to be seen.' Almost immediately we spotted someone in the same red jacket, we walked around the corner and spied another one, then another....! The lads, led enthusiastically by Alan Horner, gave me hell; far from being the fashion icon I thought I was earlier in the evening I'm.....This was not a good introduction to my new colleagues.

Buckley Hall was a former public sector prison that had been moth-balled. We were a public sector group chosen to make a bid to re-open it as a Category C prison, we were in competition with a number of private sector companies with the same aim.

We operated from a large open plan office in the centre of Rochdale.

When I'd originally turned-up in Rochdale I'd been pleased to realise that I knew two people on the team. Peter Earnshaw who was in charge of the whole process had been my boss at Wakefield and Alan Horner had been a fellow officer at Brixton. Madeleine Moulden was our team leader.

She explained that our brief was to look in detail at everything a category C prison was required to do and find the most cost effective way of accomplishing it.

The basis of our approach was to show that greater use of prison auxiliaries allows the service the opportunity to take a closer look at staff before employing them as officers. That this had the benefit of allowing individuals to get a flavour of the service to see if they wish to make it a career. A full appraisal of staff in the working environment must be more effective from the point of view of selection than a short test and a twenty minute interview. Our approach acknowledged that we would have to declare in advertising that some prison auxiliaries might be recruited as potential officers, to comply with open competition rules. This would effectively mean operating a dual recruitment policy, similar to one operated by the police.

I was already beginning to have doubts; my experience to date, particularly in the high security estate but also in a busy 'local' like Brixton had taught me that having a solid core of experienced staff was essential to the maintenance of order, control and security.

I had long believed that Swedish psychologist Professor K Anders Ericsson had it right when he proposed that many characteristics once believed to reflect innate talent are actually the result of intense practice extended for a minimum of ten years, a theory based not only on studies of sportsmen but on the practice habits of, among other groups, violinists and typists. Ericsson's idea has been taken on and popularised by the Canadian journalist Malcolm Gladwell, who proposed his 10,000-hour rule in 'Outliers,' the story of success, citing The Beatles experience in Hamburg in the early 1960's to support his belief that world-class expertise can be attained in many fields through sustained practice over a period of ten years. The private sector was starting from scratch, they could and would be able to undercut us on wages, eighty percent of a prison's budget. It soon became obvious that for us to be able to compete with the private sector in the future would require us finding a way of enticing our most experienced and expensive staff, referred to as 'two for ones.' to retire. We could then replace them with new staff, a cheaper option. There were clear risks in this approach as far as I was concerned, I began to feel a little uneasy. I'd just left a prison where the lack of balance between experienced and new staff had been weighted in favour of the latter, with near disastrous consequences for order and control.

I was still in regular touch with my old mate Dave Turner and he knew where I was working, he'd mentioned that he occasionally got 'up north' as he was now on the Yard's Fraud squad, he said he'd look me up if he got the chance.

So it wasn't a complete surprise when I got a phone call one evening to say: 'I'm on my way to Bradford to interview a Nigerian, where are you staying, we'll have 'a meet.'

I got back to the hotel to be met by the receptionist with whom we'd agreed a good deal on arrival on the basis that the group would be there for six months! The truth was our full subsistence rate only lasted for three months and if the project lasted longer we'd be moving to a cheaper option. The Met's finest had turned up mid-afternoon and asked for 'the same rate Phil Obrien's on!' She was not amused. I introduced Dave to the group in the bar whilst we were having a pre-meal drink.

We all sat down for the starter and to open the conversation and to include Dave, I made the mistake of asking if he thought his forthcoming interview, and therefore the journey, would prove positive and worthwhile.

'He was a member of a group operating a 419 scam, the advance fee fraud, on our manor. I'm not sure about this particular one. We'll be discussing tomorrow as it happens, but he's well overdue so he's going to have it no matter what. Do you want that last roll gov?' I looked across at the accelerated promotion member of our group he had addressed, his mouth open, clearly aghast at what he had heard, unable to fashion a reply as his soup dripped slowly down his tie....

My fault was I should have known he wouldn't behave. I already knew that when they had started splitting up the Flying Squad following corruption allegations, they had put him back in uniform, a shift Inspector at some small south London station. He'd lasted about eighteen months: 'WPC's Phil, always going sick, women's problems, I can't be doing with them.'

Old style with no use for women in the job and if given the option preferred to bring his suspects in unconscious!

We had two high-flying Governor 4's on the team and this exercise was tailor-made for them, their drafting skills were first-class and they were full of ideas. William Payne had a first-class degree from Oxford and Shane Bryan the same via Cambridge. However, in many ways they were like 'chalk and cheese.' William was the best of British, arch-type civil servant from a bygone age, imbued with old fashion standards, wouldn't take a taxi if he could walk, conscious of cost and public duty, sober-suited.

Shane was something of a dandy, immaculately turned-out, a smile never far from his lips, favouring dickey bows but extremely able. I was working with Shane one day on the Facilities management/ Works Department part of the bid when I got a glimpse of his CV. A law degree, a Master's degree in Criminology, an MBA, Master's degree in Education....a number of which had been added since he had joined the Prison Service in 1986. He had noticed me scanning it: 'Shane, when did you get chance to do any actual governing whilst amassing all these degrees?' The room was quiet with people concentrating on what they were doing, I hadn't taken this into consideration, laughter broke out amongst the other ranks, Peter Earnshaw and Madeleine Moulden, looked over from their shared office at the end of the room. William Payne pursed his lips and smiled: 'Do shut up O'Brien,' was the learned Shane's response.

Joan's father used to work for the legendary Middleham race-horse trainer Sam Hall. We'd often mused that if we ever got the chance we'd love to have a horse in training at his former base, Spigot Lodge. I joined the Racegoers' club when I noticed in the sporting press that members were being given the opportunity to join a syndicate with a horse in training at Spigot Lodge.

The horse's name was Chantry Beath and it was trained by Sam's successor, Chris Thornton.

Madeleine had given me the afternoon off to go over to Doncaster to watch the horse make its racecourse debut. All the team wanted to back it but I had cautioned them that the trainer felt it would need this run but that if it came through the experience satisfactorily, he had ear-marked another race at Carlisle in a fortnights time for it because he felt confident that track and distance would suit him better and therefore we could expect him to be more competitive.

As predicted the horse clearly needed the run and never looked like making the frame. It didn't stop me puffing my chest out, displaying my owners' badge, enjoying the benefits it bestowed.

A fortnight later I was up at Carlisle with a betting bank supplemented by every member of the group. Chris had said that the stiff uphill finish would play to our horse's strengths, he was confident he would be placed at least. As he predicted, the old bugger made the frame and ensured us a nice each way profit at 16/1, everyone was very happy when I returned to Rochdale and 'divvied-up.'

We were granted more time to complete the project and myself and Alan Horner ended up in a back-street pub within walking distance of the Buckley Hall site. A couple of pints, fried breakfasts, pie and chips most evenings, soon had us piling on the pounds! Mine hosts looked after us too well but after we'd been there a short while we found out that they were promising locals looking for work that they'd have a 'word with us and get them sorted out when we'd won the contract!'

They clearly had more confidence in us than the national press. An article appeared in the Independent stating that Buckley Hall would go to the private sector.

Despite this we subsequently went to London to present our case. Building on our initial ideas on the use of Auxiliaries to reduce cost and make us more competitive we recommended more intensive programmes for training them. We demonstrated how this would develop them to support their wider role in the prison establishment and lead to greater job satisfaction. We would introduce a PPRS system of appraisal which would allow all staff, particularly those in supporting grades, to appreciate fully their role in the organisation and the importance of quality in their work.

We sought to show that with the enhancement and development of professional skills within the prison Auxiliary group, the performance of tasks by Auxiliaries, traditionally undertaken by unified grades, and the increased reliance on overtime as a service arising from increased numbers of Auxiliaries as a proportion of total staff, would provide an opportunity to extend Fresh Start pay arrangements to this grade. We suggested an appropriate remuneration rate scale of £12,500. A more effective management of Auxiliaries would be encouraged rather than inherent dependence on overtime as a pay enhancement. We would provide clearer career structures for prison Auxiliaries.

We outlined the parallels between prison Auxiliaries and Special Constables, though the latter group were essentially unpaid volunteers. Both groups acted in a supporting role and were increasingly used as a pool for recruitment to officer grades. The Metropolitan police had recruited a hundred constables from the Metropolitan Special Constabulary in 1984. We noted that the power of Special Constables was limited by the Police Act 1964 but that their power was similar to regular constables.

We demonstrated the parallels to the use of Prison Auxiliaries from within the Police with the use of support staff by many Forces to perform routine custody duties in police stations, in support of police officers.

The presentation appeared to go well but I'd nagging doubts, not helped it had to be said, because the quality press seemed to be confident that the private sector had the contract 'in the bag.'

Because we'd received a time extension the project had extended into the summer holiday period. I jetted off to Florida immediately after the presentation and before the contract was awarded.

I missed the inevitable 'post-mortems,' Group 4 won the contract, the office had been closed and my colleagues had moved out before I returned. I'd been replaced at Full Sutton but received an offer of a post at Low Newton almost immediately, I readily accepted!

I was sad, I'd looked forward to working in Lancashire for the first time. I'd enjoyed the bid process and I'd learned a lot. Skills that I knew would serve me well in the years ahead.

Chapter 9 (1995-1996)
Nowt so queer as folk

'Phil can I have a word with you later after you do whatever you do when you leave your office just after ten? I've got a meeting now but I should be clear by eleven?'

'Certainly Governor.'

'Thanks Phil see you later.'

Mitch seemed intrigued about where I vanished to each mid-morning. In truth I started my 'rounds,' education, workshop, the gardens, just like I'd been doing ever since I became a manager, it's clearly not the norm, 'managing by walking about,' mustn't have been be part of the accelerated promotion curricular I remember thinking.

I had realised since becoming a manager that if I met all the staff I was responsible for daily I could prevent problems festering and being brought to my office at a later date.

Low Newton was built in 1965 and was situated in Brasside County Durham, it was about two miles from the city centre. Its capacity had increased from 65 to 215 by 1975. It held young remand prisoners as well as a separate wing of female adult sentenced prisoners.

On my first day at Low Newton I'd been welcomed by the Governor Mitch Egan and her Deputy Jim

Willoughby. I would be standing-in for the Head of Inmate Activities who was on long-term sick leave, and my posting was temporary in the first instance.

On the Sunday of my first weekend at the prison I was put on standby to attend Liverpool prison, as a control and restraints commander as trouble was expected.

I was despatched to Liverpool at 16 30 hour the following day and we returned at 21 00 hours on the Tuesday. The threatened disorder never materialised. Mitch Egan had rung Joan on a couple of occasions, to keep her updated on the deployment, and to make sure that she had her contact details: 'ring me anytime, night or day, if you have any concerns.'

As Joan said later: 'I was flabbergasted. In twenty four years in the job this is the first time I'd felt 'considered.' Mitch was special, she got it!'

At Low Newton I was immediately impressed with the education department. Prisoners' needs were being properly assessed before they were allocated to classes, there was a clear structure in place. Classroom behaviour was good from what I experienced on my daily 'rounds' and from what the adjudication records showed.

The clear priority was teaching the basic skills of literacy and numeracy. The department was self-contained, safe and airy; I had dedicated officer patrols. When I wasn't on duty my deputy Alan Bainbridge would tour all our areas of responsibility.

However I did smile wryly when I began explaining to Alan that I wanted to see staff, 'taking their personal officer responsibilities more seriously, progress reports on prisoners are crucial to this process Al, it's an essential part of the sentence planning process, it increases an officer's skill set and if we don't do them they'll bring somebody else in who will, that's the future!'

I could tell by the look on his face that whenever this 'heresy' had been mentioned in the past, the immediate reaction had been to organise a bus and ship them out to Deerbolt, where, I remember a couple of officers telling me: 'they are used to doing reports.'

Some of the chaps are going to get a culture shock I remember thinking, Mitch is charming but she's also determined.

And so I wasn't really a surprised a couple of days later when the Newcastle Evening Chronicle led with a headline that suggested Low Newton was on the verge of a riot. The previous day a couple of prisoners had removed their shoes and were tardy in banging-up at the appropriate time in a short-lived protest that appeared to have no aim. Nevertheless, Mitch was upset, who had planted the story with the press? Disgruntled staff or prisoners or a combination of the two? Having been at Full Sutton in its riotous heyday I was confident I knew when trouble was imminent. You feel the atmosphere change, prisoners who would normally acknowledge you, start to ignore you, those that avoid trouble remain in their cells, the mood changes...None of this was happening, we were certainly not on the verge of a riot.

Mitch was trying to change attitudes, bring them up-to-date, introduce more meaningful work for officers, enhancing their skills. She met some resistance from die-hards with a local prison mentality, 'happiness is door-shaped.' In truth they were a minority, young staff were eager to embrace change and welcomed greater one-to-one involvement with prisoners.

You only need a few disgruntled staff in a small prison, and if they are of sufficient seniority, they can manipulate prisoners and a have bigger negative impact than their numbers warrant. They would be challenged!

We were still involved with the horses and off we went to Haydock Park one Saturday for the Bollinger Champagne Handicap. Chris Thornton was confident of a big run, 'he's never been so fresh, so fit!' I went hunting for a bit of 3/1, Chantry was oscillating between that and 11/4. I got my price and the old horse scooted up, winning by 8 lengths. My son John capped a great day off by getting Mickey Quinn's and Lester's autographs, my winnings paid for the journey and the meal at the course before we left and we got some excellent photos taken professionally in the winners' enclosure.

The primary objective Mitch gave me was to establish an incentive scheme for prisoners. The establishment that appeared light years ahead of any other locally in this respect was Deerbolt. As an ex Borstal they had a long history of developing incentives for prisoners which they constantly reassessed, refined and updated. Les Frost my punting partner from my ECR team at Wakefield was a manager at the establishment and he arranged for me to take a look at their practices. Enthused by the visit I returned to Low Newton full of ideas.

I came up with a system that rewarded positive behaviour with additional privileges and which removed privileges to discourage inappropriate behaviour.

There were three levels:

1)   Enhanced: when a prisoner actively participates in all aspects of the regime including offender behaviour programmes. OR

2)   Standard: When he or she behaves in an acceptable way, follows the rules, takes part in prison activities and helps keep the prison safe and orderly. OR

3)   Basic: Where his or her patterns of behaviour falls below the standards required.

The Incentive and Earned Privilege system
    All prisoners entered the prison on Standard level unless there was evidence to show that they were on enhanced at their previous prison. They were subject to a review a month after arriving at the prison.
    3 warnings, adjudication or a combination would trigger a review.
    Prisoners could appeal against a decision that placed them on Basic.
    Warnings were recorded.
    They would be personally informed by the wing PO when placed on this level.
    IEP levels determined which earnable privileges they could have.
    Visits-how many?
    Access to private cash.
    Enhanced earnings might include a bonus.
    Time out of cell.

Wing notice boards explained in detail how the Incentives and Earned Privileges scheme affected the individual.

Mitch quickly approved the proposals and got it up and running. It immediately enhanced the role of the personal officer, which had been a main management aim, because prisoners quickly realised that he or she was crucial to their progress.

I was asked to attend an Inquest at Chester Le Street. We'd had a suicide on Jim Willoughby's weekend. It was sad and a surprise as the lad was from a notorious West End (Newcastle) family. They had taken offence, they claimed, to something Jim had said. I didn't always agree with Jim but this was clearly a misunderstanding or they were looking for an excuse; he was much too decent and professional to have said anything to upset them.

Anyway threats were issued and I was asked to attend the Hearing in Jim's place.

A few staff who had been present at the scene, including Healthcare staff, were required to attend and give evidence. I'd travelled up from my home in Yorkshire, the car-park had been empty when I arrived. I did a recce, spoke to the clerk of the court and the ushers who were helpful and sympathetic.

I had arranged for a mini-bus to transport the staff to court, it remained with us for the duration, taking us away for a pre-arranged meal at the lunch recess. It eased the tension and allowed us some privacy.

The family's lawyer had travelled up from London, he did his job competently but he wasn't a Michael Mansfield or Rock Tansey whom I had known as fearsome human rights briefs from my 'Bailey' years. Nevertheless, the staff acquitted themselves well faced with some intense questioning. The outcome was reasonably favourable to the prison.

I quickly saw the staff off the premises, before giving a prepared statement to a BBC North East TV reporter. The lady interviewer clearly fancied herself as a latter day Robin Day and was preparing to get stuck into me big style when messages started coming to her from BBC North East HQ, that Mike Neville, their long-term studio anchor man was defecting to ITV!

Cue, I became yesterday's news, a forgotten man. 'Cheers Mike,' I remember thinking.

I breathed a sigh of relief until I looked at the car-park. Many from the West End had come to support the family, the reason I had got the staff away as soon as possible. A significant number stood chatting and smoking near my car. Oh dear, nothing for it, I strode purposely towards the car, heart beating, sweat pouring from my brow I'm sure. I walked through the middle of them, something they clearly hadn't anticipated, I nervously inserted the key in the door, turned the ignition, said a quick 'Hail Mary,' hoping it would start immediately. I breathed a sigh of relief as I pulled away, a quick glance in the mirror showed a myriad of single-finger salutes as I vanished into the distance.

'A little bird tells me your horse is running today what are you doing still here?' 'I'm duty governor Mitch and I want to be around whilst the IEP system is bedding-in.'

'What time's the race?' '2.15 Ripon.' 'Well give me the radio get down to a bookies and watch the race, I'll cover until you return.'

An uncut diamond Mitch, for sure.

I went down to a local Independent Bookies, Charlie Chisholm; it was near a Working Men's club used mainly by retired miners.

Our horse had risen in the weights after the clear-cut Haydock success and we didn't fancy it. Nevertheless, it was at the head of the market and I remember thinking I don't want these old boys doing their dough on this when I know it's not going to win, but what can I do? I loved listening to their burr and stories, There was another race at a southern meeting due off ten minutes before ours, all the big-name jocks were involved in that and it had clearly captured the imagination of the others in the shop, they appeared to be ignoring our race; I breathed a sigh of relief.

As our trainer had indicated, our horse ran an honest race but could never get competitive off its revised weight. It finished out the back, sixth in a fourteen horse field. We would have to wait until it came down the handicap before we went the well again!

Mitch was clearly being lined-up for progress and rumours soon started that she was in line for promotion and a bigger prison. She came to see me one day to offer me a permanent position, confirming that the person I had been substituting for had accepted an early retirement package.

'Thanks Governor I'd be delighted to accept.'

'Well we're losing Mike Webber on promotion to Head of Works at Frankland Phil, we will need your experience to keep the Establishment moving forward.'

I was running every day to keep fit for football, I would often run with an SO or a particular Works officer; I had stamina in abundance but without the competition I would idle and not get the full benefit.

We used to have football training at the Riverside near the cricket ground at Chester-Le-Street and Mitch used to regularly come down to watch us. To say she was popular with the staff by this time was an understatement, the initial silliness by some staff had given way to a genuine respect for the opportunities she had provided and her loyalty, she was going to be sorely missed.

It was confirmed Mitch was to leave us on promotion to take up the Governor's post at Leicester prison.

The acting head of works confided in me one day about his fears that the Area manager would draft-in Mike's replacement from a nearby prison and it 'will be bad news for us all, Mitch and Jim won't like it they both knew him at Frankland when they were junior governors and he caused havoc!'

'Well I'm afraid if he is the only one in the area of the required rank and he applies for the vacancy I don't know how they can deny him the post.'

'Not whilst Mitch is still here Phil, mark my words.'

Mitch's last day arrived, I'd booked-in at the Newton Grange Hotel where we were having her 'leaving do,' I'd anticipated a late night!

Just after five pm with most of the staff gone, I heard a noise of metal on wood. My office was directly opposite Mitch's and when I went to the door she was using a screw-driver to remove her name and title from her door. I went to help her and I noticed a tear in her eye as we completed the removal: 'means a lot, my first in-charge, are you coming?'

I parked next to her in the hotel car park. Though it was teeming with rain and the car windows had steamed up I could see tears streaming down her cheeks.

I waited by the side of her car, she got out apologising, 'What am I like?' 'Don't worry but get ready to meet your fans because this is going to be a celebration not a wake!' 'Here Phil, I got you this, Van Morrison in Ireland, a music video of the great man we both adored.

The place was heaving, all the staff had turned out, it was a truly memorable well deserved send-off.

Mitch was replaced by Mike Kirby, Sunderland born and bred, a nice guy. He was followed closely through the door by Mike Webber's replacement.

Mike Kirby was quick to sit me down and give me a new objective, I had to make contact with a senior manager at Nissan HQ at Washington Tyne and Wear to see if they were willing to contribute to an anti-car crime initiative we were planning.

Many of the kids we were holding were in custody for car crime, indeed if I remember rightly nearby Gateshead was then considered to be the car-crime capital of England.

An officer to front the initiative had been approved and when we pitched up at Nissan and explained our objective to combat car crime involving the Police, Victim Support, the Fire Service and local paramedics, the Company immediately agreed to help and supply a Four by Four chassis!

Our aim was to highlight the deadly dangers of car crime to those involved in it and to prevent them from re-offending.

The officer fronting it was keenness personified but quickly developed an inflated view of his own importance and managed to alienate a number of teachers. Make no mistake he was good and quickly enthused the prisoners but as the Education Department was the ideal place, indeed the only place, to hold the course, I needed to keep the teachers onside!

I had him up against the wall in my office on more than one occasion but he didn't appear to be able to help himself.

True to their word Nissan supplied us with a fantastic chassis for the kids to work on. I had to put the Establishment in a patrol state whilst it was manoeuvred over the wall using a powerful hoist. The Company did us proud!

The new addition started off wanting to be friends, he occasionally joined me on my lunch-time jog.

I returned from my run one afternoon to find Mike waiting by my office door.

'Phil we've got a problem, looks like we've wrongly released someone, I want you to investigate, I'll draw-up terms of reference.'

My investigation uncovered a catalogue of errors by an officer who should have known better. He wasn't a rookie, he had even worked at Frankland prior to Low Newton, a Category A prison.

In essence two brothers were on remand occupying a communal cell. The officer had been tasked to pick one up, the court had granted him bail. The officer had called out the name on the paperwork as soon as he opened the cell, one of the lads immediately answered his call and followed the officer out of the cell down to reception. There the senior officer had asked him his prison number before supplying him with his property, he then discharged him from the prison.

His brother waited an hour before ringing his cell bell then told the startled officer who answered it that 'I've been granted bail boss, you're holding me illegally!'

It was a clear pre-planned conspiracy by the two brothers. All the 'absconder' had to do was memorise his brother's prison number and hold his nerve!

However, to avoid this happening the officer picking him up should have checked with the regular staff on the landing that he was picking the right one up, particularly important when dealing with two brothers of a similar age and build occupying the same cell.

The reception senior officer was also culpable, he should not have accepted what the prisoner had told him at face value, he should have carried out further checks. A close inspection of the relevant 1150 showed that the brother granted bail had distinctive tattoos on both his arms, whilst the other had none. This simple physical check would have prevented the escape. Two people faced disciplinary action for failing to carry out the most basic security checks.

By this time we'd added to our racing string, a filly called Contract Bridge, she was of limited ability but she had a lovely attitude and was a stable favourite. The staff nicknamed her 'Bridget;' she always tried her hardest to please both in her home-work and on the track. I remember going off to Carlisle to watch her one day, Chris had given her a couple of runs already in better class company than she faced that day. She'd finished down the field in these races and had been dropped a few pounds in the handicap as a result. We now felt we had her on a mark that she could win off, Time to 'bet like men' to paraphrase that doyen of racing correspondents, The Guardian's Richard Baerlein after he'd seen Shergar win his Derby prep race by a distance.

The filly didn't let us down winning her race at a juicy 8/1! 'Twenty, forty, sixty, eighty, a hundred, four more times, fill my pockets Mr Bookmaker, get my money ready, I remember calling out in joy!'

Things were changing at home. My eldest son had successfully completed his 'A' levels and was about to go to University, my middle son was about to spend some time at school in the US, my daughter had just become a teenager and my wallet was about to feel the pinch! Because Low Newton was closer to my home than Rochdale, my previous posting, I didn't qualify for travel allowance, the journey to Durham was about to become financially prohibitive when I took into consideration these future costs. My old friend Alan Brown was the deputy governor at Kirklevington but was about to move on promotion to another of my old prisons, Castington. He was aware of my need to move closer to home and advised me to put in for his post when it became vacant.

I mentioned it to Mike, who understood my position, he promised his support.

When the Kirklevington position was advertised, I applied, was interviewed and subsequently was offered the post.

In the meantime, the newly arrived manager was reverting to type. He was bullying his junior staff according to his PO who worked with me on my weekend on and he had even begun to poke his nose into my areas. Mitch and Jim had mentioned how he had sought to undermine his fellow managers at Frankland by picking/seeking to find fault in their areas to 'neutralise' their effectiveness. I realised that's what he was seeking to do again. He started trying to bully some of my staff, particularly my catering manager, who had achieved a fair bit during Mitch's time. Mitch had introduced me to a contact on the Sunderland Echo and through him we had ensured innovative work in the kitchen had been acknowledged through the media. This crank, working locally at the time, would have been well aware of this.

A policeman had turned up at home one evening to find out if we knew anything about an air gun that had been fired at our neighbour's property. A family with three teenage boys lived opposite us, the eldest had been remanded in custody on a number of occasions for assaults occasioning actual bodily harm, he knew what I did and had made it plain to the kids that he didn't like me. I began to wonder if I was the target. Our neighbour Barbara lived alone, she kept to herself, sweetness personified, I couldn't find a reason why she would be targeted.

Though a date for my move to Kirklevington had not been agreed between the two Governors, circumstances were soon to accelerate it.

I heard the clown walking into Mike's office one day bad-mouthing Tony Brown my catering manager. I'd heard enough, I burst into Mike's office and let the clown have both barrels! Mike certainly didn't deserve to witness it, I was out of order! Mike being the superb diplomat that he was brought the situation to a close.

He arranged for me to leave at the end of the month and sent the idiot on leave until then.

His clear intention was to keep us apart. I had not covered myself in glory; an inauspicious end to my time there!

Chapter 10 (1996-1999)
This is how prison should work!

My first day at Kirklevington went well, I was given a warm welcome by the Governor Pat Midgley who had been one of the G4 facilitators of my Diploma of Management Studies course. I was immediately placed in a dilemma.

An advertisement for a G4 post at Frankland, the prison next door to Low Newton, appeared that day and I anguished over whether to apply or not for most of the day. I'd just left that area because of travel costs but this would be promotion!

I took the application home and typed it up. With some trepidation I handed it in to Pat the following day. Initially shocked, she handled it with grace and fairness, wishing me well but acknowledging her disappointment, 'I think the time's right for us to take this place to the next stage.'

I applied, was granted a board which went reasonably well but the 'whisper' was that a young accelerated promotion graduate was a 'shoo-in.'

Phil Copple was selected, the next generation was on its way! I returned to Kirklevington for the first time in three decades. It had changed its role in that time and I was about to embark on the most satisfying period of my entire career.

Kirklevington was an open prison for adult male offenders and those intending to settle on release in the North East of England. Its focus was on helping longer term prisoners resettle in the North East of England and Yorkshire. This it did by actively encouraging them to participate in community work in the first instance, before progressing to paid employment and/or attendance at a local college or university.

On arrival at the prison every prisoner was interviewed and a case file, which he would have access to, was opened. Each prisoner was assigned a personal officer, who was the prisoner's first line of contact, he/she would closely monitor his progress and compile reports on him. After six weeks a conference was attended by all those who had had contact with the prisoner, along with his family and his home probation officer. This conference was a first step in risk assessing his suitability for release to work in the outside community.

A prisoner by this time would have already successfully completed voluntary testing for substance abuse. He then underwent a further period of development by doing voluntary unpaid work in the local community. This took the form of painting and decorating and gardening work for the old or infirm, giving back to the community. A lesson in considering others rather than just self! The Establishment had built up an impressive list of local organisations keen to utilise its help and skills.

The next stage was for the prisoner to find work or further education opportunities, most opted for paid work.

Many worked at a local chicken-processing factory, an ice-cream wholesaler or at carpet factory.

The personal officer would carry out random monthly work spot checks to ensure that the prisoner was where he was contracted to be at all times. The chicken-processing factory was about twenty miles from the prison and involved shift work. Prisoners were allowed to keep their own cars on site to get them to and from work, all documents relating to these vehicles we would carefully check, we also took it upon ourselves to ensure they were roadworthy.

Once a prisoner had been passed-out to work he was also allowed a town visit with his family each weekend. The prisoner had to be back at the establishment by 18 00 hours but this curfew time had not always been enforced, I determined to change that immediately. I used to have a weekly meeting with prisoners, I used it to inform and receive feedback from them. I reinforced our duty to our local community who provided so many opportunities for us to continue to progress.

I constantly reinforced our need to maintain the highest standards at all time, we all, staff included, had to accept personal responsibility. We would ensure our commitment to them by delivering what we said we would to the process and they would ensure they returned to the establishment at the published time or face sanctions! Once we lost the trust of the local community we might as well go back to 'bang-up and slopping out!'

I would compare this with prisons in general where a prisoner might or might not have been told what he had to do to progress towards release at his reception interview; only to be consistently failed because progress reports were not completed on time if at all! Where personal officers were not 'paired' so that the prisoner always has a point of contact, particularly important for him or her in an emergency. Where families and visitors were too often viewed as irritants rather than a crucial part of the rehabilitation process. 'At Kirk all the above are in place and crucially will be monitored closely by managers who care and who aren't scared! You have work that is productive, interesting and most importantly pays! This place is brilliant and it won't be destroyed on my watch be very clear! Any questions?' A chorus of 'no boss, thanks boss.'

This was surely how prisons should work!

Hopelessness in my experience breeds desperation so you need to build incentives into the system to encourage even men with nothing to lose to obey the rules. I was making it clear to prisoners that if they obeyed the rules they got privileges, if they broke the rules they lost them. If they broke enough rules they would end up in segregation with only one hour's exercise per day, then I'd ship then out, back-track them to a local prison.

Man is a social animal and the threat of solitary confinement is usually enough to keep the most troubled inmate in line.

I had worked in every kind of establishment and I firmly believed you should be able to determine those who will cause mayhem and those who will conform on reception.

That you could safely send the latter to the most progressive prisons with unlocked rooms and the ability to move freely around dormitory halls within weeks following risk assessment due process. Teach them to cook for themselves, buy food with money earned from prison work only, not via private cash which disadvantages the least wealthy. Kirklevington offered all this and more. There should be more prisons like it and they should be part of a seamless progressive sentence for most prisoners. Terrorists, organised criminals and serial sex offenders are the exceptions.

You have to get them to a position where they stop feeling sorry for themselves and start to see for the first time what is happening to them. To journey inside themselves, into their souls. For many it was painful but it made them realise that they had been living a life of self-delusion. They had done bad things and they were now paying for it with a sentence, but that the payment comes with the realisation of what it's all about.

With clarity of thought comes a realistic appraisal of the present and the future.

Once they'd reached this stage in their development they were ready for the outside world as far as we were concerned. We were rarely wrong, the establishment did work, it was a jewel in the prison estate.

Pat sat me down towards the end of my first week to give me my immediate objective.

She tasked me with reviewing the work of the PE department to ensure it was being used to its full potential. It was well resourced.

My first priority was ensuring that it catered for all, particularly those less gifted at sport, and those working out. I met with the PE PO and agreed a way forward, publishing a plan of action to meet our requirements. Pat approved it before going on leave till the end of the month, off to New England; I would be in charge, getting the kind of experience I craved!

Because of its location and the relaxed atmosphere, the Area manager started using Kirk to hold his monthly meeting with his Governors.

Ivor, who was by then the Governor of Acklington, caused a bit of consternation early on with staff, by refusing to give up his mobile phone at the gate. The 'big man from Strabane' would have to be challenged.

The Governor's secretary Jane came up with the idea of providing a buffet. The conference room was often vacant and we could charge for its use. The Area manager approved the idea, and we were soon adding to the establishment's coffers by hosting meetings for other public sector organisations within the region and charging them for the privilege; our catering staff supplied the buffet.

I was soon introduced to 'my duties to the local community,' Pat had a smile on her face, I'm sure, as she despatched me to judge a thimble competition at a nearby WI hall! This and addressing local Rotary organisations were some of the extra-curricular activities I found I was expected to perform. As far as Rotary was concerned, I was in effect 'singing for my supper,' I would give my talk before 'breaking bread' with them! The WI's of course, made sure I was never short of quality home-made cake and buns! I remember thinking, as I drove home from one of these commitments, Full Sutton this isn't, I wonder what 'the chaps' on D wing would say if they saw me now!

Shortly before I had left Low Newton, Mike Kirby had asked me to write-up the officer fronting the car-crime initiative, for the prestigious Butler Trust award, Jim Willoughby had kindly lent me a copy of a submission he had made the previous year, as a template.

The course had been a great success, this officer had played his part in all fairness, though he was keen to ensure everybody knew about it. In truth, without Nissan and our partner agencies, the police, paramedics, the fire service and victim support plus the way the prisoners had embraced it, it would have turned out a damp squib!

I started getting mildly chiding letters from officers at Low Newton, mainly people I had been close to in the staff football team, complaining that I had made the officer impossible to live with now that he had been awarded the top Butler Trust award and it was all my fault! Apparently, he will spend some time at Nissan in Japan, Canada, giving talks.... Oh dear! I could imagine their angst!

During Pat's summer leave I'd been negotiating with the POA about how we could manage more prisoners at nil cost. The prison estate was bursting at the seams and I'd spent most of the day fending off HQ who wanted to send us a couple of buses full of prisoners without any assessments of their risk in open conditions!

Luckily, I had Ray Mitchell, the Area manager onside. We'd done a re-profile to enable us to man another couple of portacabins where we would house those working out, this would free up an extra fifty places inside the prison. We would not have to reduce our standards, or abandon our selective assessments of risk prior to acceptance and we would continue to take from/serve prisons in the area concentrating on prisoners determined to re-settle in the North East and Yorkshire on release; not people 'dumped' on us, phew! Ray Mitchell's unstinting support for our aims was crucial to this 'success.'

We only needed a couple of high profile escapes and the Press would have had a field day and all the establishment's previous good work in the community would have been compromised. Pat supported the stand I had taken on her return and because of our economies of scale we managed to reduce our cost per prisoner place from £22,000 to £11,900 in the first instance!

I had a call from my counterpart at Leyhill prison in Gloucestershire one day. He was seeking to relocate a former policeman. He explained that the man had spent many years undercover working with and against football hooligans, principally, Birmingham City's Zulus. He had also worked in London with the Chelsea Headhunters!

He had however 'gone native' was how it was put to me; he'd been caught dealing drugs. On remand at Birmingham prison he had been spotted as soon as he came out of his cell for his breakfast, and threatened! They had segregated and moved him up country to Wymott prison near Preston, as soon as he was sentenced. There he was immediately recognised and threatened again; they had fast-tracked his category C status and moved him to Leyhill, a semi-open prison, like ours, but still he wasn't safe!

'Will you take him Phil, he's clearly too well known in the west, he's never worked up your way, he should be safe?'

I had reservations, I remember thinking he should be safe at Leyhill as it's for compliant inmates like our place. If I ever heard about any of our prisoners issuing threats I would relocate them to closed conditions post-haste!

I kept my counsel and accepted him, despite my reservations.

It didn't take long for my reservations to be realised. He had an edge to him and the other prisoners were clearly very wary of him, I've no doubt they soon learned about his past but this wasn't an issue with them. The majority of our prisoners stopped thinking and behaving like conventional prisoners or they didn't last long! They became focused on release and behaviour that was acceptable in the outside community.

His personal officer and our resident probation officer were unsure about him. He avoided eye contact, he didn't willingly engage with the process, he failed to make category D at the first attempt, we had worries about him working out.

He hadn't convinced us by the time of his next sentence planning board and remained a category C. In retrospect the warning signs were there. I had him in and told him to buck his ideas up or I would ship him out.

He made it on his next board, he was passed out to work. I ensured that his personal officer did an early 'random' visit to his place of work. He wasn't impressed by what he saw, a back street garage. The subject had been a mechanic before joining the police. His 'manager' dressed in sports gear, trainers, a base-ball cap, the epitome of the white urban hoodlum!

A couple of days later a prisoner sidled-up to me whilst I was on my evening rounds, 'can I have a word boss?'

My card marked, we copped him bang-to-rights! I was told when he would be carrying, we searched him, found the drugs, segregated him, adjudicated on him and shipped him out to Stockton prison the following day.

We went through a bit of a phase. Our Health Care professional was a large lady in her early fifties who had spent many years in A & E at Darlington Memorial Hospital. To say that she could take care of herself was an understatement, the 'chaps' got away with nothing. She had taken a shine to me but that back-fired in a spectacular fashion one day.

The need for adjudications was rare, prisoners were mostly self-motivated to conform and achieve. Therefore, custom and practice was for a prisoner facing an adjudication to see the nurse 'to be fitted,' before making his own way to the adjudication room. In a conventional prison the prisoner would be picked up from his cell early on the day of his adjudication and would be escorted to the segregation unit. He would see a Health Care professional whilst segregated, to ensure he was fit to face the adjudication process.

This particular chap had returned late from a town visit for the second time. He went to see the nurse who pronounced him fit to appear before telling him:' as it's Phil O'Brien on adjudications today you've got no chance, you might as well pack your kit now.'

He left her, went straight down to the garden store, picked-up a spade, battered a hole in the fence and absconded! The police were immediately deployed, including a search helicopter but he managed to clear the immediate area.

I felt a bit of a fraud when Pat returned to duty and congratulated me on the quality of the response, we had just followed laid down procedures. Following this incident it was decided that anyone placed on report would report to the segregation unit, where they would be seen and fitted for the process by the nurse, they would remain segregated until after the adjudication.

One of the 'extras' agreed when re-profiling PE was for us to give gym time to local OAP's to play carpet bowls competitively. The PO PEI would use prisoner orderlies who would be studying for a qualification which would enable them to seek employment in gyms and in leisure centres on release, to assist and supervise. They would also help when local special needs students shared our facilities. I would go over at about 16 00 hours to observe the final stages of the competitions and to present prizes. Two superb initiatives serving our local community reinforced the message to inmates, that we must never do anything to compromise this special relationship.

One of our officers used to run an Army Cadet detachment. He held a weekend camp in the Ripon area which he asked me to visit and address. The same officer and a number of his colleagues devised an outward bound element to the prison regime. A superb bonding exercise for prisoners and staff, collectively they spent time tramping the Cleveland hills doing the kind of exercises I had done myself all those years ago at Deerbolt.

When I first arrived the CE Chaplain remembered me from my first stint all those years ago, he looked vaguely familiar but his memory was clearly much better than mine. He retired shortly after I arrived and was replaced by a newly ordained, Methodist, ex Durham University; a lovely man.

He came to ask me one day if he could use 'Nick,' one of our 'charges,' intelligent and personable, to help him run his scout group.

I approved the application and it seemed to be working well, however after a short while he told me that a group of parents had complained. Nick had done well and the kids loved him but the minister felt reluctantly that he would have to withdraw the offer. He was clearly uncomfortable, wasn't sure how to proceed: 'Don't worry,' I told him, 'I'll break it to Nick, it's unfortunate but he's met one of the realities of a prisoner's life.'

I had Nick in just before tea and explained what had happened. He coloured, clearly hadn't expected this 'knock-back.' He was a 'first-timer,' it had been an ordeal for him at his local prison when first sentenced but at Kirklevington he had immediately got his act together and progressed. The trust and time staff invested in him paid immediate dividends. He got a job for a local carpet outlet, made rapid progress with them, quickly putting this negative experience to one side.

On release he settled in our town, I still see him regularly in the High Street and we chat, he's often supplied us with carpets and his best fitters over the years; always at the most competitive of prices! He and his wife are members of a traditional dance club in the town where they socialise with a couple of retired ex prison governors and their spouses! I know prison can work, I don't need to theorise about it, I have personal experience of it!

My second year at the prison and I was working on Christmas day. It meant I got two lunches! The food throughout the year was first class, we had two superb caterers and, as many of the prisoners would be seeking employment in the catering industry on release, they were keen to gain as much knowledge, experience and qualifications as possible; they were keen to impress.

I was still playing football with the staff and jogging. My football career came to an abrupt halt shortly after my fiftieth birthday, having been given the run-a-round by a Welsh inmate that had played at a reasonable level for Durham FC I came home and fell asleep on the couch before 18 00 hours; Joan put my boots in the dustbin and retired me!

Though most prisoners made the grade, proving the overall strength of our risk assessment procedures we didn't always get it right.

I had dealt with one miscreant who had refused to toe the line, downgraded him following due process and stuck him on a bus to Stockton prison, I believed they had agreed to accept him.

Pat had left on promotion to Everthorpe, a category C prison in East Yorkshire, she had been replaced by Susan Anthony who had been a governor at HMP Durham.

Susan was on annual leave, I was covering for her and remained on-call, she would reciprocate at the appropriate time. Our horse was due to run at nearby Sedgefield and I fully intended going up to see him run;

staff would contact me via the official mobile phone if required.

It was lunch-time, I was getting my trilby and binoculars together when my Reception SO came to see me. Apparently, the SO in reception at Stockton was refusing to accept our miscreant and the Duty Governor was upholding that decision.

Local prison staff, outside London, often gave the impression that they didn't need prisoners to function, that they were better off without them, I often found!

I rang Stockton and asked to speak to the duty governor, it turned out to be Les Frost who had been on my ECR team at Wakefield and who had replaced me on promotion at Castington. I had put in a good word for him with Ivor!

I gave him a minute to trot out a lame excuse for not accepting the prisoner which really amounted to nothing more than support for the poor decision of his SO.

'Right Les that's garbage as we both know, I'm off up to Sedgefield to watch my horse run. I haven't got time for this, I'm calling in every favour, what have you got to say?'

'No problem Phil, we'll take him, be lucky.'

'All sorted,' I said to my reception SO who shook his head and left.

Ivor turned up for an Area Manager's meeting one day and burst into my office before Jane (Governor's secretary) could stop him! I just managed to hide my Racing Post in time!

'Time you thought about moving, get back into a big jail, you must be bored or you'll get bored. Think on it.' He was gone before I'd chance to tell him I thought it was

215

great, no problems from prisoners nor staff, shipped anybody out that tried to take the piss which maintained an equilibrium that suited all. I actually believed in the place and felt it fulfilled the Prison Service's duty of care to the public as much as any Cat A Dispersal... and apart from that I've only been here for two years!

He left me with the impression he had got something up his sleeve. He had got his security governor at Acklington to ring me the previous week to discuss my anti-conditioning training pack; she intended to run a similar course.

I received a cut-out from a north east paper sent to me by Acklington's Works Governor; we'd worked together at both Castington and Kirklevington.

It referred to the antics of a former Castington officer Len Bithell, a man known to us both. It was the officer I had given evidence against at Newcastle Crown Court.

He had become the treasurer of a brain injuries charity, Headway. It was now alleged that he had plundered £14,350 from the Charity's funds, thereby preventing people, including children, from getting the help they needed! He wouldn't be 'rewarded' with an expenses-paid move this time unless it was via a prison van to jail!

Sir David Ramsbottom, the Chief Inspector of Prisons paid us a visit and subsequently wrote about us in glowing terms. He gave me a personal hand-written note as he was taking his leave. In it he mentioned some pleasant things the staff had said about me. I showed it to Susan on her return to duty, she took it from me and I never saw it again.

The Area Manager Mr Mitchell came to see me prior to his next area governors' meeting, followed closely by 'the big man from Strabane.'

Before either of us could speak Ivor began: 'he's getting bored here Ray we'll have to get him back in the system.'

Ray Mitchell just winked at me and smiled, 'sounds like he's got plans for you.'

A couple of weeks later all was revealed. Ivor had been promoted and had become the Governor of Frankland top security prison. He rang me immediately asking me to join him. I told him I'd consider it.

Never one to let the grass grow, he rang me again the following day, clearly believing that a whole evening to decide my future was long enough! Phil Copple, his deputy, made contact with me later the same week; the pressure was on!

I don't know which one of us was more embarrassed Phil or me, we'd never met, he'd been the 'chosen one' on the Frankland promotion board I'd attended but he was now effectively, probably reluctantly, helping Ivor auction off the job of one of the staff that reported to him! Phil had ultimate responsibility for security, the job Ivor wanted me to head-up!

The 'big man' had no excuse to come over and 'harass' me now, he was answerable to the Deputy Director General who held meetings with his High Security Estate Governors in London each month.

In the end, he wore me down, I relented to his entreaties and agreed to apply for Frankland. I'd enjoyed myself enormously at Kirklevington and I had total belief in the regime.

However, because of its unique dangers and risks, I knew that succeeding in the High Security estate can be equally satisfying. Full Sutton had been tough posting for both of us but we'd learned a lot. It was now time to put that experience to best use. As always Ivor was full of ideas about how we could take it forward and he'd sold it well. And of course, it's nice to be wanted!

Chapter 11 (1999-2006)

Defence of Necessity

I stood on line-route with Ivor as 'the chaps' make their way to work. Prisoners are getting to know me now and a couple of reprobates who had volunteered information just before I had adjudicated on them, convinced that I would 'go easy,' passed by. They acknowledged me, took a good look at the big Ulsterman, as he did them. I could tell that neither side was impressed with the other!

'Friends of yours?' he asked with disdain.

'A business relationship, nothing personal,' I replied. 'You can't afford to let anything get in the way of business.'

At least I got a smile from him - I think, unless of course it was wind!

HMP Frankland was a member of the High Security Estate. It held prisoners serving sentences of 4 years and over, life sentence prisoners and high risk category A's. The prison accommodation was divided between A and D holding 108 inmates each and F and G wings holding an additional 206. All cells were single occupancy.

It had a number of workshops and a large Education Department that catered for those with basic literacy and numeracy needs, as well for those with more advanced requirements including external qualifications.

The 'big man' as was his way, had 'cleared out' a few managers to make way for me. Some who had been popular and not unreasonably you might think, I was treated with a certain amount of suspicion and caution in the early days. It would take time for me to shed the 'Ivor's boy,' image!

Three things helped early on in that respect, firstly I met an officer called Chick Gardner, we'd served as officers together at Brixton all those years ago.

'Hi Phil good to see you, I'd heard you were coming, I believe your lass has got a posting here as well, that's great news, I'll see you soon we'll have a catch-up.'

I toured the prison later that day and discovered it contained staff I'd known at Brixton, Wakefield, Castington and Full Sutton, I was confident then that I'd have a solid core of support.

Chick had left me perplexed! I soon learned that a new PO from Northallerton prison called Angie Hartley had started at Frankland on the same day as me, her partner was the Deputy Governor at Northallerton, where she had also served, yet though I'd lived in the town for a number years, the three of us had never met! Typical prison service staff putting 2+2 together and coming up with 6! To be fair Angie took it with grace and good humour, when inevitably she heard about it, and would ask with a smile when our paths would cross, 'how's my fiancée today?'

Ivor sat me down early on and gave me my brief: he expected me to help the Head of Residence lead a change in attitude process. I had to reinforce the need for dynamic security, something close to our hearts since getting together at Castington, for decency in the way prisoners were treated and for me to make sure staff understood the importance of a strong regime where all activities started and finished on time.

I was to ensure I selected a strong manager to coordinate movement to and from work. Ensure that all staff took ownership of the security of the workshop, education and the activity programme, when deployed to those areas.

Devise a line-route system that allowed for a secure free-flow movement to and from all activities. Put in place an auditable system to demonstrate that all activities were visited each day by the Duty Governor and the Orderly officer.

Make sure that the search teams became more proactive.

Reinforce to all that addressing risk was the core task of all Category A prisons.

Raise the profile of the Intelligence unit.

Encourage a partnership approach between management and the unions where all parties had a shared commitment to the success of the prison, a mutual understanding of and respect for each other's roles, and an acknowledgement that through consultation and negotiation the establishment would operate smoothly and effectively. As soon as he paused to draw breath I beat a hasty retreat.

The second break I got to convince staff that I was my own man happened during my first duty governor shift, midway through my second week. My security SO Denis Williams had been asked to attend visits where two brothers from a notorious West End of Newcastle family were in dispute with him and he called me to arbitrate.

A legal visiting order had been made for one of the brothers, the other was trying to 'blag' his way on the visit. I quickly returned him to his wing.

'Thanks Phil, they are always intimidating staff, including governors, so they can do as they please, that'll make them think!'

I smiled to myself a week later when on my 'rounds' I visited F wing, the two brothers were sitting eating at a table outside their cells; they studiously ignored me as I passed.

A week later they had thawed, they acknowledged me as I passed, with a nod of the head. I found out sometime later that they had asked their wing PO Harry Henson about me? He, having informed them that I was the new head of security, had suggested that I might make a bad enemy, that it would be in their best interests if they made their peace with me!

Harry had previously served at Durham prison and had met them often over the years when they had been on remand.

G wing PO Graeme Markham came to see me within my first month to inform me that one of his staff had told him that whilst he had been on a course at Newbold Revel, in the company of an officer who had just joined our staff, this officer had produced some white powder which appeared to be cocaine, on a night out. He had then offered it to the assembled company!

I asked him to submit the allegation on paper so that I had an audit trail, I informed my line-manager Phil Copple who immediately asked me to investigate, he wrote out terms of reference.

I was given a fortnight to report, I ended up travelling to Wakefield, Long Lartin, Bristol and Wolverhampton to interview witnesses.

Having considered my findings, Phil convened a Disciplinary Hearing. The officer was accompanied by the POA chair Steve Jackson.

The weight of evidence in terms of corroborative statements was overwhelming, the case was found proved, the officer was unable to offer any reasonable explanation for his actions, a career was over before it had begun. It was particularly sad for his father who was also in the service in our region.

I'd announced my arrival and silenced some of the doubters.

I sat down in my office in a moment of contemplation and compiled a list on the most important risks I must address: escapes in general, Category A escapes, helicopter assisted escapes, release in error, the need to identify and disrupt drug networks both inside and outside prisons, targeted terrorist attack on the prison to aid an escape, targeted subversion of staff, prevention of illicit items entering the establishment, particularly weapons, phones, guns, explosives or escape equipment, security equipment failure and consequence, failure of major security system and consequence, prisoner indiscipline, riot/disorder (loss of accommodation), potential threats to staff or their families from organised criminals.

As this chapter will clearly demonstrate addressing the foregoing kept me busy for the next six and a half years.

Ivor was making his presence felt as I now started to ease my way in after my 'early successes' on visits and with the swift response to the staff cocaine allegation.

I was called to deal with a matter in the segregation unit one morning during movement to work. The 'big man' had been observing line-route movement when word reached him that B wing prisoners were refusing to move because the breakfast bread was stale! I was told later that Ivor stormed onto the wing, grabbed a couple of the 'offending' slices, wolfed them down to the astonishment of staff and prisoners before declaring, 'nothing wrong with them now get to work,' which they all dutifully did! To say the staff were wary of him is an understatement, he popped-up everywhere, they had clearly never seen anything like it before. I had the advantage of knowing how he worked. He was high profile in a new post until he was satisfied that everything was running to his satisfaction.

In time officers realised that it wasn't just them he picked on; that all his senior managers would get it in the neck if they didn't perform.

To be clear I wasn't exempt from 'a tongue-lashing' if he thought I deserved it!

Category A, longer term prisoners are and act differently than prisoners in lower category prisons and as often portrayed in the media.

Their cells were invariably neat and tidy, clean with everything in its place.

They shaved, combed their hair, often looking like they were ready to go somewhere. However, in a world defined by deprivation, things that we would consider trivial in the outside world were quite often magnified to a significance beyond their street value.

As I found at Full Sutton, men who wouldn't hesitate to kill each other outside would band together to help someone going through a hard time or if they felt that they had been treated badly.

It was a world in which the forces of good and evil struggled daily with no guarantee over which would triumph. It was a world that placed a high premium on exercising extreme care in word, deed and appearance. Keeping one's word whether it's to help someone or harm them. Strangely enough a world in which inmates punished unacceptable behaviour even more severely than the authorities did.

Early in my time there a white prisoner challenged a 'Yardie' serving a sentence for a number of gang-related murders, and who had many of his outside associates with him on the wing, about a previous conviction he had for the rape of a white girl. The two prisoners had known each other at a London prison.

The 'Yardie' took exception and along with his associates inflicted a terrible beating on the white prisoner. The latter stood his ground, never complained, 'I walked into the wall in the dark governor' when asked to explain his injuries. He refused the offer of a move another wing.

After about a week the 'Yardie' asked to speak to me, his position on the wing had become untenable, other prisoners of all colours and creeds had agreed that 'that rape was unacceptable,' and he'd lost the 'support' of his own crew. They had realised that they would be in permanent conflict with the majority if they challenged the accepted 'norms' associated with long-term professional criminals, 'no rapists or child abusers on our wing.' I relocated him to a vulnerable prisoner wing for a while before transferring him south as a 'reward' for information received. I had little time for the white prisoner who had started the process. On a previous sentence at a prison in the south, he had battered a shop instructor over the head with an iron bar, 'cabbaged' him out of the service, during an escape attempt. However, he'd stood his ground on this alone, took a beating but refused to be cowed. He'd displayed a lot of 'bottle.' We were, however to clash towards the end of my time at the prison, after a massive cannabis 'find.'

Informants are like grapes; the first pressings are often the best. I've often found that once someone has yielded initial information, especially under duress and subsequent pressure, he tends to produce increasingly unreliable results as the informer tries to dredge-up what he thinks the handler wants to hear.

I started instructing some of my staff on informant handling as soon as I arrived.

Intelligence analysis was another priority. The skills required are quick and accurate assessments of reports, a formidable memory and an easy manner in dealing with people.

As the big Ulsterman would say, 'that leaves you out O'Brien.' However I was blessed with some excellent senior officers and intelligence officers, so any deficiencies I had were masked!

The job of the intelligence analyst is key, I wasn't sure it could be taught, nevertheless I tried. It's about getting the feel for reports and their sources - what was likely to be reliable and what was not, having the confidence to sell that intelligence to decision - makers. The reports must be objective, balanced, accurate and competent. Intelligence used properly can be a life-saver. Time spent turning a foe can be more constructive than merely blustering gung-ho into a battle needlessly, putting people at risk.

I was going through an intelligence file on staff corruption left by a former security principal officer now retired. It aroused my interest because it detailed this PO's investigation into the mobile phone find on the Turkish prisoner I'd received at Full Sutton and which had led to my 'stand-off' with the IRA on the SSU exercise yard.

The file made clear that the PO felt that he had identified the staff member who had trafficked the phone. It demonstrated his extreme displeasure that his report recommendations had been ignored when it was made clear that no action was to be taken against the staff member he had identified. I then noticed what appeared to be his draft resignation memo to the Governor from his security role.

He clearly felt let down, it seemed to me that he'd had to do most if not all the work on his own, presumably mindful of confidentiality issues. I felt for him and I determined there and then to find a more inclusive way of dealing with incidents of staff corruption, where the burden could be shared with a small select band of security staff.

Though Ivor was effectively the CEO of the jail he still loved 'the security game' and within my first month had

227

me delivering our 'anti-conditioning' pack to all senior managers, ensuring that I put the session on when he could attend.

I was using a TV investigation programme tape as a visual aid. It involved the infamous escape of three Cat A's from Brixton, Moody, Thompson and an IRA man Tuite.

The 'star' of the video was typical cockney 'blagger,' Stanley Thompson: "you've got to remember yer typical screw is basically a lazy bastard, give him a paper and he'll sit on his fat arse all day long and you can get on with your thing...."

These were:

- Obtaining suitable tools for breaching the cell and end walls;
- Camouflaging their activities and disposing of debris;
- Avoiding detection by prison staff within the wing during preparations for their escape;
- Avoiding detection by staff within the perimeter following their escape.

In short as Stanley alluded to in his own way, relying on and 'encouraging' carelessness by prison officers in some of the most basic "bread and butter" aspects of the work of the prison service; this extended to neglect of the procedures for the supervision and control of Category A's generally, including the need for frequent changes of location, for close searching of the prisoners themselves and their cells and for monitoring their visits. Our job as senior managers was to ensure good governance of these procedures, as Ivor was quick to remind us. 'This is the standard against which you will be judged.'

I finished the session by informing those present that Stanley was subsequently acquitted of his original outstanding charges. He did of course face the charge of prison escape when he gave himself up. Tuite and Moody escaped to Ireland, Moody returned to London years later but was shot dead in a pub, an alleged revenge contract killing!

Tuite made Irish legal history in 1982 when he became the first man sentenced in the Republic of Ireland for offences committed in the UK. He was sentenced by the Special Criminal Court to 10 years imprisonment for possessing explosives in London. Today, apparently he's a businessman in his home area in Ireland. I'm led to believe that the 'star of stage and screen,' certainly as far as our training session was concerned, Stan Thompson, lives quietly in east London working as a builder. Of course, he knows all about bricks and mortar and the removal of.... How useful scaffolding can be and now hopefully so do Frankland's senior management team!

I had the final decision on the method of progress in relation to every SIR (security information report submitted); they all passed through me. I received one from an officer on visits, shortly after my 'altercation' with the two brothers. Their solicitor, made a bit of a show with some legal correspondence which he properly wished to share with his clients: 'I suppose you'd better show this to Mr O'Brien before I show it to my clients?' In truth, contact between prisoners and their 'briefs' is confidential and I never sought to interfere with that. What I refused to put up with was anybody taking the piss! A message that was clearly getting through, I had taken a bit of pressure off visits staff, they would traditionally get it in the neck if anything went wrong or if there were any queries, in the absence of a senior managerial presence. I visited this area daily, both they and the prisoners knew that I'd always be around in support and to make any executive decisions.

My first intelligence senior officer was an extremely able ex-hospital officer from Wandsworth.

However in Ivor's eyes he had brought 'his Wandsworth POA head' with him when he transferred north. They had clashed a couple of times over staffing levels when the 'big man' had visited our unit.

I called him up and told him to stop winding Ivor up, as that was my job.

He accompanied me to a security day at Full Sutton where they put on show their intelligence procedures and security search 'finds,' it was very impressive.

When we'd arrived I'd noted the look of incredulity on his face as local staff of all ranks came up to me to say, 'good to see you Phil, fancy coming back, it's settled here now? How's Ivor, remember me to him?'

As I explained to him on the journey home, 'Full Sutton was chaotic and frightening for front-line staff until Ivor pitched-up and got a grip and the staff clearly haven't forgotten. I know he can be a crank but operationally he's a very effective crank!'

The risks of escape are highest obviously whenever a prisoner is out of the prison on escort. These risks increase when the prisoner is out for an extended period of time which normally meant in- patient treatment at one of our local hospitals.

I attended Dryburn hospital shortly after arriving at Frankland, to assess security arrangements for a bed-watch on Charlie Kray. I paid particular attention to the physical layout of the area where the bed-watch was to take place before producing a physical security check-list. When I returned the following week, after he had been admitted, I noticed that medical staff of all grades appeared to be a bit in awe of him, fussing around him. I noticed staff peering through the side-room door at him as they passed by. The Kray mystique had reached Durham!

He was quite ill and when he returned to our prison and I expedited a move south for him as soon as he was fit to travel. He wasn't a difficult prisoner, made no demands, he got on with his 'bird' with the minimum of fuss.

The professional criminal who poses the biggest risks, because they can slip under the radar if you don't keep your wits about you, is the one with no baggage, no ties, without a drugs problem, therefore no erratic thinking, I always found.

I blitzed visits with searches on my first few months, helped in no small measure by a small but willing coterie of 'sources.' All tended to be involved to a greater of lesser degree themselves, which is the reason they were able to accurately 'mark my card.'

One of the 'chaps' told me one day with a chuckle, 'I nearly gave myself away yesterday, you should have heard what they were calling you, they never thought you would target them on successive days, they were ready to write off what you found on Friday, knowing that they had a bigger lot coming in on Saturday, they couldn't believe it when you seized that as well! I had to bang-up, get out of the way I was laughing that much.'

It's good for staff morale when they are consistently successful, it also instils confidence in inmates, they quickly realise that you know what you are doing and crucially, that you are discreet.

The 'main man' nearly cried when I subsequently met him in the segregation unit. 'It's a fit-up Mr O'B they planted it!' 'Don't give me that they're not gardeners, they're the DST!' I always felt it was important to have the last word.

Those trafficking the substances into prison used to 'stuff and swallow.' Women stuffed the 'scag' up their 'fannies,' whilst the men stuffed it up their arses, alternatively they would both swallow it. They used to put it in condoms and stuff it up and swallow it down. Some 'trained' by swallowing grapes and they would dip condoms in syrup so that they could travel more comfortably, they use something called lomotil as a binder I was told. I'd have known none of this without my willing, ever growing group of 'sources.' We were up and running and it was going well!

Intelligence gathering via 'sources' was a delicate symbiosis within the criminal world, a balancing of mutual respect. I hoped to give something small to get back big. Generally if you talk to people in the right way they respond. I remember a well-documented Essex gangster saying to me privately one day, 'you never ask us straight out governor but you always leave the door open.' It was about proportionality, relevance and reliability. The informant's log was a confidential document that had to be filled-in after every meeting. The senior in rank to the handler didn't meet the informant so that he/she could dispassionately evaluate the credibility of the intelligence and form a motive for giving it. I used to carry out monthly audits of all informant confidential documents because handling informants tests a person's skills, resourcefulness and patience. I was testing what the informants said for accuracy and quality and making a constant judgement on their reliability and motive. These checks occasionally led me to decide to break contact when it became obvious a particular informant couldn't take the pressure. There should never be any emotion between an informant and a handler, a fine line I occasionally had to walk, because some I'd known so long that I'd got to know their families via visits (and occasional phone calls), shared in their little triumphs and disappointments. Prison life was a bit of a chess game, both for prisoners and staff, particularly in the High Security Estate, a case of staying ahead of your opponents by predicting the next moves. In the criminal world most know what their rivals are up to, ensuring their 'interests' didn't clash, outside feuds sometimes got fought out inside, this was an important risk I had to often address.

This occasionally helped me spot a potential informant, these clashes were really in nobody's interests and the most surprising high profile criminals would 'mark my card' to ensure they didn't.

Potential informants might be someone with a grudge, someone seeking to take out a rival, someone looking for a reduction in sentence or someone that might be tempted by financial reward. Once you have found someone who best serves your interests you have to decide how to make the initial contact. When doing so you must put some security and safety measures in place before making an approach. This might be a plausible excuse why a prisoner might be away from where he was expected to be, for example a hospital appointment, a legal visit, a cell search. It was important to select a discreet area away from prying eyes to meet.

I did occasionally use a participating informant. This could be a particularly difficult thing to handle because he must walk an incredibly difficult line between appearing to help others without breaking the law himself and/or enticing them to do so; defence of necessity.

I occasionally operated 'talking tables,' so called because they had an in-built bug. I only ever used them in the visits area. Highly sensitive paperwork had to be submitted before this was authorised. It was normally the result of a police request/operation and I used to monitor the whole process very closely to ensure that they carried out just what had been approved and didn't pull any strokes! Defence of necessity? The reader will be the best judge of that as this chapter progresses.

I became aware that a particular Category A prisoner had set off the alarm when being electronically scanned by the DST after work. I briefed them about his 'previous' explaining why we'd have to strip him and carry out an intimate search. 'He's a persistent escaper, he was implicated in planning an escape at Belmarsh in 1998, he secreted a life-sized dummy in his bed to fool the night patrols, a well-known skilled key-maker was to go with him.'

'That alarms always going off boss, there's summat wrong with it,' he cried as we put on gloves prior to the search. He quickly retrieved a drill-bit that had been secreted up his arse and handed it over.

This was the first of a number of 'incidents' between us over the next six plus years. We would 'meet' again shortly before I retired; he would claim I had it in for him; I would be 'investigated!'

Ivor decided that the public purse could afford to fund some 'bonding' activities for the senior management team. He 'bussed' us up to Slaney Hall where we paint-balled in the morning, raced around using quad bikes in the afternoon We finished the day with a slap-up meal. In between we did a series of exercises that involved utilising basic materials like logs/wood, string to cross a river without getting wet. The 'big man from Strabane' had 'absent-minded professor' Chris Di Paolo and Phil 'three brains' Copple, (on account of his First class degree from Durham University) on his team. I had Head of Works Mike Webber and a highly skilled and inventive female Head of Psychology, for whom these kind of exercises were 'meat and drink,' on my side.

It became highly competitive; suffice to say we 'wiped the floor' with them much to Ivor's growing anger. Phil and Chris took most of the blame for his team's dismal showing.

Investors in People became the vogue and our Head of Human Resources was keen for us to attain it. However an initial survey of staff, part of the process, came to the very clear conclusion that the Governor was 'a tyrant' or sentiments to that effect! This report never saw the light of day!

The survey of course coincided with the 'big man's early years when he was 'popping up' where least expected and castigating those not carrying out their duties to the required standard. I'd become used to this reaction at both Castington and Full Sutton, but as staff, particularly at the latter, had demonstrated when I returned on a visit, they had missed his presence and leadership qualities after he'd left.

We did eventually attain Investors in People status, and a lot more besides, a couple of years later when the establishment settled and staff had become more confident. I think it's fair to say the majority of prisoners also 'bought' into what we were aiming to achieve.

The minority who didn't fully occupied myself and my staff until the day I retired.

In preparation for the year 2000 we had to plan contingencies in case our computers failed, our gates didn't function, technology was fine while it worked but you've always got to have a plan B in case it fails.

If this wasn't stressful enough I'd received written information (a note in the box), from a prisoner I'd not previously had contact with, about a demonstration planned for New Year's Eve on one of the main dispersal wings.

It was organised by someone serving life for the murder of a club 'bouncer' in Manchester.

He'd been dealing drugs quite successfully before I arrived but I'd contacted someone in his 'inner circle' who I'd known previously and we'd been able to curtail his enterprises. This was to be my 'payback.' He wasn't amused.

He was violent, well connected on the 'out' and the prisoner who had written to me was terrified, I subsequently learned he owed him a 'grand' so he'd every reason to be!

He agreed to speak to me if I transferred him out, which I did, I went to see him the following week at his new prison with my right-hand man Steve Robson and he expanded on his written communication.

Most of the people on the list, those who were going to disobey the order 'to bang-up' at the appropriate time, owed him money; the rest were his 'inner circle' which included 'my man'.

I briefed Phil Copple and Ivor and they agreed with the suggestion that I 'spike the proposed demo by transferring out the 'main players'. This we did the week before Christmas. The following day I toured the wing, people acknowledged me, a couple including 'my man' smiled, and discreetly, gave knowing winks, The atmosphere had improved noticeably.

I found throughout my career that the vast majority of prisoners just want to get on with their 'bird'. Of course they want to be treated fairly, to receive their entitlements, but long-term prisoners share many of the same worries as 'civilians,' sick relatives, problems with schools, relationship break-downs; they haven't time to riot but they sometimes couldn't afford 'to lose face'. This is where we came in handy. You make it 'acceptable' by being fair, proportionate and by not 'crowing' or making a big deal about it when you've sorted it.

Everything worked perfectly over the New Year period, it went off without a hitch.

I got a lot of my information from the phone and from visitors, some of whom I've known for years from different establishments. They'd ring the exchange when they had fears for their sons, husbands, and telephone operator Janet would put them through with a, 'one of your dodgy calls.'

One woman, worried about her husband's debt one day, and as if reading my mind, finished the call by saying, 'apart from him and the kids and the weekly shop what have I got?'

I have massive respect for the majority and I try to not let them down.

Which is why it annoys me occasionally when some staff don't treat visitors with the respect they deserve.

I had a couple working in the ECR who ironically had found it difficult working on the wings but then found that they could be 'tough guys' when operating in the relatively safe area of visits. They were a pathetic embarrassment and I made sure they knew it.

To maintain a safe environment, you needed to be aware of the currents, to be constantly assessing events and the effects they can have on the states of mind of sometimes treacherous, unpredictable men.

Most days were outwardly quiet, but at any moment there could be danger. Fresh alliances and betrayals, shifting sands. Today's friend may be tomorrow's enemy; he might inform on you or even try to kill you; this was how long-term prisoners viewed life. Stand up for yourself or you'll be 'buried'!

Somebody serving 20/30 years or a whole life sentence tended to think in terms of, escape, death, survival, being released on licence!

They structured their day: food, shower, shits, writing sleeping, walking/running around the exercise yard, attending the gym; but most of all blocked-out thoughts of home and prison became their 'home' all year round. That was it!

I knew long-termers who asked their families to stop visiting. I recall one telling me at Full Sutton, 'any letter takes me a week to get over, so visits... can be particularly hard.'

A 'dear John,' or marriage break-up was another painful reality for many long-termers. On a couple of occasions over the years prisoners had described the tell-tale signs. A new chestnut perm, a different perfume. I remember one prisoner telling me at Wakefield after it had happened to him, 'anger is the easiest answer to despair but it doesn't change anything and afterwards you feel worse than before. It will pass.'

Weekend on, and in-charge. I had a dirty protest to deal with in the segregation unit. It was in support of an Asian guy who was serving a sentence for allegedly stabbing to death a white guy (one of six) in a restaurant in the West Midlands. The whites had allegedly complained about the playing of Asian music, even though it was an Asian restaurant! The Asian, who was also in segregation, had refused to go on normal location because he was protesting his innocence.

He claimed self-defence saying that he'd been attacked by racists and his case had garnered much support both inside and outside prison; indeed a well-known pop group from the West Midlands had recorded a song in support. Five other inmates had joined the protest.

We'd received intelligence earlier in the week that a bus load of anarchists would be coming from Sheffield to show their support. The leader of the anarchists was a man recently released from Frankland who'd served a sentence for an unprovoked attack on two students in a bar. A couple of kids, first time away from home and this prat had 'cut' them. Believe me he was no class-warrior! To say I didn't like him was an understatement, I can honestly say he was the only prisoner who would make me 'bristle' when he passed me. So much so that a prisoner whom I'd known for many years at different establishments, noticed my distaste and remarked on it one day.

At a meeting on the Friday afternoon, it had been decided that Adele my weekend governor grade colleague would 'manage' the demonstration from the gate, she would be assisted in this by our PLO Steve Norris who arranged support from the Durham Force. The police would restrict the demonstrators to a specific area so that visitors wouldn't be inhibited.

I had met with Steve and Adele as soon as I'd come on duty and we'd gone over the strategy to cope one last time.

I went to the segregation unit as soon as practicable, the smell was appalling, staff walking round in thick rubber gloves. The never ending stench of piss and shit made me want to wretch!

As I had no adjudications to complete I immediately started my 'rounds.' The governor in-charge had to see each individual segregated prisoner each day, to ascertain their well-being.

The first prisoner I spoke to indicted without speaking so he wouldn't be overheard, that he'd like to speak with me privately as soon as possible, I nodded my assent and moved on.

The main man was next to be seen and he immediately surprised me by telling me that he wished to terminate his protest. His fellow protesters gave me the same news as I reached their cells.

Though this was great news it did give me a logistical problem. I had to arrange for outside contractors to fumigate the cells, the use of high-powered hoses, directed into the cells, often turning the mattresses into saturated sponges.

We had to relocate the prisoners within the Seg whilst this happened, shower them and provide clean clothing.

The long-suffering, superb staff were into this when I received a call from a very competent member of our Healthcare department. This lady always appeared to be on duty with me when incidents occurred and apparently had the audacity to see me as a Jonah! In fact she'd been known to come into the gate, ask the staff who the duty governor was, before threatening to go straight back home again on hearing it was me!

'Now I know you're busy Phil, and I've no wish to add to your stress but I think we've got a barricade...'

'Bloody hell it had to be you, I'll be over in a minute,' was my terse reply.

I addressed the Segregation unit SO, ' Finish up here, I'll take Kev with me, then ring round and get me a C&R intervention team kitted-up and tell them to report to me in Healthcare.'

I received a brief from the Healthcare officer i/c on arrival before making my way over to the barricaded cell where Kevin had already struck up a dialogue. Kevin was a C&R instructor and very 'handy' but he was also an excellent communicator and well respected by prisoners.

As the governor in-charge I was supposed to keep out of sight because in these situations I would be the final arbitrator, the 'negotiation' is best carried out by those further down the 'food-chain.' If it hadn't been for the demonstration outside the establishment, Adele would have been 'managing' at the scene.

I'd been kept in touch with that by radio and I knew it was orderly and contained.

Kevin was doing a splendid job, he'd calmed the perpetrator and I eased closer to the door when I overheard him say he was going to a box to find a photo of his family to show Kev.

I noted that the bed was not jammed flush up against the door, there was room for movement.

Just then I became aware of my intervention team entering the unit, I pointed to an empty cell that I'd opened for them and went over to brief them.

When I returned to the barricade area, all was quiet, I said to Kev: 'where is he?'

'He's in the far corner making us a cup of tea.'

'He's fucking what, come on!'

Key straight in the door, a big heave and the bed's out of the way, we grab the startled perp, whip him out of the cell and hand him over to the intervention team to search, process and relocate.

Kevin then quite rightfully and respectfully reminded me of my role and responsibility as a C&R supervising officer: 'you are responsible for ensuring that all laid down procedures relating to control and restraints are adhered to. The first being that every effort must be made to enlist the willing cooperation of the prisoner and if that objective can be achieved then force must not be used. You should have no hands on function Phil, sorry...'

All true and that was me told, he then went on to remind me. 'Don't forget Phil you promised to come down to speak to one of ours later.'

Professional to the last unlike me! 'The staff here are now achieving highly in spite of you,' Chris Di Poalo often reminded me. I did go to the Seg to see the prisoner, but not before I'd been out for a run, had my dinner, rang Tote Credit and had a bet and seen the anarchists off the premises!

Monday 7th May 2000 a group of us are running from Frankland to Belmarsh calling at all the High Security prisons. Our aim was to raise money for a prosthetic leg for Donna, a member of the admin staff who suffered serious illness, although you'd never guess. I'd worked first with her at Low Newton where she'd set out trying to get me to dance with her mate at Christmas do's, she knew how to embarrass and was great fun. She also loved the job and was good at it, her attitude and attendance record put many to shame.

Two of the group, Dougie and Ritchie, had driven the route the previous week and made up superb route maps to cover the sections each individual would run. Each person would run 12 miles then rest in the van that accompanied us. Ivor had supplied us with the van and DDG Peter Atherton had ensured that the whole estate was on board and would supply us with a buffet on arrival.

The first leg was a matter of yards, Frankland to Low Newton, a courtesy call to Donna's previous workplace.

Then the serious business with calls at Durham, Full Sutton and finishing our first day off at Wakefield. We were put up and fed at the training school.

The second day found us running through the Peak District, and, as you can imagine this often involved hills. Now I don't know if the chaps took pity on me but my 12 miles were fairly flat and culminated outside Hillsborough football stadium.

Dougie got the Derbyshire hills and cursed us loudly as we roared him on, red-faced, puffed-cheeks, from the safety of the van.

We all slept soundly at Newbold Revel that night, all the prisons we visited doing us proud both in in terms of the receptions they gave us and the money collected.

I remember Wednesday was a nice day and I was running through a small village in Warwickshire, it was mid-morning, I nodded to a woman tending a hanging basket, and as I passed the Post Office a man was coming out with his paper: 'Good day for it. Have you come far?'

The look on his face when I answered 'Durham' was priceless!

We finished at Belmarsh on the Thursday and we were welcomed by the Governor and were fed.

Ivor had paid for our accommodation for the night so, despite the tired limbs, it was wash and change and out to boogie.

We started our return journey the following day with our tank roughly half-full. We were made aware of the effect a truckers' demo over high fuel prices was having, by the number of garages we passed in London with 'sold-out, no fuel' signs.

We began to worry a bit when met with the same signs on the motorway as we journeyed north.

We really started to panic when we reached south Yorkshire with the petrol gauge hovering on empty.

One of our number, a healthcare officer knew people in the area as he'd previously worked at nearby Lindholme. He made contact by phone with a local friend but the place they suggested had run out of fuel.

'What about the private prison at Doncaster, it's just up the road, about a mile and not far from the motorway?' The Healthcare officer with the local knowledge enquired.

Dougie stopped at a garage on the way and blagged a tube in case we had to 'suck' for our petrol. It was a 'good call' as it turned out.

Soon the Healthcare officer and I were striding purposely towards the prison gate lodge.

The support grade officer at the gate was not impressed. We were untidy, sweaty, dressed in shorts and T shirts; he clearly had difficulty believing our story that we were prison staff returning north after running to London 'and we've run out of petrol because of the truckers....'

Just then a load of suited chaps appeared at the gate from inside the prison.

'Right, the Dep's meeting has just finished. I will speak with Mr McCaul about you and see what he suggests.'

'Is that Ian McCaul who used to be at Wakefield?'

'Yes I believe it is,' said the gate officer.

'Can you tell him it's Phil O'Brien who's stranded?'

Within minutes I'd spoken to Ian and he'd given us permission to suck enough juice from his Cat A van to get us home, Dougie did the honours and once again we were on our way.

Ian was the ex SAS guy who had picked me up and shaken me like a rag doll during the hostage intervention exercise during my induction week at Wakefield. A top, top man.

'The trouble is the 'big man from Strabane' as you call him, gets on to me when he suspects you've been at it. Never you! It's me that gets it in the neck when he suspects you're employing your 'Ways and Means Act' which, may I remind you, is not an Act of Parliament but an unofficial set of rules you deploy to deal with a situation as you see it!'

'And reading the rule book never got some out of the library!' was my somewhat terse response. Chris continued:

'First we had that prisoner in the seg. I kept telling him you were investigating until he pointed out he'd been clean-shaven when he first saw him, then when he next saw him whilst on his 'rounds,' some seven weeks later, he'd grown a full beard you'd had him down there that long! And now, a week after our esteemed Director General Mr Narey described the prison service as institutionally racist, you conned a doctor into putting his hands up a black inmate's arse to recover some 'smack,' Ivor's going beserk!'

Phil Copple had been promoted and had moved to his first in-charge post, Deerbolt, a Youth Custody Centre. Chris had been promoted in situ and was now the Deputy Governor and I reported directly to him.

Chris lived in York and travelled daily. When I wasn't duty governor and required to stay until lock-up at 21 00 hours, I would pick him up from his office at 17 00 hours and drop him at the station on my way home.

It gave me the opportunity to brief him daily on operational matters but he clearly felt I occasionally kept a bit back, probably, defence of necessity was my excuse!

What had happened in this case was that a West African giant had arrived whilst I was on leave and had been located to G wing. He must have had a large amount of 'coke' secreted which had been missed on reception and he'd immediately started to 'trade', destabilising the existing 'market'.

Established traders took umbrage and a 'contract' was put out on him.

On my first day back on duty he was attacked by a fellow inmate with a bowl of boiling hot gee.

Despite horrendous injuries the African fought back and was winning the fight when we intervened. He was one tough cookie who then collapsed and went into a coma. We arranged for a blue light to accompany him to the RVI in Newcastle. I elected to send some of my DST staff on the bed-watch because I was told that he still some 'coke' secreted, not 'smack' as Chris had thought. I'd got them to take a drugs detector implement with them. An intrepid Consultant had asked what it was for and after the 'chaps' had explained our fear he immediately donned some surgical gloves before retrieving the drugs from the arse of our comatose prisoner.

I thought it was a right result and continue to this day to praise the RVI and its staff whenever I get the opportunity.

'There are pockets of blatant and malicious racism,' Chris went on quoting the Director General, Ivor's got him on the run, putting pressure on him. I brought him down to earth the following day by wearing my son's scarf, Jamaica's colours interspersed with the 'weed,' logo. John was a great Bob Marley fan. 'I don't believe it,' was all he could say, the truth is he knows my politics and that I got on well with black prisoners and always had. Indeed the 'Yardies' had a giggle when they saw me on line-route, proudly wearing my scarf.

A week later I was sitting in Healthcare with the big West African, who'd been discharged from the RVI the previous day.

He'd asked if he could stay but I'd told him I would be moving him on as soon as he was fit to travel. Whilst he'd been at the RVI someone had sent him a dressing gown which had quantities of 'coke' sewed on to the seams.

"Not mine Mr O'B somebody's trying to dig me out, you keep it."

The police had checked out the address but it was 'moody.'

'Hardly, you're a good 6 inches bigger than me, I could live in it!'

We parted on good terms and he even gave me a run down on coke distribution via the Continent.

'The Columbians are starting to use Africa - more coke comes into the UK that way. At least 60 drug mules arrive in Britain from West Africa every week. We expect 1 in 4 won't get through Customs. A haulier will expect 40% of his consignments will get caught. This still gives him a healthy tax-free profit. I admire what you do boss but you are, how you say, pissing in the wind?'

Well that was me told!

I'd developed a method of 'parallel governing' which understandably unnerved the powers that be from time to time. At the end of 2002 I'd suggested to Ivor that I come off security and give my very able deputy Roy Robson a chance. The big man wouldn't hear of it: "you're there to watch my back whilst I'm here, nobody knows these prisoners like you!"

So I established channels of communication with prisoners which would have been too dangerous physically and politically for Ivor or Chris to make. Links that had the advantage for them of being deniable.

I'd developed an undeclared back-channel which carried with it a kind of trust which a front channel (a more open meeting) never could.

Each side knew that the other had their own agenda, many of my best sources were actively involved and were high profile which is why they knew what was going on. Nevertheless, the DST and prisoners understood that this didn't give them a get-out-of jail card, they were subject to the same levels of searching and supervision as everyone else! It was easy then to develop that to a point where you can have some basis for trusting what the other person's telling you.

The other advantage of such talks was that they often confirmed intelligence I already had.

This back-channel soon produced some priceless intelligence.

I was standing outside G wing exercise yard with an officer dismissed by most managers as scruffy, always looked tired, was previously an OSG. He was going through a messy divorce, wasn't sure where he would be living but to me he was a mine of information. He blended in, I suspect some of the cons could identify with his personal circumstances, they would always speak to him, he would occasionally pick-up a snooker cue and have a game with them if a table was free but the needs of the job would always come first. If he was required to open a door, take one to visits, this immediately would be his priority, prisoners respected this. He was honest and trustworthy.

'He's lost a lot of weight since he came here,' he said, 'trains all the time now, all he did was eat when he first came from Woodhill.' He was looking directly at a Cat A serving 21 years for importation of drugs, £3.5m of heroin and £500,000 worth of ecstacy tablets.

'Thanks, keep your eye on him,' I said, 'he could be thinking of making one, it's a 'classic' sign, suddenly changes his eating habits, starts getting fit, keep your eye on it I'll be in touch.'

What I didn't say was that during a back-channel meeting the previous month I'd been informed that a southern Cat A was planning 'to go on his toes!'

I had three people, independent of each other, two prisoner sources and a member of staff, watching the situation and reporting back to me. An 11 year man, license-breach, very experienced, came back to me after a week: 'Looks like we were right but obviously they are keeping it tight (name deleted) is arranging things on the out through some of his people.' He mentioned another Cat A serving an 18 year sentence for a string of armed robberies in which firearms had been discharged and people injured, not a co-accused of our 'target' but from the same county.

As was my practice I fed my intelligence back to my intelligence teams, they cross-referenced background information from back-records, providing me with excellent progress reports, a job for their week-end on.

It was clear our target was having difficulty coming to terms with his sentence, its severity had just hit him: 'I have to get out of here,' he had been overheard to say.

My reports made clear that when he was initially arrested, a tactical firearms unit had been deployed because intelligence had indicated that he had access to firearms. He owned properties in the Canary Islands as well as in the UK. His counsel at trial had represented the Maxwell brothers at their infamous fraud trial. All indicators of his wealth, he appeared to have the money required to mount an escape bid.

Now he was interval-training with an A and E man who had once arranged for a gun to be smuggled into Durham prison, to aid an escape bid.

He'd lost 6 stone in a couple of months and was considered super-fit!

My most recent information was that his intent was to get to an outside hospital, a fake altercation would take place, shielded from staff via milling inmates he would stab himself deeply with a blunt instrument that would create a sucking chest wound. A tracking device concealed in a tennis ball would be thrown over the wall near the main kitchen entrance, and one of 'my men' on the Yards party would retrieve it.

I, of course had a duty of care to my source and had to remain mindful of that.

The back-record checking of the intelligence team turned up a security information report, dated 10 July, it stated that he'd been asking his escort about the lay-out of the prison, as he was on the way to the MDT Suite. He'd shown particular interest in buildings near the old reception yard.

Our police liaison officer had been working with his counterparts in Kent as well as briefing his supervising officer in Durham.

Some of the potential escaper's visitors had been seen driving slowly through a local estate, a safe house to rent?

All the indications we had were that a medical diversion would be created, a tracking device would be attached to the Cat A van. When he was in transit 'a little team' would hijack the van and rescue him.

I did an interim report for Chris who submitted it via Ivor to the DDG. The decision was taken immediately by the DDG to review his Category, he was upgraded to Category A exceptional risk and transferred to disrupt his plans. I briefed the Head of Security at the receiving prison prior to his arrival.

We had probably dodged 'a bullet' in more ways than one!

My health care contact called my attention to a Category A prisoner who had been moved from normal location to be monitored. As she understood it the doctor was more worried about his mental health than any physical deterioration.

I set my superb intelligence SO the task of doing a back-record report on him on his next weekend on, his findings put me on alert!

The prisoner had been convicted of killing a South London gangster in 1995, on behalf of an Irish mobster, whilst being observed by SERCS-SO19!

He had put up an extraordinary defence at his trial claiming to be both a member of the IRA, the INLA as well as being a police informant. However, he was found guilty and was serving 3 life sentences.

The report detailed how he had progressed from being a trouble-free hard working student from a good family to become a one man serious crime wave. By the age of 22 he had amassed dozens of convictions for larceny, burglary and car theft. A complete maverick who mostly operated alone, he had earned a reputation as a dangerous unpredictable villain. In 1969 he'd received a 4 year sentence for robbery. His reputation as a desperado had impressed other prisoners and he'd been befriended by members of a Republican off-shoot, Saor Eire.

My concerns were raised when I noted that he'd then hatched an escape plan. He had managed to inveigle his way to the Central Mental Hospital by convincing the Directors that he was unstable, before absconding. We had recently discharged a prisoner next door to him, with mental health issues, to St Nicholas's Secure Unit in Newcastle.

SIR's indicated that the two prisoners had struck up an unlikely close relationship in the days prior to the prisoners move to St Nick's.

I was certain that this is what the 'target' was seeking to achieve. Never, not on my watch, he'd remain Cat A and go back on normal location I had no doubt that within days of him going St Nick's he'd vanish into the hills of Northumberland. He had gone 'on his toes from' the Institution in Ireland, lived on his wits in the Wicklow hills, he was never re-arrested until he did that 'hit' in London!

I didn't win them all, I was walking through visits with Harry Henson one afternoon. When I got to 'the brothers' table one of them turned to his dad and said; 'this is Mr O'Brien.' Before I could react his dad was off his seat to shake my hand!

"Right under the camera, captured for posterity," said Harry with a guffaw, 'he was worse than the brothers in his day; shootings and beatings all over the West End and there you are shaking hands with him like two old mates.'

Category A prisoners moved regularly around the High Security Estate, the idea was that if they were given too much time to get used to their surroundings, they might be tempted to mount an escape attempt. This policy had its critics and had been tempered a bit by the time I retired.

We'd received the 'clown' I'd clashed with at Full Sutton when he'd been using his ample intellect to browbeat and intimidate teachers.

He'd risen to even greater heights subsequently by being a prime-mover in the Parkhurst escape that had led to the sacking of DG Derek Lewis and the well-publicised public falling-out between Home Secretary Michael Howard and Prisons' Minister Anne Widdicombe!

He and his fellow escapees had tried to steal a plane to get off the Island!

I was always there every time he made his way to the workshop, "morning Mathew," he ignored me. Whoever was following him would invariably grin and often wink at me, when this exchange took place. They knew him and knew what I was at. He will always remain an escape risk, he's not violent, but the IRA in particular had used him to carry and store things for them earlier in his sentence.

He would do this willingly, there was no suggestion of coercion, refusing point blank to meaningfully engage with staff.

His mantra: 'no cell will contain my mind, no authority figure will intimidate me, no sentence enslave me.' I never let him out of my sight!

I kept him just short of a year then 'traded him' in for one of his fellow escapers.

I called a meeting, which Chris agreed to chair, to draw up a protocol to tackle the potential for staff corruption, as I mentioned previously, I was determined not to tackle this on my own after the experience of one of my predecessors.

We decided: we would have to create a culture of staff feeling comfortable about expressing concerns about their colleagues through the SIR system.

The security department would then gather, grade and disseminate this information at this monthly meeting.

A tasking meeting would take place before any action was taken against any individual. All risks would be assessed at this meeting.

The police liaison officer would be a member, all meetings to be minuted but the minutes would not be for general distribution and would kept in the governor's safe.

The chairman would brief the Governor as necessary.

A selection board for a level 2B generalist post at Frankland was advertised.

I was eligible so I applied.

In preparation for a day like this I had taken notice of a strategy formulated by a senior Governor Brodie Clark when he had been tasked with taking control of Whitemoor prison, following the IRA inspired escape from their special unit!

He had detailed his plans in the Prison Service Journal and I'd made a note; my intention being to use some of his ideas on a presentation I would be required to give on 'successfully effecting change.'

The 'Board' comprised of Phil Copple in the 'chair,' the two other members being Chris Di Paolo and Low Newton's Governor, Mike Kirkby.

The presentation seemed to go well and I felt I handled the questions at the end comprehensively.

Chris was superbly professional post the 'board' and didn't give me clue how it had gone. Though I still dropped him at the station each evening, we would stick to talking about operational matters. I was conscious that others, both within the region and outside it, had also been interviewed.

He took me into Ivor's office on the day of the SMT Christmas meal: 'the results are in the post today so there's no longer an embargo. In fact, as we're going for a meal most candidates will know their result before you. Well done! You were successful. You were brilliant on the day, vigorous, animated Had you popped an 'e' before you started? By the way, Copple had heard the speech before!'

'The big, long, useless, trainspotting anorak' was my not very complimentary reply.

'Come on Phil that's a bit harsh, me and Mike hadn't a clue!'

By the way I told Ivor about your performance.'
'What did he say?'
'That's my boy!'

My simple intent as I moved up the management ladder was to seek to improve on what was there initially. This was impossible without like-minded staff. The successful manager needs to get his group selection right and have a solid succession plan. Don't make wholesale changes; change when you see staff getting stale remembering that succession planning is crucial and needs delicate handling. In the Category A estate there was little margin for error, you have to do simple things consistently well and cut out risk. Insist on attention to small detail but empower people, let them get on with it whilst monitoring and supporting them. It's important to also to remember that even the supervisors need supervising!

I'd no time for the 'club' that some staff of all grades were in. The one that was constantly worrying about the pension scheme, the ones that got ratty about annual leave, days in lieu or bank holidays! The 'club' that was serving out its time, the 'club' that had given up! I'd never joined that 'club' and I'd no place in the group for anyone that did. Prisoners were plotting 24 hours a day and to keep one step ahead I needed staff who were just as committed. We needed to search after hours, over meal-breaks, unsocially, to get results. If you were strictly 9 to 5, you were better off in a workshop!

It was vitally important to create an audit culture where achieving high quality work was valued and rewarded, and which emphasised the importance of doing the right thing in the public interest.

To achieve this through my managers the core skills I expected them to have were:

- Awareness of their feelings and an ability to control them,
- Emotional resilience - the ability to perform consistently under pressure,
- Motivation - the drive and energy to achieve results,
- Influence - persuasive skills,
- Decisiveness - arrive at clear decisions and drive them through,
- Conscientiousness - displaying commitment to a plan of action and match words and deeds.

I was blessed with staff who had these skills and more in abundance.

A potential key compromise; an assistant chaplain had used the toilet in the chapel at lunch-time when all the prisoners had returned to their wings. He had removed his pouched belt from his trousers, this held his keys and ID card. He had placed his belt on the floor. When he had finished his ablutions, he left the toilet leaving the belt on the floor.

At approximately 13 30 hours two officers took up their duties in the chapel, they failed to carry out an area search prior to receiving prisoners for a Buddhist meeting. At about 14 10 hours a prisoner went to the communal toilet He had been the first person to use it. The staff had been stationed at a table between the door and the toilet. Nobody else could have used it without their knowledge.

The prisoner was in the toilet for 30/40 seconds. He relieved himself standing up when he had finished he turned and saw the pouched belt on the floor. He came straight over to inform the officers. They gave the pouch to the chaplain but failed to search the prisoner, nor did they report the incident to the duty governor or the orderly officer.

The prisoner told his personal officer when he returned to his wing which is how Chris and I became aware.

We immediately despatched someone with the keys to Wetherby for forensic examination. This process proved that the keys had not been copied or tampered with in any way.

The prisoner was due for release on the 16th of the following month after serving an 8 year sentence so did not have the motivation to exploit a belt found by chance. On the contrary he was keen to avoid any trouble that might put in jeopardy his release date.

The statements taken, interviews conducted and the results of the forensic key examination were entirely consistent with the prisoner's story that he didn't handle the keys in any way.

There was no key compromise; however this was due to good fortune rather than any degree of competence by the three members of staff involved, they would be subsequently suitably dealt with.

A week later with Chris we were going through some learning points over the pouch incident along with in-charge chaplain, Liz Cummings. She was due to retire and I knew she would be missed, I'd worked with her at Low Newton and she knew me too well. She managed to be as popular and respected by staff and prisoners equally; a unique position for a chaplain in my experience.

Chris's face was a picture when we got on to general matters just before the meeting concluded: 'Phil's long been a worry to me, I've lost count of the pairs of trousers I've worn out at the knees praying for him. I always felt, no feared, that he operated just this side of the bars...'

Mr Di Paolo nodded furiously in agreement!

Mid-2002, Chris was chairing our adjudications standards committee. A senior officer from the segregation unit attends and presents any successful appeals against adjudication findings over the previous quarter. The aim is to improve the fairness, transparency and credibility of the system in the eyes of both staff and prisoners.

On the odd occasion when one of mine is overturned he will exclaim with mock horror: 'surely not, what went wrong, I thought all yours commenced 'it's a fair cop gov you've got me bang to rights, I throw myself on your mercy!'

Actually, the common thread of judgements confirmed that a prisoner, like any other citizen, had an unfettered right to access legal advice and also to court. The principle was that a prisoner retained the same rights as those in the community except those expressly taken away by statute, for example the right to personal liberty and freedom of movement. This governed how I carried out adjudications, though I'm not sure I convinced Mr Di Paolo.

I struck gold 'source-wise' in the most unlikely of circumstances; however it was a relationship fraught with danger.

I rarely acknowledged my 'sources' whilst touring the wings unless they were amongst a group of prisoners I'd stopped to converse with.

I'd talk to so many people, that people generally felt 'safe' talking to me if they had a query. If they were entitled they got it, prisoners knew that so wouldn't begrudge prisoners speaking to me, the queries tended to be about visits or property, things crucial to all, it was well known these were areas in which I had the final say.

I'd advised an older, first time prisoner, about visits shortly after he'd arrived and since then we'd always passed the time of day whenever our paths crossed.

However, he surprised me one day when he asked, 'can I have a word in private boss?'

The substance of our conversation was that one of his daughters had struck up a relationship with another prisoner on the wing, they had first noticed each other on separate visits. The prisoner he identified was a Category B with a dreadful prison record for assaults on both staff and fellow prisoners, and now I'm told he was in regular touch with paramilitaries. 'He wants to break with them boss but he doesn't know how to do it, I told him you were approachable but I don't think he's ever asked staff for help, it's not in his nature!'

I returned to my office to refresh my memory about the Cat B he'd mentioned.

He was now in his mid 20's, serving a life sentence for murder. He had originally been sentenced to HMP, (detained at her Majesty's pleasure), a life sentence for young prisoners and had received this sentence when 15 years old.

From the West Midlands, he'd been sent initially to Aylesbury, the long-term youth custody in the south.

This establishment held many black gang members from the London area and had a reputation for violence.

Though not very big, he had developed a fearsome reputation for violence, in fact his record demonstrated that he'd proved so hard to handle that he'd been 'starred-up' before his 21 birthday and sent to Whitemoor adult prison.

Then, rather than fading into the background he appeared to attach himself to the IRA contingent and others with violent tendencies; appearances before the Governor and long periods segregated became the norm for him. He had been at Frankland for 10 months. He had been placed on report shortly after arriving, there were threats to staff, but his behaviour in recent months had improved dramatically. Funny what love can do!

I had the lad picked-up by a couple of my intel staff and they delivered him to me at a discrete location and left us. He was a bit nervous at first describing his initial experiences at Aylesbury. It probably helped that I had lived and worked in south London and knew something of black gang structures and cultures.

'No excuse for the way I behaved but coming down from the Midlands I knew I'd have to make my mark immediately or they would swallow me up. On the second day at the servery one spit in my food so I picked-up a ladle and did him, one of his mates left the queue before staff could react, and came for me, I cut him with my tray, then the bell went. Staff jumped on me but it took

6 of them to get me down the seg, I gave a good account of myself though I knew I would get a hiding in the end, they needed to see that I was game!'

When I finished my punishment, I was put on another wing and a rival group to the one I had rucked with 'adopted' me even though I am white. I got into everything they were in to, drugs, 'taxing' people and, as you know, when one of your own is attacked, retaliation has to happen, no matter what the consequences or repercussions, it has to be on. And it was often which is why I spent so much time in the seg and I suppose why they 'starred' me up.'

'Then you went to Whitemoor and got involved with the people our mutual friend is worried about?'

'Yes I can lip-read so they used to ask me to watch staff to interpret what they were saying, particularly when PO's or Governors were on the wing. They also got me to teach them back slang, but they didn't pick it up very well. You need to be from my area, I used to carry things for them.'

'What did they do for you?' 'They made sure I had private cash, they put me in touch with people in Ireland who wrote to me. My mam couldn't afford to visit me down there, or to send me regular private cash.

'So presumably you are still on good terms with them, so what's the problem?'

'You know I am writing to Pam, my first real girlfriend, I'm thinking different now and I don't want to put that at risk.'

'They are at peace now?'

'Some of the ones I knew have gone on the run, they might still get in touch, they told me this might happen years ago, I agreed that if it was necessary and they came over here, I would 'supply' cars and somewhere to stay for them. They advised me to settle down, calm down and conform, get better reports, work towards Cat C and release.'

'Have you any proof of this on-going connection?'

'I've got cards and some money sent last week.'

'Okay I'll check this out, are you okay to speak again?'

'Yes.'

This latest 'source' quickly proved a boon to me, his street credibility was such that people wouldn't think twice of discussing nefarious activities in front of him which helped me no end.

Word soon reached us that the cons had nicknamed me Columbo. Now whether this was because of my detached retina (a long not particularly edifying story) or my dodgy mac we never did determine.

More interesting was that word reached us via an SIR that the chaps were so impressed/unnerved by our recent success that they had started 'a de-briefing' process, a discussion on who I talked to when I toured the wings, in an effort to uncover my 'sources.'

Shortly after this incident there was a bit of media palaver over one of our inmates who'd recently been released to Glasgow on license. He'd clashed publicly in the street with a rival in which knives had alleged to have been used and he was now returning himself to Durham, to 'give himself up,' closely followed by the media.

Just before he had been released he'd asked me, 'is it worth a tenner for a freedom of information app to see what you have on me or will it be too heavily redacted?'

I'd advised him to buy his youngster a bigger present which he accepted with a grin.

He was fairly quiet on the wing but he was close to an Irish prisoner who had escaped from Pentonville and had been recaptured in the Netherlands. He was reputed to have links to a Republican offshoot but I strongly suspected that this was just a badge of convenience. He was a robber pure and simple, one who showed a taste for antiques.

He did however have a sense of humour, I was walking past the prisoners' kitchen on F4 where one of the notorious Newcastle brothers was frying something, the Irishman was standing in the doorway.

'Mr O'Brien, I'd love to get all your grasses over a flame like this and burn them.'

'Steven you'd be surprised who speaks to me.' As the Geordie quickly turned his back on me, the Irishman cracked a grin and started pointing animatedly!

Paul Ferris wrote to me from Durham prison asking if he could return to Frankland to finish his sentence. I expedited the move as he was serving a long-term sentence. It was where he should be.

My paramilitary 'source' proved to have the current 'contacts' he'd described, cards and photos sent by prominent members of Sein Fein. I soon found myself looking at photos and correspondence from people I had got used to seeing on TV going into Stormont for meetings.

Special Branch, briefed by police liaison officer Steve Norris, soon took a keen interest but not before my local dividend paid off 'in spades.'

His 'street-cred' because of his previous anti-staff stances and propensity for violence meant people never thought twice about dealing in front of him.

He had marked my card about a visits favourite and as a result the DST captured a load of gear and the traffickers.

Visitors were filling two or three little water balloons filled with 'weed.' They cut a hole in the bottom of their pockets, putting the balloons in their pants. They would then go to the toilet in visits to retrieve them before passing them via a kiss.

Like others it seemed to amuse him when he heard them slagging me and couldn't wait to tell me what they had said: 'why don't I get a proper job? when am I going to retire?'

A little bit of inter-agency working, special branch was keen to have 'my boy' nearer London, so we re-categorised himto C and moved him to a Training Prison in the South.

Unable to help himself he'd escaped within weeks!

The following month he rang me from Woodhill, closed prison, back as a Cat B with E man stripes!

'As soon as I got to my new prison I met a 'lifer' I'd known at Aylesbury. He and another con already had a plan in place and they asked me if I wanted to come. Before I knew it we were through the fence! They nicked a car, they were making for London but I was having second thoughts. I left them on the outskirts of London and called a contact in Ireland. I was told to make my way to Glasgow where someone would arrange safe passage for me across the sea to Belfast.

I was having second thoughts by this time, so I gave myself up, giving the name of my special branch contact helped with the local police.'

Of special interest to our PLO Steve Norris was the fact that when he'd been remanded to Woodhill, he'd met a group of lads from Luton who were serving sentences linked to Islamic terrorism. They had been found in possession of a load of 'moody' passports, driving licences and so on.

'I had some knowledge of these through my paramilitary contacts, they made me laugh, they were trying to convert me but the one I'd known loved his 'weed' and his 'hooch,' but got embarrassed when I reminded him.'

I got him back up to Frankland as soon as I could. Steve Norris was keen to interview him.

I was talking to a Cat A I'd known for years one day when he said: 'I'm surprised you've still got so much glass in the canteen, all the others have plastic or are going that way! Do you know (name deleted) keeps an empty sauce bottle above his bed on his window sill in case anybody tries to take him whilst he's snoozing and another on his wash basin next to his tooth brush in case anybody tries to take him whilst he's shaving?'

'No I didn't. Thanks I'll sort it.' Phew!

Our brave young Donna died and there was deep depression across the Establishment, replicated at our neighbouring prison Low Newton, where she had also served.

Her requiem mass at Ushaw was packed out with staff from both prisons, a celebration of a short but productive life, a life well-lived.

The previous month I'd ran a contingency plan exercise and I'd assigned her a major role which she

267

played to perfection. The sheer commitment and joy in her face, particularly at the subsequent de-brief as she described how the exercise had gone from her perspective, was a joy to behold!

The objective of that exercise was to test our contingency plan in relation to a hostage situation. As usual there were learning points that we incorporated into the plans.

All staff had to undertake computer training, centrally organised and facilitated by instructors who were on-site for about three months.

I'd completed the course early on though it has to be said I'd proved the most inadequate of students. Suffice to say the younger members of my staff could often be seen peering inside my office to observe my feeble keyboard attempts. On more than one occasion I rose and chased them down the corridor!

The big man from Strabane must have suffered, similarly, he'd failed to attend until the very last session. He'd made sure Chris waited with him.

Chris had rung me mid-afternoon to say that the big man was busy at the appointed start time and the session had been delayed till he could attend.

'Don't bother waiting for me Phil, I'll get a taxi, that's providing we finish before midnight, otherwise I'll sleep in the office...'

I'd been receiving intelligence on a proposed escape involving the screwdriver, file-up-the-bum, dummy-in-the-bed man, another head-the-ball Cat A murderer from Gateshead and one of mine.

A former prisoner related to one of the conspirators was supposed to supply a gun, he'd successfully accomplished this at Durham prison some years previously.

I'd been on leave so I was having a catch-up: 'don't know when the gun's coming in yet but you might be interested in this.'

It turned out that the file man had been observing the beats, changeover points/times of the dog handlers and had produced a chart of which any HR department would have been proud!

I put details of my meeting in an in-confidence SIR for Chris and left it with Governor's secretary Sue Johnson.

On a beautiful summer evening I decided to ignore the motorways where possible and take the scenic route home.

I was just leaving Scorton on the Northallerton road, windows open, the wind in my hair, 'Who's Next,' in the tape deck.

'Out here in the fields I fight for my meals, I get my back into my living..'

Suddenly my pager sounds, 'ring the ECR'.

'I don't need to fight to prove I'm right I don't need to be forgiven...'

Again the pager, 'ring Chris Di Paolo.'

I haven't a phone, I'm nowhere near a phone box, I'll be home in fifteen minutes I thought.

'Don't cry don't raise your eye, it's only teenage wasteland, it's only teenage wasteland oh yeah, they're all wasted..'

Off went the bloody pager again, 'ring Ivor.'

I'm beginning to realise that this might have something to do with the SIR.

I'd left for Chris. We had an unofficial protocol in place when I had something 'sensitive' going down. I would 'filter' through Chris who would 'judge', let's say when to alert the big man so he didn't go over the top, 'bring in the SAS, contact the Pope, Kenny Dalglish..'

Queer my pitch in effect. Looked like we'd failed this time!

'The song is over it's all behind me
I should have known it she'd try to find me
Our love is over, they're all ahead now
I've got to learn it..'

My pager was still indicating but I was nearly home. I ignored it.

'No one knows what it's like to be the bad man, to be the sad man, behind blue eyes.'

I turned into my drive, Daltrey's in full voice, Moonie was really going for it.

'We'll be fighting in the street, with our children at our feet and the morals that they worshipped will be gone, and the man that spurred us on, sitting judgement on our wrong.'

My wife met me at the door: 'what's going on, I've had Ivor, Chris and an SO from the ECR ring?'

I rang Ivor's number, Chris picks it up and gets as far as saying: 'Hi Phil.'

When the phone's clearly snatched from his grasp and a Belfast accent appears: 'I can't believe it, all these years we've known each other and you've left a smoking gun on my desk?'

In hindsight I should have thought about it instead of launching into: 'No worries. The gun's not come in yet. The escape's not imminent.'

'And you can guarantee that can you? If not you can clear your desk in the morning.'

Chris came back on trying to reason: 'look we are going to have to move a few, do something, what do you think?'

'Look I understand but these are seriously naughty people and I have a duty of care to mine.'

I quickly made an assessment, gave Chris a list of names, including the three perps for this. We relocated all, including mine (temporarily).

I took the bull by the horns the following morning and went to see the big man.

Fair play to him, as always when we had 'a tiff,' it was immediately forgotten, I didn't 'have to clear my desk.'

Chris did mention on our way to the station the following evening that 'Ivor's position was complicated by the fact that he was standing in for the DDG last night. 'Peter's on leave so just imagine it Phil, three murdering Cat A's escape from his establishment, on his watch!'

There was another escape find shortly after the above and I'd no advanced warning of this.

We became suspicious of a letter, it appeared to contain something solid so we X rayed it. The X ray showed up three flat pieces of metal approximately ½ inch x 4 inch. We resealed the letter which had been marked 'subject to R39,' it was ostensibly from solicitors. We sent an OSG to the wing with the letter, following a briefing.

He was instructed to get the prisoner to open the letter in front of him, we would be in close attendance but out of sight.

The prisoner opened the letter but was seen clearly trying to hide metal objects within accompanying carbon paper. When he realised he'd been rumbled he fled to his cell with us in pursuit, the OSG was left holding three hacksaw blades!

When we reached his cell we caught him trying to hide other items.

I immediately ordered a lock-down search which uncovered a laundry bag containing a rope made from green cellular blanket, roughly 30 ft in length, some clothes, a badminton net, a shortened mop handle and a bracket, 9 wooden coat pegs, 2 metal hooks, a plastic knife, a piece of wood, sharpened and shaped like a dagger.

We also found a quantity of hooch, which was unrelated to the escape equipment, so somebody else had been unlucky!

The 'chap' was segregated and I began an investigation. I quickly determined that there wasn't going to be a mass-break-out, the letter recipient was acting alone. He had a history of assaults, dirty protests, threats to staff using home-made weapons and most pertinently, he had attempted to slip his cuffs during an escort after feigning illness. His back history from Full Sutton and Whitemoor showed a single-minded drive to escape. He had tampered with cell fabric by removing bricks, had befriended a known key-maker and had been found in possession of hand drawn maps of the prison and a photograph of a fence section.

Totally uncooperative when questioned, I re-assessed his risk and provided recommendations.

He'll move again, and again and again, he's too big a risk to be allowed to settle, tough but that's just the way it is with a small minority....

We learned many lessons: we reviewed the need for a Yards Party, it had been set-up to keep the prison clean but it had been a conduit for the gloves and the discarded netting at least. In the interim, Yard's Party gloves will be accounted for each day and will only be exchanged on a one-for-basis. Wing grills will be made part of the cooking inventory and would be accounted for each day.

The selection of Orderlies as can be seen from this and previous incidents, is often crucial to the success of prisoners' plans.

They rely on relative freedom of movement and access to important areas. Prisoners selected for Orderly posts should always have their positions ratified by a security governor grade so that he or she can satisfy themselves that more junior staff had not been 'conditioned' when recommending them. The governor grade then had to ensure that once appointed the Orderly was properly supervised and controlled.

The solicitors were made aware of how their name and legal privilege had been abused.

Just another day in a Cat A Dispersal.....

Weekend off and I'd been all over the Racing Post since 08 00 hours. I'd managed to get a bit of 2/1 about a horse I intended backing in the Champion Hurdle at the Cheltenham Festival later in the season. Rooster Booster was special I felt sure, and as the race this day would be much easier than its target race at Cheltenham, to my mind it was a 'penalty kick!'

The tapes were about to go up, 15 15 off time, it was now trading at 11/8, I'd had £200 to £100 so I was feeling really happy when suddenly the phone rang it was the Governor. 'Phil can you just give me a few, I'll ring you back after the race...' He could clearly hear the race commentary in the background.

Weighed-in and so had I, lovely jubbly.

When I returned the call I found that Roy Robson and Graham Markham had been complaining to the Governor about Steve Robson who had moved a violent prisoner to the Seg. 'I'll sort this on Monday but I strongly recommend that he stays where he is. On a previous sentence he tried to seriously assault a couple of our PEO's and we have intelligence that he still bears a grudge against the PE department and Steve is obviously aware of this.'

I had a meeting with Steve, Roy and Graham as soon as I returned to work, and the 'misunderstanding' was resolved in minutes. Steve had come in like a bull at a gate in their eyes and had made himself unpopular with a few. It was a matter of presentation; he should have liaised with Roy in the first instance, as the Head of Residence he had overall responsibility for the wings.

However the decision he had taken was correct, he'd untapped potential, loved security and intelligence gathering, he just had to improve his presentational skills.

Roy and Graham were strong, fully committed members of staff, extremely talented in their own right, in truth these inter group disputes rarely happened, the success of the establishment meant too much to everybody.

Steve however was to soon make an important discovery.

Later that year, on 11 March 2003, I went 'to the well' once again on my old favourite Rooster Booster, he bounded up the Cheltenham hill to win the Champion Hurdle at 9/2, landing some lumpy bets for yours truly in the process.

We'd often wondered, when we'd broke up a drug dealing group and transferred them out, how within days the same system seemed to be seamlessly up and running again. It was Steve who helped us join-up the dots.

He'd received information that all the payments for drugs were going via relatives to the brother of one of our Cat A's whose brother had a Lawn-mower repair business.

Our investigation determined that he was acting as the 'Banker' for all the drugs transactions throughout the Cat A estate until the police put a stop to it.

He'd made enough from these illegal transactions to sell his business and retire early I subsequently discovered.

We'd been watching a relationship develop between a young female staff member and a Sunderland rapist. We were originally alerted by concerned wing staff; they had become suspicious of the time they spent together. It was particularly difficult for her fellow officers because to all intents and purposes she was an excellent officer. Competent, cheerful, flexible, always willing to go the extra mile either for her colleagues or prisoners.

Her future mother-in-law worked in the prison for one of our partner agencies and her father was in the police.

We then received intelligence that the prisoner was expecting a 'consignment of drugs and it won't be coming in through visits.'

The clear implication was that a staff member would bring it in.

I was aware that John Burnett, a wily old operator who was due to retire soon, had 'a source' on the wing. John tasked his 'man' to find out where the drugs handover would take place. He came up trumps and got an address and the PLO set-up surveillance.

John couldn't wait to tell me when he'd suggested to his 'source' that I take over from him as his handler when he retired. He said: 'are you sure JB, he's a bit slippery?'

The surveillance paid off, the officer was picked-up entering the prison and was taken down to Durham police headquarters, I was left with the unenviable task of breaking it to her prospective mum-in-law who was expected on duty soon.

2003 proved a vintage year for my 'betting bank.' My dad, who was a keen student of the form book, had heard through a contact in Ireland about a horse called Monty's Pass that had been laid out for the Grand National.

When I pressed him about the bona fides of the informant he assured me 'he knows 'the time of day,' believe me. He's in the unsinkable Titanic Thompson class,' name-checking a notorious 30's American gambler he'd often told me about. 'And you know what someone once said about Titanic: if he had offered one to two that he could eat sugar and flower and crap a birthday cake, they would have bought the candles!'

That was good enough for me, I started backing it ante-post a couple of months before the race at 33/1, 'seagulls' in racing's sometime secret language. I decided to 'press- up,' and ended up having £1000 to £30 three times.

I was walking around B wing Friday 4th of April, the day before the race when an officer who used to work in security asked me what I fancied for the National. I told him. 'I'll back it,' he said, I noticed his wing governor, Adele making a note.

The following day Monty triumphed and I was considerably richer. As I liked to do on the occasions when I 'd had a decent 'touch' I went to Tesco and bought all their extra-large tins of Quality Street sweets so that all my 'troops' could share in my good fortune.

I distributed them to the various areas as I did my 'tour' the following day.

I met the officer who'd asked me for my tip; he coloured and admitted he hadn't backed it, scaredy cat I remember thinking. Not so Adele, she couldn't wait to tell me she'd backed it at the starting price, 16/1. She'd 'cleaned up,' and admitted dancing around the betting shop as Monty powered home. Good for her, it showed real 'bottle.'

I was Acting Governor one day as both Ivor and Chris were on a course. I'd received a call from a lady in Lancashire who managed NHS pensions. She asked me to call-up Dr Shipman to inform him that he would forfeit his pension rights. She faxed the relevant paperwork over to me and asked me to confirm as soon as I had done the deed.

I went straight over to the Healthcare department, where Shipman was housed, to do the deed.

He was reluctant to accept the paperwork at first and got noticeably irritated as I explained what was happening to him.

I then rang NHS Pensions HQ as requested, to confirm the task had been completed satisfactorily. I placed the prisoner on a suicide watch immediately because I was aware of a note in his file which warned that he had threated to take his own life if his pension was forfeit.

My phone monitoring staff couldn't wait to tell me the following day that in a call to his wife that evening, he'd described being given the up-date on his pension by 'a minor prison functionary!'

'Hey Mr Tamborine man play a song for me.' My tape-deck reacted as I turned on my ignition, and the Byrds burst into song.

'You still listening to Dylan,' asked Mr Di Paolo with disdain? 'My my this is quaint' he said, as he fiddled with the manual windows of my ancient VW Polo!

'I'll throw you out of the bloody car if it's not good enough for you,' I threatened, I reached across the passenger side for the door, as we sped past county hall in Durham, on our way to the railway station, causing Mr Di Paolo to yelp!

Earlier that day I'd attended his office and found him buried behind a mountain of records. 'Anybody there?' 'I'm here darling but you might have to dig me out,' was his reply. Ivor was now delegating more and more work to him as the Establishment continued to make progress on all fronts. I carried out regular unannounced exercises to test our procedures as well as at least two major contingency plan exercises each year. These and my daily 'rounds' had helped us maintain standards, achieve highly in our annual security audits and the Big Man was content. I knew the Big Man wouldn't be with us much longer, he'd achieved what he' set out to achieve and he needed a new challenge, I'd seen it all before.

He left us shortly afterwards, joined the private sector, taking over as Director of Forest Bank prison in greater Manchester, a prison operated by UKDS.

'Anything happening?'

'They've got a new one boss, have you heard, Holland and Barrett?'

I'm talking to a 'Lifer' inmate who after many years of drug abuse has turned his life around and had made solid progress.

'You know we can order supplements from H and B from private cash? Well (name deleted) makes a note of all the private cash identification details and they are sent on to an outside contact in Heaton. The contact rings up the H and B store in the Midlands somewhere, identifies the private cash orders from the prison and has the goods redirected to a sub-postie in the West End that they have 'straightened.'

When notified by the sub-postmaster that the parcel has arrived. They pick it up, insert heroin, scan it via the computer, pack it as if new and send it on here!'

'Full of smack, cheeky bastards?'

'How do they get it up to the wing?'

'It's pretty new but I think they rely on (name deleted), not sure if they pay him but he likes to be around gangsters, you can see he likes it when they make a fuss of him and call him by his first name.'

I'd organised a change of personnel in reception where all property was initially received. I'd put a lady in charge who was like a rottweiler, nothing got past her; she couldn't be intimidated.

I briefed her, knowing confidentiality was assured. The parcel duly arrived, we removed the 'smack,' sent the bone fide stuff up to the wing via the officer my source had identified as the weak link, and awaited the fall-out!

The prisoner who was first to the 'doctored' box was clearly a 'patsy'; a heavy user. The main suspects stayed at arms-length, I put the 'patsy' down the seg and questioned him but it was like talking to the wall, his brain and speech was so addled with drug use and abuse. He did tell me 'I was the hardest lad in the toon when I was fifteen!'

The 'chaps' weren't happy of course and one actually had the audacity to claim that: 'you're breaking the law boss if you're bugging our cells!'

Word got out inevitably and all the staff began talking about it, the officer that delivered it to the wing, with the rest of the property was clearly embarrassed. He started nervously hanging about the office, keen to let me know he knew nothing about it...

After a couple of weeks he went off sick and never returned.

Two of my managers, Graham Foster and Harry Henson made the trip to H and B HQ to apprise them of the situation and to agree a protocol with them and our

Finance department to make sure this never happened again.

My 'boy' had served his 'penance,' and had been transferred to a prison in the South Midlands. I got a 'message' from him one day, he'd needed to see me urgently. I'd mentioned it in passing at my morning briefing to my staff, it had been picked-up by our police liaison officer Steve Norris.

Steve asked to speak to me privately the following day, having got clearance from the 'highest-level' I was to subsequently discover.

He'd been authorised to tell me about a proposed high-profile, but as yet secret visit, to our area by a VIP!

He'd reported to his superiors that one of my 'sources' with proven links to terrorists, both Irish and Islamic, was desperate to pass on some information to me, they wanted me to make the visit to him as a matter of extreme urgency so that they could discount a terrorist risk. I could have a police escort and the Force area I would visit would provide me with anything else I needed. We had permission to inform my Governor Phil Copple, Phil gave his approval for me to proceed but I detected he was nervous. I have little doubt that this was because he recognised the potential risks to the prisoner.

Within a week, in company with Steve and another policeman, I made my way south.

Armed with a 'moody' movement order we 'sprung' my man and interviewed him at a local police station. His info concerned a bit of drugs trafficking with staff involvement which I promised to pass-on; he took great delight in telling me what a young Irish tearaway, who I'd got rid of prior to the proposed 2000 F wing sit-in demonstration, had to say about me! Three years later and he was still complaining about me: 'An obsessed, fit-up-merchant who clearly didn't have a home to go to. When is he retiring?'

A couple of months later, 22 November 2003, I'm watching Tony Blair and George Bush on the national news, eating fish and chips in Sedgefield, knowing that I'd played a small part in facilitating the visit!

We suffered a death in custody, a heavy-duty heroin supplier. I'd first met him at Full Sutton, well capable of looking after himself and always kept himself busy, working in the Kitchen, and 'working out' both in-cell and in the gym.

It appears to have been a heart attack brought on by stress.

It turned out that his wife, son and daughter were trying to keep his 'business' going but had been caught-up in a police 'sting.'

His wife had been remanded to Low Newton and I'd given them permission to speak the day before he collapsed. The truth be told he'd been subject to a bit of 'talking tables.' Properly sanctioned and he'd almost beaten it.

He'd gone into visits, sat as directed in the first instance but as soon as his daughter joined him, he asked to move tables, 'the light's in my eye gov giving me a headache?'

Surveillance conscious as ever!

He was immediately directed to another table, similarly 'covered.'

Take a bow Hughie C my man Maximum respect!

As I'd noted earlier Ivor had joined UKDS and had been replaced by Phil Copple on promotion.

In his first week Phil had published what amounted to a rallying cry to all the 'troops,' via a Governor's Notice to staff.

I'd returned my copy to him with a note attached which said: 'excellent sentiments which I fully endorse but haven't I read them somewhere before? Brodie Clark circa 1999?'

'Cheeky bastard' was the reply I received!

The Daily Mirror then printed a front page article suggesting that Harold Shipman was 'acting in a caring role,' in Healthcare.

It was nonsense but quotes from his LSP3E report were undoubtedly genuine.

The Mirror continued to drip-feed information about Shipman that contradicted the prison service press office version of events, which the Service subsequently had to admit were true. This caused acute embarrassment and had the effect of keeping the story high-profile. I began an investigation.

Their information was so accurate that I became convinced that they must have had a copy of his lifer report, his LSP3E.

I couldn't believe that Shipman himself was the source because he had continuously sought to minimise the immense media attention he attracted particularly because it so obviously pained his family. This was obvious night after night as we listened to anguished phone-calls.

Indeed my niece was in same year at University with one of his kids, studying the same subject and reported first-hand how difficult life was for him. I believe he subsequently had to defer for a year. She shared a flat I'd bought in Jesmond, with my kids, they were all studying at Newcastle University.

There was however a strong possibility that the source was the document itself.

The paper kept saying 'you wouldn't believe who the source is, you wouldn't question it if you knew the source.'

I was pretty confident then that somehow they had managed to get a copy of the document.

A copy could have been smuggled out of the establishment by a rogue staff member and passed to a press contact.

A copy could have been provided by 'a rogue' member of staff at the Lifer Unit at prison service HQ.

One of my governor's went down to see how the documents were handled at Lifer Unit HQ. He found files left on desks until read and located in the Core Lifer Record, files not put away, and everything depending on trust. The offices were large open plan areas which he felt would provide easy access for a 'rogue' staff member.

I had our IT company EDS check out all our phone extension numbers and they found one 'contact' with a local paper but it turned out to be legitimate contact by our personnel department in relation to a recruitment campaign.

Our procedure for requesting LSP3E reports was as follows: a memo was sent to all key staff members who had contact with the prisoner. They were asked to complete an enclosed blank LSP3E. This was sent with a template which outlined the areas the report writer needed to cover. A letter was also sent to the home probation officer asking for a report following agreed guidelines.

When a progress or parole report was requested by Lifer Unit, a file was started and all completed reports were kept in an individual 'pocket.'

When all the reports had been received and typed-up, they were given to the Lifer manager at Frankland to write his conclusions. The report was then typed- up. As soon as the completed dossier was received by the Lifer Clerk it was photocopied and sent to the prisoner for him to make representations (7 days for a progress report and 28 days for a parole report).

The full copy of the dossier was then sent to Lifer Unit HQ, recorded delivery.

A copy of the report was kept in the prisoner's sentence planning file in the Custody office.

Harold Shipman's case was no different from any other except that he sent his set of reports back the day after receipt via a Health Care officer (name deleted).

A copy of the reports were sent to Lifer Unit on 2 May.

The reports are typed and are password protected, hard copies not distributed were locked away in a steel cabinet overnight.

The reports were held in Custody, Healthcare (a copy was returned to them for their file) and the Typing pool. They were held on a typist's computer for three months).

It would have been possible for a 'rogue' member of staff to withdraw Shipman's file from the Custody office and copy any information the Daily Mirror sought.

The booking-out system relied on the user completing a record card.

My task was to devise a more secure system both locally and at HQ for the files/reports which related to the Country's most notorious prisoners.

Other news soon replaced Shipman on the Mirror's front pages and sometime after this event he moved on to Wakefield prison.

However this wouldn't be the last time I was to feature in his life story.

We extended the jail to make room for long-term prisoners with severe personality disorders, a DSPD unit.

Building work on this scale is always a risk. You have outside contractors to manage, walls removed, tools and debris, it's a security manager's worst nightmare!

Luckily my security senior officer Denis Williams was due to retire and I managed to get him to come-back as an OSG and be my permanent 'eyes and ears' on site through-out the process, either myself or one of my managers visited the site at close of play each evening to ensure it was left in a risk-free state. Overall the project went smoothly, but we did, however, have one major risk to manage.

A prisoner who had previously been involved in a high profile successful escape, approached his wing governor for guidance, and he was referred to me.

'I've been approached by a group of Geordie prisoners who have asked me to advise them on how to escape via the DSPD site. I've got an appeal pending and I've told them that I don't want to be involved. Look, I've had similar approaches at other places because of that business on the Island, but when I turn them down, they normally forget about it after a couple of weeks.'

'These are more persistent because they feel the 'contract' gives them a better opportunity than they could normally expect and they feel that Cat A's will be moved prior to Christmas before the wall is breached for the next stage of the building.'

The wall was to be breached prior to Christmas and we were considering moving Cat A's...staff's loose lips?

I arranged for a couple of intelligence unit staff to be allocated wing evening duties so that they could specifically observe those taking an interest in the DSPD site. I had my regular wing staff contacts, independent of each other, watching the targets and reporting back to me during the daytime state.

I also had prisoner 'sources,' unknown to each other, watching those showing interest in the site, 24/7!

I briefed Denis Williams and along with Chris Di Paolo we re-evaluated the security of the DSPD site.

Our enquiries determined that the prisoners had noted what they felt was poor camera cover on the south side door on F wing. That their intention was to grab an officer with a view to taking his/her keys in order to escape through the south side door.

This action was to coincide with the wall breach and the expected availability of a lorry nearby.

The intention had been to drag the driver from the lorry a take it over.

A local gangster had agreed to act as 'quarter master,' to supply safe houses, cars, materials to aid the escape. A diversionary 'fight' would 'keep staff occupied' whilst the escapees made their break!

Clearly, we couldn't let this progress any further so we wrote it up for the attention of the DDG. People's categorisations were re-assessed and were moved on.

This included the original informant, to protect his integrity, it was however to a place that satisfied his needs.

An experienced 'source' had marked my card about an officer on my group who was 'managing' a number of club doormen.

'Some of those clubs are providing ready-made point-of-sale outlets that are secure and highly mobile for drug sales boss.'

I discussed it with Chris and he signed and circulated a Governor's Notice to Staff about secondary employment. It reiterated the point that unified grades must seek permission from the Governor before taking up secondary employment.

It emphasised that permission would be refused where work would conflict with the interests of the department or would be inconsistent with their position as civil servants. It made it clear that employment in nightclubs or at sporting events where the duties might require physically restraining members of the public and the use of control and restraint techniques was not appropriate.

I was actually recuperating in hospital following an eye operation but senior members of my team came to visit me and we agreed a strategy, I received regular up-dates on their progress.

Graham Foster and Harry Henson spent a fruitless evening in Bishop Auckland trying to catch our man flouting the Governor's order. We'd given him ample opportunity to seek permission before we acted.

We'd been told this is where he would be on this particular evening.

My fault, I should have insisted on street clothing or clubbing gear for our amateur sleuths.

British Legion blazers and cavalry twills didn't quite cut it.

It freaked the 'bouncers' out so much when they entered the clubs that they reversed the process, they ended up speaking into their radios and following our erstwhile 'Poirots' about from club to club, up and down the High street! Graham and Harry gave up after an hour and went home. I was later told that our 'man' had been in town but had spotted Graham and Harry and kept out of sight.

He was subsequently subject to an investigation and disciplinary action and left us.

Chris left on promotion and got his own jail at last, a category C establishment in Rutland. Dave Gant had 'worked out' my best retirement date to qualify for maximum benefits and still have a life and hopefully good health, when we were senior officers together at Wakefield. I'd be retiring in February 2006, soon I'd be just a distant memory and those staff at the prison who were starting to make even me look competent, could take it to the next level.

This is what I told Phil Copple when he asked if I intended seeking to succeed Chris. I would be retaining my '2 for 1 retirement rights.'

Got a delicate problem one day; a contracted-in professional from a partner-agency broke down in tears in my presence - she was being harassed!

It appears that a governor senior to me, who had oversight in her work area, had been making her feel increasingly uncomfortable.

He would invite her into his office, ostensibly on business then say: 'when I saw you this morning I just wanted to take you in my arms!' A provocative suggestion?

It was clear that she couldn't cope with it, she was sobbing.

This wasn't a consensual affair, it was a misuse of power, an attempt at coercion.

I had to act quickly, I knew it was a conspiracy of silence that allows sexual harassment to stay routine, that incuriosity and cowardice leaves too many victims, I informed Phil Copple immediately.

In truth I'm not sure it was ever resolved to her satisfaction because she left soon afterwards.

Public protection and safe-guarding children was a crucial part of the establishment's role. We had a significant number of sex offenders amongst our population and their release had to be managed. We operated a multi-agency approach with important input from the police and probation services. We had a key role in working with these agencies in protecting children from dangerous offenders through an appropriate response to any disclosure of abuse. In communication and referral of concerns/allegations to social services and the police. Assessing the risks identified offenders might pose to children, monitoring their contact with children through telephone, letters and visits.

This determined the work of our public protection meetings, admirably chaired by our senior probation officer Karen Blackburn and astutely written-up and managed by Sue Rafferty. This was another area we scored highly in, we were the only High Security prison to regularly achieve the Resettlement KPT.

The complexion of the High Security Estate was changing. I remember touring F wing one day and being approached by a couple of giant Russians.

'Excuse us Mr O'brien, but we have been told that you could advise us about visits?'

Their intelligence file had informed me that they had been convicted of shooting a Russian 'businessman' down south.

Excellent English speakers, very confident with KGB/FSB backgrounds, or so the Authorities suspected.

Now over here taking contracts from filthy rich oligarchs who had made their money in banking, oil, or mineral exploitation during Russia's post-soviet privatisation.

Conducting vendettas against each other whilst at the same time buying-up some of the south east's finest property.

MDT was my principal method of testing for, and detecting the use of drugs. The prisoners referred to it as 'the piss test.' We took a urine sample, the trouble was we could only detect cannabis, amphetamines or other soft drugs that remained in the bloodstream for 28 days after use. The mandatory drugs test could only detect hard drugs, such as heroin, cocaine or 'crack' for up to 3 days after use!

Therefore a soft drug was more likely to be detected on an MDT than a hard drug. This was a point hammered home by the drugs' barons' and their 'gofers.'

291

This was another reason why good intelligence was crucial to me, I could 'target test.' I would occasionally attend the MDT suite, those that were worried about a potential result were often willing 'to talk.'

As far as I was concerned intelligence collecting had one moral law; it was justified by results.

Following a tip-off, Steve Robson and the DST found a replica gun. Crafted carefully in wood, copious amounts of black boot polish to it to give it a more authentic look. A crude map of the Durham was found with it.

A subsequent investigation found that a couple of very dangerous lunatics had intended taking a prisoner hostage before making for the gate using the replica gun. In the evening dark the gun would have looked authentic, it was skilfully made.

Their intended hostage had been found guilty of murdering a little girl who had been camping out in a relative's garden in Wales.

They had reckoned that the hostage would attract little public support and had intended 'topping the nonce' to slow the police down if they managed to escape.

Not very well thought out but as one later pointed out to me: 'sometimes even the daftest ideas work boss.'

They were segregated, re-categorised and moved on over a period of time.

I travelled down to Whitemoor prison in Cambridgeshire at the request of one of my 'sources' who was subject to an adjudication.

My 'fiancee' Angie Hartley's career had soared and she was now the Head of Ops at the prison.

She met me at the gate and gave me a tour of her areas of responsibility. Indeed she embarrassed me when taking me into the security office by introducing me as 'that nuisance that Peter Atherton is always telling you to contact for advice virtually every time he visits!'

I've got to admit they gave me a warmer welcome than I might have felt able to give them, if the boot had been on the other foot. Made me a cup of tea, got the biscuits out, I had maximum respect for them.

In the end my 'boy' didn't need me to go witness for him he must have struck some sort of plea bargain. He did wave at me through Perspex however.

A couple of months prior to this visit we'd achieved the highest security rating within the whole estate following an external security audit.

Not unreasonably Phil Copple was over the moon and immediately posted the audit results at the gate for all to see.

As I was driving back home I found myself contrasting the treatment he'd received with what I'd just experienced from the security team at Whitemoor.

Phil had described a rather frosty response from his peers at the DDG's monthly meeting with his High Security Estate Governors, in the immediate aftermath of our audit triumph, when Peter had congratulated him. I remember thinking I know which group I'd rather be in the trenches with!

My intelligence team was impatient to see me one Monday morning.

They had been monitoring the phone calls of a recently received Category A prisoner.

He appeared to be discussing an Area Manager in intimate terms. I was a bit sceptical at first because the prisoner had been in custody for a significant period already and surely if there had been a connection/relationship, his previous prisons would have picked it up.

No, they hadn't, and on listening to the recorded conversations I decided that this was dynamite!

I told Phil who demanded a transcript for the DDG, oops!

The prisoner was an ex public schoolboy who had been sentenced to 25 years in 2002, for helping to smuggle cocaine worth £100m, a record at the time. The Judge called him 'vain self-interested, arrogant, greedy and ruthless.' His wife had received a 24year sentence for the same offence.

Looked like a child from each family were an item Can you be held responsible for who your children fall in love with?

What complicated it for this area manager was the fact that the prisoner intimated that he had advised him about different prisons and discussed prison personnel with him, something I'm sure the Director General pointed out to him before accepting his resignation!

On the latter I had to giggle as I handed Phil the transcript: 'a bit difficult for me as I could be seen as the one most likely to gain from his demise!

Next stop, area manager, then Mr Copple, I remember thinking?

About once a month it appeared that the main dispersal wings were suddenly flush with 'weed.'

My 'sources' were aware of it after it had arrived but didn't know who the prime movers were nor how it had come in. It was clearly a small, discreet cell in action.

I was pondering this as I observed searches using metal detecting archways and X ray machines at the gate.

Hand luggage and bulky outer garments had to be placed on the X ray machine conveyor belt.

At the metal detection archway, the person visiting was asked to open his or her pockets into the tray provided. All the items on the conveyer belt were scanned.

I needed to be sure that there was no cross-contamination of sterile and dirty areas. It was crucial when we were consistently achieving so highly that staff did not feel that they'd done enough, it was time to rest on their laurels! The risks attached to this in high security jail were too high!

Nevertheless, I'm sure that my frequent, unofficial audits got on their nerves from time to time!

I had the DST came on early unannounced to search. Regularly searched areas in the establishment whilst it was in a patrol state, all without success.

I'd briefed Graeme Markham and I'd given him carte blanche to go ahead on his own accord if a situation presented itself.

It didn't take him long to 'strike gold.' He was handing a form to a Cat A, a major player, so that he could make parole representations, as the prisoner was about to leave his office, Graeme mentioned the weed epidemic and asked if he could help. He told him that I would support his career progression if he was in a position to help us. The prisoner looked most put out, he'd never been a 'source,' had lots of prison and street cred, communicated with staff on his terms, only when he wanted something.

'Think about it you don't have to say anything now.' He left the office with a scowl.

However, he'd thought about it for a few days before returning with his submissions and some priceless information.

At a 'tasking' meeting the following day Graeme was able to inform us that the first of three consecutive 'drops' had come in that morning, a 9 bar!

That a little 'firm' had come up from Manchester the previous day and met a member of staff in a layby near the Nissan factory in Sunderland.

I forewarned Phil Copple and got his blessing to act, we made plans for an early morning search the following day. We would need to be discreet because our 'suspect' would be in very early as he worked in the kitchen. Obvious extra cars on the car-park would probably 'spook' him.

Sweet success; we caught the 'target' with the 9 bar, and when the police searched his house they found £11,000 in a safe that he was unable to account for.

As the day wore on he admitted his guilt, claimed that he'd felt slighted because he was only employed on a temporary contract 'whilst I do most of the work!'

A prisoner had picked-up on this unhappiness with his lot and exploited it.

'Provide a little service for us occasionally and earn a bit of tax-free?'

'I did try to stop but they told me once you are there, there is no way out, except jail!'

As a result, he's suspended, 'nicked' and facing a 2 to 3 year prison sentence.

Phil had asked me how confident I was of getting a result. 98% was my tongue in cheek reply!

I was able to identify the prisoner organiser from the description I was given so I 'segged' him questioned him and got nothing. He was an ex High Risk Cat A who had badly injured an instructor in 1994 during an escape attempt. I moved him on.

Then I got a letter from his solicitor telling me I've got it all wrong, where's my proof, I make it up as I go on...?

I confronted his mate on F wing, a contract killer who I'd helped find a ballistics expert when he was struggling with his appeal, much earlier in his sentence.

'He tells me I've got it all wrong, so I'd better bang everyone up and we'll start again, don't arrange anything special for the next week or so, think about visits, and we'll search for clues.

Look I'm not bothered about his 'brief,' I've got letter templates for every day of the week to answer clowns like him if that's how he wants to play it. You know I'm not looking for an OBE, the gear was coming in, I've plugged the gap, got rid of the 'originator' and the idiot staff member that was bringing it in.

We both know I haven't got everybody involved, neither inside nor out, if that's what he's suggesting. So be it, we'll start this afternoon, don't make any plans.'

'Got you boss, I'll get in touch with him, that's the last you'll hear of it. And it was!'

11 April 2005 I was in Leeds dodging Yorkshire TV cameras. I was there to give evidence at the Coroner's

Hearing into Harold Shipman's death in Wakefield prison.

The questions had been innocuous rather than hostile. I was asked about how I gave him the news about losing his pension and to confirm that I'd immediately put him on a suicide watch. All this was documented, dated and timed and wasn't questioned.

I don't really know why I was called.

I'd had it on good authority that a young black south London gang member had a mobile and I was interviewing him in the Seg with Gary Hassan. We'd been going round in circles for about 15 minutes, him telling me he hadn't got it and me telling him that I know he had. There was no animosity, we got on well, in fact it used to amuse him and his friends that whenever I appeared on the wing, those with something to hide could be seen scurrying away.

I happened to mention that, whenever I heard someone had a mobile I immediately thought that they were planning an escape and I started to mentally re-risk assess them!

'You mean Cat A Mr O'B?'

With that he whipped a mobile from his nether regions with great alacrity.

This took myself and Gary by surprise. He regained his composure more quickly than me probably because he was much younger.

My natural reaction was to reach out for the offending object, but before I picked it up it up the kid was up off his chair, ' Just a minute Mr O'B,' and he brought me some tissues from a neighbouring table. Gary was gob-smacked and then started to grin.

I remember thinking that was extremely thoughtful, but they are starting to look after me now. It's not supposed to be like this, maybe it is time to retire.

I'd been using DST managers to man a High Risk escort to Newcastle Crown Court. It involved a powerfully-built mysterious yank who had shot and killed a police officer in Leeds, before attempting to kill two others. The trial had transferred to Newcastle because of the revulsion surrounding the crime in Leeds, it was felt he would get a fairer hearing on Tyneside.

He was subsequently found guilty and received a whole life sentence.

When someone received such a heavy sentence we opted to keep them in Healthcare overnight in order to assess their mental well-being. Sometimes 'gangsters' resented this and sure enough 'our man' told his senior officer 'I won't be going anywhere,' when he returned from court. As soon as I was informed, I made my way over to see him.

My two 'minders' Gary Hassan and 'chopper Harris' stayed out of sight but within hearing.

He greeted me amiably when I arrived at the Cat A unit kitchen.

'We aren't going to fall-out are we Mr O'Brien?'

'That depends on how long you keep me here, I will be falling out with either you or my Mrs, I'm already late home waiting for you to be 'weighed off.' I'd prefer to fall-out with neither of you but if I have to choose it's going to have to be you, now get your kit and come with me.' Which he immediately did, much to Gary's and 'Chopper's' amazement I later discovered.

Sometimes, at least in your head, you have to link arms with Doc Halliday, and the Earp boys and stroll down to the OK Corral and chat up the Clantons in a way they understand. Deal with the world in kind or be its victim.

Seven months before I was due to retire there was a serious incident at Wakefield prison, Phil Copple was tasked with investigating the circumstances that had led to it and he asked me to be part of his team.

It was an escape attempt and it involved my nemesis the 'abrofile/fake body in the bed/waiting for a gun to come in before I go man!'

The one that almost caused the large gentleman from the province of Ulster to sack me.

He'd almost succeeded this time, he'd managed to get onto the workshop roof with a weighted rope and a suspect car was awaiting him in a street nearby.

My brief was to look into the apparent lack of security intelligence about the escape.

Early in the process Phil had asked me if I would be willing to go to Wakefield on detached duty in order to lead a radical improvement in security performance and I agreed. He included this recommendation as part of his interim report.

I began this work on 7 November and it continued into February 2006 when I formally retired.

In the interim Phil carried out an investigation on me! Our erstwhile escaper recognised me as soon as I went to interview him and complained about having a biased reprobate like me on the team. I'd already proved over the years I had it in for him... Anything bad that had happened to him since he came to the High Security

Estate could be laid at my door... I was obsessive, impervious to reason...

Phil may well have agreed with some, if not all of the foregoing but as he pointed out on this occasion it was he that had cut a hole in the ceiling of the workshop's recess. He, that was on the roof with the grappling hook inserted into a weighted tube, with 48 foot of webbing material attached. He that had a small section of reinforced cardboard tubing with more webbing secured to it...could any of this be really my fault?

He got the picture and withdrew the complaint.

My priority over the next three months was to improve decency and dynamic security, ensure there was greater investment in intelligence work, strengthen security instructions in the workplace, strengthen management checks, to raise security awareness generally; in fact to convince the Director General to keep Wakefield in the High Security Estate.

I'm pleased to say the staff embraced the change necessary and Wakefield is still performing its Category A function to this day!

I returned to Frankland on the 7 March 2006 to the obligatory stale twiglets, cold sausage rolls, leaving presents and warm words. As I drove up from Yorkshire the words of the Training PO at Leeds all those years ago came to mind: 'welcome to the first day of the rest of your life,' then just like that I was gone.

Three months later I was working in Marks and Spencer in Northallerton.

Chapter 12 (2006-2008)
The Private Sector

I'd always wanted to work for Marks and Spencer, a company I'd long admired, and I got the chance shortly after I'd retired when they opened a Simply Food store in Northallerton.

I joined them in July 2006 and worked mainly in the cold store. It was my job to unload and store the daily delivery and to help out on the tills when required.

Then in early September I got a phone call from Ivor out of the blue.

He wanted to know if I would consider a mentoring role for his inexperienced staff. This was on the back of a negative Inspection Report which had noted that staff and many prisoners, were in fear of a significant minority of organised criminals who appeared to be doing as they pleased. A member of staff had been 'potted,' had excrement thrown over them, in the presence of the Inspectorate!

I told him I'd consider it, but never one to let the grass grow he rang me again the following day.

We discussed the establishment's needs at length and agreed that a full-time position was what was needed if I was to have the necessary impact quickly.

We agreed a salary package, I gave my notice to M and S and I moved to Manchester to a flat provided by the company.

HMP Forest Bank was in Salford, Greater Manchester, The 25 year design, construct, manage and finance contract was won by UKDS in 1997 and it opened in January 2000. It was a local prison holding 1040 adult and young offender men. It served the courts in the North West and sat in a country park with a lake and a meadow which were for public use.

- 'Make your issues, wants, needs clear and factual and identify your/their adversaries, the dealers, the bullies etc.
- Always have reasoned answers prepared for any questions that they may ask and get your view across.
- 'Name the opposition and hold them personally responsible for what's wrong.'

I'm explaining the early stages of informant handling/witness questioning techniques to my security group.

'And when interviewing, if the witness is belligerent, you wear him down with greater belligerence. If the man shows fear, you offer calm comfort. When he looks weak, you appear strong. When he wants a friend, you crack a joke. If he's confident, you are more so, assuring him that you are certain of his guilt and are curious about a few small details. If he's arrogant, if he wants nothing to do with the process, you intimidate him, 'I'm going to have to seg you till I get this sorted.'

'How do you know you've got the right man?

Nervousness, fear, confusion, hostility, his story changes, contradicts itself. What patterns of behaviour indicate deception? He's uncooperative, too cooperative, talks too much, talks too little, gets his story perfectly straight, fucks his story up, blinks too much, avoids eye contact.'

My team are looking at me now as if they think I need serious psychological help or a better grade of marijuana!

The first couple of weeks had been difficult, true to form 'the man from Strabane' had made a guy up to Head of operations the week before I arrived, only to demote him once again as soon as I arrived to take his place.

To say I wasn't popular is an understatement, my phone had been sabotaged, my team were taking things to their old boss, showing a reluctance to engage with me. A further complication was that Ivor's deputy Steve Taylor was close to the 'deposed' so this was a dynamic I needed to be wary of.

Then as usual I got a 'win!'

On 'my rounds' on one of the wings I spoke to an officer who told me that he was a prosecution witness in an upcoming court case in relation to a serious incident that had happened in the prison. He was clearly terrified, he'd had no support nor guidance.

I spoke to my security managers about it but they were nonplussed, I made it clear we needed a protocol to support staff in these circumstances.

I got hold of our police liaison officer and we went straight down to Manchester Crown Court, the court staff and in-house victim support officials could not have been more helpful and a strategy was agreed.

The court usher seated me where the officer witness could see me whilst he gave evidence and it went well. The judge agreed with counsel that the witness could be released as soon as he had given his evidence. I positioned myself between him and the defendant's family as he left court, but in truth this wasn't necessary, they didn't give him any grief.

Ironically, I recognised the patriarch of the family from my time at Full Sutton, he nodded at me and smiled as we left.

Word quickly got round and the vibes I got from staff when I next toured the wings was noticeably much more positive. Now to build on this.

I'd been reviewing past security information reports about an officer who appeared to be 'bang at it!'

On Friday 2 June 2006 an officer had been carrying out a routine cell search when he came across two letters, clearly left for him to find, which detailed the names of prisoners involved in drugs and bullying. Another SIR submitted later the same day, named other prisoners on the same wing involved in various criminal activities. The informant left his name and number. At 14 00 hours the following day this inmate was so badly assaulted he needed treatment at Hope Hospital. Whilst there he had confided to his escort that officer (name deleted) was passing information to prisoners on the wing for payment.

On Monday 5 June 2006 I noted another SIR which claimed that the officer was forewarning prisoners about cell searches!

A couple of days later another prisoner 'source' was assaulted by a group of prisoners the officer had been seen talking to just before the assault took place.

A member of staff overheard him telling the group, 'come on lads I can't cover for you anymore.'

An officer was told by a prisoner that the previously named member of staff was bringing in mobile phones, needles and ink to make a tattoo gun, for prisoners.

That prisoner's families had his home address and sent payment there by post!

I held a tasking meeting with my security group where we reviewed all the evidence to date and we came up with a plan to deal with it. It was obvious to me that the reason he was allowed to flourish was because there was no structure in place to deal with him, that was about to change I told the group.

Staff told me that one of the difficulties was that though they carried out early morning unannounced searches, the staff member with ill intent, knows something is up if he or she notices more cars on the carpark than normal at this particular time, or they note a queue of staff snaking around outside the gate, waiting to get in, suggesting a search is taking place in a small ante-room near the gate. All they do then is leave the illicit items in the car, or turn around and take them home, bringing them in when they consider it's safe to do so.

I explained that it's going to take a bit of ingenuity. Use the prison van to bring the search teams into the prison early; park our own cars elsewhere off site until we've done the business.

I checked our man's shifts, anticipated when he'd bring the gear in and bingo, caught him in the act

We kept a low profile until he came through the gate then I directed him and everyone who followed him into visits where my search teams were waiting.

He was found to be in possession of ten lighters which he admitted, 'I was bringing in for the lads!'

One down, how many more to go? Quite a few I remember thinking.

Another 'win'. The staff was impressed, I'd won a few more over, I could tell.

Following this incident I arranged a meeting with my security managers and we devised a system to deal with staff corruption on the lines I'd instituted at Frankland.

We agreed that firstly we had to make staff comfortable about telling us about concerns they might have about a member of staff.

We would investigate, gather information, grade and disseminate this information at a monthly meeting. The police liaison officer would attend.

A tasking meeting would take place prior to any action being taken against individual staff, all risks would be assessed.

We'd received information that a solicitor would smuggle in some 'smack and weed' for a twenty year old armed robber. We were ready to pounce but she cancelled the visit at the last moment.

She turned up the following day and we were waiting. We found her to be in possession of 8g of cannabis and 10g of heroin. She was nicked. A trainee solicitor with a firm in Glossop; a career over before it had begun.

Later that year she was found guilty at Minshull Street Crown Court of trying to smuggle drugs into the prison in her boots and knickers and was sentenced to 5 years in prison.

Ironically when I went up the wings later that day the expectant recipient was chipper, 'plenty more fish in the sea Mr O'B.'

But it was another win, good for staff morale, as Napoleon used to say, 'the morale is to the physical as two is to one.'

We'd tightened up movement to work and education, increased observation. Duty managers toured all work areas twice a day.

A recent reception who was considered 'a player' and who had last been in the prison in 2005, told one of my managers Lindsey Wright. 'This place has changed. Staff are now in charge!'

I was impressing on my managers that leadership was not rocket science. That what produces effective leadership can be found in basic principles which focus on people, quality and a positive culture. That leaders do not turn bad into good of vice versa, they magnify what is already present.

Then, as if just to prove that I'd still some way to go to convince some staff, I got a timely reminder that I was still a work in progress.

Steve Robson had rung me from Frankland asking if I could give them a rest from a Cat B prisoner we'd both known for years, Durham prison had taken him for a while but had returned him.

I had to admit, he could be a pain in the arse and that wasn't a technical term.

Having said that he'd done well over 12 years and would have to be released in the not-too-distant future.

I decided to give him a chance on the basis that he should be 'tested' in less secure conditions before his release.

I made sure I met him in reception on arrival, he greeted me like a long-lost friend, proudly telling everyone within earshot about how long we'd known each other.

I noticed that my reception senior Dave Armstrong was looking with alarm at the size of our man's record, suicide warnings spread across the front.

'It's up to you, you've been given a chance, seize it and you could be finished with Dispersals,' I told him.

Sometime later I'm looking out of the window and I saw the manager I'd replaced striding up to the Dep's office with the recent reception's 1150 under his arm, I awaited the call.

Sure enough Steve Taylor asked me to attend his office before giving me a minor dressing down for accepting 'this dangerous prisoner, totally unsuitable for our type of prison, arrange his return forthwith.'

He was a Cat B prisoner and we're a Cat B jail but I could tell by his tone it was futile arguing.

I was up and in early the following day to do my own dirty work.

He was devastated when I told him he'd be returning to Frankland, I found it difficult to justify, what could I say? We were going to have to get used to handling these type of prisoners if Forest Bank was to be taken seriously.

Though I felt at the time this was personal, and I let Ivor know that I wasn't happy about the Dep undermining me in concert with one of my managers, he agreed.

I was soon investigating a complaint by a Mr Kevin Sinclair, Director of the National Gay Prisoners Support and Advisory Service. He claimed to have been racially abused by a member of staff whilst visiting the prison.

He was supported in his claim by a case worker for a local solicitor. I interviewed all concerned.

I determined that the incident took place and the erring staff member would be dealt with at a later date by the Director. I had established that the case worker was an independent witness, that she'd never met Mr Sinclair previously.

As well as sanctions against the individual I had a duty to ensure that these attitudes were not institutional.

There were undoubtedly racist beliefs and behaviours among both prison officers and prisoners.

Though legislation provided safeguards for groups rendered vulnerable by discriminatory conduct and it assisted in securing coercive compliance, at the very least. It can also ensure that people's attitudes do not get translated into behaviours and actions that discriminate, but you can't leave it at that, leave things to chance as this incident proved conclusively.

Managing equality and guaranteeing people's rights under the law required us managers, as well as those we manage, to demonstrate what proactive steps we would take to combat discrimination, promote equality and value diversity.

I would include it in prisoner compacts in relation to the earned privileges system and also into staff appraisals.

It's then incumbent on senior managers to ensure that people's rights are guaranteed, and the law is upheld by their rigorous management of those systems. Where standards slip they would be challenged immediately.

Ivor asked me to suggest a couple of things we could do to build on what we had already achieved.

Senior managers, talking and listening, making sure that they were there for staff when things got difficult, providing a more pleasant environment with the best equipment, tapping into the huge reservoir of talent we had by offering rewards, both financial and in terms of recognition. Using our best staff as mentors for new staff to reinforce the positive culture we were creating and to raise standards, awards for innovation, an in-house journal, were some of the things I suggested.

But it was the idea of a yearly staff meeting where high-performing individuals and groups could be recognised, and which offered managers a platform to feed back on their year's work to date and where they could outline their group's priorities for the following year, that most enthused him.

We'd introduced something similar at Frankland. A programme was produced, with speakers given a timed slot. We had the hall professionally wired for sound, refreshments supplied for the break. As at political conferences, we had an amber/red light warning for those who had taken to the stage. Amber to begin to wrap-up whatever you were saying and red, the equivalent of a red card, i,e., get off your time's up!

The only one who refused to recognise the 'warnings' of course was 'the big man!' He would open the event and sail merrily on and on and on, to the increasing chagrin of his Dep Phil Copple who was vainly attempting to time manage events. Numerous speakers invariably lost their slots as that 'man from Strabane' warmed to his task.

To be fair, because security was crucial in the High Security Estate, I never lost my slot but much more important to me were tea/coffee and my favourite wagon wheels, served up during the break.

Young Rachel from the Secretariat used to put a clump of them away for me and for weeks, indeed months after the event I would cry out, 'Rach can I have one of Ivor's wagon wheels with my coffee?' When I'd returned from my rounds of the prison.

In fairness Ivor had learned his lesson by the time he'd taken over at Forest Bank and he gave us all ample time to get our message across. It proved a popular yearly event whilst I was there.

I rang Chris Di Paolo at his new prison for a catch-up. He howled with laughter when I told him about our up-coming Christmas staff meeting. Following Phil Copple's move to Deerbolt, Chris had taken over as Frankland's Dep, the responsibility to time-manage the event passed to him. He'd even lost his own slot on a couple of occasions as Ivor's opening epistle went on and on.

I came on duty one morning and the previous day's duty manager, Ian Whiteside asked me to speak to an ex Frankland recalled life sentence inmate who was refusing to leave the Seg.

I called to see him on my 'rounds' and he was amazed to see me, 'Columbo what are you doing here?'

I quickly established that his probation officer had arranged his incarceration because, it was alleged, he had failed to comply with Probation Hostel requirements, something he vehemently denied.

He was reluctant to come on board initially until I explained 'look I'm not making a judgement, the appropriate outside agencies will decide whether your recall was necessary, but either way it is better to fight your case on normal location. If your appeal against the recall fails then you'll serve the rest of your considerable sentence in the High Security Estate and I will reallocate you as a priority.

However, if you chose to remain down here, I will move you Segregation Unit to Segregation Unit.'

He immediately agreed that would be a mistake and expressed himself happy to be located in the main prison.

A couple of days later a wing staff member came to see me to ask me if I wanted a letter stopped! The ex-lifer had mentioned that I was working at Forest Bank, in a letter to an inmate at Frankland called Paul Massey.

Massey was well known in the area in which Forest Bank was situated.

'Unless there is anything derogatory or threatening in it let it go, I've already met a couple of people from Full Sutton I know, it's becoming well known that I'm here now.'

A month later I went up to the wing to inform the lifer he would be returning to Frankland. His re-call decision had been upheld and he had come to terms with it.

'Paul says hello he bets they put the red carpet out for you?'

'Tell him crime pays when you see him, I need a wheelbarrow to take my wages to the bank each month.'

I was still reviewing historical information concerning a named prison custody officer who was allegedly bringing in weed for prisoners for £150 and £250 a time depending on the quantity.

An SIR dated 24/3/07 claimed that this PCO had told a colleague that he intended bringing drugs in for a prisoner to gain information.

Another SIR submitted later in the month said that a prisoner had overheard another prisoner arranging for the PCO to bring in a mobile phone and drugs for another prisoner. He had reported this to a member of staff.

We started to carry out 'random' searches of staff built around his shift pattern. Within a fortnight his wing senior came to tell me 'he has failed to turn-up for his shift and has told a mate on the landing, 'that's it I've had enough, I'm not going back!"

On the back of this latest incident I submitted suggestions to Ivor that we introduce pre and post-employment checks, we develop an anti-corruption culture and training, provide better support to vulnerable staff, promote a culture of openness (whistle blowing) and review our code of conduct and discipline.

Early February I received a phone call from Frankland informing me that Chris Di Paolo had been involved in a serious accident on the A1 near Doncaster, on his way to a conference.

He died in 21 April in hospital in Nottingham, a terrible tragedy.

Ivor and I made arrangements to travel to the funeral together until we discovered it was invitation only and I wasn't included.

I satisfied myself with raising a glass to him alone in my flat on the eve of his funeral, playing The Byrds 'Eight Miles High,' a tribute to what he constantly told me was 'your appalling musical taste old boy,' as I drove him down to the station in Durham.

And still it continued, staff being more confident that things were getting done were submitting SIR's and contacting security managers with information with greater regularity. A recent SIR named an auxiliary who worked in the stores who, it was alleged, had brought in a phone for a named prisoner.

He apparently gives them to a named cleaner who distributes them. Our information suggested that a named prisoner's girlfriend would drop off two phones with the storeman to bring in the following week.

The going rate for bringing the phones in was £300 per phone!

The storeman and the auxiliary storeman work in tandem, one will enter the prison 'clean,' the other will wait in his car until his colleague rings him from inside the prison to confirm that no staff searches are taking place.

We were watching them closely, both left the prison together one lunch-time, they returned via the railway track side. We put on a staff search, they had nothing on them but when the DST went out to search the exercise yard close to the trackside, they found three parcels containing 'weed,' batteries and a phone!

At lunchtime three days later Mr (name deleted) entered the prison and went to the stores, he immediately asked for an outside line. Mr (name deleted) was seen inside his car answering his mobile phone before making his way to the gate. I appeared once he'd entered the gate and directed him and all those following him to visits to be searched.

He was found to be in possession of a quantity of mobile phones and steroid tablets. Both suspects were cautioned by our PLO who arranged for their transfer to Swinton police station. They 'folded' once questioned and directed the police to a cannabis 9 bar at one of their home addresses. I completed my witness statement. Further intelligence provided us with the name and address of the main prisoner organiser. I joked with my PLO, 'twenty years in the job and you're still a PC, you should be a Chief Super at least with the amount of 'collars' I've given you in the last eight months!

I was contacted at home one Saturday in August by my SPCO Lindsay Wright. She had received a call from a Mr Nicholas Hopkins of the News of the World about an article on one of our PCO's that they were intending to publish the following day.

I confirmed to Lindsay that the staff member was not one on our radar, she told me that he'd asked to speak to me but she'd confirmed I wasn't at work.

He had told Lindsay that he'd been 'stitched up' by the paper. That he'd met an ex prisoner for a drink in Tenerife. The prisoner had told him that he'd been offered a job in Dubai, would he come with him to the interview and act hard and agree to anything!

He admitted he'd agreed to bring heroin and cocaine into the prison, 'but I would never have done it!' 'I now realise it was a set-up and the press are camped outside my house, what will people think of me, I'll lose my job?' He was crying, clearly distressed.

Though I doubted he'd be with us for much longer he was still our responsibility, we had a duty of care. I asked Lindsay to ensure he had family support and to tell him not to report for his night shift that evening but to report to the Deputy Governor's office at 10 30 on Monday morning.

Our PLO went to London subsequently on our behalf and met with Mazher Mahmood, the 'fake sheikh' to discuss the sting he'd instigated on the gullible PCO. He was forthcoming and provided us with the audio and other physical evidence and that was the last we heard about it. The PCO resigned following his meeting with the Dep!

Ivor used to chair a 'wash-up' meeting of senior managers each Friday afternoon.

He mentioned at one of these meetings that himself and the Dep were to attend a local jobs fair the following Monday.

'And we know don't we Phil that this will be the perfect opportunity for Forest Bank to take the lead. The public sector will send staff who are not of sufficient rank to make decisions, and they'll be full of doom and gloom, negativity?' I looked away and hoped that he was wrong.

We were planning a resettlement wing and outside work opportunities would be a big incentive for prisoners to conform and progress.

Sure enough the big man couldn't wait to tell me on his return, 'HMP Manchester had sent a couple of PO's who were full of doom and gloom, we haven't got the staff to cover that, don't think we have the resources for that kind of initiative, it would take us ages to risk assess...' Apparently he and Steve had lined up plenty of opportunities for the resettlement wing. I despaired of my old employer sometimes, they could be so predictable. Steve had also been responsible for some pioneering work with the Cooperative Bank that had made it easier for our inmates to get bank accounts, find accommodation, pay bills, gain employment on release. The local media were now being much more supportive, they weren't starting every report on the establishment with the negative Inspection Report and the 'potting' incident as used to happen. Tangible improvements had been made, we'd renewed purpose, a clear structure was now in place.

I'd been trying to 'cultivate' a young Moss Sider, he was closely related to the leader of one Manchester's most infamous crews. We had got on well and I had helped him out a bit when he got into a few minor scrapes. He hadn't given me anything major yet, he had his loyalties which I respected. I needed to persevere because unusually, his credibility crossed gang lines. I knew he was a potential mine of information if 'our needs connected,' which is what I was waiting for.

We'd developed a strategy for managing inter group rivalries and tensions.

We questioned younger prisoners on reception on any gang affiliations, selling this approach on the basis that we didn't wish to locate them with people that 'would slice them up!' They understood and were extremely honest, from our perspective it allowed us to build-up a data base of local gangs. Occasionally it gave up some priceless intelligence on a 'major player,' who they were keen to avoid, someone neither ourselves nor the police, through the PLO, had previously been aware of.

At the time I'm considering I remember we held, 1 Norris Green, bitter enemies of the Croxteth crewe, 5 FMD bitter enemies of Doddington, 2 Gooch, bitter enemies of Doddington, 1 RSG bitter enemies of Doddington, 2 LSC, bitter enemies of Gooch/LSG, It took careful management to keep them apart but we managed it.

In October we organised a family Eid day, Forest Bank had a larger Asian population than I'd known anywhere else.

It went really well and I got a dozen letters subsequently from visitors telling me how much they had enjoyed it, which I really appreciated.

I had plans for an enhanced visits area with a free coffee machine, magazines, tables with flowers, a water fountain. This would be for the benefit of those who had seized the opportunity to progress and their families, those who fit the criteria and who were coming towards the end of their sentence. Prisoners could also then meet with outside agencies responsible for their resettlement in a more comfortable and appealing area, more professional and business-like.

We were moving forward, carrot and stick or hearts and minds as we had termed it since our Castington days. We were planning family days when prisoners and visitors had more freedom to interact, where they could 'break bread together' on tables outside, when the weather permitted.

Rewards for positive behaviour and nobody's been 'potted!'

Ivor and Steve Taylor were pleased by the progress and made sure I knew it, however, not one to be complacent, 'the big man,' had asked me to deliver my anti-conditioning package to all staff, all civilian staff including teachers. 'If you stand still and admire Phil, you end up going backwards,' ever the pragmatist.

I had agreed to take over a control problem from one of our sister prisons, Peterborough.

He would arrive late evening so I told the duty manager to locate him in segregation overnight to give me chance to assess him.

When the Duty Manager told him he was to be located in segregation overnight on my instructions he replied,

'Well I'm not going, who's Phil O'Brien? I'll knock him out!'

Lindsay couldn't wait to show me the duty manager's SIR explanation as to why my instructions hadn't been carried out, when I came on duty the following morning.

I went straight down the wing to see him. A member of staff pointed him out to me, he was sitting on a table in the middle of the landing. I went over to join him.

'Alright gov, who are you, the Welfare?'

'No, I'm not. I'm Phil O'Brien and I've been told you're going to knock me out!'

'No, no I was only joking.'

Well I'm not, get your kit and come with me.'

When I got back to the office I found that my security team for the day, Ms Wright and Ms Webster had drawn up chairs in front of the CCTV that covered the wing, made themselves coffee, got out the biscuits, before settling down to witness the action.

'What if he had knocked me out?'

They just giggled, getting close to my sell by date again when I'm amusing gangsters (Paul Massey) and prison staff alike.

Security manager Tim White had expressed concerns about the attitude of a new recruit whilst he was giving the security input to an Initial course.

Tim rightly decided to monitor his progress.

An SIR submitted shortly after he took up his first post indicated that this PCO was 'lending burn' to prisoners who would pay him back at the end of the week. The informant further suggested that he had heard prisoners inviting the PCO into their cells for a smoke! A further SIR described him as 'a con with keys!'

A month later we received information that he had been paid £500 for bringing in 2 phones and half a bar of cannabis and that he would leave the goods behind the washer on F1. The drugs were split between F1 and A1 prisoners when they reached the gym. We then were told that he wanted a £1000 for the next 'drop' because security had just arrested two staff! (we believed he was referring to the 2 storemen).

A couple of days later he came on duty, found that he had been reassigned to an outside hospital bed watch, told his colleague in that case he needed to get a book from the car but returned empty handed. Was he becoming surveillance conscious before a 'drop' we asked ourselves?

Then 'our needs coincided' as I always knew they would!

My Moss side contact needed to see me urgently, he was down the block.

He'd failed a drugs test, 'It was only a bit of weed but my girlfriend has been threatening to finish with me, if you put me on closed visits it will be the end, please...'

He offered up some low level stuff but I made it clear who and what I was interested in.

He still prevaricated, I knew that the PCO was dealing with another major 'player' on another wing but I was equally sure that my man knew what was happening because of his family connections and the fact that I knew he was on friendly terms with the 'player.'

We reached an accord and I called a tasking meeting.

We were to expect a decent size drop the following day. All my staff were strategically placed to observe the target. He was observed going into the locker room, he subsequently came out carrying a red cup, he asked a member of the security team if he could take it into the establishment. He appeared very nervous.

I asked the passive drug handler Mr Hunter to take his dog around the staff locker room, it 'indicated' at locker 308.

I then asked pro-active dog handler Mr Sosa to 'sweep' the locker room with his dog, it also 'indicated' at locker 308.

Arrangements were then made for a prison service union representative to accompany, Tim White, and PLO Steve Waite to observe the PCO open his locker. Inside they found 62.9g of cannabis resin, 7.9g of cannabis leaf, 14.2g of heroin. The PCO was arrested and taken to Swinton police station.

I was convinced a 7 'stretch' awaited him and that's what he eventually drew.

I got stuck into our PLO again,'Waitey, you should be an ACC with the amount of bodies we've served up for you this year!'

And then, just like that, it was over again. Ivor had been promoted and was to take over Regional Operations Director for Scotland and Immigration. We'd just had a positive unannounced Inspection report. The report accepted that the Establishment was no longer under siege from a minority of powerful inmates, that we'd established order and control and things on many fronts had improved, still they criticised Security/me for carrying out too many strip searches on visits! How we were expected to achieve the former without the latter was beyond me! Keep that in your mind as you watch on your TV screens, the scenes of violence and abuse suffered by staff and compliant prisoners, at the likes of Durham, Birmingham and Stoke Heath.

However I was ready to go, we'd got some good young managers, who had just required purpose and structure, how could they progress if old buggers like me were still in place? Front-line private sector staff were just as competent as their public sector colleagues, with consistent support and supervision, if anything they sometimes exhibited a more 'can do' attitude.

Private sector managers were much more budget aware than their public sector counterparts.

As far as the Chief Inspector was concerned I'll leave it to Edmund Burke:

'those who would carry on great public schemes must be proof against the fatiguing delays, the most mortifying disappointments, the most shocking insults and most of all the presumptuous judgement of the ignorant upon their designs.'

Says it all really?

Decision making is what sets people apart in this profession; making a decision and then owning that decision.

Nobody will ever convince me otherwise.

Postscript

I have previously described how the Press had published a story claiming that Harold Shipman was running 'surgeries' at Frankland. The 'sting' perpetrated on the gullible, potentially 'bent' PCO by the Sun newspaper's 'fake sheikh. In January 2008 I was asked by the Company to investigate the circumstances which led to photographs of Rose West ending up in both the Daily Mirror and the Sun newspapers on different days.

The weight of evidence suggested that the photos had been taken by a mobile phone with a camera facility or similar device. There were clear indications that the photographs had been taken between Christmas Eve, when the Christmas decorations were put up and New Year's Day when they were taken down.

CCTV cameras did not penetrate inside cell walls so these photographs could not have been taken via stills re-called from CCTV footage.

I concluded that it was unlikely that the pictures in the Daily Mirror were provided by prisoners, a lock-down search immediately post-publication failed to locate any phones, indeed only one had been found in the previous year. I must admit I did have my reservations about this following my most recent experiences at Forest Bank.

When I first viewed the inset photograph included in the edition of the Sun, Saturday 26th January, 2008, 'Lardy Rose in the exercise yard.', I had reservations about its authenticity. Ms West was unequivocal that it was not her. 'the photo outside in the Courtyard is obviously not me, not that one.' It showed the figure wearing a fleece with a quarter zip. Her property card showed that her only fleece was full zip. This appeared to be a superimposed image designed to give credence to the accompanying article.

I determined that the main photograph featured in a national on Saturday 26 January 2008 headlined 'gross West leaves the canteen' was taken by a mobile phone camera or similar device from a CCTV image. The curser was clearly displayed in the bottom left of this photograph, and I determined the three areas of the prison where this could have been done.

I further discovered that (name deleted) a former inmate had rung the prison on 16 January 2008 to say that she had been offered money by the Sun newspaper to reoffend, so that she could get sentenced and take photos of Ms West.

The Red Top Press clearly increase sales if they can generate a story about a serial killer or presumably they wouldn't go to such lengths to obtain copy on the likes Peter Sutcliffe and Rose West. How much of this is in the public interest; how much of it is merely sensationalism. Should they consider the risks of bringing fresh trauma to surviving victims or victim's families by publishing such stories?

If they 'encourage' a staff member or a prisoner to smuggle a mobile phone into the prison for such purposes could they be considered as accessories after the fact?

I found numerous examples of members of the Press making contact in local pubs with staff members. Seeking access to visits using a false name, trying to cultivate prisoners' family members, all to generate copy on Rose West.

When is the public interest being served and when is it simply prurience, or criminal?

Certainly if prisons are not carrying out their duty of care to the public, which includes both staff and prisoners, the media has a duty to investigate and report, so that the organisation can be called to account. When prison staff are acting in a criminal manner the media are serving the public interest by reporting this.

The company also asked me to examine their procedures on Deaths in Custody on a number of occasions following in-cell fatalities.

Common failings that featured time and time again were, bullying and violence; shortages of suitable staff; a lack of training, poor record keeping and poor communication between PCO's and medical staff, courts and community health teams; inadequate risk assessments; and often poor emergency response. The inmates themselves often had a history of mental illness or self-harm. Inadequate care plans for those self-harming, failure to locate them in a safe cell were common to these cases.

Gradually these invitations to work petered out.

In December 2009 when the English Governor of Magaberry prison Northern Ireland had been threatened and resigned, I asked Ivor if he fancied us giving it a go, take on the Orange and Green but he declined. I tried him again sometime later when they were looking for a Chief Inspector for the Province's prisons, but he again declined.

We've lost touch.

I am still in regular touch with Gary Hassan and Dave Hall from my public sector days and Dave Armstrong from my foray into the private sector, as well as 'Dave Turner' who retired to his native North East, but more on him later.

Dave Armstrong contacted me in 2015. He'd met a Kiwi lady whilst working as a manager at one of the company's prisons in Scotland. They had decided to marry and live in New Zealand, he was seeking a job in a Privately-run prison over there, could he give my name for a reference.

I subsequently did a telephone interview with the HR department and he landed the job.

He contacted me again the following year, January 2016, his career had further progressed and he was now a senior manager at the Serco-run Mount Eden prison in Auckland.

They were having problems of order and control and the New Zealand Government had accused the company of mismanaging the prison. He feared that they would take the prison back into the public hands at the mid-point of the contract some six months hence.

He wondered, 'if you would be interested in coming out on a short-term contract to do what you did at Forest Bank, I reckon I can convince my boss to fund it.'

I was up for it and renewed my passport but before it could be progressed further Serco were stripped of the contract and fined a record amount, the prison was taken back into the public sector.

I note that the IRA supergrass I had de-briefed all those years ago at Full Sutton died peacefully recently whilst on holiday in Jamaica.

One of the 'nutters' we had thwarted attempting to 'make one' using a home-made weapon, had intended taking a notorious child murderer hostage prior to killing him. He managed to kill a different child murderer, whilst still in prison in 2013, so realised his dream!

My old 'sparring partner' Paul Massey was shot dead in a targeted 'hit.' This resulted in alleged revenge shootings in Salford and Swinton and other areas of Greater Manchester. Someone has recently been arrested in connection with his murder.

Dave Turner keeps trying to line me up with jobs, expert witness gigs etc.

He is on an early warning list for jobs in Justice Sector. He sent me a link earlier this year, advertising for a Governor of the prison on the Island of St Helena. It was a two-year secondment and initially that put me off, a six-month contract in New Zealand was much more appealing at my time of life.

He kept encouraging me and I decided it might be interesting to find out if they were looking for something different in terms of style.

I filled in the application form and was pleasantly surprised to be offered an interview following the completion of an on-line personality test. I was delighted to make the 'cut' and I subsequently attended an interview at St Helena's Government office in London.

Alas, it soon became quite clear that it this stage they were not looking for a different 'style,' certainly not mine!

They appointed a qualified Maths teacher with twelve years prison experience and I wish them well.

You never know, if a Cat A prisoner escapes or they suffer serious disorder, I might get a call. If not, it's been a 'blast'; I wouldn't have missed the last forty years for the world.

**

Printed in Great Britain
by Amazon

SECESSION

A. R. LAMB

By the same author

Divers (Electron Press)

Cornish translations by Ray Chubb

British Library Cataloguing In Publication Data

A Record of this Publication is available
from the British Library

ISBN 1846850754
978-1-84685-075-2

Published February 2006 by

Exposure Publishing, an imprint of Diggory Press,
Three Rivers, Minions, Liskeard, Cornwall, PL14 5LE, UK
WWW.DIGGORYPRESS.COM

CHAPTER ONE

AT MIDNIGHT he was standing on the edge of the lawn beneath a clouded sky. Rain fell on his forehead in such tiny drops that it might be mistaken for electrical tingles. From a comparison of observations made during the preceding hours he'd assumed there was no life in the house. All he had to fear now were security contrivances or gaps in his knowledge. He hoped that none of the gaps would be wide enough to contain a person more courageous than himself. He tried hard to believe that his foreboding referred neither to any specific event in the future nor to any specific danger within, that it was nothing more than the healthy dread which any initiate feels with no elders to be pushed by and no peers to be pulled by. He had to pull himself, but the mechanism was clumsy. The conversion of dream-motion into muscle-motion, fuelled by baked beans and half-baked ideas, was no easy process. His haversack, hanging limply over his back, might contain latent silver and potential gold, or it might just be an empty scrotum. His scrotum itself was tight to the point of pain. The beans in his stomach were undecided whether to carry on down or turn around and come back up. He could list a whole society of reasons for giving in and going home but only two for continuing: the possibility of profit; the fear of being afraid.

He put his hand through an open window; pulled up the handle of the larger window below; entered. His torch revealed a laundry-room. A couple of machines stood there with gaping mouths, hungry for clothes. He crept through into the living-room; froze as his foot scrunched against something. It was a box containing chicken-bones. The floor was carpeted with them. What sort of place was this? Then he heard definite sleep-breathing from the far side of the room; turned off the torch; ducked down behind an armchair; accustomed

3

his eyes to the light dribbling in through the French windows; made out a bulky form sprawled on a settee, emitting snores at random intervals. Let's get out of here, said his legs. Hold on a minute, he replied. If he's fast asleep. Terp slowly brought the torch-beam up over the body, noting on the way a coffee-table supporting a forest of bottles, eventually illuminating an old, red, bulbous face.

The eyes opened. Off went the torch. Down went Terp behind the armchair again. God, he's awake. Come on, run. Wait a bit, will you? He might be too pissed to know what's going on. And sure enough, after a minute or so, the snores resumed, this time rattling regularly with every inhalation. Terp began to fill his haversack with ornaments. He didn't care about profit now. He just wanted to get the job done as fast as possible and get out, simply in order to say to himself that he could do it. The bag was almost full when he heard a roar behind him. He turned round to see that the old man had crept up on him and was now within arm's length. He must have been pretending to sleep. A slow-motion version of a punch known as a hay-maker was now swinging its way towards his head. Terp ducked. The punch went on into thin air. The rest of the old man's body went whirling round after it, with the result that he fell backwards to the floor. Once there, he remained still. He was breathing, because occasionally a gargly sound issued from his throat, but was it a snore, or a death-rattle? Please wake up, sobbed Terp. Please. Oh God, oh God. He ran out to the front door, left it on the latch; ran up the street and on until he found a working phone-box; dialled the emergency services; gave the details of the house and the whereabouts of the victim; walked quickly home.

* * *

His career as a burglar having been terminated after this encounter, he fell into a state of despair, a state with ever-expanding frontiers, a state which governed him through the holes in his shoes. He'd thought (he thought) every thought there was to think, and not one was worth recalling. Low as he'd gone, he could still find no-one to look up to. His mother, with whom he lived, was useless. Her own despair, born of rejection and alcohol, had nothing in common with his. When compelled to tolerate her presence, he was resolutely mute. His father, who had been absent for longer than he could remember, and who had long since formed another family to oppress, was less than useless, little more than an illegible scrawl inside a cheap and inappropriate birthday-card which some years arrived late and others not at all. He had no lover to confide in, no priest to confess to. He became so sarcastic and cynical with his friends that they soon left him alone, categorising him as weird.

Occasionally he would glimpse a way out of the state but, on closer examination, would find it blocked with guilt. The thought that he might have been the cause of someone else's death was enough to send him scurrying inwards. Immediately after the event he could perhaps, without incriminating himself, have discovered the fate of the old man. But he'd become in effect a double ostrich: he didn't want to know either way. He even, as a means of inducing greater self-rottenness, began to question his memory of what had happened. After all, it didn't seem very likely that someone would fall lifeless as a result of an undelivered punch. Perhaps he had taken one of those empty bottles and, in a blacked-out frenzy, used it as a club.

With the eventual proceeds from the robbery (which had luckily included a couple of baroque gilt-bronzes) he bought himself a pretty little Japanese motorbike and began riding up to various high points on Dartmoor and walking himself to exhaustion. The moor in autumn was the only place with which he had any empathy: grey mist, grey stone, grey sheep echoed the grey void he contained. Death was the next stop. One of these days he'd be bound to get permanently lost.

He always steered well clear of other walkers, but on this occasion avoidance was not an option because he literally stumbled across them. They were kneeling on the ground side by side, the man's arm around the woman's shoulders, the woman's arm around the man's waist. They stood up. They appeared to be a few years older than himself. The man was big, both tall and broad – black leather, black stubble, black eyes. The woman was big too, the same height as Terp. They grinned at him. He couldn't reciprocate.

"Sorry to disturb you," he muttered.

He began to walk away, towards the nearest tor. He heard them talking behind him. He'd gone fifty yards or so when they caught up.

"Hold on a minute," said the man.

"What?"

"Where are you from?"

"Plymouth."

"And what's your name?"

"Terp."

"Is that a first name or a second name?"

"It's a sort of nickname. My surname's Wyatt, so my friends used to call me Terp, after Wyatt Earp, you know."

"I get it. I'm Jack. This is Demelza."

He shook hands with Jack. The grip was firm but not crushing. He shook hands with Demelza, saw the mist glistening in her eyelashes, felt a flutter in his solar plexus, was instantly smitten forever.

"Look at them," said Jack, pointing to the ground.

Terp saw nothing until he bent over. Then suddenly a dozen tiny bell-headed mushrooms 'appeared'.

He looked up to see Jack producing a sheath-knife. A stampede of fantasies rushed through his head, in all of which he ended up dead.

Jack calmly scored a faint but precise circle around the mushrooms and then put the knife away.

"Why did you do that?"

"They'll wait for me now. They won't let anyone else pick 'em. Or see 'em."

Terp racked his brains in vain for a supplementary question.

"There's something we'd like to show you," said Demelza. "You wait right here, OK?"

Terp shrugged. He had nothing better to do.

They climbed the tor, eventually emerging on a pinnacle; beneath them, a drop of at least thirty feet.

Demelza jumped first.

She landed with a sickening crunch in the ferns.

"Oh, Christ," muttered Terp, imagining at least a pair of broken legs.

But when he reached her she was already on her feet, smiling and quite uninjured.

"How could you do that?"

"Watch Jack."

They backed away.

Jack came down at the same velocity, but if anything hit the ground with a harder thump. He seemed to use no particular technique to absorb the shock: he landed on all fours, lay still for a moment, then sprang to his feet.

"That was fantastic," said Terp. "I can't believe you haven't hurt yourselves."

"It's easy," said Jack. "Well, it's either easy or it's impossible."

"Try some yourself. See how you feel," said Demelza.

"What? You can't do it without them?"

"I know what you're getting at," said Jack, aggressively. "And it's a load of bollocks. How could you hear them if they weren't calling to you? Don't give me none of that stuff about unconscious synthesis."

"I wasn't going to."

7

"They're the ones who are divine and eternal, not us. They're the ones who can transform at will. Why do you think they are everywhere? In picking them we're being picked by them. In eating them they, not we, are being fulfilled. We're just the servants of their glory. We might observe it. We might reflect it. But we don't partake of it."

Terp thought this was going a bit far. These weren't the sort of things you said out loud even if you believed them.

"It's important that you understand this," continued Jack. "Because any other attitude and you'd be using them and they'd punish you for that. There's hardly anywhere in this country where they don't grow and yet everywhere they're taboo. Why is that? Because they're a counterpower. The mushrooms are taboo to society. Society is equally taboo to the mushrooms. In order to be picked by them you have to be already alienated from society. You have to be in between the two powers... What am I blabbering about? If you do it you do it, and if you don't do it you don't do it. Just do it."

"Alright," shrugged Terp. "Why not?"

"We'll find them for you," said Demelza.

Terp was neither afraid nor particularly enthusiastic. He didn't give a toss about anything. He felt his life was over anyway. Nothing could surprise or resurrect him.

They brought him a handful.

"Give 'em a good chew."

He ate them one by one.

The taste was incomparable and unpleasant.

They sat in silence.

Terp felt no change. He kept on glancing up at the top of the tor, trying to shrink the distance between here and there. He wasn't bothered about killing himself, only about pain or paralysis.

"You'll be ready to go up soon," said Jack.

"How should I land?"

"Don't think about it. If you jump you'll know how to land."

"Whatever you do, don't force it," added Demelza. "We won't think any less of you if you climb down. It's nothing to do with courage anyway; in fact if you use courage to help you, you'll certainly hurt yourself."

"OK," said Jack, after a few more minutes' silence. "If you start now you should be ready by the time you reach the top."

Terp set off.

As he climbed, he experienced a series of quiet revelations: the granite wasn't inanimate, but vibrant; the plants which grew in the crevices weren't stupid, but sentient; even his hands had a dazzling life of their own to lead.

He looked at himself as he'd been until now as though at a mouse, as though at a stranger. A grey mousy stranger who'd somehow been deluded into thinking that greyness and feebleness and estrangement were all there was; who'd never known clarity, never known energy, never known colour, never known form.

He reached the pinnacle and peered over. From here it seemed further than it had from below, even further than it was. He didn't see how he could survive the drop. Wouldn't it be a shame to die when he'd only just discovered how to live?

He closed his eyes to try and relieve the vertigo and was immediately (there's no other way of putting it) swallowed by a tiger.

The next thing he knew he was on his feet laughing and Demelza was hugging him and Jack was shaking his hand.

"I did it!" he bubbled. "I can hardly believe it... I don't know how. I'd already decided I wasn't going to – I've never been much good at heights. I closed my eyes because I was feeling dizzy and I saw this tiger, not like a photograph or anything, this huge head facing me and then it just sort of swallowed me up."

"That's perfect," said Jack.

He took from his pocket a curved tooth, about three inches long, attached to a thin silver chain.

"For you. Put it on."

Terp drew the chain around his neck. Demelza fastened the clasp at the back. The point of the tooth hung down about level with his solar plexus.

From all the questions clamouring he selected the silliest:

"Is this a real tooth?"

"Yeah, it's real plastic. It's a real plastic tooth. It doesn't matter what it's made of. It's what it means that matters."

"What does it mean?"

"It means you've been swallowed. If the tooth is outside you then you are inside the tiger."

"Are you saying you expected that to happen?"

"We hoped."

"And that's how you jumped?"

"Of course."

He believed it, yet he was amazed by it. He was amazed he believed it, yet there was no way to disbelieve it. He wandered away for a few yards; fell to his knees in the bracken.

It was beginning to get dark.

"How did you get up here?"

Terp's attention was so absorbed by a bracken-frond that for a while he was unable to register the question, then when he'd registered it was for a while longer incapable of understanding it.

"... Bike," he said at last.

"Good, because we want you to come back with us."

"Back with you?"

He was beginning to have difficulty with the verbal. After-images of the frond multiplied behind his eyes, spawning vegetable kingdoms.

"Yeah. Where did you leave your bike?"

He looked around, vainly striving to stem the flood of greenness and remember which direction he'd come from. But he had even less idea of where he was than who.

"Don't worry," said Jack, gently. "We'll find it. It's bound to be on the same road as ours."

* * *

Half an hour later they reached their bike, an ancient black beast.

"How do you feel?" said Demelza.

"Good."

"Are you capable of riding?"

He looked around; saw a couple of ponies grazing nearby; decided that he wouldn't mind mounting the smaller of the two, the one with dancing ginger and white dapples.

"I don't think he's safe."

"No," said Jack. "Tell you what: we'll go and get your bike. I'll ride it back and you can ride pillion on ours with Demelza. What kind of bike is it?"

"Little... Suzuki... Red."

"Give us the key."

"The key. The key... Do I know it?"

Jack laughed and patted his hands against Terp's pockets until the key responded by jangling against its ring.

They donned their helmets, fired up the engine.

"Wait right there," shouted Jack, over the roar. "Don't move an inch."

They disappeared over the next brow. Soon he could no longer hear them. For a while he stood still and silent in the windless, drizzly dusk. Then he began to pace quickly back and forth on the side of the road, dissipating some of the tremendous energy within. Then he began to bellow wordlessly at the top of his voice.

Whenever a car appeared he carried on pacing, but stopped bellowing. Eventually, a single headlight over the brow implied a motorbike. And sure enough it was Demelza, his crash-helmet over her forearm.

At first he sat with his hands gripping the sides of the seat and his head back, enjoying the carnival of colours which zinged past against the charcoal sky. After a few minutes he put his arms around her waist, clasped his hands together against her belly, buried his face in her back. He succumbed to an onslaught of unknown emotions, as if twenty years of postnatal blinkers had suddenly been torn off, as if n billion years of prenatal blindness had suddenly been cured. Despite the onrushing cold air, despite the layers of leather and cloth, he could feel the warmth radiating from her, a warmth he'd yearned for forever, the warmth of another body, of another gender, of another world. Sobs rippled. Tears cascaded. She took her gloved clutch-hand and pressed it against his.

CHAPTER TWO

HE AWOKE to the yelping of seagulls, to sunshine diffused through calico curtains. The tidiness, the emptiness, the yellow-walled brightness all contrasted immeasurably with his room at home. He'd been so exhausted after his arrival the night before that they'd sent him to bed as soon as he'd eaten. He arose and drew the curtains: straight-edged patches of sea could be glimpsed between distant rooftops. He put on his trousers and softly opened the bedroom door. He had no idea what time it was, whether they were still in bed.

He emerged from the bathroom and began to tiptoe downstairs. As he reached the middle landing he heard the lilt of female voices. He listened for a while, but could discern no words. He carried on down, noisily now to announce his approach. Demelza met him in the hall, put her arm around him, kissed his cheek, led him back into the kitchen.

"This is Rose," she said, referring to the person sitting at the table. "Jack's sister."

He advanced to greet her. She seemed about his age. As she leaned forward to stand up, his glance was naturally drawn to the gap between shirt and sternum. He noticed, hanging above her cleavage, a curved tooth identical to the one with which he had been presented..

She shook his hand and looked him clearly in the eye:

"Good to meet you."

"And you."

"Well, I must be off," she said, putting on a jacket. "See you later."

"Yeah... We'll pick you up about eight."

Demelza gestured him towards the chair Rose had vacated. The cushion was still warm.

"So how do you feel?"

"... I'm not sure... Good... Weird."

"You had a big day yesterday. It's bound to take a while to sink in. But you slept alright?"

"Oh yes, wonderful. Best sleep I've had in years."

"Any good dreams?"

Nothing as good as this, he thought.

"Nothing specific," he replied. "Just a lot of greenness – like a jungle... Not that I've ever been in a jungle."

She raised her eyebrows and tilted her head, a look which seemed to say 'don't be so sure about that'.

He chuckled.

"Where's Jack?"

"Gone to work. He would have liked to take the day off, but he's got about eighteen jobs on the go and people are starting to get angry."

Terp sat back, basking in the prospect of a day alone with her.

After breakfast, they walked down to the front. He realised he wasn't even sure where they were.

"Paignton."

"Oh, yes. Of course," he said, recognising the pier from occasional trips he'd made as a child.

Most of the amenities were closed. The beach, accustomed during the season to the daily weight of ten thousand bodies, was unburdened. The sea was friendly and gentle, a light easterly breeze knocking up a few polite little waves. The horizon was mutilated by a succession of oil-tankers. They meandered down to the water's edge, then along under the pier and back towards the promenade.

"See that," she said, indicating a boarded-up little hut. "It's a gold-mine."

"How come?"

"It belongs to Jack's parents. They only sell simple things, like tea and crab-rolls, but the mark-ups are stupendous. They take enough during the season to live like lords the rest of the year... They're in Barbados at the moment."

They dawdled up the main street, which went at right-angles to the front. He was proud to be seen with her. As they passed the only open amusement-arcade, they were accosted by a dishevelled individual on crutches.

"Oh, no," she muttered.

"Hi, Demmie."

He wore a long black coat, its lapel decorated with a badge bearing the initials 'MDL'. The plaster-cast on his left foot was covered with signatures and obscenities. He emitted an odour which even outside in the onshore breeze was astonishingly acrid. The look in his eye was both disturbed and disturbing.

"Hello, Kizer. How are you?"

"Fucking awful."

"Sorry to hear that... When does the plaster come off?"

"I dunno. Keep missing the frigging appointments, don't I?"

"Well, that's just silly."

"I've got better things to do than sit around for hours in outpatients. I'll saw it off myself when I'm ready."

"I wouldn't do that. You'd probably end up with septicaemia."

"What do you care, anyway? It's Jack's fault I broke it in the first place."

She laughed and shook her head:

"How do you make that out?"

"He tricked me. He made me jump from a higher point than he jumped from."

"Come on. That's absolute rubbish, and you know it. He did all he could to stop you. He knew you weren't ready."

"He hexed me. He just wanted to keep me out... Got any money?"

She gave him some change from her purse. He hobbled back in to the arcade. The fruit-machine almost immediately coughed up a jackpot, which clattered into the tray and spilled out across the floor. Terp went in to retrieve the overflow, only to have his hand impaled by the black-rubber tip of a crutch.

"What do you think you're doing?"

"He's only trying to help," said Demelza.

"Oh... I thought he was trying to help himself."

"You shouldn't judge people by your own standards."

"Alright," he said, when they'd transferred all the winnings into his coat-pocket. "I guess we're quits now."

She narrowed her eyes and tightened her lips at the implication, but seemed to think better of further expressing her anger.

"OK," she said. "Quits. But don't you forget it."

He scowled and hobbled off towards the cashier.

They continued up the street.

"I could have done without that," she said.

"What was it all about?"

"I can't stand him, or any of those people."

"What people?"

" The so-called Mushroom Defence League. We thought at first they might be allies, but we've really got no more in common with them than we have with the police. They stuff fifty or so into their stupid gobs, then smoke a load of dope, then go down the pub and drink gallons of beer and vodka while yakking on about sacredness. They wouldn't know sacred if it gave them a black eye."

Terp was disconcerted by her vehemence, though comforted by his own apparent immunity.

"Jack tried so hard with that Kizer, long after I would have given up. Trouble is, he only sees the good in people. No, that's not true: he sees the bad, but he always acts as though it doesn't exist..."

* * *

Terp was used to doing nothing; he wasn't used to enjoying it. Yet the afternoon slid serenely by, unsullied by so much as a speck of boredom. She'd apologised for having to work. She would have preferred to give her whole attention to him, but she must finish this particular piece because the agreed deadline had passed. Her craft was called 'pyrography'. He'd never heard of it before, and probably would have laughed at it if he had, but now that he worshipped the cause (her) and had inspected the effects (geometric, organic, Celtic-looking designs upon discs of sycamore, pregnant with inextricable meaning) he was certain it was the highest artistic endeavour. In a sense she concurred with his assessment, yet she refused to claim any credit, or even any talent. The designs had come to her, complete and unbidden, from the mushroom; all she had to do was transfer them, first with pencil onto paper, then with heat onto wood. There was no difference in kind between the devotion she felt when executing the work and the devotion her customers felt when contemplating it.

Jack came home just after dark. He greeted them both with equal warmth, although he didn't kiss Terp. They went out around eight, picking up Rose on the way. Terp felt good, wedged between the two women on the front seat of the van, although he sat a little stiffly, not wishing to commit any inappropriate acts of touch. He had no idea where they were headed, only that he was going to be 'shown something'. Conversation was impossible, given the racket of the diesel engine, so he enjoyed the urban light-life. It was fascinating, but perhaps too gaudy and cartoonish for his new tastes. They drove through Paignton and most of Torquay. They stopped outside a terrace, Jack returning a few minutes later and lobbing a bunch of keys onto Demelza's lap. They drove on another half a mile, parked and walked a further hundred yards or so until they arrived at the entrance to a place called Kents

Cavern, which Terp had heard of but never visited. They let themselves in. The other three produced small torches and led the way down into the caves.

"We want you to wait here," said Jack.

They went back the way they'd come. Soon the last glimmerings of torchlight were engulfed and he found himself besieged by that rare phenomenon known as absolute darkness.

At first he kept it at bay with projected images and delusive worries: he was the victim of a cruel and incomprehensible joke; they'd gone; he was locked in; the caves were probably closed for the winter; he would die of terror; if he survived the terror he would die of starvation. But after some consideration, during which he concluded that if he couldn't trust them then he was back where he'd started and didn't want to live anyway, he opened his mouth and began to breathe deeply, allowing the cold, damp darkness to come into him and wash away all the remaining detritus of his former life.

When the first alleviation arrived he was neither surprised nor incredulous: a pair of goldfinches, who soared and swooped around him, their flight-paths intertwining, leaving radiant trails of red, white and gold etched into the black air; who hovered side by side in front of him for what seemed like ages before finally flying off.

Momentarily he believed they'd been real, in the sense of possessing bones and genes and feathers; that somehow they'd become trapped in the caves. But of course if they'd been real they would also have been invisible.

The second alleviation came in the form of a single torchlight, accompanied by a softly humming voice. After a while he was able to discern the bearer of the torch: it was Rose, definitely Rose. She placed her left hand in his right hand, turned off the torch, ceased her humming. Only when he felt the intense heat of her hand did he realise how cold he'd become. A charm of delicious, unprecedented feelings flew up his arm and down into his ribcage.

She turned the torch back on and played the beam around the rock-face in front of them until illuminating the impression of a white, curved tooth.

Nearby was a framed caption, upon which she now focussed the beam, long enough for him to read the following:

Fossilised tooth from a sabre-toothed tiger, who lived in this locality   upwards of ten thousand years ago.

"Now take the tooth from round your neck," she whispered. "And rub it against the tooth in the rock."

He did as he was bid.

CHAPTER THREE

"TELL me where to turn," shouted Jack.

Terp, jolted out of his reverie, was disappointed to see how close they already were to the music he must face – the ghastly, predictable cacophony conducted by his mother. (Jack had offered him a job. They were now on their way into Plymouth to pick up a few of Terp's things.)

"Next left."

Even worse than the prospect of the approaching showdown was the thought that he must soon relinquish this delicious proximity to Demelza. She'd fallen asleep soon after they'd left Paignton. At first she'd leaned against Jack, but he'd pushed her away as she was hampering his gear-changes. Ever since, the top of her head had been pressed against Terp's neck, her face buried in his shoulder. Whenever he'd closed his own eyes he'd found it easy to imagine that their actual souls were in chaste yet intimate contact.

"Second on the right."

There might be other music to face as well, the music of doom. Having heard about the possible stain upon Terp's psyche, Jack had been unreasonably sympathetic. He'd understood Terp's initial attitude - not wanting to know. He'd agreed with his present attitude - needing to know. He'd volunteered to try and find out what had happened.

"Next right... Just here."

They pulled up outside the little half-house, sitting there wizened and grey from a surfeit of misery. He saw the curtains still closed upon his own room, predicted with a shudder the mess and stench inside.

"OK," said Jack. "How do I get to the scene of the crime?"

"It's not funny," said Terp, drawing a crude map in Jack's notebook.

He and Demelza disembarked. Jack drove off.

They walked up the short path. Terp unlocked the front door.

"It's only me," he shouted, from the hall.

"Don't let her get to you," he whispered.

They went into the front room. His mother sat in a preliminary sherry stupor, preceding the real business of the day, which was oblivion. At least she'd dressed.

The stare she now inflicted upon him was composed of daggers, pincers, gouges.

"Where have you been? I've been worried sick about you."

"Yeah, sorry. I should have phoned... This is Demelza."

"Very pleased to meet you, Mrs. Wyatt. I've heard so much about you."

"Oh?" she said, glancing at Demelza without taking her outstretched hand, then resuming the stare. "What have you been blabbing about?"

He was going to protest that he'd expended no more than half a dozen words upon her, when he remembered that truth was a commodity never traded in this house. Demelza must have come to the same conclusion, as she went on to say:

"He told me what a good mother you were, how much love you gave him when he was baby, how much attention you gave him when he was a child, how much encouragement you gave him when he was an adolescent, and how he threw it all back in your face."

"In my face. That's right."

"He didn't tell me what a beauty you were."

His mother frowned:

"Hardly."

"Rubbish," said Demelza, sitting down on the sofa next to her and gently lifting her fringe away from her forehead. "You're still lovely."

"Get off!" she squealed, jerking her head away. "What the hell do you think you're doing?"

22

"Sorry. I just wanted to look at you properly... You know, you shouldn't drink alone if you can help it."

His mother, in the middle of pouring a fresh beaker of sherry, pointed at the sideboard.

"Go on, then. Get yourself a glass."

Terp was astonished to see Demelza fetch a similar beaker, have it filled to the brim, empty it with a single swig, screw up her face at the taste, slam it down on the coffee-table and indicate a desire for more. He was flabbergasted when, after half-emptying the refill, she took hold of his mother's left hand and began to tell her fortune:

"You think your life is over, but it's not by a long chalk. It's just in a kind of waiting-room. You've got an appointment with destiny, that's for certain. Maybe you arrived a bit early, or maybe destiny has been delayed, I'm not sure."

"Eh?... What are you on about?" said his mother.

He could see she was teetering between blind drunken rage and blind drunken credulity.

"I expect you've been looking forward to liver-failure, or whatever else it is you think you're going to die of."

"Don't," she sobbed, snatching her palm away and using it to hide her tears.

"Come on," cooed Demelza, embracing her. "I'm sorry I was a bit harsh... Let me finish the reading. You haven't heard the good news yet."

Mrs. Wyatt dabbed round her eyes with a tissue, blew her nose, then relinquished her hand.

"It's pretty obvious," continued Demelza. "Your son is leaving home. His room is free. You're going to take a lodger. I can see him now. He's got all his own hair, all his own teeth. He's a mature student at the university. His heart is waiting for you, just like yours is waiting for him. His name is Frank. He's a bit of alright. In fact I quite fancy him myself."

They shared a laugh at this.

"Excuse me a minute," said his mother, rising unsteadily to her feet. "I'm bursting for a tinkle."

"I didn't know you were a palm-reader," said Terp, after she was out of earshot.

"I'm not. It just makes it look more convincing."

"What? Do mean you were having her on?"

"Not at all. I saw what would happen before I looked at her palm, but I wanted her to believe it. Part of it coming true is her believing it will come true. How will she get a lodger if she doesn't advertise?"

He shook his head:

"It was all so specific. You said his name was Frank. What if it isn't?"

"Then she won't fall in love with him."

His mother returned. He allowed her to stroke his hair.

"Are you going to stay for tea?"

"We'd love to," said Demelza. "I'll give you a hand."

They disappeared into the kitchen. Terp listened to them chattering for a while, then went upstairs. He waded into his room, drew the curtains, opened the windows, surveyed the interior: half-finished bowls of cereal, set to concrete and sprouting furry mould; clothes stiff enough to qualify as armour; a pile of broken skateboard decks; sketchpads full of messy doodles; notepads full of murky poems. That existence, represented by this squalor, had ended less than three days before, yet already seemed implausible. The thousands of hours he'd spent in here could be described without précis in three words: nothing at all.

He heard the van draw up. He stood back, away from the window. He was still innocent until proven otherwise. He heard Jack come whistling quite tunefully up the path, heard the doorbell ring, then the sound of greetings and introductions. Ten minutes later he appeared in the doorway.

"They seem to be getting on pretty well," he said.

"I know. It's amazing."

"They're going at the brandy now... You got any decent boots for working in?"

"No."

"Never mind, we'll get you some... So this is it. Has anyone told the U. N.?"

"How do you mean?"

"Looks like a disaster area to me."

"Very funny... Did you find anything out?"

"Yeah. I feared the worst when I got there. There was a For Sale sign outside the house. The inside was completely bare. So I went next door. Luckily she was a nosy old biddy – she knew everything. Seems he was a bookie, supposed to be rolling in it. His wife had left him a couple of months before the burglary. He sold his betting-shop to Ladbrokes; apparently they'd been after it for ages. He's gone to Majorca to live, taking a nurse he met in the hospital. So all in all you didn't do him any harm, may even have done him some good."

* * *

That evening, on the way back, Jack pulled off the dual carriageway and drove up to the moor. The sky was bright with stars and half-moon.

"You coming, Dem?"

"No. You two go. I'll stay here. I'm still feeling a bit woozy."

"Come on. It'll clear your head... I'd prefer you did the dowsing. I think you'll be better at it than me."

"Oh, alright then," she said, grumpily.

Jack, muttering something about 'evil stuff', went round and opened the back of the van. He drew out a thin iron rod, maybe ten feet long. Then he scrabbled about among the mass of tools and timber until he found a coil of wire, about an eighth of an inch thick. He grabbed a pair of hefty pliers, cut off a three-foot strip, straightened it out against the road with a lump-hammer, cut it in half and bent a right-angle about a third of the way along each length.

"There you go," he said. "Just the job."

"What are we doing?" said Terp.

"A bit of surveying."

They walked into the wilderness, Jack leading, Terp following, Demelza dawdling behind. After half an hour they reached the rim of a deep bowl. The flattish bottom looked about a quarter of a mile in diameter. They went down until they reached the middle.

"Alright," said Jack, handing the wire rods to Demelza. "Do your stuff, woman."

They followed the direction suggested until the ground had risen to about forty-five degrees. Jack began penetrating the heather and topsoil with the iron rod. He made numerous attempts in a fairly wide area, but nowhere did it go in further than a couple of feet before meeting granite.

"This is no good," he announced. "You shouldn't have had all that drink."

They went back to the middle. This time Jack took the dowsing rods: they now pointed in the opposite direction. But the eventual results were no better. Returning to the centre again, Jack handed the rods to Terp.

"Hold them loosely. Clear your mind and let them do the thinking. Let them tell you what we want to know. We're looking for deep soil. Deep soil."

Terp held his arms outstretched in front of him. He felt the rods begin to move. He followed them round until eventually they settled on a direction roughly in between the previous two.

Now, after a couple of failures, the iron rod began to penetrate for the whole of its length.

"Great," said Jack. "This is it. Well done, boy."

"Beginner's luck," said Terp.

CHAPTER FOUR

"THIS country stinks," said Jack. "This whole fucking world stinks."

Terp grinned into his sandwich. Jack's militant alienation always inspired and baffled in equal measure.

"Respect to the travellers. Respect to the tepee-dwellers. At least they're trying. But they've still got economic ties. They're still parasites on the stench. We're after total secession."

Terp nodded, his mouth full of bread and cheese. Although he wasn't sure whether they'd ever really migrate to the moor or whether the obstacles would prove too daunting, he'd go along with anything Jack prescribed, trusting him to be infallible. Jack's present life here in Paignton seemed centred, rooted, virtually idyllic, so his determination to terminate it became all the more incongruous and all the more infectious. They'd been working together for a month now, during which Terp had been constantly amazed by the warmth Jack engendered in almost everyone they'd come across. At first he'd assumed that this kind of belonging, which he'd never experienced himself, must be a property of every small town, but soon came to believe that Paignton was a special case, a special place, different in kind from other resorts, and that its inhabitants were peculiarly blessed.

"I don't feel the people who originally went up there were driven by fear," Jack continued. "...Of strangers, of stronger strangers. I think they were drawn by the moor itself, which yearned for someone to appreciate its sacred places... Not that I particularly trust the type of person who goes about saying 'wow' to stone circles... Golden ages can't always be in the past, can they?"

"Of course not. If they were, we'd all have to become archaeologists."

They were sitting on a stack of plasterboard in an extension to a house on the outskirts. Jack had been working here in spasmodic bursts for the past two years. The plan was to finish up all existing work before they began excavations on the moor. New jobs could be declined with difficulty, as Jack had never said no before, but it was impossible to prevent the whimsical expansion of existing jobs. Sentences beginning with 'Would you just...' or 'Could we have...' were commonplace, and since the clients were all friends or relatives, or friends of relatives, or relatives of friends, Jack felt obliged to comply. Nevertheless, as a result of hard graft and long hours, the number of jobs was slowly beginning to shrink.

They'd finished eating their lunch and were just enjoying the last few sips of tea when they became aware of a powerful smell accompanied by wreathes of smoke coming in through the doorless doorway.

"Must be a skunk outside," said Terp.

A moment later the skunk leaped into the room in the form of a small dreadlocked white man with a huge grin on his face and a huge joint in his hand.

"Ah, caught you!" he shouted. "Skiving again, you lazy buggers"

"Don't talk to me about skiving," said Jack, jumping up and hugging him. "We've been at it since seven this morning."

"Yeah, sure. I know your sort. You charge by the hour then sit around smoking dope and spouting philosophical gibberish."

The skunk spoke with some kind of Scottish accent

"Don't give other people your own addled brains. I haven't even had a single drag since I saw you last."

"You won't believe this, but neither have I. We only got this stuff last night on the way down. The tribe we were with in Wales was pretty strict about the herb. We've just been living as simply as we can... Kind of rehearsing for the future."

"Good," said Jack. "So do you think you can do it? Go forever without the herb, without the Special Brew, without the schoolgirls?"

"No problem. I don't need nothing. I'm not sure about Rhiannon, though. You know what a hedonist she is."

They shared a laugh at this last remark, then he gave the joint to Jack and came over with grimy hand outstretched:

"You must be Terp. I'm Glen. I heard you got swallowed and made the jump. I'm stoked for you, man. Put it there."

From beneath an amazingly emaciated jumper he produced a sabre-tooth on a silver chain. Terp reciprocated with his own, leaning forward to allow the two teeth to entwine.

"It's great you've come now," said Jack, passing the joint to Terp with dragon-plumes emerging from his nostrils. "It's time to start learning the language. It's no good just being able to speak it. We got to be able to think in it."

"Think in it?" queried Glen. "Are we going to carry on thinking?"

"I'm being realistic. It may be impossible to stop."

"We won't need to think, because we're going to be thought."

"That follows," Jack nodded. "We won't need to dream, because we're going to be dreamed."

"Right. And we won't need to smoke, because we're going to be smoked."

"Yep. And we won't need to drink, because we're going to be drunk."

Terp decided to risk a contribution:

"We won't need to eat, because we're going to be eaten."

They both stared pokerfaced at him as if he'd said something crass and irrelevant, then bellowed with laughter.

"Good one," said Glen. "Except that if you're going to be eaten you ought to eat, otherwise you won't make a very good meal."

Terp looked down. Oceans of self-pity beckoned him, but he decided not to bathe.

Glen yawned:

"Listen, I've got to crash. I've been driving that bloody heap all night and most of the morning."

So he curled up in the corner while they put in the noggins between the ceiling joists, oblivious to the sawing, the hammering, the swearing, the singing, the joking. Nor did he stir when the two little girls of the house came home from school and charged into the extension full of high-pitched exuberance; when they plaited his dreadlocks, tweaked his nose-ring, rubbed sawdust into his jumper, tied his bootlaces together.

"Who is this?" said the younger one, after about half-an-hour, once Glen's properties as a plaything had been exhausted.

"Oh, just a stray cat," said Jack. "We're going to take him home with us tonight."

"He's not a cat."

"He is. He looks a bit like a man, but he's really a big cat in disguise. That's why he's sleeping on the floor. Do you know what a disguise is?"

"Something that makes you poorly?"

"No," laughed Jack. "That's a disease. A disguise is like when you wear a mask."

"I've got a tiger mask," said the older one. "It makes me feel poorly."

"That's probably because it's made of something nasty. No, a really good mask fits so well you don't notice it."

They proceeded to feel all round Glen's face for the join, even pinching his skin. Still he did not stir.

* * *

That night Terp was bemused to find himself sitting on the sofa with Rose's left hand in his right hand. They'd left off speaking some ten minutes before, yet the silence which surrounded them showed no signs of discomfort, seemed to relish its self-sufficiency. Apart from the oasis which her hand contained, the house was deserted. Everyone else had driven off to a pub to meet some friends of Glen's, who might be likely candidates. As the front of Jack's van could take no more than four and the back was impenetrable, Terp had volunteered to stay behind; Rose likewise. He'd seen her a few times over the past month, although only in company. He'd grown to like her without feeling any profound attraction, his romantic faculties having been fully occupied with worshipping at the foot of Demelza's plinth. But now Rose's hand drew him back to the night in the cavern, to the goldfinches, and forward to the prospect shimmering just above the horizon, the possibility of love.

Earlier, after the six of them had eaten together, Jack had conducted a semi-serious discussion about their future. Although the optimal matrix was octagonal, four of each gender, they mustn't use their present deficit as an excuse for procrastination. There was no doubt that the other two already existed; whether they arrived sooner or later, together or apart, was immaterial. So the eclipsing of English by Cornish should begin right away. He'd been through the dictionary and blacked out the words they would not need. Since Cornish was a dead language, there were many ways of resurrecting it as a vocal entity. To avoid arbitrariness, he proposed that they adopt the Welsh system of pronunciation, as the two languages were related, and as Rhiannon had been brought up bilingual in North Wales. Her parents had learned Welsh from their parents and so on, in an unbroken line back to whenever. Therefore her speech was authentic and she would be their teacher. He hoped the language would eventually become less of a tool than an outlet. The mushroom communicated without speaking, so they also should aspire to muteness. He himself would be happy never to say another word. At this he'd been greeted by various expressions of incredulity. How would he lay down the law? Glen had enquired. He'd pretended to resent the implication. For a start, any law worth obeying could lie down perfectly well on its own. And law which could only be mediated through the voice would always run the risk of distortion by subjective influences. His ideals were muteness, thoughtlessness, leaderlessness. What would then be left but the core, containing the seeds of a new way of life, discontinuous with the rest of human history? They might not reach it fully themselves, but the next generation would know nothing else.

CHAPTER FIVE

A SINGLE-SEATER Air Force jet is plunging towards the clouds. The pilot gives up hope of regaining control. He ejects. His parachute opens and he descends in comparative silence.

He lands on the moor. Visibility is about twenty yards. A couple of small, bulbous-bellied ponies move away from him. A few sheep look across without curiosity and then return to their grazing. He releases his harness, removes his helmet. He tries to activate his homing-beacon, finds that it is unserviceable.

A number of people materialise single-file from the mist. They come straight towards him and yet when they arrive they don't address him directly but carry on talking among themselves in a language of which not one word or even intonation is familiar. They're all fairly young, fairly dirty; dressed in greens, browns and blacks – military-mediaeval fashion. They fold up his parachute. They beckon him to follow them. He asks who they are. They smile in a friendly way but don't reply.

They move with lithe, springy steps. He hobbles along behind, his back sore from the ejection, his ankles sore from the landing. Towards the bottom of the slope a door – covered with tufts of grass and therefore previously invisible – is pulled open. Before he has time to react he is grabbed and pushed inside. The door is slammed in his face and barred. He hammers and hollers, unhinged by what has happened. After ten minutes or so he slumps to the floor.

There is a little light squeezing in between the grass-shutters covering the window, enough for him to now realise that he isn't alone. He crawls over to the corner, ignites his lighter, reveals a frightened face surrounded by a mass of sheepskins and hair.

"Hello," he says.

No response.

"What's going on here?"

She shakes her head.

There are candles by her side. He lights one. He feels in his flying-suit and brings out a bar of bitter-dark chocolate (part of his survival kit). He offers her a chunk. She accepts and eats.

"Don't worry," he says. "A bunch of miserable peasants like these aren't going to hold us for long."

He unzips more pockets, producing maps, a compass, a multipurpose knife etc. These he hides beneath the sheepskins.

"Tonight," he says. "We'll wait until they're asleep and then we'll get out."

She shakes her head again.

"Why not?"

She reveals her ankles, encased in mud-casts.

"Broken?"

She nods.

The door opens and a couple of the troupe (one male, one female) enter. They carry dried grass, peat blocks, a bowl of steaming meat. They address her in their tongue. She answers with apparent fluency. For about five minutes the pilot looks on in amazement. Then he makes a run for the door. The female casually reaches out, grabs his wrist and turns him through the air onto his back. he lies there groaning with pain and humiliation. She kneels above him, smiling and shrugging as if to say that she hadn't meant to hurt him. They go out. The door is barred again.

The woman asks him if he's alright. This is the first time she spoken in English.

"I'll live," he replies, dourly. "... How come you're speaking now?"

"They've given me permission."

"That's very good of them."

"They saved my life."

34

"Well, they didn't save mine. I could have been home by now."

"You'd never have made it. You'd just have walked round and round in circles until you were exhausted."

He laughs incredulously:

"Not with a compass, I wouldn't."

"Your compass won't help you if you don't know where you are in the first place."

"Of course it can. You just decide on a course and then follow it. The moor isn't that big."

She shrugs:

"Try it if you like."

"Don't worry, I will... But what about you? Are you a prisoner here, or what?"

She thinks for a while:

"I'm a prisoner in that I couldn't go back if I wanted to. I'm not a prisoner in that I don't want to go back."

"What's that supposed to mean?"

"It's a long story."

"Tell me. I've got plenty of time. It's not even dark yet."

* * *

She talked while he set and lit the fire, while he reviewed his own events. He'd never know what had gone wrong, could only suspect a bird-strike. He hadn't ejected before. The aircraft had certainly carried on into the sea. No-one would have seen his parachute, because of the low cloud: he'd be assumed dead. People who did eject were often looked upon with some mistrust: are you sure you did everything you could before you consigned n million pounds' worth of hardware to the sea-bed? He'd been in voluntary spins, of course, but this one hadn't resembled any of those. What if it had hit something? There'd be no medals for sinking a ship, even if it were laden down with Japanese cars. He'd abandoned at the lowest possible altitude. He knew he

35

was blameless, but no-one else knew – he'd lost radio-contact.

At the same time he was listening to her describe how she'd got here. She must have been pretty unbalanced to start with. A few months before, she'd driven to Newton Abbott railway station and left her car there. She'd then taken a bus up to Dartmoor with the intention of literally walking herself into the ground. She'd had enough of everything and totally intended to die. It had been neither a cry for help nor an act of revenge. She'd wanted her husband to believe that she'd run away. If he knew she'd committed suicide he'd blame himself, whereas if he thought she'd run away he'd be able to blame her and hopefully get over it a lot quicker.

She'd walked until she was exhausted and then she'd lain down to wait for the chill of the night to finish her off.

The next thing she knew she was here in this shelter. The peat-fire was flickering and Demelza was sitting at her feet. For a while she really believed she'd died and been resurrected in a different world, or a different era. Although they treated her with kindness and gentleness they wouldn't speak to her, didn't even appear to understand her questions.

The first day and night she slept between sips of mutton-broth. The second morning she felt well enough to sit up when Demelza and Jack came in. They brought with them a black, steel, padlocked box. They set it down beside her, handed her the key. Inside, she found a Cornish-English dictionary, a couple of phrase-books, a grammar, some original texts. They indicated that she was to immerse herself in study.

"... They gave me this as well," she said, producing a piece of card from beneath the sheepskins and handing it to the pilot. "It was my first assignment - to find out what it said."

The card was ornately bordered with botanical motifs. In the middle were two words, hand-written in red and gold capital lettering:

DYNARGH DHYS

So what? thought the pilot.

"So what does it mean?" he said.

"It means 'you are welcome'. It meant I was welcome. You can't imagine how I felt when I understood. To be welcome. Nothing else. Just welcome... The possibility of belonging... I set to work with real enthusiasm, like I hadn't felt for years. Learning the language was the best therapy I could have been given – instead of thinking a lot of useless and feeble thoughts, which was what I had been doing, I had something concrete, something specific to get my teeth into... All those chewy consonants... I used to love languages when I was at school-"

"But why Cornish?" interrupted the pilot. "We aren't even in Cornwall."

"I think they felt it was the only language which had any claim to be indigenous to the peninsular. It would provide a direct link to the land. But the main thing was to get away completely, not just to cut themselves off from society in space and feeling, but in time and thought as well. That's why they're so strict about not speaking a word of English – in the end it'll just wither away until it's completely forgotten."

The pilot shook his head. It might have crossed his mind that this desire to isolate themselves was in some way similar to his own ambition, which had always been to fly; but if the comparison existed it remained trapped beneath the surface. He was only conscious that these people weren't even worth despising.

The hierarchy over which he'd crowed in the twenty odd years since receiving his wings was indisputable. Now, a navigator (a man with only one wing) was always worth looking down upon. Medical officers and chaplains (men without wings) occasionally attained the standards demanded by his contempt. As for civilians, they didn't enter the picture. If he was forced to consider them he might assume they possessed petty little hierarchies of their own in which to coalesce, but these people here, these layabouts, these outlaws, these dregs, were beyond even that pale...

"For ages I did nothing else except learn," she continued. "They helped me with the pronunciation side – Rhiannon especially was so patient. And the more I learned the more I understood what they were doing here, and the more I understood the more attracted I felt. There was nothing for me to look back on with any regret. They positively wanted me to join them. They didn't look at my arrival as an accident. Of all the thousands of uninhabited square miles the fact that I'd walked here and collapsed, so the next morning they saw me – or rather they didn't see me but four or five sheep huddled together in a way that looked strange and when they came up to investigate they discovered that the sheep were surrounding me and keeping me warm – far from being an accident was simply an answer to their prayers or incantations or whatever you like to call it. You see, when they first arrived there were only six of them, but they felt they needed eight, four of each gender, as a proper foundation... Of course, now you've come they're cock-a-hoop. They told me just now how they got you."

The pilot, who'd hardly been listening, perked up:

"What was that? Say that again."

"They said they shot you down."

"Shot me down?" he exploded. "What the hell with?"

"I don't mean literally... But it's not just the land they own – it's the air above it as well. They plucked you out. They rescued your body from all the technology in which it was – what's the word? – encumbered. They sent the plane on into the sea. They brought you down safely. No-one's hurt by it, are they?"

He was now seriously concerned for her sanity.

"You don't really believe all this?"

"Why not? What other explanation is there? I'm here. You're here. If we're here we're meant to be here."

"Listen. I don't know what they've done to you, but whatever it is is not good. I'm going to get you out of here. Don't worry."

She sighed; raised her eyes to the ceiling.

"You haven't understood a word I've said, have you? I'm here because I want to be here."

She raised her arm and pulled a string which led up through a hole in the wall.

"What's that for?"

"They've got a little brass bell attached to the end of the string. I just ring it if I want anything and they come as soon as they can."

Sure enough, a couple of minutes later the door opened and Jack and Terp appeared. They exchanged a few words with her and then Terp stood between the pilot and the door while Jack pulled her upright and equipped her with the crude wooden crutches which up till now had been leaning against the wall.

"Where are you going?" said the pilot.

"For a shit, if you must know."

He winced. He wished he hadn't asked. Never before had he heard a woman refer quite so unambiguously to that particular function. But now was no time for amending or even analysing his squeamishness. As soon as they'd gone he retrieved his things from beneath the sheepskins, pocketing all except the knife. He then stood by the door on the side it opened from, pressed his back against the wall; unclasped the knife; cleared his mind for action.

He wasn't keen. The thought of stabbing another man held no attraction whatsoever. Yet he was obliged to. It was his duty as well as his right.

The door opened. The pilot held his breath. Whichever one of those scum came in first...

Nothing happened. There was no sound from outside.

What the hell were they doing?

As he turned to investigate he felt something at his throat. He started back, saw a huge blade and groaned.

This is it, he thought.

But Jack only grinned and shook his head reproachfully. Then he clasped and pocketed the pilot's knife; sheathed his own; laughed; patted the pilot on the shoulder; helped the woman back down onto her bed; went out.

The pilot sank to the floor, relieved that he hadn't had his throat cut, annoyed that he'd been outwitted.

"Did you tell him about my knife?"

"No. I forgot you had one. I would if I'd remembered. Luckily he had a feeling you might try something."

"Great," he said. "I don't believe this."

"You're not going to get away," she said, quietly. "You'll just have to come to terms with that. They couldn't afford to let you go even if they wanted to... Just think, though – in a few months you'll have forgotten all about how you feel right now. You'll be wanting to pass the test as much as I do."

"What test?" he muttered.

"There's a tor a little way from here. All you have to do is jump off it and land without hurting yourself. If you succeed, you're in."

"How high?"

"When you're up there it looks about forty feet, but it's probably no more than thirty. That's how I broke my ankles."

She paused. A look of consternation crossed her face.

"I made all the right preparations, but in the end I was too eager. I jumped too soon. I forced myself when I should have waited until it came naturally. I'll know next time."

"What? They made you jump thirty feet?"

"No-one made me do anything. They all six of them jumped before me. They all landed beautifully... I can see now why I wasn't ready – there'd have been no-one here to help you, to speak to you. I don't think you'd have had the patience to learn the language on your own. We'll jump together. By the time my ankles have mended, you'll be ready. I know you can't conceive it at the moment."

The pilot was silent. Tonight he would escape. Tomorrow he would return with police to rescue her and arrest the rest of them. He couldn't take what she said at face-value. These people were extremely sinister. They must have brainwashed her. She was lucky she hadn't broken her back. He knew all about landing on feet as well as on wheels.

"Here," she said, reaching down inside her jumper and handing him a tiny, wizened mushroom. "You probably think I'm not in my right mind, but that little person will prove otherwise."

He would have laughed if he'd been in a better mood. As it was, he merely raised his eyebrows:

"Oh yes? How?"

"It's a counterpower. As soon as I became fluent enough to understand they gave me some. I swallowed them but I didn't eat them. That's important. You don't eat mushrooms. Did you know that? Because you can't digest them. But some species have developed the ability to communicate as they pass through you."

What was she on about? He didn't care. Her words were just symptoms, of no interest except in so far as they cast light on the mechanics of her subjugation.

"They're communicating continuously, but sometimes it's easier to hear what they're saying if you swallow them."

"I see."

"Just look at that one in your hand. Look at it for a while and tell me if you don't feel anything."

He pretended to look at it.

"I don't know what you're getting at," he said, handing it back to her.

She shrugged;

"That's understandable. You're too agitated and too prejudiced at the moment. Everything it represents is meaningless to you just as everything you represent is meaningless to it... But there's plenty of time."

He gritted his teeth, turned away from her and stared into the fire.

He had to keep reminding himself that she wasn't one of them, in order not to react against her as if she were.

It was difficult, because it was like talking to two people: the person they'd deluded her into thinking she was and the person he assumed her to be – a rather weak, middle-class 'wife' who'd 'got a bit depressed'...

CHAPTER SIX

OF COURSE at first he didn't stop to consider their smell. He just dismissed it out of hand as disgusting. He'd always been something of a hygienomane. He liked to shower and change his clothes at least twice a day.

"What do you do for a wash around here?" he asked, on the first morning.

He was already beginning to itch all over.

"We don't," she replied, without any embarrassment.

"You can't be serious."

"Afraid so. You might find it unpleasant at first, but that's only because you're nervous, or wearing artificial fibres. After a while you'll begin to smell exactly how you're supposed to, how we do."

"I think I'll decide how I'm supposed to smell," he declared, pompously. "When they next come in would you ask them for soap and water, and a razor."

He'd always repressed his beard, although allowing his moustache to flourish within conventional limits.

"I'll try," she shrugged. "But it won't do any good."

He heard noises outside, accompanied by whistling. Then Terp poked his head through the paneless window; grinned; exchanged greetings with the woman; nailed some wooden battens across the frame; then came in and replaced the pane and the beading, which the pilot had removed the night before.

(For the first ten minutes, he thought he'd succeeded. He'd squeezed out under the grass-shutters and made it to the top of the slope. He'd just set off east when he was suddenly and silently surrounded by the three men. Surrender had been the only option.)

He suspected that she'd pulled the bell-string. But when he accused her she just chuckled:

"They don't need me to tell them what's happening. There's no way you're going to get out. The sooner you realise that the better."

About noon, unable to contain himself any longer, he asked her to ring the bell so he might be taken to the latrine.

On the way back he dawdled, scrutinising the environment.

They were situated near the bottom of a bowl. (Late dawns and early sunsets were the order of the day.) On the skyline he could see files of figures, silhouetted. He remembered now, from low-flying exercises, how Dartmoor, instead of being a wilderness, was invariably thronged with walkers. He'd always classified their gaudy colours as visual pollution – second only to nasal pollution in his book.

He'd never understood walking for the sake of walking. You walked to your car, from your car to the crew-room, from the crew-room to your aircraft, and that was about it.

"If we were designed to walk more than a few yards," he used to say. "We wouldn't have invented the wheel, the propeller, the jet."

And now these walkers, who were more or less insane, represented his only hope.

He ran, yelling at the top of his voice.

Jack caught him; tackled him; clamped a huge black stinking paw over his mouth.

* * *

If you can't beat them, pretend to join them.

This was the strategy which the pilot, after a few more escape-attempts, adopted.

The more amenable he appeared, the less vigilant they would be.

There was also the possibility of rescue. Having discovered that they lived entirely upon sheep, which

44

the men went out at night to kill, he felt sure it was only a matter of time before they were caught. The sheep weren't there simply to annotate the moor: they must be owned: the owners must in the end come looking for the thieves. He didn't reckon much to their converse belief, that they were protected from intrusion by an intangible wall. He thought it merely comical when she told him how the men would circumambulate the rim of the bowl, pissing every few feet in order to maintain the efficiency of this defence.

There was also the inevitability of disease. Although mutton may provide a reasonable diet for a while, deficiencies were bound to build up. As he was by far the last to arrive he'd surely be the last to succumb...

Meanwhile, he began to learn the language. Aside from showing willing it was something specific to do. Until then, when she wasn't irritating him with her lectures on the glories of mushroom-consciousness, his time had been filled with moody silences, incredulity, anger and despair; with scratching at imaginary flea-bites; with searching for imaginary lice. His only amusement had consisted in planning his revenge: prison was too good for them: he'd be doing society more of a service if he just flew over one day and bombed them all to high heaven. They were more of a threat than the Communists ever had been, than the Mohammedans ever would be.

The language was innocent. The other six were the only people in the world speaking it full-time. It was dependent upon them for this new lease of life, but that didn't make it party to their criminality. There was nothing in its grammar to encourage filth and degradation. They, including her, were his enemies. The language could be a friend; a bit of a peasant, but a friend all the same, with whom he could look forward to spending the day, with whom familiarity bred respect and, eventually, affection.

Moira declared her delight with his progress. When the casts came off her ankles, she issued him with a challenge:

"How long before you'll be fluent?"

"Why?"

"I'm dying to jump again. If I exercise properly I'll be ready in a month. Can you be fluent by then?"

"Easy," he said.

"Gans es," she corrected him.

"Gallaf, my a-yl y wul gans es," he said, after a moment's hesitation.

They laughed.

She held out her hand.

The pilot, without thinking, reciprocated.

This was the first time they'd shared a laugh, the first time they'd touched.

He recoiled immediately, but it wasn't one of those touches which die as soon as its physical components have been removed. It crept up his arm, across his chest, into his heart. Here it began to agitate subtly for a revolution in his feelings, which until now had not departed from the strictest animosity.

CHAPTER SEVEN

WHATEVER else was confused between them after the handshake, this much was settled: they would jump together: he would be linguistically qualified by the time she was physically fit.

He would jump; he would be accepted; and then he would escape. Nothing could be more straightforward, than feigning one purpose and intending another. —

So now, instead of half-heartedness, he concentrated hard upon the learning. With her enthusiastic assistance, he expanded his vocabulary, aligned his syntax, honed his pronunciation.

But as he approached fluency he discovered that the border between means and ends became less easy to maintain. The language invaded him more and more deeply. He struggled to think in English, to resuscitate concepts like 'brainwashing', but the accepted meaning was always drowned by the literal meaning, which evoked if anything a pleasant and necessary act of mental hygiene.

He conducted a daily programme for the reinforcement of her ankles. At first it wasn't that he wished her well, just that he no longer wished her ill. He couldn't see her condemned to another few months of pain and immobility. Whenever any of the others came in he was friendly and talkative and they, believing in his commitment, were friendly and gracious back. Having approved his recommendation that she needed as much calcium as she could get, one of the men would go off with a pail each night and walk miles to the nearest dairy herd. The pilot couldn't help being impressed by this sacrifice. Nor could he help being touched by the eagerness and warmth with which the dual initiation was anticipated. It wasn't just any two people who were needed, to make up the numbers, but

47

specifically himself and her, whose separate arrivals had been governed by destiny rather than by randomness.

Somewhere deep and long ago inside him they were creating the person they wanted him to be. That person would form one half of a 'breeding-pair'. Jack, he discovered, was realistic enough to realise that they weren't going to create anything genuinely aboriginal in themselves, no matter how outlandish they became. No matter how many strings they severed, some (for example, childhood and adolescence) would remain inaccessible to scissors. The best hope lay in the next generation. The babies who were born here would be the first to stand a real chance.

It was nearly October now and the bowl was often swathed in mist, so that when he went to the latrine the isolation of this place from all other places appeared even more pronounced and indisputable than when he was inside. He found he was no longer able to feel they were sinister, so much as misguided. Their beliefs were utter hogwash, yet he could almost begin to admire the sincerity and consistency with which those beliefs were held.

Now and again he would shake himself to try and disintegrate these new feelings, but his hold on convention had never been particularly strong. From as early as he could remember he'd wanted to do nothing except fly. He'd conformed, he'd allowed himself to be conditioned, for the sake of this single purpose. Before he'd flown his closest friend had been the idea of flying. Since the day of his first flight his only love had been flying itself. Although he could always respond appropriately to what the next man was saying, his sense of camaraderie had never been more than superficial. Other pilots alone commanded his respect, and even then that respect was often alloyed with questions (How much does it mean to him? How good is he at it?), rarely tempered with affection. He was forty-five now. Provided he passed his medicals he'd have at most another ten years in the air. The Service was changing. The new men were a different type altogether. They weren't inspired by the glories of flight, but by competitiveness, technology and speed. They didn't go gliding at weekends: they went jogging or shopping. They didn't drink themselves delirious in the Mess every night: they went home and watched television, or hung wallpaper, or played Mickey Mouse games with their wives. Nevertheless, despite his disinterest in the barbaric side of his occupation, despite his disappointment in what the Service had become, despite his dislike of taking orders from career-minded individuals far younger than himself, he wouldn't for a moment consider coming out unless and until he was grounded.

During the last twenty-five years he'd spent little time alone with a woman, most of his encounters having been brief and sweet. So all and every day with Moira had seemed initially far worse than solitary confinement. Yet since he'd begun pretending to tolerate her he'd found that the pretence had required less and less effort to sustain. Although she had presumably accepted the kind of partnership in which they were going to be engaged she'd never displayed the slightest hint of anticipation, for which he was grateful. At first he'd slept on the floor. After the handshake he'd moved onto the dried-moss mattress – beneath the sheepskins, but with his head at the opposite end from her head. When it grew colder it seemed silly to waste energy so he'd begun to sleep the same way up as her, still without ever touching. Then one night about a week before the jump he'd woken to find his arm around her and astonishingly no wish to remove it. The heat poured from her shoulder as though her whole body were focussing upon his palm. The smell of her, which until now he'd resolutely categorised as repellent, became a fertile pleasure to inhale, making the most irresistible perfume seem a fraud. He turned away in order to disarouse himself, to ask himself what the hell he thought he was playing at. Yet the morning brought no reversal. All day he wanted to touch her. All day he questioned her eyes and all day they answered in the affirmative. After they'd been locked up for the night they gazed for a while silently into the fire and then there on the sheepskins, with flames flickering in the fireplace and the shadows of flames dancing on the walls, they began to succumb.

They awoke as close as they'd gone to sleep. The pilot was exultant. The night had been a series of revelations. His regrets could hardly get a look in until she announced that she was pregnant. He was incredulous. When she assured him that she was sure, that a woman can know these things immediately, he felt protective and resentful, proud and guilty, wonderful and dreadful. He wanted to confess his falseness, to explain why he had to go back, yet he couldn't for fear of the consequences; so he hid his ambiguity, while she lavished him (lashed him) with all her untapped delicious tenderness and love.

* * *

The night before the jump Jack sat down with them after bringing in their meal. He began to talk about the sabre-toothed tiger. He explained that although everyone else had been swallowed without any prior inkling of its existence he didn't consider this unexpectedness to be a crucial part of the test and so he was dispensing with it in their case, to maximise their chances of success. He'd been testing the tiger more than the candidate, making sure that its presence was objective. He didn't want to be under any delusions. He felt they should all have a clear view of what was outside themselves. He described the mushrooms as 'cleg byan' (little bells). He described them as 'sylwysy' (saviours). Apparently they'd stood and watched without much enthusiasm while the so-called higher animals had evolved. For billions of autumns they saw nothing to excite their admiration, nothing which they hadn't already imagined and rejected. The mushrooms were capable of great love, but only when the sabre-tooth had begun to walk this land did they find a worthy object. From then on, whenever they saw it coming, they would swoon and beckon, but for further aeons the sabre-tooth ignored them until one day a young and curious cub happened to swallow a few. After this first consummation the mushrooms were laughing. The sabre-tooth's dreams, instead of being limited to rehearsals of its hunts, were invaded by other realms, where food was not an issue. These realms, greener than any visible green, brighter than any reflected light, the mushrooms offered to the sabre-tooth, to rule over. In the end they loved it to extinction. But it would have become extinct anyhow. This way, instead of disappearing, the sabre-tooth could live on in the mushrooms, could stalk the realms which the mushrooms contained, could become divine, could become in truth the local god, the god of the peninsular, in whom no-one had until now believed, yet with whom it was possible to achieve far closer contact than any other god alive. Between the sabre-tooth's extinction and now the mushrooms had waited patiently for the right people to come along. Sometimes they'd be taken up by minorities; even today plenty of people out there were gobbling them down by the handful. Maybe some had caught glimpses of the sabre-tooth, maybe not. He supposed not. He knew from experience that they were mostly the wrong people, at worst looking for kicks, at best imagining the mushrooms to be a mere tool, a key which might unlock something valuable inside themselves. Whereas it was the other way around. The person contained the key; the mushroom the door. There was nothing worth unlocking inside anyone. It was the greatest error to mistake the mushroom's consciousness for your own unconscious. But they weren't mean. No matter how insulted they might be by these attitudes, they'd give everyone something, even if it was only a bad time. In order to receive the sabre-tooth you had to make yourself worthy of it, you had to sacrifice yourself to it, you had to allow it to eat you. After that you'd be able to do everything it could do; you'd have access to everywhere it had access to. In being eaten by it you'd inherit its strength, its awareness, its suppleness, its springiness and all the realms of its dreams. But you had to give yourself up completely. You mustn't jump with hope. You mustn't jump with courage. You must jump with despair. You must jump as a victim. Moira's mistake the first time around had been too much of both courage and fear. Her fear of the drop had been so great she'd used her courage to override it. She'd jumped too soon, before the sabre-tooth was ready to catch her. Tomorrow they must stand on the edge and wait and not care what had gone before and not care what was to come...

Since he'd started speaking Jack had looked neither at Moira, nor at the pilot, but only into the fire. Much of the time his eyes had been half-closed. His voice had grown quieter and slower. All that could be heard now was an indescribable low noise – not quite a hum, not quite a purr. Then the eyes closed fully and stayed closed and the noise ceased. He was lying on his side, on his elbow, on the sheepskins, utterly still.

"Esos ta ow leverel ny goth dhyn stryvya?" said Moira. (Do you mean we must not strive?)

No response.

"My a dyp ef yw a gusk," she whispered. (I think he's asleep.)

The pilot wasn't so sure. He hadn't seen anyone sleep with their head erect before. Yet if he was asleep...

The door was unbarred.

The pilot stood up, took a few test steps.

Jack didn't move.

Then Moira reached out and took his hand. This threw him. He saw in her eyes pure love, fidelity, a lifetime's companionship – not the remotest suspicion of his intentions. And anyway, if he failed, the consequences would be disastrous. He smiled down at her, went over to the fire, stoked it, replenished it with a few peat blocks. As he returned Jack sprang to his feet, looked hard into the pilot's eyes, grinned, nodded, squeezed his shoulder. Then he embraced Moira and left.

They began to discuss the information they'd been given. Of course the pilot couldn't express the full spectrum of his reactions. He must confine himself to the narrow band which corresponded with her enthusiasm.

* * *

They were woken at the crack of dawn. Each was given a handful of fresh wet *sylwysy* and a bladder of water. The pilot didn't swallow them: he hid the masticated mass beneath his tongue and between his lower teeth and cheeks before taking a drink. Then he followed her outside to where the rest of the troupe were waiting. They set off up the side of the bowl. The mist was thick. The pilot prayed that it would not lift. When they reached the rim and began to walk on level ground she threaded her arm through his. He wanted to push her off. He couldn't bear it. He couldn't bear how much she meant to him, how much the new life inside her meant, how little they both must mean. The mulch in his mouth tasted unfriendly. It tasted of all the bad decisions he'd ever made. It tasted of burning bridges.

They came to the tor. The others wished them luck. Moira led the way. The pilot concentrated on quelling his vertigo. He hated any kind of climbing. Three rungs up a ladder had always seemed far more perilous than thirty thousand feet. At the top she saw his fear and offered to go first. She stood dead still on the edge for a couple of minutes before disappearing. He peered over. She was on her feet: laughing, shouting, beckoning. He raised his right hand. Then he stepped back, scrambled down the other side of the tor and ran for his life.

CHAPTER EIGHT

HE was overheating. There was a terrible stitch in his left side. After a couple of miles he collapsed. If they found him now they could have him.

When he'd recovered his breath a little, he looked around. The scene reminded him of where he'd come down: the same high plateau, the same soft mist, the same vague ponies. Only this time, no-one appeared. Either he was being pursued inefficiently, or not pursued at all. He began to realise that he might have succeeded but, instead of exuberance, felt bewilderment.

His immediate future ought to have been clear. He must get off the moor. He must go to the police. He must return to his station and explain to the C.O. what had happened. The first stage was easy enough: he still had his compass: knowing that he was nearer the eastern edge, he began to walk east.

Although his feet seemed convinced, his sympathies had already set off in the opposite direction. This should have been a day of glory for Moira, but his cowardly refusal to follow her down must have instantly eclipsed her joy in achieving the jump. His guilt and sadness were colossal. She wouldn't understand. He hardly understood himself. They might be captured. They might corroborate his story. Yet he could still so easily be barred from further flying: he could be distrusted; he could fail his medical. Even if he was lucky, what would the remainder of his career boil down to? A few hundred hours in the air, at most. He was giving her up for that. He knew there was no question of having both. She might forgive him for not jumping. She would never forgive him for betraying them.

He tried to admonish himself for oversentimentality, but he couldn't help it. He hadn't before felt such closeness to another being, hadn't even imagined such tenderness was possible. The voice that was calling to him came not only from back there through the mist but from deep within his soul. All the skies he'd ever shot across were now infused with her; all his take-offs somehow take-offs towards her; all his landings landings upon her...

After an hour or so he came out beneath the mist, began to approach farmed land. Below huddled a higgledy little town, looking like so many sweepings just shovelled down off the moor and left at the lowest point. He found a road and descended further. The sign at the outskirts said: ASHBURTON. He remembered that this was where she'd lived with her barren husband. One of these grey peripheral houses might have been theirs. No wonder she'd got so depressed, he thought, unable to understand how she'd stuck it out as long as she had. But then all civilian existence except the purely rural was incomprehensible to him.

People stared as he walked along the main street. He caught sight of himself in a shop window: his hands, his flying-suit, were streaked with dirt. His beard, his hair, his eyes, were wild. He ducked into a public lavatory and washed his upper half as best he could with cold water and liquid soap. He was vainly attempting to wipe his suit clean with his cravat when he felt something unexpected in the breast pocket. It turned out to be a debit-card. He frowned with astonishment. How the hell did that get there? he wondered, thinking back to the day of his last flight. There was no explanation except absentmindedness, perhaps combined with prescience. The card certainly made a lot of difference to his present dilemma. The postponement of a decision was now possible.

He found the kind of shop he was looking for. It sold sturdy clothes, camping equipment etc.

"Can I help you?" said a woman, with disdain in her voice and disgust upon her neatly stencilled face.

He coughed and produced his suavest timbre, his plummiest accent:

"Please excuse my appearance, but I've just been survival training on the moor. I missed the other chaps I was supposed to be meeting up with so I've got to make my own way back. I need some clothes for a start..."

Having selected boots, socks, vest, longjohns, shirt, trousers, jumper, jacket and hat he took them into the cubicle provided and drew the curtain.

He emerged in shades of green and brown.

"They'll do fine. I'll keep them on, OK?"

To these purchases he now added spare underwear, a knapsack, a box of candles, an Ordnance Survey map.

"I think that's just about it."

While she was putting the card through the machine he felt as though he were committing a serious fraud, and yet the money which would be drawn upon was his, had been honestly earned in the service of Her Majesty. Nevertheless his unease affected his hand, which wrote a signature so unlike the one on the card that she compared them with reluctant suspicion.

"I'll just have to make a phone call," she said.

"Sure," he shrugged, although he really just wanted to snatch the card and run.

This illusion, that he was impersonating himself, was persistent. He could only put it down to the disorientation produced by his months of captivity.

When she returned she asked for his address. As soon as he mentioned the words 'Officers' Mess...' she relaxed. She wanted to make the sales as much as he wanted to make the purchases. They both knew that any quarter-witted criminal would have practised the signature assiduously beforehand.

Having stuffed all his dirty clothes except the flying-suit into a litter-bin he went along to the hotel and took a room for the night.

* * *

It was the longest, hottest, weirdest, saddest bath of his life. All that was left of her, all that had migrated from her skin to his, was now adulterated with soap and shampoo and diluted with water. So alienated did he become that for a few moments he left his body and looked down upon it from the ceiling through a film of condensation. This event worried him. He'd seen himself without a mirror before, but only when flying. He'd sat on the wing of the aircraft and felt neither wind nor cold, an experience he'd marvelled at until the shell in the cockpit had urged him back. For all he knew this was a common occurrence, although he'd only heard one other pilot mention it when drunk. But then to talk about such extreme detachment would be to advertise a potentially disastrous incompetence. The closest legitimate activity was gliding, where you were accompanied by no more than a slight and constant whoosh. It was quite acceptable to declare that gliding was real flying and powered flight crass by comparison. It was also acceptable for aircrew to dismiss parachutists as idiots. Whether they 'free-fell' or 'broke their fall' or 'slowed their fall', all they ever did was fall. He'd once been compelled to go on a parachute course himself. The total lack of vision in the eyes of the instructors had appalled him as much as the absurdity of climbing a tower and leaping from the top. He'd detested and feared every minute of it. The practise of jumping voluntarily, in cold blood, when there was no emergency, let alone for fun, had always seemed to him demented. Whereas in a glider your compromise with gravity was of a different order – although you always fell in the end, in the meantime you could climb. He tried to remember exactly what gliding was like, but all he could see in his mind's eye were buzzards – the way they'd soared and miaowed above the bowl while he'd stood at the window of the cell, peering up through the grass-shutters.

He emerged from the bath white and wrinkled; dressed; went down to the bar; had a few drinks; went into the restaurant; had a good meal; went back to the bar; had a few more drinks; went to bed.

The inner warmth induced by alcohol and food, the outer comfort produced by sheets and blankets and radiators, were nothing compared to the bleakness created by her absence. When he thought of alternatives (his room back in the Mess, any room anywhere in the world) he couldn't conceive of them being less desolate. The damp, dirty, dark cell had already, although less then sixteen hours ago, become paradise.

* * *

In the morning he made a few phone calls from the Yellow Pages; paid his bill; went to the bank; bought some oranges; took a taxi to the so-called 'Flysport Centre'; asked the driver to wait.

Twenty minutes later he emerged with a blue plastic cylinder about seven feet long and eighteen inches in diameter, which they managed to fit in between front windscreen and rear window. He showed the driver the place on the map where he wished to be dropped and then got into the seat behind him.

For once the western sky was clear, the pressure high, the breeze easterly.

"How'll you get back?" said the driver, staggered by the amount of change he'd been told to keep.

"Don't worry – I'm meeting some people up here."

"See you again."

The pilot grinned. As the taxi turned around a voice in his head was saying 'this is stupid' – a tiny voice, easy to ignore.

He shouldered the cylinder and marched swiftly away from the road.

Two hours later he was crawling through the heather towards the west rim of the bowl and peering over and realising for the first time just how well-camouflaged they were because it took an effort, despite the perfect visibility, to convince himself that there was a settlement down below.

He opened the cylinder and assembled its contents into the simplest flying-device ever invented, otherwise known as a hang-glider.

* * *

Terp was squatting red-faced over the latrine when he saw the delta silhouette circling above – an instant laxative. He divined either a monstrously mutated buzzard or some uncategorised primitive creature as he ran to rouse the others. They emerged dreamy-eyed from their noon naps. Their reactions ranged from fear to defiance. Moira, who came out last, was the only one able to recognise what they saw. Her face changed from white to red; all the lines which had sloped wanly downwards now sprang back into life.

As he began to descend the host of small birds which had been mobbing him dispersed. He landed running on the far slope, unshackled his harness and carried on towards them.

She came to meet him halfway with her forgiveness. They returned arm in arm. The others hung back, apparently waiting to see what attitude Jack was going to take.

Jack asked him where he'd been.

"Ashburton," said the pilot, grinning.

"Fatel wreta omacontya?"

(What have you got to say for yourself?)

The pilot explained that he'd never meant to escape; he'd only meant to evade the jump; without wings he suffered from the most dreadful vertigo; the only qualm he'd had about staying had been the loss of all opportunity for flight; and now he'd solved that problem. Couldn't they make an exception in his case?

Jack was silent for a while. In front of him Moira pleaded with her eyes. Behind him the votes were mostly in favour.

"Ny a vyn predery adro dhodho. Ty a yl godryga rak tro."

(We will think about it. You can stay for the time being.)

The pilot assured them that they wouldn't regret it.

After he and Moira had gone off to consummate their reconciliation the other six crowded into Jack and Demelza's cell, where they all lay down. The meeting was for the most part silent. Jack had always encouraged them to discredit thought and discussion, to trust the bright red caul by which they were surrounded. Anyway, it was obvious what had happened. The pilot had intended to escape. The mushroom had brought him back. His return hadn't surprised them, so much as the method. It seemed he'd been swallowed by a buzzard instead. It seemed the mushroom had listened sympathetically to his desire for wings rather than forelegs, lightness rather than power. Who were they to question such compassion? The alternatives were unpalatable: they must either kill him now or build a separate cell for him and lock him up in it for the rest of his life. Besides, their prime hope lay in the unborn, and as Moira was the only one who'd so far succeeded in becoming pregnant her equilibrium was paramount. (The way she'd behaved during his absence had not augured well for the rest of her term.)

The meeting was dissolved, having sanctioned two simple decisions: the pilot was to be admitted to their midst; rabbit was to be added to their diet.

* * *

He lay awake after Moira had drifted into jellysleep, from where she issued occasional half-moans which spoke of contentment, love and security. Inside him steam condensed into liquid, liquid relapsed into ice. He was aghast at the enormous insanity of what he'd done. When he reviewed his actions it seemed as though they'd been committed by someone else. Having absorbed him, she'd split him, ejecting the part of him which was riddled with doubt and deceit. He wanted to rouse her. He wanted to talk. But he knew she hadn't slept while he'd been away, that all last night and this morning she'd quivered in a siren state. Now she'd cancelled the spell by which she'd automated him. He was free to lie there frozen with disbelief. He was free to panic. Yet he remained aware of the one who was still inside her, who was exploring further into her jungle, who was sheltered by her sunspeckled canopy, who was supported by her pulsating earth, who was swathed in her dark green light.

He shivered.

CHAPTER NINE

THE cell which had been their prison was now their home. Winter hovered beyond the bowl: the last mushrooms had been gathered, dried and stored; the first snows had already attempted to settle on the tors. Moira was beginning to swell. The rift in the pilot had healed. Her eyes were now his only thirst, her breasts his only hunger, her hands his only prayer, her lips his only law. He was with her as much as he could, because he loved being with her, yet when he was compelled to be away from her he hardly felt less complete. Wherever he went, whatever he was doing – searching for firewood, digging for peat, setting or emptying snares, flying the hang-glider, collecting the idiosyncratic herbal delicacies which her body demanded – a constant glow radiated from his solar plexus.

His doubts had migrated gradually, the first exodus taking place during the 'Kern', held in Jack and Demelza's cell a few days after his return. The ceremony, celebrating the final achievement of their octagonal matrix, had been silent and simple. They had each slit their wrists in turn and bled into a copper dish. The dish had then been passed from mouth to mouth.

The pilot was the last to drink. He hesitated. He fought to quell his revulsion. The small amount of blood left seemed to be visibly quivering with all sorts of lethal diseases. And yet Moira was already contaminated. Realising that he had no desire to live a minute longer than her, he screwed up his eyes and swallowed.

Once he was confident he wouldn't vomit he lay back. He felt light, as though embedded in a cloud rather than a sheepskin. Moira's body was to his right, Demelza's to his left. Their heat ignited him. If he closed his eyes he could feel them in bright tints of red. If he opened his eyes the darkness swirled with conflagration. His prejudices against Demelza surrendered, and hence his prejudices against Jack, against Rose, against Terp, against Rhiannon, against Glen. The distinctions between himself and them seemed no longer worth maintaining. At first he thought he might be feverish, but then this weak hypothesis was swept away by a series of revelations beyond dispute: they really were at the beginning of something discontinuous: a positive catastrophe had taken place, leaving them absolved from the rest of human history, future as well as past: whatever happened to them hereafter their life here was already endless.

He'd always vaguely suspected the tradition he'd inherited, but had never been perceptive enough or curious enough to find the fault. Now he knew. The complex of ideas which had spread from the Middle East like some dismal imperialism should have stayed in the Middle East. It didn't apply here. Their own tradition – suppressed, preserved, untapped – awaited them.

All this he seemed to grasp in an instant. Energy effervesced inside him. He wanted to run and leap and yell. He sat up. To his astonishment everyone else sat up as well, each to their own astonishment, and even while they were all laughing at this coincidence of motive they were jumping to their feet and charging through the doorway and streaming out over the bowl.

They reached the plateau still exulting. Jack caught up with one of the scattering ponies, grabbed its mane and rode around shrieking until it tossed him off. He landed in a heap of mirth, emerged with flailing arms. They carried on east towards an intermittent moon. They reached a vantage point from where they could watch the lights glistening all the way across the belowlands to the sea. These lights meant nothing to them. They turned away and ran back into the moor. When eventually the energy subsided they lay down on the vast mattress of heather and slept.

* * *

The pilot was now known as 'Bargos', or 'Barg' for short. He'd learned how to trap rabbit on survival courses, so he was happy to gain exemption from sheep-stabbing by putting this skill into practise. About a fortnight after the *omgemysky* (mingling) he'd been on his way to check one of his snares when he noticed a buzzard standing nearby. His first reaction was annoyance. He realised there was a possible flaw in his method: local raptors, instead of having to dive on the living, could simply land next to the dead or dying.

He was amazed the buzzard hadn't taken off. He knew them to be extremely wary. He'd never come closer than twenty yards to one before, yet now he was near enough to see a rabbit strangled in the trap – otherwise untouched. The bird stood motionless, its head turned away from the rabbit, apparently watching him with its right eye. He challenged himself to see just how close he could get. He became soft and slow, oozing forwards as imperceptibly as possible.

He might even be able to stroke it. He began to put out his left hand. The buzzard still showed no sign of apprehension. Perhaps there was something wrong with it? Then, just as his fingertips were about to reach its throat, the beak came down hard on the underside of his wrist, tearing off the scab which had formed over the cut made two weeks before, unleashing a gush of bright blood. He jumped back with a yelp, but his anger died as he saw the buzzard wipe its beak across its breast, saw a thin trail of his own blood spreading out pinkly as it was absorbed by the pale soft feathers.

He gripped his wrist to staunch the flow and lay down on his back to watch the majestic helix with which the buzzard was now inscribing the sky.

* * *

A few days after this personal confirmation Barg had been out again marching through the shrouded afternoon when a big cat emerged from the mist on his left, bounded along softly and quickly in front of him and disappeared into the mist on his right. At first this manifestation merely reminded him of the stories which abounded around each of the three moors on the peninsular. Many sightings of outsize cats had been claimed, but the scanty photographic evidence was at best inconclusive. Only later did he deduce that he'd seen their tiger, the most contentious of the premises he'd been expected to accept.

He was now cured of all unhealthy scepticism: everything without was also within. He listened to Moira as to an oracle. He flew along in her slipstream without effort or argument. During the long evenings they sat together making rabbit-skin hats for the whole troupe and in the silence of scissoring and sowing they realised that this was it, as far as they could go, as far as anyone who still occupied a particular portion of space, who still subscribed (however loosely) to a linear theory of time, could go. Yet while they thus hovered on the edge of divinity, they were forced to acknowledge that all was not well with the others. Rhiannon began to visit them, each night regurgitating larger and larger chunks of her unhappiness.

Glen was the cause: his eyes had become hard, his lips evasive, his cock mechanical. She wasn't even a person to him any longer, merely a receptacle into which he could deposit his daily duty. During their earlier nomadic life together, she'd tolerated his frequent diversions; at least when he'd returned to her he'd been passionate and remorseful; the good had by far outweighed the bad. But now enforced monogamy had deprived her of the good. Worse, he refused to talk about it, refused to admit that they were living anything less than the ideal life they were supposed to be living.

Barg was shocked by these disclosures, having assumed that the other pairs were as deliciously enfolded as Moira and himself. Just as he'd never before known warmth, so coldness. Besides, this kind of relationship-speak was a new experience. Perhaps the occasional fellow-officer's wife had confided her discontent to him in the past, but only as a prelude to adultery, never in such intimate detail. When Rhiannon cried, he wanted to cry too. She seemed such a waif, especially in contrast to Moira's pregnant blossoming. He wanted to hold her to him and soothe her. At the same time, he felt a small revulsion: the paleness of her face in the candlelight, the wispiness of her voice, the smell of her turmoil, kept him at arm's length. So he expressed his sympathy by means of looks and nods and murmurs. He let Moira do the talking. She advocated perseverance. Thwarted fertility could express itself in many unpleasant ways. Glen's alienation was merely biological. Conception would change everything. Once achieved, he would return to her, body and soul, for good.

Whereas Rhiannon expressed dissatisfaction with her partner, Rose, who also began coming in to see them, expressed dissatisfaction with herself. She was letting Terp down. She was letting her brother down. She was letting everyone down. The first few months had been wonderful. She had truly loved Terp, had surrendered to him with unprecedented frequency. Their lovemaking had often attained the status of sacrament. (Apparently, the mushrooms adored sex, something outside their own experience. They couldn't get enough of it - the more ecstatic the better.) But her own desire had gradually transmuted, through intermediate stages of apathy and disdain, into disgust. After all, there seemed something incestuous about their union: if Jack was in a sense Terp's father then she was in a sense his aunt. So now the only way she could continue giving herself to him was to pretend that he was Glen, who she'd long secretly fancied.

Again Moira advocated perseverance, explaining that womb could sometimes override heart, that womb unsown might quite naturally look elsewhere for seed, although she admitted afterwards to Barg that her advice was feeble and probably futile. But then what else could she say without initiating the disintegration of the troupe?

* * *

The next time he saw a buzzard close-up, they were both airborne, taking advantage of the thermal emanating from the fires below to soar above the rim of the bowl. He was astounded to glimpse the trace of red on his breast and recognise this as the same buzzard, his blood-brother buzzard, his beautiful blood-brother buzzard.

When he got back down Jack was waiting impatiently. He'd promised to let him have a go.

Jack ran down the slope and managed to get off the ground, but only briefly before crashing. He was too heavy.

"Eskelly gosek!" he shouted, when Barg reached him. (Bloody wings). "Pyw yn bys re glowas adro dhe dyger a y nyj?" (Whoever heard of a flying tiger?)

Barg laughed, seeing he was unhurt. He wanted to make some joke about the fact that he himself had been flying a jaguar when they'd shot him down, but the expression was beyond him.

CHAPTER TEN

JACK was sick. He hadn't been seen for a week, during which Demelza had headed off potential visitors to their cell by warning that he was in a deep exploratory trance and must not be disturbed, for fear that his soul be prevented from return. But her face, which each day appeared more stricken, betrayed her, until she was forced to admit the truth.

Not so long before, Barg would have rejoiced at this news; now, he became almost as distraught as the others. Jack was the mushroom pope, the vicar of tiger, from whom all their resolve derived. Weakness in one so strong could not be ascribed to a random attack by some blind bacterium. There must have been at least a tremor in the other world.

On the night of the ninth day, Demelza called everyone in. There were no candles burning, only a quiet glow from the fire, yet the changes in Jack's appearance were so extreme that they induced a collective gasp: his beard and hair white; his cheekbones and shoulderbones stark; his eyes huge and luminous.

"Oh, God," blurted Terp, "We must get a doctor."

Jack slowly shook his head. His expression conveyed condemnation of the lapse into English, dismissal of the concept of outside help, understanding of the lapse, sympathy with Terp's alarm.

He nodded to Demelza. She gently drew out his arms from beneath the sheepskins. These arms, which once might have felled whole societies, were now mere brittle twigs, their Celtic tattoos shrunken and distorted.

They all lay down around him. Rose held one hand, Terp the other; Rhiannon held one forearm, Glen the other; Moira held one upper arm, Barg the other; Demelza caressed his head.

"Da yw genef agas clowes oll," he said, his voice hardly more than a whisper yet somehow clear and strong. (It's good to feel you all.) "My a vynsa cowsel orthough kens, mes bys yn hedhyw nyns en vy sur yn py forth a vynsa mos maters... Kyn ny won vy pandra a wharfa my a vyn y dhesmygy kens pell... Ty a yl gasa cumyas pypynak uer a vynta... Ny vynta ow gasa hag yndella ny vynnaf vy dha asa. Le pypynak a wreta mos my a vyth ena dhe'th gwytha... Nyns yw hemma trajedy, ytho, na wra y wul yndella... Ny wrussyn fyllel. Ny wrussyn ma's camgemeres agan rannow... Agensow my re assayas nyja yn un ankevy nyns en vy genys ma's dhe lamma... Res yw dhym lemmyn bos genys arta dhe lamma... Lemmyn res yw dhym bos kelmys der lamma... Ues wharth wosa mernans?... Hep mar... Ow beth yw ow lesk hag ow lesk yw wherthyn..." (I would have spoken sooner, but until today I was not sure which way things were going to go... Although I do not know what has happened I will soon find out... You can leave when you want to... You will not be leaving me, just as I will not be leaving you. Wherever you go, I will be there to guard you... This is not a tragedy, so do not make it one... We did not fail. We just mistook our roles... The other day I tried to fly, forgetting that I was only born to bound... Now I must be born again to bound again... Now I must be bound by bounding... Is there laugh after death?... Without doubt... My grave is my cradle and my cradle is mirth...)

In the awful interval between the last words and the last breath, Barg saw with his own eyes, with everyone else's eyes, a white tiger arise through the sheepskins. He saw the colossal mouth half-open, to reveal gleaming teeth, glowing tongue. He saw the tiger lick Demelza hard across the forehead, then slowly turn around above them and with one leap depart airborne through the closed door.

* * *

He was the first to emerge, the first to discover that in the meantime snow had fallen and settled, enough to cover all but the tallest tufts. The cloud had cleared away, unveiling stars and half-moon. The wind had dropped to zero.

He stood in the midst of the still white glisten and felt both blessed and bereft.

Twenty feet in front of the door the virgin snow had been impregnated by paw-prints.

Terp came out and fell to his knees, his body shaken by sobs. Barg crouched down beside him and enveloped him.

* * *

When he awoke he momentarily couldn't understand why the hand he reached for felt so alien. Then he remembered what had happened. Moira had remained in vigil around the body with the others, while he had soothed Terp to sleep.

He arose quietly and went outside. The sky was again clear, the sun just beginning to peer over the rim of the bowl, but more snow had fallen overnight, obliterating the paw-prints.

After half an hour of good grief, he was joined by Moira and Demelza.

"Y a vyn mos," said Moira. (They want to go.)

He looked at Demelza for confirmation, saw the vertical scratches across her forehead, kissed her there.

"Ny allaf perthy gortos," she said, the tears glistening in her eyelashes. (I cannot bear to stay.)

He nodded.

"Pandra wren ny gans an corf?" (What about the body?)

She shrugged:

"Ny welaf ethom y remuvya." (I do not see any need to move it.)

"Na my na fella," he agreed. (Nor do I.) "Y mava yndan dhor solabrys... Nyns yw ma's mater gora an gweras yn y le... My a vyn y wul." (It is already underground... Just a matter of putting the earth back... I will do that.)

"Muer ras dhys," she said. (Thank you.)

* * *

An hour later, he stood with his arm tight around Moira, facing east. Leading away from them, a jumble of boot-prints. Halfway up the far slope, five forlorn silhouettes. Beyond the rim, the sun.

They went back to their lair, lay down together and mourned.

At dusk he arose, leaving her fast asleep. He cleared the snow and tufts from the roof of the death-cell, tore up the felt and prised off the boards. Then he began the long task of filling the cell with earth, two buckets at a time, some of it no doubt the same earth which Jack and Terp had excavated in the first place. Whenever he felt like flagging, he reminded himself that this was nothing compared with the immensity of what they'd achieved, given that all the materials needed for the construction and waterproofing of the cells had been carried three miles at night over rough terrain.

By dawn the body and the sheepskins were submerged. He replaced the boards and the tufts, camouflaged the places he'd been digging from. He estimated another six nights of similar toil before the cell was filled.

He joined Moira for breakfast, his wrists sore from the countless occasions when pick had clashed with stone. She'd heated up some mutton-stew. There was half a sheep left; after that had been devoured, they would be limited to rabbit. He looked anxiously at her, hoping that the trauma of Jack's death would not have affected her profoundly enough to hurt the unborn one. But this morning, now that she'd caught up on her rest, he could find no flaw in her blooming perfection, and indeed no chink in her cheerfulness.

Between breakfast and sleep, he fretted about the future. He half-heartedly devised a way of getting back: a story of Jack as a giant psychopath who had kidnapped them both and held them inescapably captive up here until his own death had intervened. With as reasonable an explanation as this, he would be restored to his squadron; they would be married; their child would be born under the supervision of efficient machinery and competent medics. He tried to imagine her living in quarters, mixing with fellow-officers' wives, making small-talk at dinner-parties; failed. Nevertheless, he offered her the story, adding that it wasn't what he desired; he'd already sacrificed his career for her and had no wish to undo that sacrifice; he just felt he ought to give her the choice. She laughed and refused. She wanted them to stay as long as possible. What could be better down there than up here, apart from a few physical comforts? How could they start a new life on the basis of a lie?

She seemed to have everything sorted out. They were here because they were meant to be here; they were a bridge between worlds: she, who had intended to die; he, who was officially dead; Jack, who had actually died. One day perhaps they would be forced to go down, but when they did so they would elongate, not abandon, the bridge.

In these musings of hers, which to him almost certainly corresponded with the truth, true comfort lay.

CHAPTER ELEVEN

SO they went on, through winter to spring, in a state of feline equanimity: hunting, eating, playing, grooming, sleeping, dreaming. Only when she'd entered her seventh month did he again begin to fret. His confidence, although high, might not extend as far as midwifery. It was all very well, as she advocated, relying on instinct and intuition, but when two lives were at stake he felt knowledge and experience would be more useful attributes. Cats have been known to bite through a new-born kitten's tail, mistaking it for the umbilical, and although he was unlikely to make this exact mistake he could easily make another just as catastrophic. So he began to nag and she, when the nagging did not abate, gradually shifted from vehemence to acquiescence. He promised that they would return when the baby was three months old.

So the next fine dry morning they set out, their only luggage a bladder of water and some strands of dried rabbit. They walked steadily towards the sun, with frequent rests and rubbings of her back; with feelings of astonishment when the first car passed them, of trepidation when they passed the first house.

The sun had moved round to the south-west by the time they arrived on the outskirts of Ashburton. She opened a gate; they walked up a drive; she knocked on a door. A woman appeared and frowned at them.

"Carla," said Moira.

"Moira?" said Carla, after a few moments of unrecognition. "Oh, my God. I've been so worried. I thought I'd never see you again."

After they'd hugged, Carla stepped back – to confirm with her eyes what she'd felt with her stomach.

"You're not?"

"Yes. Isn't it wonderful?"

They hugged again.

"This is Bargos."

He shook hands:

"How do you do?"

The words had slipped out of him naturally, the first he'd spoken in English for ages. But after they'd gone he wondered if he'd got them wrong. It seemed a strange way to greet someone, with an imponderable problem.

The interior of Carla's house smelled of incense, of cat-piss, of coal-smoke, of mould, of bleach, of tobacco. Carla herself smelled of hormones overlaid with rose-musk. She gave them bread and cheese and camomile tea while Moira outlined all that had happened to her since she'd 'disappeared'.

"It sounds unbelievable," said Carla, shaking her head. "...Still, I knew you weren't dead."

"What about other people? What about Tim?"

"I saw him at a party a while back. We didn't get to speak much... The bimbo he was with was all over him like a rash."

Moira smiled and sighed. There was no doubt about the genuineness of her relief.

Carla stood up:

"I hope you don't mind if I leave you for an hour or so. I've got an appointment that really can't be cancelled. Make yourselves at home... There's loads of hot water."

Although his nose had been twitching ever since he'd arrived he realised now it had only been giving him a partial picture: the two most powerful smells in the kitchen were undoubtedly those of Moira and himself.

Carla's bathroom was big and bright. They stared at themselves in the mirror and decided that radical changes were required. Their hair was so filthy and so matted that nothing could be done except cut it down as far as they could with scissors and shave the remainder.

Carla's bath was deep and long. After they'd scrubbed off most of the dirt they sat facing each other

76

and sweated out the rest. Shorn, she was even more beautiful. Her eyes, without their hair-curtains, seemed even bigger, even more magnetic; there was nowhere else to look, nowhere else to go, but into their shining darkness.

There was no interval between suddenly feeling light and finding themselves on the ceiling. They gazed down through a film of condensation upon their own heads, which from here looked like two white eggs nestling in a nest of foam.

The door opened and another head appeared, that of a blond boy. He stared transfixed and open-mouthed at the bath. They fell back into their bodies. Within a few seconds she'd gathered herself enough to smile and say:

"Hello, Jude. It's me, Moira."

The boy put his hand on his heart and sighed in a way which is sometimes transcribed as 'phew'.

"I'm sorry. Hi. I haven't seen you for ages... I thought I'd really flipped then. When I opened the door I just saw these two eggs floating on the surface."

"Only bad eggs float, Jude," she said. "We're good... So what are you on today?"

"Nothing, honest," he laughed. "I'm as clean as a whistle... Anyway, where have you been?"

"Did you miss me?"

He looked bashful, glanced at Barg.

"I did, actually. I used to enjoy talking to you."

"Yes, but did you enjoy listening to me? I seem to remember lecturing you rather too much."

"Not at all. I used to like the sense you made."

"Well, thank you... This is my new man. We've been living up on the moor, underground."

"Far out."

"Yes, it was. And now we've come back in."

"So how does it feel?"

"Alright, so far. Mind you, we only arrived a couple of hours ago."

"Will you be staying till tomorrow?"

"I hope so."

"I'll see you then, then. Could you tell Mum I've gone over to Tots and I'll be back in the morning?"

"Right... Before you go, do you think you could find us a couple of towels?"

* * *

They wandered barefoot about Carla's garden, his towel acting the part of a sarong, hers that of a sari. They'd tried nakedness for a while but, realising that they could be overlooked by neighbours, had covered up for Carla's sake. They loved the garden. Their visual diet had been limited for so long to heather and gorse, bracken and grass, that the luxuriance of species entranced them. Now, as twilight took over, things began to simplify: leaves verged on silver; flowers edged towards black. In the west a Scotch pine, silhouetted against indigo and magenta, somehow reminded them of heaven.

They heard hello being shouted. They slid back in through the French windows. Carla, at the other end of the dusky living-room, yelped.

"Oh God, it is you," she sighed, turning on a light. "You keep freaking me out today."

"We had to shave it right down," explained Moira. "It was just like felt."

Carla approached:

"Actually, you look beautiful."

They embraced.

"What about me?" joked Barg.

"You just look brutal," said Carla.

"Leave him alone," laughed Moira. "... All our clothes are in the machine. That's why we're wearing towels."

"Don't worry. I can sort you out and Luke can sort him out."

"That's good of you."

They followed her upstairs, into her bedroom. She opened a wardrobe, pulled out a few suitable voluminous garments and threw them on the bed for Moira to choose from. She opened another wardrobe and told Barg to help himself.

"Are you sure?"

"Of course I am. It's not a bloody shrine. I should have got rid of this clobber ages ago."

He took a long collarless shirt from a hanger; put it on over his towel; looked down to admire the whiteness; looked up to see Carla staring at him; felt, for the first time, a pang of attraction; began to shake with uncontrollable wholebody sobs.

His eyes and nose pouring, Carla handed him a tissue. He buried his face in her neck, pressed his chest against her bosom. She pushed him away, turned to Moira for help.

"We grieve as well, you know," he said. "It's just we don't get much chance to express it."

"What's he talking about?"

"At least this shirt has stayed faithful to me until now, which is more than I can say for you."

Carla's face collapsed into anguish. She ran from the room.

"Dywysk an crys," said Moira. (Take off the shirt)

He obeyed, fell onto the bed. She draped herself around him and held him. She smelled odd, having donned one of Carla's caftans: a mix of washing-powder and old perfume along with a tinge of Carla herself.

"Yth ens y ow dagrow," he said. (They were my tears.) "Mes nyns o my esa owth ola." (But it wasn't me who was crying."

"My a wor. Luk o. Yn nep forth Luk." (I know. It was Luke, somehow Luke.)

"Ny wruk vy scullya dagrow aban an tro dewetha esen vy dhe Ashburton, an nos spenys adhyworthys ha kens dhe henna ny won pana. Yw Ashburton tyller pur vorethek?." (I have not shed tears since the last time I was in Ashburton, the night I spent away from you, and before that I do not know when. Is Ashburton a very sorrowful place?)

"Yw," she said. (Yes.) "Kepar ha pup le oll... Res yw dhym mos dhedhy ha styrya." (Like everywhere... I must go to her and explain.)

After one last caress of his forehead, one lingering press of his hand, she was gone. He turned onto his back, rearranged his genitalia, sighed and closed his eyes.

He sat up sharply when the women returned.

"I wasn't asleep," he claimed.

"Sure," laughed Moira.

"I know what happened now," said Carla. "At the time I thought you were taking the piss."

"What was Luke like?"

"Like a fruitcake."

"He was sweet?"

"No, he was mad. He wasn't sweetly mad very much either. He could be, but most of the time it was just nasty."

"I'm sorry."

She shrugged:

"I'm over the worst."

Barg was glad to see that her attitude towards him had changed. Before she'd been bitter, brittle, choppy; now her eyes told him he was accepted willingly in his own right, not just reluctantly as Moira's appendage.

"How about this until your clothes are dry?" she said, taking a white towelling dressing-gown from a hook on the wall and handing it to him. "I'm going to cook now."

After a brief embrace, he asked Moira what she had thought of Luke.

"He was a mastic," she replied.

"Eh?"

"A bit like a mystic, but stickier. He got stuck in all the wrong places."

"What's a mystic?"

"A non-stick mastic."

He laughed, without knowing what he was laughing at.

"Did you grieve for him?"

"I didn't then because I was so angry at what he'd done to Carla and Jude. But now, today, I just feel sorry for him. I think he misses her more than she misses him."

Barg agreed.

CHAPTER TWELVE

THE next day she felt like resting, a feeling underpinned by all sorts of complex reasons for not wanting to see Demelza just yet, so he drove over alone. At first it was interesting to be master of a machine again, but when he 'floored it' up the dual carriageway there was little thrill, perhaps because Carla's car was a very old and portly Japanese dog.

Having arrived in Paignton and got lost for an hour or so he finally asked directions and discovered the address Demelza had left with them. When she answered the door, each initially failed to recognise the other, he because her previous black mane was now a bright green crop no more than two inches long.

"Yua ty?" he said. (Is it you?)

"Bargos!" she exclaimed. "This is unbelievable. I went up to see you yesterday."

"Yesterday?" he repeated, unable to grasp the meaning. "Yesterday?"

He was still having trouble with the occasional simple word.

"Nobody there. Where's Moira? Is she alright?"

"Yeah, fine. She's in Ashburton. We left in the morning. She wanted to stay, but I persuaded her to come down for the birth - while she could still manage the walk."

He followed her in, amused by the chips and shavings of wood sticking to, dangling from, her jumper.

It turned out that the motive for her abortive visit had not been strictly social: Terp had disappeared and she'd been looking for him. He'd taken Jack's death worse than anyone, and that was saying something. He'd refused to adapt, had never spoken a word of English - something to do with Jack's last admonition to him that night. His behaviour had become increasingly spasmodic. He'd been weeping a lot and eating a lot of psilocybin. When he wasn't doing one it was the other. On the mushrooms he was radiant, raving, ranting. He said all they lacked were arms and legs and that's what he would provide. He would become *lader war-dhelergh* (an upside-down thief). They didn't have to be swallowed; they could work from the hem of a curtain, from beneath a rug, from inside a pillow-case. He talked about coming in from the wilderness, about bringing the wilderness in from the wilderness. His references to Jack became worryingly reverential, as though Jack were some kind of god when he was only a white tiger. One evening a couple of weeks before he'd gone out and never returned. She feared he'd killed himself. She feared he'd become confused about which world he was supposed to be spreading the word to.

"I'm sure he'll turn up," said Barg. "Perhaps he just needs to work things out on his own."

"Mar qureta consydra yn y gever ny yll ef bos marow," he added. (If you think about it he cannot be dead.)

"Pyth yw dha styr?" she said. (How do you mean?)

"Res yw saw predery yn town." (Just focus.)

After a few moments, she smiled:

"I know what you're getting at. He is around somewhere. I can feel it now. Down here things can get overlaid. You lose sight of the truth. You forget who you are. Anxiety proteins and whatnot."

He nodded, though not sure what she was talking about.

"So did you go up on your own?"

"Yes."

"What was it like?"

"It was awful. It was wonderful. Such a perfect day, weatherwise, wasn't it?... I wanted to come and see you before but I couldn't face it. I couldn't face seeing Jack. I couldn't face not seeing him. I felt guilty for leaving so soon afterwards, but at the time I had no choice."

"Did you see him?"

"No. But I felt him... I felt I felt him... I didn't feel alone, or rather I felt less alone up there than I do down here."

"So you haven't had any other contact?"

"Contact schmontact. I wouldn't believe it if I did."

"Why not?"

"What would be the point of going if he wasn't really going to go? He was called and so he went. They don't stay around because we need them, only if they need us. He was never a needy person. Nor was I, for that matter."

She went on to confide in him. He was pleased to be able to listen and honoured to be asked. At first she hadn't had time to touch her own grief because of the neediness of the others. They'd all gone more or less berserk. Only when things had quietened down a little, after Rose and Glen had left together, could she begin to dissolve herself... They certainly weren't acts of love, or even lust, but mere obliteration. Looking back on that series of motley men, she was ashamed at what she'd done.

Barg expressed understanding, but didn't feel it. He wasn't so much shocked or disapproving as incredulous at such a reaction, sure that if he were to lose Moira he'd be celibate forever.

Jack's parents had been consistently good to her, even after the rift with Rose; never an inkling of blame for being alive when their son was dead. They'd given her oodles of money, as if in reparation for her loss. Underneath all the sorrow she believed his father was proud of what Jack had led them into. (He knew about everything except the mushrooms.) He'd always respected his son, rarely complained that his own ambition for him – to take over the business on the beach – would never be fulfilled. He'd always expected him to go out in a 'blaze of glory', was relieved that at least it hadn't involved a motorcycle. He looked at

Jack's life as complete and exemplary. What could be more understanding than that? What better way to channel his grief than through a process of idolisation?

So eventually she'd settled down into a kind of angry serenity, helped by carving for eight or ten hours a day. It was something she'd always been meaning to get back to. She'd had timber out there drying for years, yet the pyrography brought in the money, took all the time. Now, with enough to live on, she could devote herself; with a mallet in one hand and a gouge in the other she could close a circuit, bridge a chasm.

"Come and see."

He followed her out to the back-garden and found – spanning three saw-benches beneath a clear polythene awning – a tree-trunk, half-transformed into a twist of crawling babies. He helped her lean it upright against the wall so he could see the overall idea, which was musical, contrapuntal - a triple-helix. Up close, some were intricately detailed, down to tiny toes and tender ears; others still rough. The finished faces even bore distinct expressions: fear, wariness, pleasure, surprise, distress, laughter.

"I'm carving the children we never had together."

He did wonder when she said this whether she'd lost her marbles, but her look seemed both to recognise and refute his suspicion, challenged him to suggest anything better to do.

"This is the baby-pole. Next I'll do the infant-.pole, and so on. We would have had three, we should have had three and now we will have three... My life will be their lives."

Standing back again, he remarked how egg-like the heads were. He knew little about babies, less about carving, yet enough to appreciate the poignance and the magnitude of her achievement. If only it were endless, he thought. Then they could climb all the way to heaven. This was his sole criticism. He put his arm around her. She briefly leaned her head against his neck.

"It's amazing," he murmured. "Miraculous."

"Oh, it's not just pure inspiration – I've got friends with a baby. They let me study her, draw her, photograph her, measure her, even model her in clay. I know the form and the pose so well now I can just go with the flow... It's keeping me sane."

Loud dreamy music began to issue from an upstairs window.

"Rhiannon," she explained. "She must have woken up. Why don't you go and see her? I'm sure she'll be pleased. She respects you... I might do a bit more."

Having helped her re-cradle the pole, he went upstairs. The music, although synthesised, sounded somehow natural, evoking whales, depths, darknesses. He knocked, half-opened the door, peered into the room. Rhiannon sat up in bed, reached across and reduced the volume, her hair-spikes silhouetted against the calico curtain.

"It's me, Bargos."

She groaned and put her arms out. He leaned forward. She clung to him. On the surface, stale perfume; below, the same smell of despair.

"So how have you been?" he said, gently disembracing.

She groaned again, grabbed his hand, made him sit on the bed.

"Bad, eh?"

She nodded. The tears welled.

"You'll recover... Just give it time."

"You don't know what I've been through."

"However bad it is, it's got to get better."

She slowly shook her head.

"You've been strong before, haven't you? So you'll be strong again."

"Rose is pregnant."

His stock of platitudes already exhausted, he had no response to this news.

"First she gets him, then she gets his baby."

He squirmed inside, while still trying to convey sympathy.

"You don't care."

"Of course I do," he said, sliding away from her eyes. "I just don't know what to say."

The cassette-case on the floor bore the title '*Songs of the Killer Whale*' and the subtitle '*Soothing Sounds for the Oceanic Soul*'. Various items of underwear were strewn about, including some he'd rather not look too closely into. The hand he was holding began to apply meaningful pressure. The other hand crept up over his thigh. As she leaned toward him the duvet lowered to reveal the beginnings of her breasts. Not sure what was coming next and not wishing to find out, he stood up:

"I've got to go now. I'm sorry I couldn't have seen you for longer. The car I'm in is borrowed and I've got to get it back."

He kissed her dryly on the forehead. She lay down, turned away, muttered a sad goodbye. Promising to return soon, he left the room and bounded down the stairs, with the distinct perception that there'd been no real desire on her part, only the need to feel worse about herself.

As he came into the kitchen he heard a sound which could have been mistaken for a woodpecker. It was of course Demelza, astride her work, bending away from him, so that one line of babies seemed to be disappearing into her baggy-trousered behind. She was embalmed in concentration. Unwilling to interrupt, he watched quietly from the open doorway.

She's right, he thought. It's not creation but revelation, continuous revelation. The conventional chain of causality – mind to hand to tool to wood – could just as plausibly be reversed.

Like all good labours, there was pain as well as love involved: eventually she straightened her back, dismounted, stretched her legs.

"How long have you been standing there?" she grinned, when she caught sight of him.

"Oh, ages."

She punched him playfully in the chest:

"I thought you were still with Rhiannon."

"She's in a bad state, isn't she?"

"Yeah... She's beginning to get on my wick. She seems to go out of her way to make herself rejectionable."

He nodded:

"I don't know how to deal with her... I'm old enough to be her father."

"Then be her father."

He laughed.

"Because I'm tired of being her mother."

"But you won't throw her out?"

"Oh, no," she softened. "I'd never do that... Do you want to see the others?"

"Where are they?"

"On the beach, learning how to work the gold-mine. They're going to take it over soon."

* * *

Having parked as near as he could, he walked to the front. The season was just getting under way. The promenade was on the verge of bustle. Beyond the sparsely-peopled beach a calm sea glistened with late afternoon sun. He drifted along towards the pier, towards the sound of harmonious brass, his eyes glazed from the shock of so many strangers, most of them speaking English with Scottish accents. By the time it came into view, the Salvation Army band was playing 'Abide with Me', compelling him to blink back the tears. They stood in higgledy ranks on the sand. One girl in particular focussed his sorrow: she was wearing a uniform she'd long grown out of, embracing a euphonium she'd yet to grow into.

The recital over, he glided on in a state of wretched beatitude until he reached the hut. And there they were, two unrecognisable beings who must once have been the Glen and Rose he knew, administering to the needs of a small queue. Glen – clean-shaven, short back-and-sides, an embryonic paunch evident behind a florid shirt – bantering chirpily with his customers. Rose – brush of red hair, gingham dress - spreading baps, pouring tea, occasionally laughing at Glen's quips.

"Crab-roll, please," said Barg, having reached the front of the queue.

"Crab-roll for the egghead. Anything else, sir? Nice warm wig perhaps?"

"Cup of tea."

"Nice cup a tea for Baldilocks."

While his order was being fulfilled, the side door opened and a huge magenta-cheeked man appeared.

"Whoops... It's the boss," said Glen, bowing down in mock servitude.

The colossus cuffed him lightly across the ear. Glen feigned great pain, appealed to the queue:

"See what I have to put up with? Corporal punishment. Mental torture."

Although her father maintained his grim expression, Rose smiled and shook her head. She even caught Barg's eye as she took his money, yet still she didn't know him.

"My re glowas del esos ta gans flogh," he said. (I hear you're expecting.)

"Bargos!" she blushed. "... You look so different."

"Hey, man," said Glen. "Good to see you. Sorry I didn't recognise you."

After negotiating a five-minute break, Glen came out and put his arm round Barg. They found a bench and sat down side by side. Barg felt a little estranged, although he'd always got on well with Glen up there. He hadn't even known he was Scottish.

"So how do you like your new life?"

"It's fantastic. No, really – it is fantastic. The Crabman is such an amazing bloke. You know he's stood there every summer for about the last forty years, getting fatter and fatter, wealthier and wealthier. He's got this thing where he pretends to be really grumpy all the time, but you can see behind it he's full of mirth. Yeah - he knows all the answers. There's so many weird things going on in there. Did you see the teapot? Huge aluminium job. It's been colonised by a squad of spacelings. They've got spin but no mass, so they can live inside it without taking up any room. Whereas the crabs have got mass but no spin. You get those working together inside you and you're laughing."

"What do you mean, spacelings?"

"Little beings, voyagers, missionaries. They've got benevolence but no power, mind but no brain, humour but no jokes. People always imagine they're going to come in vaguely human form, flying some kind of high-tech craft, but that's just projection. These guys are the real thing."

"The old man told you this?"

"Well, not in so many words, but I sussed it. He's their chosen host. They pass on the vibes to the customers. Some of them come down here every year, from as far away as Glasgow or even Inverness. How do you explain that?"

"Inertia," said Barg.

"Oh, come on. You know what an effort it is to get here. You know how long it takes on the train? If you'd done it once you'd realise it needs much more than inertia to keep on doing it. The place is gross and tacky, like any other resort, but that's just a mask. Underneath, it's actually paradise."

Glen's hypothesis, although unnecessary, certainly possessed predictive power: Barg, having ingested his crab-roll and a few sips of acrid tea, was laughing.

CHAPTER THIRTEEN

TERP sat in the day-room, his tears dripping onto his trousers. The noises around – of balderdash from the television, of contrariness from the patients, of impatience from the staff – did not impinge. He was elsewhere, watering the autumn earth, beckoning the mushrooms forth, trickling, cascading, flowing all the way down from moor to sea.

When he felt he'd done enough he lifted his head; took a big swig from his water-bottle; smiled beatifically. He considered crying a valid vocation. Everyone else in here was permanently dry-eyed, except once a female nurse he'd come across in a cubby-hole; but he'd judged her tears substandard, trivial, unworthy of consolation.

He looked around, noting the states of the patients, deciding who was most in need of attention. An auxiliary he'd never seen before approached him, having misinterpreted the wetness of his trousers:

"Come on," she said. "Let's get you cleaned up."

"Gwra omwolghy," he retorted. (Clean yourself up.)

"I know," she cooed. "You couldn't help it, could you?"

"Yth esos ta ow flerya." (You smell bad.)

He squeezed his nostrils with the thumb and forefinger of his left hand.

She nodded understandingly:

"Not very nice, is it?"

She grabbed his right wrist and attempted to pull him up. He yanked his arm back in reaction. She fell towards him and, twisting to avoid landing in his lap, hit the floor. He laughed, fuelling her anger. She got up, gripped his wrist and forearm with both hands and began a more determined tug. A sickly sweet sweat broke through the ranks of perfume and deodorant which had until now surrounded her. This he could relate to. Now he almost wanted her in his lap.

A repeat of her previous indignity was forestalled by Jim. Having glanced in through the doorway and seen the incident, he came rushing over with the words:

"What's going on?"

She relinquished her hold and stood back, puffing.

"I was only trying to get him cleaned up."

Jim laughed:

"Oh, that's nothing worse than tears. He always has a good cry about this time. Don't you, Pete?"

Terp nodded, rubbing his palms against his trousers and making as if to wipe them on her uniform. She jumped back with a yelp of disgust. Jim took her out of the room.

Terp stood up. He'd been motionless for hours, but now the muscle-action had ignited him. He felt pretty sure that poor Matthew was most in need, having earlier today suffered a barbaric blow to the head, otherwise known as electro-convulsive therapy.

On his way over to Matthew's corner, he lingered behind the door.

"... there's no need for you to interact with him unless he wants to," Jim was saying in the corridor. "... he can see to all his own needs... we're just trying to give him some space... and some time... we can't help him... so we're hoping he can help himself..."

Terp grinned. Jim was a good bloke, the only person working here with whom he wanted to relate. Of course even Jim didn't know that Terp was speaking a viable language, but had logically assumed some disturbance to the motor-function which resulted in scrambled words. A couple of weeks before Jim had brought in a book of Christian names and asked Terp to point out his. Terp's actual name was Maurice, which he had no wish to be called ever again, nor even Mo, so he had chosen Peter, as much for its symbolic significance as anything. After this 'breakthrough' Jim had tried to tempt him with other reading-matter, but Terp had politely resisted. Although there was no specific rule to prevent him from reading - as opposed to speaking - English, he wasn't interested in anything that newspapers or magazines or books could provide.

He squatted in front of Matthew and looked into his downcast eyes. Behind the blankness he saw terror, hate, defiance, disintegration. It was going to be a big job.

"What you fucking staring at?"

Terp was shocked by this hostility. They'd recently established a kind of rapport. They had a lot in common, both about the same age, both sectioned about the same time, after committing remarkably similar 'crimes'. Matthew had attempted to put some ten-pound notes into the coat-pocket of an old man in the street. The old man, thinking he was being robbed, had kicked up a stink. Some passers-by had detained Matthew until the police arrived. The violence of his resistance, the implausibility of his explanation, along with many other signs of psychosis, had soon led him here, where he continued to kick out, both literally and verbally, at all who came near, with the occasional exception of Terp.

"My a wor an pyth a wrussons dhys," he murmured. "My a vynsa y hedhy mar pe possybyl. Porth cof yth of abarth dhys. Yth eson ny owth araya war-dhelergh. Gwra assaya bos moy heweres, ena ty a vyn scappya a'n le ma." (I know what they have done to you. I would have stopped it if I could. I am on your side, remember. We are inverting the order of things. Try being a little more co-operative, then you will get out of here.)

"I don't know what the fuck you're saying."

Terp sighed. Their relationship had been a haven, in which they communicated by monologue. If Matthew wanted to speak, then Terp would patiently listen. If Matthew wanted to be silent, then Terp would quietly talk. Of course as far as Matthew was concerned, Terp was speaking gibberish, but he'd never complained before, probably because he'd been absorbing the meaning into some metalingual region of his soul.

Terp tried again, lowering his voice even further in an attempt to make it more hypnotic:

"Ty a wor an pyth a lavaraf. Saw yth esos ta ow predery na wodhyes ta. Porth cof ow dhyscosow dhys. Ny yllyr cafus olow-paw hep pawyow. An tyger a vew. An tyger a worta. An tyger a vew rak dha sylwel. An tyger a worta rak dha dhybry. Nyns yw res saw omwul tam moy saworek..." (You know what I am saying. You just think you do not know. Remember all I have taught you. You cannot have paw-prints without paws. The tiger lives. The tiger waits. The tiger lives to save you. The tiger waits to eat you. You only have to make yourself a little more appetising...)

"Hoi!" shouted Matthew to the auxiliary. "This prannock is hassling me. Get him away."

Terp sighed and stood sadly up, at last accepting the truth: Matthew no longer even recognised him. The ECT had blown their haven to smithereens.

* * *

Often it would be dawn when they got back to the van. They would see the sun rising beyond Torbay and then they would drive dazzled down towards it, their hard labour of the night before condensed into delicious fatigue. This routine had gone on for months. But work looked back upon is work with the tedium taken out. From all those nights of digging and building he could now create, or perhaps perceive, an ideal night in which they worked side by side without error, without frustration, without doubt, like two well-oiled dreamers; a night whose ending was always golden. The leaden skies which characterised a majority of the actual dawns had been retrospectively transmuted.

He could revisit this night at will and find again the strength Jack had given him: the strength to bend, the strength to comply, the strength to persevere. His position here was intolerable, and yet it must be endured. He'd rather wait for release than have to escape: a failed flight could mean a crucial setback to his plans. His sole crime had been 'breaking and entering'. Having successfully secreted a mushroom into the hem of a curtain, from where he believed it would transmit, he'd been caught by the house-owner and mistaken for a burglar. He'd been passed on first to the police, to whom he patiently recounted what he'd been doing and who he was - *lader war-dhelergh* (an upside-down thief), a giver and not a taker. But of course his explanations, reasonable as they were, had fallen on stony ears, the number of Cornish-speaking policepersons in Devon being even tinier than in Cornwall. His bag of mushrooms (the only identity he carried) was confiscated and he was delivered into the hands of the Health Service, sectioned for his own safety under the Mental Health Act, and ensconced here in the Haytor Unit of Torbay General Hospital. Since then he'd experienced the rigours of an oscillating regime. The day-shift led by Jim wasn't too bad, Terp being mostly left to get on with his work. But Jim's counterpart on the other day-shift was a sadist, an imbecile and probably – even if he didn't know it himself – a homosexual, the intensity of his dislike for Terp being otherwise inexplicable. This character expected Terp to be his valet, his tea-maker, his bacon-sandwich-maker, his punch-bag and the butt of all his crude and pathological wit. Terp mutely absorbed the insults, bovinely obeyed the commands. Retaliation might have entailed an extension of his section and a programme of ECT, both of which he dreaded. His only strategy, when pushed over the edge, was to become motionless, rigid, until the tyrant tired of his taunting. However, he dare not use this recourse too often, realising that from the outside it must appear very much like the behaviour of a genuine patient. With Jim he sometimes felt guilty for not speaking English, with the other often angry. Yet he had no choice in the matter. He'd several times attempted to break the vow, made on *erghmemansnos* (snowdeathnight), after his outburst about fetching a doctor, but had discovered that his tongue, his teeth, his lips, his larynx were made of sterner stuff.

Jim remained determined to establish communication. Working on his theory that Terp's problems were motor, he began to appear with various items of remedial equipment, the most hilarious being known as a 'Macaw'. Designed for people with speech impediments, this was a species of tape-recorder featuring a grid of exchangeable phrases on its upper surface. When a phrase was pressed it would instantly emerge as a voice. Terp was touched by the sentiments which Jim had written and recorded on his behalf, for example:

> *I'm crying from grief*
> *I'm crying for love*
> *I know why I'm here*
> *Leave me alone*
> *I don't like it*
> *I don't know why I'm here*
> *Hi, I'm Peter*
> *I need a walk*
> *I can't remember*

He pressed each in turn and out spoke a good approximation of Jim's voice. He laughed until the tears came.

"These are just for a start," said Jim. "It's a shame you can't write your own."

He nodded in agreement, having already established that the vow extended as far as the fingers of his right hand. When provided with notepad and pen he'd been unable to formulate a single word.

"Do you think you can use it? It might help you to interact."

He shrugged.

"Shall we try and think of some other phrases?"
He shook his head.
"Leave me alone," said the Macaw.

* * *

Acting on another brainwave Jim had one
afternoon brought in a map of the U.K. and asked Terp
to point out where he came from. Without thinking of
the consequence, Terp had indicated Plymouth. So of
course the next day, Jim had appeared with a street-
map. Terp had scowled and walked apologetically away.
The last thing he wanted was anything to do with his
mother, or anyone else he knew for that matter. The
solution to getting out was right here at the top of his
head, in the form of Demelza's phone-number. He only
had to ring her and explain what had happened and
she'd be sure to rescue him. But he couldn't bring
himself to do it. He'd been discovering recently how
much he hated her. At the time, he'd tried to ignore or
understand her rash of promiscuous behaviour, yet
now, looking back, he became more and more appalled.
Her love for Jack must have been a sham. If she'd had
any depth she'd have buried herself in black for the rest
of her life. As for Rose and Glen, great comrades they'd
turned out to be.

Although lavish with those three, his hatred was at
its most generous when focussed upon Bargos. The
others were guilty after the catastrophe - if it hadn't
happened, the pairs would still be together. He might
not have loved Rose as much as he should, but he'd
loved her enough to stay with her. Whereas the pilot's
guilt was entwined in the event itself. Somehow, he was
responsible. And Terp, as the only one who'd stayed
true, had been appointed avenger. His first job when he
got out of here, perhaps his only job, was to kill the
killer.

When he'd originally felt this command he'd
dismissed it as ridiculous. He wasn't the type, wouldn't

hurt a fly, wouldn't say boo to a goose etc. He could hate without wanting to hurt, let alone wanting to kill. But as the command became more insistent he realised it must derive, if not from Jack, then from some other entity in the world to which Jack had migrated. So he gradually forced himself to forget how much he'd liked the pilot, forget his compassion on *erghmemansnos* (snowdeathnight), and expose the anomalies surrounding him: he'd fallen out of the sky; he'd escaped and then returned; he'd never been swallowed, never made the jump, yet he'd managed to wangle his way into the troupe. And now he sat up there, unchallenged king of the moor, probably laughing.

CHAPTER FOURTEEN

IN the end he had to admit there was a sexual element to his crying. The assumption of altruism was flawed. Since arriving here he'd succeeded in quelling all manifestations of libido. He'd also succeeded in stripping his soul and transforming it into a bell-headed mushroom. Yet there was still a way to go before arriving at desirelessness, never mind selflessness. He realised that his reabsorbed semen was being used to augment his stock of tears. Crying, which once seemed so noble, had become a form of masturbation and must cease. A mushroom is not, should never be, a phallic symbol. A phallus may sometimes be a mushroom symbol.

Faulty also, the idea that a mushroom can communicate without being swallowed. The practise of this idea had led to his captivity, but now he was ready to recant. After his last experience with Matthew he'd abandoned the talking-cure, which took account of each individual character, and instead tried standing in the middle of the day-room and transmitting telepathically to the patients as a mass. If he could strip them as he'd stripped himself, of all postnatal gunge, they would reach unanimity. They would rise up and break out together. He would lead them to the moor, test them on the tor. With those who made the jump he would take over the settlement, killing the pilot and making Moira their queen. But although he spent many afternoons concentrating on this endeavour there were no noticeable results. He began to realise that however clear the transmission, if the receiver is untuned or broken or non-existent the message will not be heard. He also began to understand that these psychotics, apparently such good material, having abandoned and been abandoned by society, were the most difficult to subvert. Solidarity was an unfulfillable dream. The one thing they had in common was that they had nothing in common, their isolation from each other being even more profound than their isolation from society. You could call the staff a body in that they were often capable of working together, especially if someone needed restraining. You could never call the patients a body, except for administrative purposes.

As a consequence of this new-found realism he relinquished all therapeutic activity and only wept in bed. From having had one foot in each camp he now had neither in either. During the days he was invulnerable and amenable, concealing his disrespect beneath conventional manners. He washed and shaved every morning. He ate his ghastly meals with the prescribed grace, at the prescribed pace. Inside, he immersed himself in yearning: for the feel of coarse heather against his cheeks; for the rasp of peat-smoke against his throat; for the company of dappled ponies; for the nourishment of dumb sheep.

But most of all he yearned for the cry of a dying buzzard. Only then would Jack be vindicated, his death balanced. Meanwhile his death must go on falling. Whatever world the buzzard belonged to, it wasn't their world: it was an antithesis. Only when the buzzard's death began to fall could Jack's death begin to rise again. Only then could Jack become a true *sylwyas* (saviour).

As the restoration of his liberty drew near, he grappled with the problem of method. Yearning for something is rarely an effective means of bringing it about. Ideally, he would like to shoot the buzzard in flight. That would be a proper death, a heavy death, a symmetrical death. He came in by being shot down and so that was how he ought to go out. But this solution would entail, somewhere between here and there, stealing a shotgun and some cartridges. Given his record (of being caught) he didn't much rate his chances. So he went through the tools he knew to be up there and imagined the sort of weapons they might become: axes, shovels, picks, chisels, saws, hammers. Each brought a scowl of revulsion to his face. Then he remembered his sheath-knife, which he'd left in the wake of their stricken departure. After all, the pilot had once tried to stab Jack. They must meet face to face, perhaps in a fair fight. Even though he knew this was the answer, the thought of plunging his knife into the buzzard's gut still caused considerable trepidation.

* * *

On the afternoon of the penultimate day Jim came over as soon as his shift began.

"You know your section expires tomorrow?" he murmured.

Terp nodded and grinned.

"But they won't just let you walk out of here on your own, with nowhere to go."

He groaned and thoughtlessly grabbed Jim by the lapels.

"Hold on a minute. Don't get het up... How would you like to come home with me?"

He frowned.

"They wanted to give you six months, but I've offered to be your Guardian and they've accepted that. It's a legal thing, you understand? Won't really mean anything as long as we trust each other."

He was so touched by this offer and the sacrifice it implied that he gave Jim a hug.

"Muer ras dhys," he whispered. (Thank you)

He would go home with him for a night and then he would go on up.

"I've talked to my partner about it. She's dying to meet you."

* * *

Three weeks later, at about the same time of day, he was standing motionless in Jim's conservatory, leaning west towards the September moor. His arms were out above him, halfway between horizontal and vertical, as though in supplication. His palms were pressed lightly against the glass. He was naked. A fan-heater crouched at his feet, exhaling warmish air. The sun only shone between frequent showers splattering in from the Atlantic.

The greyness of the tors merged with the greyness of the clouds. He tried to project himself up there, to perceive what they were doing. The settlement was less than ten miles away as the crow flew but he found he was incapable of getting beyond the tree-line. So he tried to imagine instead. He felt sure Moira would have had her baby by now, his previous uncertainty about this event being one of his reasons for procrastinating. The argument, which he'd redecorated several times, being that once she'd given birth the buzzard would spend more time away from her, flying and hunting, therefore he could be more easily accosted. He also reasoned that the loss of her mate would cause her less grief after the completion of their breeding-cycle. She might even be receptive to a change. Once she learned what a Judas Barg had been she'd soon understand both the justice and the necessity. She was always such a zealot. And now she was the only one, apart from himself, who'd stayed true to the tooth they wore.

"You alright?" said Marianne.

He nodded.

"Give me ten more minutes?"

He grunted.

Stillness and silence were a piece of cake. Nakedness was a little less edible, though he was beginning to get used to it. By hard exercise he'd already eradicated much of the pudge acquired during his internment. If not yet proud of his body, he was at least no longer embarrassed. He closed his eyes and concentrated on analysing nasal information. He discerned two main streams: mould-spores from the damp and rotting timbers of the old conservatory; hormonal molecules from Marianne. She was sitting about ten feet away, half-shielded by her drawing-board. His feelings about her were confused, perhaps because of the complex way she treated him. Sometimes she allowed him to penetrate her armpit with his nose; other times she kept him at arm's length. She variously regarded him as a feral mascot, as a dumb oracle, as an autistic son. If she was painting she might question him about a particular tone of green and he would sign his opinion. If she was going out she might wonder whether her hair should be up or down and he would indicate a preference. Sometimes, like now, she looked upon him as a mere arrangement of light and shade.

Today's stream was so powerful and so delectable he felt sure she must be ovulating. He wished them luck. They were hoping to have a baby together, having previously procreated with other partners. Jim had had his vasectomy reversed. They were both imprisoned by the same idea: that their love would not be profound or even valid until it produced a living emblem of itself. Only then would their former partners be properly eclipsed. He already knew more about some aspects of their relationship than either of them, because they both separately confided in him. His vow made him an ideal repository. Their worries, their dissatisfactions, their insecurities were exotic and fascinating. He responded with laughter, with sympathy, with incredulity. Life here was seductive. In the mornings, after a run and a session on their rowing-machine, he would help Jim with the restoration of the Victorian ex-vicarage. In the afternoons he would model for Marianne. He could hold a pose for hours without boredom or discomfort. He was only anxious to finish today because he'd decided to try and communicate with her, to give her some notion of his identity.

Although he might be repaying their kindness by playing all the roles they wanted him to play, he still felt himself ungrateful and dishonest in withholding what could be given, no matter how tricky the giving.

"OK," she said. "Come and have a look."

He went over and examined her sketch, a study for a painting she had in mind. He pursed his lips, raised his eyebrows, nodded his head, to show approval. He didn't doubt her talent. He just couldn't see the point of figurative art. Why remove something from three dimensions to two, but in such a way as to revive the idea of three? He tore a blank leaf from one of her sketch-books and crudely drew a bell-headed mushroom with a slightly crooked stalk. He pointed at her drawing, then pointed at himself and shook his head. He pointed at the drawing of the mushroom, then pointed at himself and nodded his head.

"Looks like psilocybin to me," she said. "Do you mean you want some? I don't think that's such a good idea."

He shook his head a few times, again pointing back and forth between the drawing and himself.

"You mean that's what caused your problems? You had too many?"

He shook his head a few more times and even more vehemently. He repeated the mime, this time placing his sketch over hers.

"You mean you're not a man. You're a mushroom?" she concluded, unable to keep the mirth from her mouth.

He nodded, trying hard to look stern and sincere, but her giggles were highly infectious.

"Looks more like a stink-horn to me," she said, playfully tweaking his penis.

Louder laughter followed. He, not knowing what a 'stink-horn' was, hooted mainly at the idea that something could look more like something else than itself.

As soon as he'd recovered enough, he began to put his clothes back on, realising as he did so that the idea, although still hilarious, was banal. Lots of things can look like other things. A planet can look like a star. A frog can look like a fallen leaf. A harmless snake can look like a poisonous snake. An insect can look like a stick. There were countless examples of mimicry in the animal world. Indeed, there were probably thousands of species so well-camouflaged that no-one had yet discovered them. When he'd finished dressing he signed to her that he'd soon be back, then went through into the room where they kept most of their books. Drawing a tiger was beyond him, so he was hoping to find a photograph. As he scanned the shelves his eye was arrested by a spine which bore the words CORNISH ORDINALIA. Glancing at the back cover, he learned that the volume contained one of a fourteenth century cycle of mystery plays, dealing with the Passion of Christ. He looked inside and discovered that the left hand of each pair of pages was printed in a fairly recognisable version of his own tongue – apart from the names of the speakers and the stage directions, which were in Latin.

He flicked through, greedily gulping the phrases. The spelling was a bit odd and some of the words unknown, but by and large he could understand and feel nostalgic for an epoch he'd never inhabited, for a faith he'd never possessed.

He jumped up and ran back to the conservatory. This could say more on his behalf than a whole flock of Macaws. She was still working. He waved the book in her face.

"What now?" she chuckled. "Are you saying you're Cornish?"

He opened the book at random, crouched down beside her and declaimed from the top of the page, under the name 'IHC':

"*My a lever gwyryoneth:*
onen ahanough haneth
re'm gwerthas dhe'm yskerens.
Nep us genef ow tybry
a'm tullvyth, yn surredy,
ha sur a'm gor dhe'n mernans."

He pointed to the opposite page and she, suddenly serious, whispered the translation:

"*I say the truth:*
one of you this night
has sold me to my enemies.
One who is eating with me
will betray me, assuredly,
and indeed will send me to death."

She looked into his eyes, her mouth open, her forehead baffled.

"So that's what you speak?"

He nodded. Her breath smelled of the hummus she'd had for lunch.

"I always thought your words were just garbled. You understand English but only speak Cornish? How come? I thought the language was long dead."

He didn't respond. He was beginning to freak out at the passage he'd just read. Wasn't it a message to him? Why had it opened on that particular page? Etc. He put his arms around her, laid his head on her lap, sobbed.

"I wish I could help you," she said.

He wished she could as well, but he was beyond help. What he must do, he must do alone, and he must do it immediately. He must forsake their warmth and go up into the grey and wet. Snippets of the mystery play expanded and merged inside him. Perhaps he was the guilty one, the Judas, and Barg merely the faltering one, the Peter? Their combat would decide. He was just as prepared be killed as he was to kill. She stroked his hair. The top of his head pressed against her belly; his left ear pressed against her thigh. This heat, this shelter, he must forsake. He disentangled himself, kissed her cheek, then stood back and cleared away his tears. That was the end of that. Now it was time to grow up.

A particularly heavy shower began to din against the glass roof. They went through into the kitchen. She raised one lid of the range, put the kettle on, then stood with her bum against the rail. He sat down at the long table and began going through the play for something else to say, but soon realised that any statements he extracted were bound to be either misleading or empty. Although Jack might be a saviour, he died lying down, not upright on a cross.

"I'm still not any the wiser," she said.

He closed the book, pushed it away, spread his palms, shrugged his shoulders, grinned. Perhaps it was best to leave things as they were. From their point of view as well as his own, tonight was a good time for him to depart. Tomorrow she would be pregnant; the day after tomorrow he would have been in the way. They might worry about him for a while after they found him gone, but in the end they'd be relieved. They'd remember him, if at all, as a ghost.

The kettle began to huff and she made tea. They sat and sipped at opposite ends of the table.

"I think you've got the right idea," she said, after ten minutes or so. "Silence is the best conversation. I don't believe I could know you any better than I do now... It's great having you here. Don't ever think you're unwelcome... You've stabilised us. It was quite difficult before you came. Just the two of us after having lived with so many other people... I hope you don't think I'm exploiting you with all the modelling. I'm so pleased with that study I just did I'm going to start on the painting tomorrow - so you can have a rest... A lot of people hide themselves behind the words they speak, don't they? Just as clothes conceal the body, so words conceal the soul. Who said that?... Whereas you're naked all the time, whether you're dressed or not."

He banged the table and yelped. He was lapping it up. It was good to be projected upon, good to play the part of her ghost-son, good to have the attention of a warm-blooded mother.

"I've got to get some shopping? Want to come?"

He stood up. He usually refused invitations to go out with her, but this evening he didn't want to be alone for a moment. There'd be plenty of solitude to come. Meanwhile, he needed as much company as he could get.

They trundled along through overhung one-track lanes, down to the nearest supermarket. He even went in with her, as if to remind himself what he wouldn't be missing.

"You OK?" she enquired, after a couple of aisles.

He pointed at the lights, then mimed the act of puking.

"Go on back to the car, then – I won't be long."

But he stuck it out, despite the discomfort. Apart from faint waves of nausea, he felt as though his cheeks no longer fitted his face. Presumably the lighting had been designed to addle the brains and encourage profligacy. His forehead prickled with anger. He wanted to sweep his hands along the shelves, clattering all the products to the floor, but restrained himself for her sake.

When they emerged, the clouds had cleared, to be replaced by darkness. The return journey was punctuated by intermittent remarks from Marianne concerning her daughter, who might be coming tomorrow. She hoped this visit would end a period of estrangement. The daughter had never seen Jim and her together.

"You'll like her – she's a real wild child."

Although his curiosity was aroused, he resolutely squashed the temptation to once more postpone his departure.

After helping to put away the shopping and then chopping a few vegetables he sat back down at the table while she slowly continued with the preparation of the supper.

At about nine, they heard the scrunch of tyres against gravel.

Sometimes the turmoil of Jim's job meant he arrived home a little ratty, but tonight he was in a good mood. He opened a bottle of wine and filled beakers for Marianne and himself.

"Peter and I have made a breakthrough today."

"Oh, yeah?"

"That book on the table. I assume it's one of yours. I've never seen it before. He read something from it – that's the language he's been speaking."

Jim came over, picked up the book, frowned:

"I haven't actually opened it since I bought it."

Terp dutifully read out the first few lines of the proffered page:

"*Govy y vones ledhys,*
kemmys dader prest a wre.
Y dhader yudrok dylyd,
pan y'n lathsons dybyta."

The translation opposite said:

'*Woe's me that He is slain,*
Who was constantly doing so much good.
His kindness is ill-requited,
since they have killed him without pity.'

Jim slowly shook his head:

"I can't believe this. How do you know it?"

Terp tapped his forehead with his forefinger.

"I've got it!" exclaimed Jim, turning to Marianne. "He must be a Breton. I know their language is very similar to the old Cornish and some of them are still speaking it. He doesn't come from Plymouth – that's just where he came in."

He turned back to Terp:

"Is that right?"

Terp nodded enthusiastically and slapped the side of his head with his left palm. Better to be a Breton than a ghost. And more truthful. After all, the Bretons were simply Britons who'd chosen to emigrate from the

111

peninsula, rather than be subjugated by the Saxons. Through their proud stock the original language had survived until today, despite perpetual persecution by the French; whereas among those who had stayed behind the language had inexorably been usurped by English, before dying out completely in the far west over two hundred years ago.

This subject saddened him, reminded him of their first few weeks of study, of Jack's discipline and intensity. By the power of his will alone, he'd enabled them to expectorate the whole wretched, shabby culture and free their tongues for better things. How intrepid they'd felt as they penetrated the barbed thickets of the new vocabulary. How superior they'd considered themselves to other revivalists, whose interest was merely academic or nostalgic. Their own interest was crucial: the language represented a bridge over which they could slowly learn to walk. Jack often held up the Bretons as a bit of an example. He and Demelza had been across a few times with their bike and had got to know a militant group who, although still for the most part earning money within the state system, spent all their spare time on the Francophobic edge.

"So if we take you to Brittany," said Jim. "You'll be able to show us your home, your people?"

Terp nodded again, knowing his bluff would never be called.

"So how come you understand English, but don't speak it or write it? Is it a political thing? Some kind of Celtic thing? You hate the English as much as you hate the French?"

Terp shrugged at these questions. Even if he could speak, the complexity and clarity of his position would still be incommunicable.

Jim replenished his beaker, coming back to say:

"Oh, I forgot to tell you. Your friend Matthew did a runner last night."

Terp grinned and clapped his hands.

"That's all very well. I just hope he doesn't hurt someone."

He earnestly tried to sign that Matthew was no danger, pointing at his solar plexus to suggest that he was like himself.

"Hardly," said Jim. "You never kicked anyone when you were in there. You never threw hot tea at anyone. You never shit yourself out of sheer malice towards the people who'd have to clean you up."

Terp shook his head slowly and sadly. Poor Matthew must have gone downhill fast, no doubt thanks to the ECT and the medication, because up until three weeks ago he hadn't shown the slightest disregard for the conventions of continence. He'd started so innocently, so idealistically, in his role as an inverted pickpocket. Now he was out there alone, the generosity gone from his heart. The system he adhered to had been blown away. Rage was all that remained.

He tried to send Matthew a message in the form of a pair of goldfinches, which he now called *scafheoryon-tewlder* (darkness-alleviators). He saw him slumped in the corner of a bus-shelter. He set the goldfinches gyrating luminously in front of him; hoped they might help.

Although quite pretty, Matthew had no leaning towards homosexuality, or even any particular liking for homosexuals; yet he'd spent the early part of the summer renting his body to older men. The proceeds, apart from the little needed for his own sustenance, he'd passed on to even older men. He once solemnly told Terp that if everyone were to act like him, there'd be 'no more war, no more poverty, no more overpopulation'. This was among the more lucid explanations of his behaviour. Other times he would mutter incomprehensibly about 'infinite ingress', about 'nullification and exaltation', about 'living death to the full'.

Terp acknowledged some metaphysical merit to Matthew's system but believed it had failed because its components were arbitrary. He'd obviously had an unrewarding relationship with his father. He might just as easily become a killer instead of a benefactor.

"Perhaps we shouldn't worry too much," said Jim. "They're bound to find him soon."

"Let's eat," said Marianne.

* * *

After a silent, peaceful supper they both began to yawn ostentatiously, preparing the ground for an early night. This suited Terp, as he hoped to get up there before daylight. He followed them to the foot of the stairs, contriving to touch them both.

"Night, Peter," said Marianne. "God bless you."

"Night," said Jim.

"Dumostadha ha muer ras dhys," he murmured. (Goodbye and thank you.) "Re bo concevyans warnas. Re bo dha yssew cawr." (May you conceive. May your offspring be a giant.)

CHAPTER FIFTEEN

NOT long beyond dawn he was crawling through the heather and peering down over the rim of the bowl. He'd walked strongly all night, fuelled by Marianne's vegetable-crumble, only beginning to flag after relinquishing tarmac for rough ground.

The settlement was virtually undetectable from here, but that was part of the design; even the chimney-system had been arranged in such a way as to diffuse smoke through the tufts above the cells so it might, if ever noticeable, be mistaken for mist.

Still warm after the fifteen-mile trek, he settled down prone to watch, his chin resting on his forearm.

When he awoke, the sun had moved round to the south-west. In the meantime there must have been at least one heavy shower, because he was soaked. He crawled away from the rim, then ran and stamped about for a while to revive his circulation.

He was annoyed at having fallen asleep; he'd arrived early so he could spend the day observing Barg's movements. He was also irritated with himself for having ignored the practicalities of the mission; he could at least have brought bread and water, a waterproof jacket or coat, a box of matches, a torch. (He'd felt squeamish about stealing from his hosts.)

By lying on his side, he managed to transfer some moisture from heather to tongue.

He watched until dusk, then began to make his way down.

He went into the cell he'd shared with Rose; felt for and found his knife; attached the sheath to his belt; came out and pressed an ear against the grass-shutter of Barg and Moira's cell: no sound. He walked over to the latrine and sniffed: no indication of recent use. He returned to Barg's cell and slowly pulled open the door;

inside, darkness and the stench of mould. He felt about: the sheepskins were wet, the fireplace cold.

He finally accepted what he'd been avoiding all day: not only were they not here now, they hadn't been here for some time and may never be here again.

He came out and bellowed wordlessly at the cold, clear sky.

After this outburst, his anger gone, he was able to calmly contemplate his fate. What was so bad about dying? Jack had done it willingly, easily, even humorously. After all, it was a simple procedure, to slip across from one world to another.

The purpose had been false, not the path. If he'd known the true purpose, he might have put it off indefinitely.

He was relieved that his personal consumption, barring a few more lungfuls of air, was over.

He must leave just as Jack had done, on his back, on Jack's bed; that way he'd be sure to find him.

He opened the door to Jack's cell and screamed: the darkness was solid; the darkness was wet. He recoiled and ran off, sobbing and stumbling.

When he fell he did not rise, but began to writhe convulsively, with white light searing behind his eyelids and foam gushing from his mouth.

The whiteness remained after the storm had passed, after the heat had dissipated. The whiteness could coalesce into fur. The fur could induce a pair of emerald eyes. He could make his home inside that fur, behind those eyes.

He took out his knife; pulled up his shirt; held the knife out in front of him with both hands; plunged it into his belly.

For a few moments he fancied he was bounding tremendously away across the bowl. Then the icy dampness in his back recalled him. He was still behind his own eyes; when he opened them he saw the half-moon, the stars.

He peered down at his midriff, imagining a splurge of intestines: nothing there but a shadow of blood. The knife had hardly broken the surface. He ran his thumb across the blade: *pensogh avel quallok.* (Blunt as arseholes.)

He went back and lay down in his own cell. He was going to have to suffer before he died.

* * *

His earlier sleep, in daylight, had been as uneventful as it was unwanted, the hours between falling and waking compressed into a single, empty moment. This sleep now, if sleep it was, in the absolute darkness of his cell, became vivid as soon as it began.

He found himself in his room in Jim's house. There was a young woman sitting on the edge of the bed, cradling the pillow, rocking from side to side, humming monotonously. Her eyes were closed, her head tilted. He hovered above her, entranced. The upward curves of her brow, the downward curves of her lashes, touched him where he'd never been touched before. She made him feel like a swarm of butterflies. He even saw a few strands lift from the surface of her hair in response to his multitudinous wings.

The door opened and Marianne came in.

"Any luck?" she said.

"I think so," said the siren, who he now realised must be Marianne's daughter. "I've got something, but only that he's here."

"He can't be. We've searched everywhere."

"I can feel him. I can almost see him."

And indeed, at this moment, she was looking vaguely towards him. Although he gyrated and jittered in an effort to augment her perception, she soon turned to meet her mother's gaze.

"Yth esof vy omma!" he shouted. (I am here)

His words made little impression on the air.

He tried to place himself in their eyelines, but the thought zinging back and forth between them repulsed him, dejected him - if he was here, then he was dead.

* * *

He awoke to pain in all his joints, to the beginnings of a fever. Sunlight seeped in through the gaps in the grass-shutters, illuminating the debris of his life with Rose: directly above him, pinned to the ceiling, the god's-eye she'd made as an aid to fertility; leaning in a corner, the crude spinning-device he'd fashioned for her; lying here among the sheepskins, the jumper she'd half-knitted for him. All his bitterness about her had evaporated. He felt gratitude for their time together. She'd been good to him, if not for him. They'd each known, probably from the start, that the other wasn't the one. They'd come together to please Jack and for that reason they'd stayed together, would be together even now if he was still around.

From the depths of a half-remembered dream he retrieved the will to live. And if he wanted to live, he'd have to leave. He couldn't subsist here on his own. He'd never be able to kill a sheep single-handed; it had always taken three of them. The only other source of protein was rabbit, pony being unthinkable as well as uncatchable, but he didn't know how to trap.

He would go back and prove that he wasn't a ghost.

Having risen somewhat tentatively to his feet, he went out into the breeze; lifted the lid from the buried rainwater-butt; drank; splashed his head; dabbed the wound in his belly, which was beginning to look nasty, surrounded by yellow frills of pus.

"Holy Mary," he moaned, then realised what he'd said.

"Mother of God," he muttered.

"Fucking Ada," he shouted.

These additional ejaculations weren't so much expressions of alarm as tests of tongue. It seemed he'd finally been released from his vow. This must be a sign, a confirmation that he was right to go back. When he got there at least he'd be able to explain himself. In the meantime, he could swear again. They'd never learned any swear-words in Cornish, and although they'd tried making some up the neologisms had never fulfilled quite the same function. Swearing was one thing, perhaps the only thing, that Saxon was better for.

He stood up; went over to Jack's cell; slowly and fearfully pulled open the door; then flung it wide once he was sure that the interior was filled, not with some dimensionless horror, but with earth, pure, simple and black. He laughed at his panic of the night before. They must have buried Jack where he lay; his deathbed had become his coffin. He climbed round to the top of the cell to confirm this hypothesis and discovered, growing directly above where the body had been, the biggest, whitest, most heart-startling bell of a mushroom he'd ever seen. He squatted down, but found that this position hurt his wound, so lay on his side with his face up close to it. The gills were dry and perfectly defined; the stem sturdy and as thick as a little finger. He closed his eyes, opened his valves, asked for guidance.

Ten minutes later, he set off towards the south-east, inspired by the messages he'd received. He'd been forbidden to eat. He was weak and the mushroom strong, strong enough to be lethal. Besides, there was no longer any need for him to swallow, or be swallowed. It was time to speak instead. But first he must get his own strength back. He must become sturdy enough to carry a whole church on his shoulders.

Although he began by walking fast, he was soon overtaken by an irresistible lethargy. The skyline was already, despite the earliness of the hour, marred by the silhouettes of walkers. If he could just reach the rim of the bowl he might get help.

After catching his foot in a rabbit-hole, he fell over. After falling over, he crawled. After crawling a little higher, he collapsed. After collapsing, he surrendered.

* * *

The next thing he knew, he was lying in his cell. The door was open. He could hear hammering outside. Then the doorway was momentarily filled with a silhouette. The silhouette, as it entered, became a woman with green hair, a woman he almost recognised.

"How are you feeling?" she murmured.

He tried to reply, but his mouth was too dry, his tongue too swollen.

She placed an icy palm on his forehead.

"We're just making a stretcher. We're going to carry you back to the van."

He grunted. The words 'back to the van' were incomprehensible, a paradox.

"I'll get you some water."

The next thing he knew, his head was being pulled gently upright and the cold rim of a cup pressed against his lower lip. After sipping as much as he could, he flopped against her, his face nestling into her bosom.

"There, there," she said, stroking his hair. "You'll be alright."

The next thing he knew, there was a twilight-blue sky above him. He seemed to be travelling on his back, feet first, through the bumpy air.

"What the fugging hell's going on?" he slurred, before relapsing into oblivion.

* * *

The next thing he knew, he was cool and dry - surrounded by linen and daylight. On his right, the panes of a tall window ran with rain. He became aware of other beds, of nurses swishing past, of a drip attached to his wrist, of Demelza.

She was asleep upright in a chair at the side of his bed, her hands clasped patiently on her lap. He gazed at her without worship or desire. He gazed at her as a sister. She'd obviously looked out for him - that's why they were both here. It was time he started looking out for her. All he'd ever thought about was his own grief, yet hers had been infinitely worse. He had three half-sisters who he'd never met. Her presence in his life, as a whole-sister, more than made up for that absence.

She opened her eyes; made contact with his; smiled; reached under the sheet for his left hand.

"How do you feel?"

"It just comes naturally."

She laughed, more with relief than mirth.

"I'm sorry," he said, referring to his attempt at a joke, but hoping also to encompass his period of unjust hatred, the trouble his obsessiveness had caused.

She shook her head slowly:

"You couldn't help it."

"What's wrong with me, anyway?"

"You're a nutter."

"I mean, physically," he chuckled.

"Septicaemia... But antibiotics..."

"Oh... Do you think he?"

"No."

"Why not?"

It seemed absurd: all those millions of people, now including himself, whose lives had been saved by a fungus, yet Jack had died from the lack of one.

"You know why not."

"Did you see it - growing above him?"

"Yes."

"Did you leave it?"

"Yes."

"What are we going to do?"

"Survive."

"We can't just let it go."

"We have to. It's over. There's no connection between up there and down here."

"Why don't we make one?"

"What do you want to do? Start a religion?"

"Why not?"

"Because it wouldn't work. What we had was true. If we tried to spread it, it would become false."

He nodded, although he didn't agree.

"I blame that bloody pilot. He never made the jump. We shouldn't have let him in. He was the – what do you call it? – spanner in the works."

"Don't be silly. If it wasn't for him you'd be dead. He was the one who traced you."

"You what?"

"I was worried you'd done yourself in, but he showed me you were still around... We hoped you'd eventually come back of your own accord, after you'd sorted yourself out. Then later on we thought maybe you couldn't come back, even if you did want to... Yesterday morning after a lot of blind alleys he came here to the loony unit and found that was where you'd been all along. He picked me up and we drove over to the people who were supposed to be looking after you, but of course you'd gone. They seemed to think you might be making for Brittany, but we thought we'd try the bowl... So that's how we found you... I don't think you'd have lasted another night."

"I was trying to get back."

"I know you were. But now you're back for good, aren't you?"

"Looks like it," he said cheerfully, hoping to hide the rips in his soul.

"You'll come home with me when they discharge you, won't you?"

"I don't know."

"I need you."

"In that case..."

"I'm going loopy there by myself. It's like I'm the one who's dead."

"Don't," he implored. "Of course I'll come... Where's Rhiannon?"

"She's living with Barg and Moira. They've got a winter-let just above Ashburton... I really couldn't cope with her any longer."

"What about the baby?"

"He's a wonder of the world. They've called him Piran."

"So why did they leave?"

"They were worried about the birth. They're intending to go back up when he's older."

"Ty a wor del ve comondyes dhym ladha Bargos?" (You know I was told to kill Bargos?)

She laughed:

"What are you talking about? Who told you?"

"They did. The people on Jack's side. Even if he's innocent. An innocent Judas is better than no Judas at all."

"Oh, don't be so ridiculous."

He repressed any further theological observations, seeing the look of shocked disappointment in her eyes.

She leaned forward, kissed his forehead, stood up;

"I'm going to go home now - I didn't get any sleep last night. See you tomorrow."

Without looking back, she walked wearily away.

"Drat," he muttered.

* * *

For the rest of the afternoon he oscillated between consciousness and coma, between bad dream and good dream, between good dream and no dream at all. Meanwhile, the assault of fungi upon bacteria passed its turning point. By teatime he was able to take some solid food. Afterwards, he enjoyed the banter which circulated among his fellow-patients before the waves of evening visitors began to roll in.

He noted that many of the relationships now depicted - husband and wife, son and mother, father and daughter – were sustained by love, a contrast to those he'd observed in the Unit, where visits usually ended in blankness or rage.

The relatives had for the most part departed when Jim appeared:

"You just can't keep away from this place, can you?"

Terp grinned, then frowned and tried to look less well than he felt. He'd hardly had time to worry about this encounter, had certainly not foreseen it happening tonight, so he was relieved by the jauntiness of the greeting.

Jim sighed and sat down.

"Hard day?"

"You're telling me. My head is throbbing."

"They get to you, don't they?"

"Yeah. I'm in the wrong job."

"No, you're in the right job. It's all your colleagues that are in the wrong job."

"That's unfair."

"Most, then."

"Still unfair."

"Some?"

"Maybe."

"You realise this is the first conversation we've ever had?"

"Doesn't seem like it."

"No, it doesn't seem like it at all. You can know people without hearing them speak intelligibly. You knew me, didn't you?"

"I thought I did."

"I'm sorry for leaving like that, but I had no choice. There was something I had to check on."

"So what happened? I got a very brief picture from your friends. How come you're speaking English now?"

"I was released from-"

He ummed a little, censoring the word 'vow', remembering that their relationship still possessed both legal and psychiatric components; so, although he wanted to tell the whole truth, he now presented an abridged version of events, which included no lies, but emphasised the secessionism, the Celticism, and skated over mushrooms and tigers.

"Wow," said Jim, when he'd been filled in. "Sounds like something worth doing... What a terrible way for it to end."

"Yeah. But the thing is, he didn't think it was terrible. He was pretty light-hearted about it himself... If I look back to his actual death, it was an easy thing, a simple thing - just slipping across from one state to another... Even though he looked weak, I'm sure he was just as strong as ever."

Realising he'd strayed onto dubious ground, he scanned Jim's face for signs of distaste; found none.

"That's how I felt at the time. But of course since then it's been overlaid by so much heaviness..."

"You must cling to it as it was, and I don't mean that in a therapeutic way. I mean, really cling... You were privileged."

"Thank you - for everything. I always knew you'd understand."

"So what are you going to do? We'd love you to come back, but you don't have to. The guardian thing is no problem."

"I'd like to go and stay with Demelza for a while. She's had no-one to help her and she's suffered far more than any of us. But if you still want me to work on the house, I'd love to do that."

"Great," said Jim, standing up. "I'll look forward to it. You just make sure you get better first. I talked to the nurses on the way in. They think you'll be able to come out tomorrow."

* * *

Just before lunch next day, he took a shallow bath, having been advised to keep the dressing on his stomach dry. At two o'clock, Marianne arrived with a bag of clothes and her daughter.

"This is Hannah."

"Hello, Peter. Good to meet you."

He looked at her dumbfounded. A swarm of butterflies bombinated inside his abdomen. She lowered her eyes in response to his stare and he saw the opposing curves of brows and lashes.

"I thought you were speaking now," said Marianne.

"I am," he grinned. "I'm sorry."

"We're going to drive you over to Paignton."

An hour later, he was lying on the sofa in the living-room. Hannah sat in the armchair opposite. Demelza had taken Marianne out to the back-garden, to show her the baby-pole, which was now permanently vertical.

"You know I saw you the other night," he began. "When was it? Three nights ago? Or four? I can't remember."

She looked puzzled.

"You were sitting on the bed in the room I used. Cradling a pillow?"

Her eyes and mouth widened as she realised.

"Mum asked me to try and divine where you were. I'm supposed to have this power. But I didn't see you, not properly, although I did sort of feel that you were there."

"You must have summoned me. And I came without even knowing that I'd been summoned. How about that?"

"It is amazing," she murmured.

There was so much warmth in her voice, in her eyes, he could have stripped there and then.

"Well, it's amazing now. At the time we thought it meant you were dead."

"I know you did... Maybe I was... And if I was, then you resurrected me."

She laughed and waved the idea away:

"So what was it like, being a ghost?"

"Frustrating mainly. I couldn't get any closer to you than about this."

He indicated with his hands a distance of a few inches.

"The aura."

"You think so?"

"Must have been."

"You know what I would have regretted most about dying?"

"What?"

"Never having touched you."

"Ah," she murmured, sliding out of the chair, kneeling beside the sofa, taking his hand.

The most astonishing current of delight came in through her palm, ran up his arm and down into his solar plexus, his stomach, his groin. He closed his eyes and, perhaps for the first time in his life, felt whole.

Then, without warning, she took back her hand and stood up.

"What's the matter. Didn't you feel it?"

"Yes, but I don't want to. It's too much. I'm not ready for anything like that."

"Suit yourself," he shrugged, baffled more than irritated. "No hurry."

CHAPTER SIXTEEN

"I MUST have been firing blanks," he said.

The news of Rose's pregnancy had led him to this diagnosis. He wasn't worried on his own behalf. He only mentioned it because he was interested in discovering Demelza's attitude. The issue had hardly been discussed when they were up there, although he did remember Jack once muttering something about the sparsity of souls over the moor.

"I think that's all it was. I bet if you and Rose had stayed together down here it would have happened straightaway... That's the pity of it. He wouldn't bring children into this world, only that. So I took the Pill for ten years, right up until the time we left... But they were here all along, just waiting to be born."

"Do you mean here in the house?"

"Yeah. Or in the garden."

"And you never had any inkling?"

"I can't pretend I did... I'm glad I didn't. It would have been unbearable."

"Is it bearable now?"

"I don't know," she sobbed, burying her face in his chest.

He stroked her hair with a brother's hand, dislodging a few wood-chips. He concocted caressing sounds in his diaphragm. There was nothing more he could do, nothing more he ought to do. Since his return he'd tried hard to annul himself when he was with her, to become a culture on which her grief could grow. She hadn't had a chance to mourn properly until now, given the turmoil in which everyone else, especially himself, had indulged. For the first two days she'd wept and raved; sometimes angry with Jack for leaving; sometimes angry with herself for letting him leave; sometimes even hinting at an imbalance in their relationship, an inequality which Terp had neither observed nor suspected. Today, feeling calmer, she'd spent most of the daylight hours in the garden, roughing out her infant-pole with the help of a chain-saw. Tomorrow, he hoped to see her smile.

He enjoyed the passive role. It was better to hum than to speak. This afternoon, while she worked, he'd started composing a sermon on behalf of the ranter who still lived noisily inside him; but, after inflicting little more than a dark and repulsive doodle on his piece of notepaper, had soon given up. Who would listen? If anyone did listen, would they hear? If anyone heard, would they follow? If anyone followed, would they make the jump? If anyone made the jump, would they learn the language? Considering these improbabilities, perhaps it was better not to bother. After all, Jack himself had rarely preached, never to the unconverted.

She raised her head. His shirt-front was soaked.

"At least I've got the next one started... I'm looking forward to hearing them speak."

This was how she talked about carving – as though it belonged in a category equivalent to but distinct from life and death. Unlike his own, her cosmogony was both innocuous and rewarding, might even correspond with the truth. Who was he to say how the unborn spend their timelessness? He admired the baby-pole as a sensual, spiritual, technical achievement and anyway disdained the concept of insanity.

"Do you ever think it was all a big mistake?"

"Never," he replied, without hesitation.

"I do sometimes. If we hadn't gone up he wouldn't have died. Surely you'd exchange that for this?"

"It might be better for us. But what about him? He'd be like a fugitive from his own fate."

She sighed and slowly nodded:

"I know what you mean."

* * *

After a week's convalescence, he revived his motorbike and then began using it daily to travel over to the old vicarage. The job was much easier now: options could be discussed; instead of simply carrying out Jim's orders he could make his own suggestions as to ways they should proceed; and often these suggestions, whether based on structural or financial or aesthetic factors, were accepted. At first he worked hard enough, yet without any deep enthusiasm, discomfited by the suspicion that he was procrastinating again; but once the processes, the tools, the materials regained their hold on him he began to realise that this existence wasn't necessarily second-best to another. If Jack had led at all, it had been by example; and one important facet of his example had been the fifteen years he'd spent building, during the last of which - first in Paignton by day and then up on the moor by night - Terp had worked alongside him as his labourer, his pupil, his receptacle. In a sense the apprenticeship continued, even in the absence of the master: in order to imitate him fully perhaps he should complete another fourteen years before moving on. In another sense his own behaviour constituted a real, though minor, aspect of Jack's immortality: all his actions - the way he held a hammer, wielded a trowel, planned a day; even the terms he used in talking to Jim or organising a delivery on the telephone - were imbued with Jack's spirit. Although formally trained in bricklaying, Jack had picked up the other trades as he went along. He'd once talked about being 'drunk with carpentry'. Now, as Terp tackled the restoration of the staircase, he began to experience the same intoxication.

He refused to take more money than he needed for food and petrol, explaining that he was still an apprentice. This arrangement, instead of an hourly rate, meant he could repay them by ensuring that the greatest possible proportion of their surplus income went on materials; it also meant he could take his time.

Marianne was even more attractive to be with than before. Every day he could see Hannah in her. He remained for the most part silent when they were together. This was how she liked him – a pool into which her stream could disappear without judgement or repercussion. Mother and daughter (according to Jim) had fallen out again, cause unknown, so for the first few days, to Terp's disappointment, Hannah was hardly mentioned. Then one afternoon, as they sat in the kitchen, the cause burst through: Marianne vehemently disapproved of Hannah's relationship with a person old enough to be her father, or even her grandfather; a person she herself had hated and despised for years.

Terp clenched his teeth, his buttocks, his fists. So this was what he was up against. Some dirty geriatric was pawing his future wife.

"I really thought you two were going to hit it off and she'd come to her senses... He's just some little tinpot guru type. He hasn't got an ounce of spirit himself, but what he can do is recognise it in others... And then he leeches for all he's worth... Ugh, I'm too angry to talk about it."

She stood up, drained her cup and began vigorously wiping the surfaces. Terp sat a little longer, shocked and infected by her vitriol, then went back to work. The next day, at the same tea-break, the story began to emerge. She'd met him first about a year after Hannah's birth. In those days he was known as 'Muktananda'. (Today, having been through his Indian and then his Native American incarnations, he insisted on being called 'Zed'.) She'd been to one of his crummy lectures and afterwards had been introduced to him by the friend she'd gone with. He'd told her he was looking forward to seeing her paintings. She'd assumed he was mistaking her for someone else, as in those days she couldn't even draw. Hannah's father having just left her for someone else, she was at 'rock bottom'. He'd started coming round, taking her in with his insidious altruism, pretending that her spiritual development was his sole concern, convincing her that she was destined for better things than maternity; the eventual sad result being that Hannah was sent, at the age of one and a half, to live with her father, while Marianne embarked on her vocation. He undertook to guide her himself, although he knew 'eff all about it'. After a few months of ceaseless drawing, of painting, of studying how others had drawn and painted, she was ready for her first project - to complete thirty-six crucifixions, in oil, on canvas, for the first of which he posed with a torn pillowcase over his loins. When she'd completed it to his satisfaction he took it away and ordered her to start on the next, using no reference but her memory. So the work went on for nearly a year. She struggled to gain facility, then she struggled to lose it. Boredom was forbidden. She must focus always on the importance of what she was doing, both for herself and for the world. She must live the anguish. There was no celebration when the thirty-sixth had been completed. The world was no different. He paid her pittance and left with hardly a word. She didn't see him again for ages - a couple of months, when he'd been coming more than weekly. Having known anguish so well, she now knew desolation and self-loathing. Somehow, she'd failed. Never did she doubt that in forsaking her, he was still guiding her. After weeks of torpor she forced herself to start painting again, now taking as her subject the deposition, inspired by a wax model made in the sixteenth century. She hoped this was the answer: only beyond the deposition and the entombment could there be the resurrection.

At this point she left the kitchen, returning in a few minutes with an open book.

"There it is," she said. "Isn't it amazing? So dynamic. It wasn't made to last and yet it has. It was made to be painted from."

He stared at the photograph: three crosses, three ladders - in wood; the waxen bodies of Christ and the two thieves being lowered to the waxen ground.

"Sansovino," he read. "Never heard of him."

"Jacopo. I owe him a lot. He really saved me... See, he did it simply as a guide for a friend of his who'd been commissioned to paint the subject. The picture hasn't survived, but the model has."

"Mmm," he went, feebly trying to echo her sense of wonder.

In truth, he wasn't that interested. His vision was fully occupied by the ugly image of the charlatan.

"So what happened – when you saw him again?"

"Nothing much. He turned up out of the blue, after all that time, but I was still overjoyed that he'd come, dying to show him my new work. He pushed me away. He wouldn't even come in. He handed me a terracotta what-do-you-ma-call-it? Thing with a lid? An urn. Told me my enlightenment was inside and walked away. I opened it – ashes. I ran after him, still loving him, caught him at the gate, asked him to explain. Your pictures, he said, what else? As though I was an idiot. Only then did I realise, not just that he didn't care, but that he was actually malicious. When I saw that smug little woman sitting in the passenger-seat of his car, done up like a gypsy, I went berserk and smashed the urn against the windscreen."

She giggled at the memory.

"It was so funny, but not at the time. The ashes blew back all over me... He grabbed me and sort of threw me away. You've really blown it now, he said... Got in behind the wheel, punched a hole through the windscreen and drove off. That was the last time I had anything to do with him. Of course, I'd heard stories about him over the years, knew he'd changed his name to Zed, but really I'd hardly thought about him until Hannah told me she was involved... I'm so worried... What he might do to her... She's not the strongest tree in the wood."

Terp shook his head slowly, sadly; imagining his frail Hannah in the clutches of this monster.

"Does she know? About you and him?"

"No. Definitely not. I'm sure she would have said. And I don't want her to know. She'd just think I was jealous or something... Oh, I realise you should let your children make their own mistakes, but not exactly the same mistake you made and not when it's putting their lives in danger... There must be some way to stop it."

"I could kill him," he murmured, deadpan.

"Hadn't thought of that," she laughed. "Great idea. You could get away with it as well."

"Yes. I could."

"I hope you're not serious. No, I just thought perhaps you could be a bit more persistent. You seem to have given up... I know you're pining for her."

"You're right," he said, pushing back his chair and rising, resolute. "Give me her mobile number. I'll ring her this minute."

He took the phone outside, indicating that he'd be inhibited if she were to listen. Hannah answered quickly.

"Can you talk? Where are you?"

"In my car."

"Where's your car?"

"Just approaching Cumberland."

"When will you be back?"

"Tomorrow night."

"I'd like to meet Zed. Will you introduce me?"

"Why?"

"I've heard a lot of good things about him. You know I lost my own teacher. I thought maybe he could give me some advice."

"He's always willing to help. It's a good idea. I'd like you both to meet... I thought Mum would have turned you against him."

"No, not at all. She was just a little concerned about the age-gap."

"What's age got to do with anything? His body might be a few years older than mine, but for all you know his spirit is a new moon."

"Alright, alright. Keep your hair on."

She laughed:

"I suppose I am a bit touchy about it... Tell you what – I'll give him a ring and then call you back."

While waiting, he vaguely surveyed the outside work which he would start in the spring. The roof was passable for the moment, having been coated by the previous owners, but the chimney needed repointing, the cast-iron gutters and down-pipes replacing; then there were all the window-frames, many of which resembled sponge more than wood. The job was endless, deliciously endless...

After twenty minutes or so, Hannah rang to say that Zed would see him at seven the following evening. She herself wouldn't be back until much later, though anyway she thought it best if she wasn't around when they met...

He was astonished at how quickly and easily everything had fallen into place: the omens were good. He went in and, after pleasing Marianne with the news that he would see Hannah next day, began to sharpen his sheath-knife.

* * *

When he pulled up at home that evening, one rear door of the van was open and someone was rooting noisily about inside. Imagining a thief, he kept his helmet on, undid the clasp around the handle of his knife, crept up the driveway and slammed the door shut.

"Oi!" came Demelza's voice from within.

He opened up and apologised; asked what on earth she was doing, fearing that she'd finally flipped.

"Looking for Three-in-One," she said. "Mine's run out. I thought Jack might have some."

"What do you need it for?"

"Sharpening my gouges."

"Why not use this?" he suggested, unearthing a container of engine-oil. "Anything will do for that job."

"I like Three-in-One," she said, and began to sob.

"Come on," he cooed, helping her out. "Leave it till the morning. You can't work in the dark, can you?"

"Some of those things in there he touched more than me."

"So? You're not jealous of his tools now, are you?"

She giggled through her tears. He put his arm around her and ushered her into the house.

"You spent more time with him in the last year than I did."

"Possibly. But I didn't sleep with him - at least, not very often."

She guffawed and punched his shoulder. The crisis deflated.

After supper, he asked her if she'd heard of Zed. She hadn't, but apparently there were hundreds of these 'small-time gurus' out there in the South Hams. Years before, when they were about Terp's age, she and Jack had dipped their feet into what she now called 'all that pick-and-mix nonsense'. They'd sat in a sweat-lodge with a 'public-school shaman'; practised the 'feeble rituals' of neo-pagan magic; attended a Tantric weekend run by a 'tubby little voyeur'; hovered on the edges of a group called *Buddhists for Jesus* (or it might have been *Christians for Buddha* – she couldn't quite remember). They'd met a lot of 'phoneys', a lot of seekers, no finders; concluded there was nothing to find.

"Oh, I've heard of worse than that," she said, when he'd told her of Marianne's experience with Zed. "I mean you could say he started her off. Look at her now – she's a perfectly reasonable person and a fucking good painter."

Terp frowned, quickly rejecting the possibility of disguised benevolence. He didn't want any ambiguity to pollute his attitude, which was pure, righteous, perhaps even chivalric. Revenge for Marianne, rescue for

Hannah: these were motive enough; added now a blow for truth, for the way they'd discovered against all the other 'ways' he'd just glimpsed, which were nothing but delusion.

He went to bed early, needing to temper himself for tomorrow. If his plan worked out, he might subsequently become a serial avenger, clearing the land of false prophets...

CHAPTER SEVENTEEN

AT SIX the next day, having left his bike in a corner of the Co-op car park, he came into the village Fore Street and began counting down the numbers. He wore sunglasses, a black baseball cap, a maroon shirt and black trousers with each pocket swollen by a glove. His scheme was failproof. Once inside alone with the monster, he would stab it through the heart; return to his bike; put on his waterproofs and helmet; then ride noisily back for seven as if to keep his appointment. He'd seen everything so clearly the night before he felt sure that, in some sense, in some dimension, it had all already happened: after ringing ostentatiously for a few minutes, peering in at the windows etc., he would rouse the neighbours, raise the alarm. He would thus be present, shocked and distraught, when the body was discovered.

The first flaw in his precognition became apparent as soon as he reached the right house: instead of a single doorbell, there was a panel of buzzers and names.

"You looking for Zed?" said a youth, as he was letting himself in.

Terp took his finger off the buzzer and nodded.

"In the pub."

He looked across the street to where the youth had gestured with his thumb.

"Fucking shit," he groaned, after the door had closed.

The lounge was empty. There were a few people in the saloon: some youngish workers standing by the bar; three old men sitting at a table. Two of the old men were playing crib; the other was looking on. They were dressed similarly, with jackets and ties and cloth caps and ruddy faces, the rustic effect being somewhat spoiled by cheap trainers.

He was just about to go and check the lounge again when the onlooker said:

"Peedur?"

Terp glanced round to make sure there was no-one else in the line of sight, then pointed quizzically at his chest.

"You early, boy. I were just going to finish this yer pint, then go over 'ome."

The accent was strong, but not quite recognisable.

"Now you'm 'ere, I'll 'ave a rum an' shrub."

Terp drifted fogbound towards the bar. The landlady gave him such a disdainful look that he pocketed his shades and tried to smile as he ordered the drinks.

He sat down on the bench beside the old man; put his hands behind his back to hide their shaking.

Zed emptied the rum in one go, chasing it down with a large swig from his pint of mild.

Terp racked his brains for something to say, but his brains were busy trying to deal with a deluge of incredulity. How could this codger ever have been the satanic figure described by Marianne?

Zed rapped his empty short-glass lightly on the table and made a slight noise in his throat, sometimes transcribed as 'ahem'.

"Would you like another?"

"I don't mind. I'll have a large 'un."

"Two rum and shrubs, please," said Terp, returning to the bar. "Make them doubles."

He followed the old fellow's suit, swallowing the rum whole, then washing it down with ale.

"Thass it, boy," said Zed, nudging him with his elbow. "Only way."

Terp gawped open-mouthed around the saloon, his head levitated by the infusion of alcohol.

"Fifteen two, fifteen four, fifteen six, two's eight and one for his nob's nine," said the cribbage-player diagonally opposite, picking up a peg and registering his score on the board. "I'm in."

He looked across to Zed:

"You backed the wrong 'orse agyen."

"Blimmin' 'eck," moaned Zed, opening a little leather purse and emptying out a few coppers.

"Thass all I got. Can you make it up, Peedur?"

"What to?"

"'Tis only a pound."

Terp produced all that he had left: between them, they possessed ninety pence.

"I'll owe 'ee tenpence," said Zed to the victor, scooping up the change and passing it over.

Terp wanted to laugh, mainly at himself. So much for his career as a fearless avenger. He'd only known the guy ten minutes and already he was paying his gambling debts.

After his companions had embarked upon a new game, Zed moved a little closer to Terp and murmured:

"Hannah say you lost your teacher up air."

He waved his right hand towards the moor.

"Yeah."

"Want me to help?"

"If you can."

Zed turned to face him, first removing his own cloth cap, then lifting off Terp's baseball cap:

"Let's have a look at 'ee."

So they scrutinised each other, Terp desperate to find behind the white soft hair, the well-creased laughter-lines, the sparky blue eyes, some sign of lurking evil.

Zed pulled out of the stare, grinned, nodded and turned away to fill his pipe.

"Well?" said Terp. "What's the verdict?"

"You lucky, boy. You don't need nuthen..."

"Really?"

"... Except what I got."

"How do you mean?"

"...I got what you need... I might give it to 'ee."

"Oh," gulped Terp, reaching for the safety of his pint.

141

Zed stood up; took leave of the cribbage-players with a few affectionate words and squeezes; raised a hand to the bar.

"S'later, Dorothy."

"Alright, Zeddie," said the landlady. "You take care now."

"Drink up, boy."

Terp swallowed his remainder, then followed Zed, who was swaying gingerly towards the door.

They crossed the street and stood on the threshold while Zed searched for his key. After going through about a dozen pockets he gave up and began pressing buzzers at random.

"Who is it?" came a female voice over the intercom.

"Sme. Let us in. I've forgotten my key."

He pushed the front door open. They went up the first flight of stairs and into a small unlocked room which smelled like an amplified version of Zed himself.

Terp's baffled glance took in a gate-leg table and two upright chairs; an ugly great wardrobe; two single beds, one with a lime-green, corrugated counterpane, the other with a bare mattress surmounted by an open rucksack; unadorned, woodchip-papered walls; a grimy, curtainless sash-window. There seemed to be no television, no radio, no reading-matter; not even a clock.

Zed spun his cap into a corner; hung his jacket over one of the upright chairs; yanked off his tie and let it fall to the floor. He sat down and felt in the jacket-pockets for his pipe and tobacco. He began to fill the pipe, then abandoned it. After sitting head-bowed and motionless for a minute or so, he crawled and flopped groaning onto the bed.

"You alright?"

"I shall be in a minute," he whispered. "It don't last long."

His ruddiness had been replaced by pallor; his half-closed eyes were showing only whites; his breaths were slow and rattly.

"Have you got any medication?" said Terp, loudly. "Any tablets?"

No response. Zed was now apparently unconscious. Terp rushed out of the room. One of the other doors on the landing was open.

"Hello!" he shouted, knocking.

A woman wearing two towels, one covering her body from the armpits down, the other around her head, emerged from an alcove.

"Sorry to barge in, but I'm worried about Zed opposite. He seems to be having some kind of turn. It looks serious. I don't know what to do."

"God," she said, whooshing past him, flavouring his nose with mandarins.

He followed her across to the room. She sat down on the edge of the bed; placed a palm on Zed's forehead.

"Shouldn't we get a doctor?"

"Shush a minute," she whispered.

At the end of the minute, Zed opened his eyes and grinned up at her.

"Nice turban," he murmured.

"Thank goodness for that," she sighed, tweaking his cheek. "I thought I was going to have to give you the kiss of life."

"Didn't you fancy it?"

"Not really."

He began to slide his hand in between towel and knee. She stood up, chuckling:

"Nothing wrong with you... When's Hannah back?"

"Tonight."

"Good... I'm going to get dressed."

Nodding at Terp as she passed, she closed the door behind her.

Zed sat up.

"Sorry about that, Peter. I'm all yours now... I'll just stay here for a bit, if you don't mind."

He rotated his pillow through ninety degrees before sandwiching it between his back and the headboard.

"What happened then? What's wrong with you?"

"Nothing wrong. I'm dying, that's all... Just putting it off for a bit... These little deaths keep me in credit with the big death."

As well as losing a lot of its accent, his voice seemed to have deepened by a few tones.

"So that was a little death?"

"That's what they call it."

"Who?"

"The people who talk about it."

Terp grinned and shook his head:

"Are you sure you're OK?"

"Positive... I'm good for another few hours at least."

"You are joking?...You seem so different now."

"Wouldn't you be different if you'd just come back to life?"

"I don't know," laughed Terp. "Depends who I came back as."

"Exactly... Why don't you sit over there?"

He pointed at the foot of the other bed.

"That's it. Lean up against her rucksack, then we can both be comfortable."

Having done as he was bid, he began to feel amazingly relaxed. The muscle-pains from his day's work seemed more like pleasures. His head rested against Hannah's rucksack, filled with Hannah's clothes, exuding Hannah's scent. She was here in all but body.

"I know why you came."

"What do you mean?"

"I wasn't born yesterday... I was born today."

They both laughed at this as though it were hysterically funny.

"I'm sorry that I ever had the thought, really sorry," implored Terp. "I imagined you were some kind of monster."

"You don't need them."

"What?"

144

"Imaginary monsters. You can use the space for something else."

Terp wanted to defend himself against the implications of this charge, but could hardly do so without involving Marianne.

"You don't need any of that negative stuff. You love each other. Isn't that enough?... You know I've never touched her, don't you?"

"Really?"

"I've been inside her many times, yes, but I've never touched her. I know her like a verger knows his cathedral. Now I must retire from that duty, that wonderful duty."

He held out his right fist, palm down.

"Look at all the keys on this ring, the size of them, the age of them. They're yours now. Here, catch."

Terp joined in the mime by cupping his hands and grunting as though the impact hurt.

"She was only staying here because she thinks I need looking after. And I was only keeping her here because I think she needs looking after. Her work makes her very vulnerable."

"Her work?"

"You know. What do they call it nowadays? Remote viewing. She's using it to help find missing people. You can guess what a tricky job it is. Say I give you something belonging to someone who's disappeared – a sock perhaps. You tune in to the sock. If you do it the way Hannah does it you can then see the person. You can tell the relatives or whoever's sent for you whether their loved one is alive or dead. But you can't prove it, unless the person happens to be buried beneath a signpost, or else living somewhere you recognise. You're limited to a radius of about twelve feet around the body. Beyond that, the resonance fades and all you get is fog. See the problem? She's tried using maps, but you know what women are like with maps. All the time she's tuned in she's defenceless. Her own existence is negated. She's got no space to protect her. It's dangerous to stay too long. So, if the person is alive, it's not possible just to follow them about until some evidence of where they are appears. Sometimes she's lucky. Letters are useful, at least the envelopes in which letters come. Then of course she can pinpoint them. But often she gets no clue at all."

Zed rose from the bed; tapped his chest a few times with an open palm; inhaled noisily.

"I feel a hell of a lot better... You hungry?"

"Could be."

"Well, I'm bleddy starving. Let's go and see if there's anything we can scrounge. The stuff she left me with has run out."

Terp followed him down to the communal kitchen. They peered into an aluminium saucepan containing half an inch of congealed stew; agreed it was unpalatable.

One of the cupboards contained a slightly stale French stick.

"This'll do," said Zed.

They broke the bread and ate.

Terp munched avidly. Despite the dryness, it still tasted of heaven. He'd had nothing for ages.

Zed stopped after slowly ingesting no more than a morsel.

"I thought you were starving."

"I don't need much to fill me up. Your stomach shrinks along with everything else, you know."

"Is that right?"

As they left the kitchen the towel-woman, now dressed and made-up, arrived at the foot of the stairs.

"I'm just going out for a couple of hours. Will you be alright?"

"I feel fine, Maddy," he said, putting his arm around her. "On top of the world... And anyway, I've got Peter here to look after me."

They ascended into the room and resumed their previous positions on the beds.

"So you're pretty much sorted out."

"Am I?"

"Course you are. She'll come to you very soon."

"If she wants to."

"I know she wants to."

"And you and she never...?"

"I already told you. Don't you believe me? I gave that other job up years ago, or rather it give me up. She's more of a virgin now than when I met her."

"Glad to hear it... So how did you meet her?"

"I was walking back along the road from Totnes one evening. She stopped and offered me a lift. She'd just split up with her boyfriend... I had a bit of a turn in the car. She brought me home... My only real talent is seeing other people's talents, which are often hidden from themselves..."

His remarks were interrupted by an abysmal yawn.

"Oh, God... I think I'm going to have to have a nap."

"Do you want me to leave?"

"No, don't... I only need forty winks, then I'll be right as rain... Must have been all that food..."

He trailed off into sleep.

Terp very slowly reached his left hand into the rucksack and drew forth the topmost garment. It was a kind of vest. He laid it over his face; breathed deeply; breathed blissfully.

* * *

She was drumming with her fingertips on the steering-wheel, in time to the savage music from her system. The car was at a standstill. He swarmed around her, found he was able to get far closer than before; so close he could no longer see the dashboard-lights, no longer see her, no longer hear the music.

He sank to his knees in awe at the majesty. Stained-glass light poured over him like balm. Pillars branched into arches; arches soared into vaults. Far away, a silver cross shimmered above a white altar-cloth. The space was vast, yet thronging with presence; the silence, absolute; the flagstone on which he knelt, hot.

The next thing he knew, the door was being knocked upon; the door was opening; Maddy was appearing; Zed was swinging his legs around and rising from his bed.

"Hannah's just phoned. There's been a pile-up on the M5 and she's stuck behind it. Doesn't know when she'll be home."

Terp stood up after Maddy had departed:

"I better go."

"You're welcome to stay."

"No. I'm pretty knackered."

He didn't want to be there when she got back late.

"It's such a pity. I'd have liked to have seen you two together."

Zed went over to the wardrobe and, after rooting around for a while, produced a flat brown-paper package.

"I want you to have this," he said, tearing open one end and unsheathing an unframed canvas.

Terp beheld a rudimentary crucifixion: no thieves, no centurions, no nails, no beard, no Mary, no blood. The paint seemed to have arrived on the surface in a state of confusion, as though insulted at being handled with such ferocity, yet somehow it had organised itself to allow the image to emerge. The downtilted face alone expressed more anguish, more forsakenness, than ought ever to be depicted.

"It's a bit harrowing," he said.

"There's more to it than meets the eye."

"How do you mean?"

"Abandonment isn't an eternal state."

"I hope not... Who was the artist?"

"Oh, some bird I knew ages ago. She did a whole series for me. This is the only one left. I think I flogged the rest."

If he'd detected the slightest glimmer of duplicity in Zed's eyes, the attack might now have begun. But all

Terp could feel was affection and all he could discern was affection returned, in far greater measure than it was given: the old man's cheeks glistened with tears.

"Goodbye, boy."

* * *

The funeral was an ecological affair: a cardboard coffin; a grave in a meadow; an absence of priest. In silence, they carried him, lowered him, covered him. Once the turf was restored, they embarked on a rendition of 'Abide With Me' - words from photocopied sheets handed out by Hannah, tune from the collective memory of the mourners. The last hailstorm had settled around them, giving the illusion of snow. Terp trembled. He hummed inaudibly, whereas Hannah's singing voice was strong and euphonious. With nudging elbow and shining face, she exhorted him to join in. He stared at the sheet, but the words were blurred by tears; and besides, the melody seemed far more meaningful.

Of the twenty-odd people there, he recognised only Maddy, the two cribbage-players and the landlady of the pub; the rest were mostly in their forties or fifties, a slight majority of women. From overheard conversations in the farmyard and on the walk down, he'd gathered that many of them had been followers. A few appeared in the pub later on. One, a bald bloke with a smoke-wizened face, nodded at Terp as they stood at the bar and asked him if he was a relative.

"I was his son."

"I'm sorry."

"It wasn't biological. In fact, it was only for a few hours."

"Oh, I see what you mean. You were entranced."

"Something like that."

"So he never lost the knack... Marcus."

"Peter," said Terp, shaking the offered hand.

"You knew him recently?"

"Yeah. I only met him a few days ago. He was sitting right there..."

"Really? He never went in pubs when I knew him. Mind you, it was a long time ago."

"Were you a disciple?"

Marcus laughed:

"That's a good word. Depends on the meaning. Did I worship him? Or did I have the discipline for total obedience? It's difficult to remember. I loved him and then I hated him and then I more or less forgot about him. It's funny: now that he's gone, the love seems to have returned..."

"That's good. He was very loveable."

"I never really knew what made him tick. We had a close relationship, but one-sided. He was interested in me. And I was interested in myself. I suppose I never thought of him as a person, only as an authority... an oracle. I wish I'd seen him again. I know he renounced all his previous life. He even told someone he'd just been in the business of exploiting the incomers. I don't believe it myself. He certainly didn't mind taking money off those who had it, but then he also gave his time free to those who didn't."

"He was penniless when he died – literally."

"I'm sure. Of course, he was an incomer himself. You know there are more people living in Devon who weren't born here than there are who were? The difference with him was that he was from the west, whereas almost all the other incomers are from the east or the north. His antecedents were Cornish through and through..."

Hannah came and stood between them, helping herself to one of the sad-looking sandwiches which the landlady had provided in honour of the occasion.

"Do you two know each other?" said Terp, putting his arm around her.

"I think so," she nodded. "You're the organ-man, aren't you?"

"That's right," grinned Marcus.

"What's an organ-man?"

"I work on them – repair them, restore them."

"Oh, yeah? What kind?"

"Church, mostly."

"Good job?"

"Oh God, yes. Couldn't stop anyway, even if I didn't love it. I've got work for years ahead. Sometimes it seems like security and sometimes like a ball and chain... So you must be Marianne's daughter. It's ages since I saw her. How is she?"

"She's doing fine. Except she's gone and got herself pregnant."

"You're not pleased?"

"I don't care. I just think she's getting a bit old."

"Hannah was living with him until the end," interpolated Terp. "It was only because of her that he lasted as long as he did."

"That's rubbish," she protested. "He lasted as long as he wanted to."

* * *

The next day, she insisted on leaving for a new assignment in Norfolk, despite his miscellaneous objections.

"I can't not go. I might be their only chance. How would you like it?" she'd said, to which there was no reply.

He had to admit that the claims she made about her own well-being were confirmed by the physical evidence: she'd put on weight; there was colour in her cheeks; her eyes and hair shone; her asthma had all but disappeared. Those last few hours with Zed had apparently precluded the possibility of grief. She'd found him waiting for her in the yard of the defunct railway-station (where she parked her car). She'd been both touched and appalled. Two o'clock on a clear

November night in nothing more than shirtsleeves seemed like a recipe for hypothermia, yet when they'd got back to the room his forehead had burned her palm. They'd gone to bed straightaway, she in her sleeping-bag, he beneath only a sheet. On the road since morning, she was now beyond exhaustion. When she closed her eyes all she could see were red lights receding from her, white lights coming towards her, and all she could feel was motion; so she kept them open, hoping the room and its contents, duskily illuminated by a compound of streetlight and moonlight, would convince those inertial forces inside her that the journey was over. Very little had happened. He'd cried out once to God, at which she'd got up and pushed her bed against his so she could hold his hand. She'd just settled down again when he began to murmur. He seemed to be concerned about someone called Piran, this being the only word she could dislodge from the unintelligible stream. After that he relapsed into silence, his breathing regular and serene. When she awoke to daylight, his hand was cold. She'd been totally unprepared and yet totally accepting. Although she'd seen no visions, hadn't even had a memorable dream, she felt somehow almost blissful. She'd phoned Terp first. His sense of guilt, which on the ride over superseded all other senses, so that by the time he reached the village he was quite prepared to be accused, and to accept the accusation, of murder, atrophied as soon as he saw her. She was calm, clear, loving. By her actions she made it obvious and irrefutable not only that they were now, but also that they always had been, a couple. When she pulled back the sheet, he found Zed's face locked into a vaguely humorous expression; felt a little fear, a little repulsion, a lot of light-hearted reverence as he bent to kiss the stone forehead.

There was no need to miss her after she'd left for Norfolk. He spent the rest of Sunday trying to inject some colour into the blackness of Demelza's mood. The previous afternoon, anguished at having made a carving-mistake, she'd rammed the chisel into her palm. He helped exchange her bloodstained bandage for a clean dressing; brewed feverfew tea; lit an aromatic candle. He couldn't accept the seriousness of the catastrophe. She'd merely lopped off the tip of an earlobe. He would have just glued it back on and forgotten about it, but for her the world had ended. The infant-pole, nearly complete, must now be abandoned. She maintained that there were only two sins in carving: not going far enough and going too far. Going too far was the mortal sin. Glue and filler were anathema. The only possible redemption lay in starting again from scratch. He argued that she was in a perilous position, that she ought to try and 'get out more'. She scowled, blanketing everything 'out there' with disdain. She'd been sentenced to solitary purgatory, sundered from Jack on the one side and her unborn children on the other. Staying home at least meant being where he had been, where they would have been; at least made the loneliness just about bearable. Despite these unpromising indications, he set about persuading her to come to work with him next day. The job he had in mind – for which he genuinely needed her help – involved restoring some of the decorative plasterwork on one of the vicarage ceilings. Five hours later she relented, a decision she tried to retract at seven the next morning when he went in to wake her up. He refused to leave her alone. She wanted to die. He threatened to fetch a doctor and have her sectioned. Coming from him, she took this for a joke. Nevertheless she promised to be down in ten minutes.

When they arrived, Jim was in the kitchen and Marianne still upstairs. He seemed genuinely joyed to see Demelza, embracing her as though she were his oldest friend, even though they'd only met once. He set about absorbing her distress with the skill of a master. Slivers of her old strength, rudiments of her old banter, began to reappear. In no time she was criticising Jim's lifestyle, characterising him as a 'petit-bourgeois' and an 'Aga-lout'. Jim in turn accused her of being a 'lumpen' or even a 'bloody hippy'. She punched him on the shoulder. He grabbed and squeezed her arm. Terp was astonished to realise that they were actually flirting. Marvelling at Jim's capacity for sympathetic magic, he left them to it.

The largest space downstairs had originally comprised one room, which at some time had been turned into two, and now had become one again. The ornamental border running around the ceiling was interrupted by gaps where the partition had crossed. This border consisted of a relief-pattern representing leaves and acorns, enclosed by a simple moulding. Demelza, having assessed the job, went off in the van to fetch what she required, returning a few hours later with some dental plaster and a retardant. She then started to reproduce, by a process of building up and paring down, the missing sections.

"I knew you could do it," said Terp, at the end of the second day, when only the final smoothing remained. "It's a piece of piss compared to straight carving. Didn't you like being able to add as well as take away?"

She shrugged. She'd shown no interest in stages which have to be gone through, in the healing powers of time, in the possibility of light at the end of a tunnel, in changes which are as good as rests, or any of the other platitudes with which he'd been pelting her.

"Look at it like this: instead of carving into the bare, dead trunk and trying to bring it to a life that was never its own, you're creating the expressions of the tree itself, its leaves, its seeds, its present and future...."

He tailed off, noticing that she was shaking her head dismissively. She wasn't going to be swayed by any twopenny-halfpenny symbolism.

"Plaster is death," she declared.

"Oh, come on. Remember what Jack said when he gave me my tooth. It's not what it's made of that matters. It's what it means."

"That was different... I'm going to do another infant-pole, so you may as well stop trying to put me off. That's the only way I'll agree to live."

"In that case, there's nothing more to say... Funny, isn't it? When you were together I went to pieces and now it's the opposite. It's like we've just got enough strength for one between us... Maybe the only way for you to come up is for me to go down again."

At last she smiled:

"Don't you dare."

She spent most of the third day, having finished her work off early, with Marianne. After struggling in the attic all morning, Terp was headed towards the kitchen to get some food when he heard them talking. He halted in order not to interrupt. In order not to eavesdrop, he should also have retreated, but curiosity got the better of him.

"...I think you're absolutely right to carry on," Marianne was saying. "Some of us deal with the living. Some deal with the dead. I never heard of anyone representing the unborn. It's a whole new field and you've got it all to yourself."

CHAPTER EIGHTEEN

AT first they adhered to their original intention, of returning when the baby was three months old. Bargos remained enthusiastic about the subsistence side of the venture. Since coming down, he'd often considered the mass of protein running around inside rabbit-skins, even tried to calculate the yearly tonnage killed by cars and eaten by magpies or killed by cats and eaten by flies. The figures he came up with always towered over the modest quantities killed by buzzards and eaten by buzzards. This was the one principle on which he'd asserted himself: if they were to be genuinely self-sufficient they must devour nothing that was not freely available. Mutton should be excluded, because the taking of sheep involved depriving some poor hill-farmer of his livelihood. Moira had scoffed at this qualm, claiming that the hill-farmers only pretended to be poor, that they were subsidised to the hilt, that they probably got more in compensation for a lost sheep than for one they took to market. Nevertheless, she agreed to leave all practical and moral considerations to him, just as he allowed her to dictate their metaphysical arrangements. Barg didn't have a system of his own, never had had: when you're flying you don't need one and when you're not flying you don't want one; so he had no grounds for any objection to her new synthesis, where Piran became the pinnacle towards which all previous human progress had aspired. The other three 'breeding pairs' had been infertile, therefore they were meant to be infertile. Yet the other three had aligned themselves voluntarily whereas she and Barg had been forced together despite strong mutual repulsion. Perhaps that's why their partnership was so perfect now: they'd got all possible hatred out of the way to start with.

"Oh, I don't think I ever hated you," he said. "I just felt at the time you were misguided."

"Well, I hated you. You were the most pompous, repressed person I'd ever met."

"Charming... You were a bit of a pain in the arse yourself, always lecturing me about something or other... Still are, come to think of it."

"Only for your own good," she said, punching him. "You were like a blank slate. You needed covering with runes."

"What are they?"

"Never mind," she said, putting her forefinger to her lips. "Ny goth dhyn usya tavas an dyscryjyk." (We should not be using the language of the infidel.)

She'd made it a rule to speak only Cornish if either or both of them were alone with Piran. Sometimes they lapsed when he was sleeping, as he was at this moment, blissfully, in his crib beside their bed. She'd become even more imperious since the birth. Her status as a milkflowing mother seemed to have augmented her power. Her pronouncements had always been infallible. Now, her orders were undisobeyable. Barg chuckled to himself. It had just occurred to him that she had single-handedly replaced the whole of the Royal Air Force, under whose slightly less rigorous authority he had previously consented to live.

"Lavar dhym," she said. (Tell me.)

He shook his head, grinning. It would be both linguistically difficult and emotionally unwise to communicate such a comparison.

They were lying, clothed, on top of the duvet, the room dimly lit by a red-shaded lamp. She sat up and poked him in the gut.

"Res yw dhym gothvos an pyth yw mar wharthus." (I want to know what is so funny.)

"Travyth." (Nothing.)

She swung herself round to straddle him. He grunted. She wasn't getting any lighter. He pulled her down and rasped his chin-stubble against her neck. She screamed. The baby woke up. She reached across and began to vibrate the crib, cooing a little lullaby:

Marak dha ven melyn
Oll an forth aberth
Oll an forth aberth
Oll an forth aberth

Der newl hag hager awel
Oll an forth aberth
Oll an forth aberth
Oll an forth aberth

Ow tremena run ha morhogh
Oll an forth aberth
Oll an forth aberth
Oll an forth aberth

(Ride your millstone/All the way in... Through mist and tempest/All the way in... Past seal and dolphin/ All the way in...)

When she was sure sleep had returned, she stopped singing and looked earnestly down at Barg:

"Nyns ues dowtys dhys?" (You have no doubts?)

He shook his head in surprise. This was not the kind of question she usually asked. Their empathy, their identity of purpose, had always been taken for granted. Doubts were anyway pointless without alternatives, and there was no alternative. The money to which he had access, in his current account, would run out if they didn't go soon. He hoped to leave some as a fallback in case they couldn't survive on the moor. There'd been talk about her getting something from her husband as a one-off payment for all her years of barrenness and slavery, for all his years of carelessness and infidelity, but 'Tim' had failed to keep either of the appointments he'd made to come round and thrash things out.

Beside the lack of any alternative to returning glowed a constant truth: Barg had fallen to earth exactly there. A split second earlier or later with his ejection, a fraction of a knot more or less wind, he'd have landed miles away and this little family would never have existed. So the place was certainly crucial, probably sacred.

"Saw ponvotter my a'm bues ef dhe dhos ha bos claf ha ny vyth gallos dhyn y sawya." (I only worry that he will get sick and we will be unable to cure him.)

"Prag a vynsa ef? Ef yw mar yagh. Ef yw mar gref.." (Why should he? He is so healthy. He is so strong.)

"Jak o yagh ha cref." (Jack was healthy and strong.)

She nodded blissfully:

"Destnans Jak o dyffrans." (Jack had a different destiny.)

Barg laughed.

"Ef o cref lowr dhe verwel," she continued. (He was strong enough to die.) "Peran yw cref lowr dhe vewa." (Piran is strong enough to live.)

"Gront e ewn os ta." (I hope you are right.)

"Yth of pupprys ewn. Yma Jak ow provya car ha seyth margh gwyn rag y halya adrus dhe'n bys aral hag yth eson ny ow provya kert ha dew vargh-kert rag y halya adrus an onen ma." (I am always right. Jack is providing a chariot and seven white horses to haul him across the other world and we are providing a cart and two old cart-horses to haul him across this.)

Barg grinned, although he couldn't quite make sense of her words:

"Mar qureta leverel yndella." (If you say so.)

"My a wra leverel yndella," she murmured, smothering him with kisses and caresses. (I do say so)

He had to admit that Piran's equanimity was beyond question: he was a great suckler, a great sleeper, a great smiler; his fingers and toes were enfolded in antiquity, his eyes illuminated by eternity. Being totally ignorant about babies, Barg might have assumed that

160

they all suckled and slept with the same regularity, that they were all suffused with the same serenity, but he'd been assured by Carla that this was far from the case. Of course, her explanation was more mundane than Moira's: it was just a matter of pot-luck.

The relationship between the two women had gone through many hoops, the most recent of which still crackled with painful fire. Carla had argued vehemently against their intention to re-emigrate, calling Moira 'irresponsible' and 'deluded' and finding herself called, in eventual retaliation, 'jealous' and 'negative'. They were now estranged. Barg was now a buffer between them. Carla, at first apoplectic at the accusation of envy, had today confessed to him that their togetherness did accentuate her loneliness, that she sometimes felt like an intruder in her own home, particularly since Jude had moved out and English had become a minority-language. So there were no selfish motives behind her opposition to their plans. She feared for Piran's physical health. She feared for Moira's mental health. Lots of mothers, especially late-bearing mothers, 'think the world' of their offspring; few weave such an elaborate and dangerous myth around them. Barg had carried on sanding while she showered him with strictures. He noticed that he felt resentful of her presence in the workshop and wondered with a silent chuckle whether this feeling belonged originally to Luke. He only turned his head to respond after she'd mentioned the word 'myth'. He quietly declared that she was taking the wrong tack, that he'd never known anyone saner than Moira, that they needed to get back to their homeland, that they were misfits down here. Whatever had happened to them had happened forever. If she saw it the way they saw it, as true, then her objections would become groundless. He didn't usually talk like this and she didn't usually listen like this – without interrupting. She seemed to be staring at the grimy apron he was wearing. Her eyes were beginning to bulge with tears.

He stopped speaking when he noticed her condition. She swayed for a few moments, then fell forward into him. He put his arms around her to prevent her from further collapsing to the floor. She smelled strongly of rose-musk and garlic. The rose went straight to his libido. A huge wave broke above him, swamping him in sorrow and guilt for all the hurt he'd caused her by cutting himself off from her forever. He heard himself groan. She raised her head and began to kiss him blindly on the mouth. He reached down from eternity to reciprocate. Their tongues became indistinguishable. His fingers plunged avidly into her buttocks. She tore herself away and jumped back, her eyes aghast. She screamed at him, asking what the hell he was playing at. He frowned. He couldn't help glancing out of the window to check that Moira wasn't in the garden. After removing a Stanley-knife from the pouch, he untied the apron and handed it to her, blaming it, apologising for having worn it. She accepted the explanation with a limp wave of her hand. He didn't need to expand. He didn't need to tell her that his body had been under dual-control, nor how differently things might have gone if he'd been usurped completely. If Luke had burst into his cockpit and knocked him out, her marriage might even now be resurrecting itself on the floor of the workshop and he himself would have nothing to remember and nothing to feel remorseful about. Because there had been definite desire on his part, hard to believe as he looked at her now - wan, deflated and severely disturbed, nestling the apron against her cheek. He couldn't do anything to console her, so he was relieved when she turned without a word and departed, still clutching the apron. He resumed sanding down the chair he'd recently repaired. He liked it out here. She'd presented him with the key a week or so after their arrival, having learned of his interest in woodwork, an interest he'd managed to maintain throughout his service career. Most of the stations he'd been posted to had possessed a workshop he could use when he wasn't flying or drinking or playing bridge or philandering. He'd specialised in labour-intensive objects such as inlaid jewellery-boxes which fellow-officers would buy off him for a nominal sum to give to their wives. This pastime was the only connection he'd retained with his past, his father and many of his uncles having been joiners. He'd quickly repudiated all other family-feelings once he'd received his wings. When asked by others or by himself about the wisdom of such a schism he would point to nature, where as soon as you can fly properly you fly away and never return.

* * *

Early on the morning of departure, Barg had already packed Carla's car with sacks of oats and millet and cartons of fruit-juice - these provisions intended strictly for Piran, to enable him to bridge the gap between breast and rabbit. The mid-September day promised many hours of sunshine once its mists had dissipated. He went upstairs for a final shave. Moira called him into their room:

"*Nyns yw ef compes.*" (He's not right.)

His little nose was oozing, his eyes weeping, his cheeks flaming, his forehead boiling, his throat whimpering. This complex of symptoms was unprecedented. Postponement was unavoidable. The women took him to the doctor. (They'd become fully reconciled the night before, during the course of what should have been their last supper together.) Barg, left alone, felt himself in limbo, felt himself unhinged, wished he'd gone with them. He drifted out to the workshop; gazed vacantly down over the garden; began to sharpen a quarter-inch chisel which was already quite sharp enough. Yesterday he'd said farewell to this weird hiatus in his life. He'd found renovation congenial, worryingly so, since it had involved a negation of himself: taking over a dead man's job, restoring the work of other dead men. He couldn't contemplate starting anything new now, but if they did have to stay on there was still plenty for him to do. He'd managed to clear about half the backlog which Luke had left. Carla had sold most of the pieces on to other dealers, keeping a few for her own shop. As far as their 'board and lodging' were concerned, she'd been content with the income his efforts had realised. Apparently, Luke's contribution had flagged in the months leading up to his end: he'd produced less and less, although spending more and more time cooped up out here.

He ran back to the house as soon as he heard them return. Moira, smiling, handed the baby over. Barg cradled him tenderly, looked down into those blue-beyond eyes and wanted to weep. He hadn't known how anxious he'd felt. The diagnosis was uncertain: by the time they'd been admitted into the doctor's presence the symptoms had disappeared. Moira put her arms around him, lightly sandwiching Piran between breast and chest.

"Mmm," she cooed, glissando.

"I may as well go and open up," said Carla.

They disembraced at once, but she'd already grabbed her bag and gone, leaving behind a whiff of hostility which made their noses twitch, which made them frown with regret: wrapped up in their trinity, they'd offended her again.

Next morning, Moira announced a new dispensation. She was sitting up in bed, Piran serenely suckling from her right breast. Barg, still prone, pressed against her left flank, his right arm around her waist, his left index finger gripped with slowly oscillating pressure by the baby's right hand. She now realised that yesterday's episode had constituted a veto rather than an indication of susceptibility. Given that Piran was unable to articulate his wishes into words, how else could he so effectively have prevented their departure? She proposed that they extend the postponement indefinitely. When he was old enough to do so, he would tell them when they should return. Meanwhile, she saw no reason why they couldn't stay down here and at the same time stay true. She had it all worked out. Winter-lets were now becoming available. They could still live as devoutly and as frugally as they'd intended. He could carry on working here. She could, if necessary, resume her old profession of counsellor. She was sure she'd still be able to act the part, even if she no longer believed in the precepts. They would have Rhiannon to live with them. She was still in a bad way, had hardly stirred from her room in Demelza's house for months. If Terp ever turned up, he'd be welcome too. It was right they took some responsibility for those whose lives had been wounded on their behalf.

Barg merely grunted when she asked him what he thought. All this revolution had been a lot to take in when still only half-awake. She elbowed his shoulder. He sat up and shrugged:

"Pypynak a leveryth ta." (Whatever you say.)

* * *

Later that same week, 'Tim' at last appeared. It was early evening. Barg had just collected a heavy and elaborately ugly desk from the garage. He didn't respond when asked if Moira was in. He put down the desk; straightened his back; stared; scowled.

"Did you hear me?" said the other man, coming closer.

Barg was repelled by the smell of his deodorant, by the smoothness of his face and hair and clothes, by the shiftiness of his eyes.

"*Ke hag omgyjya ganso,*" he muttered, gesturing towards the front door. (Shove it up your arse.)

Not wanting to see them together, he walked away, out onto the road. A smug and opulent car sat there. He was just about to give it a kick when Carla drew up.

"He's here, is he?" she said.

"Yeah... I'm leaving them to it."

"Fancy a drink?"

He got in beside her.

"Did you meet him, then?" she asked, as they pulled away.

"Sort of... I didn't like him."

"Oh, nobody likes Tim."

"I'm not happy about it."

"I wouldn't worry. Her money set them up in the first place. If she took him to court she'd get a hell of a lot more than she's asking for and he knows that... Anyway, good news – I've found a nice place for you. Vacant from this weekend. It's virtually on the moor."

"Great," he muttered, monotonously.

"I thought you'd be pleased. I put a lot into getting it for you – the owners didn't really want children."

"I'm sorry. Thanks a lot. We owe you so much... I wonder if I should have left them together... What if he attacks Piran?"

"Don't be silly. Even if he wanted to he wouldn't be able to. Moira's much stronger than he is."

They pulled in to the pub car-park. His pockets were empty. She passed him a twenty-pound note.

"You order them. I'll pay for them. I sold the Queen Anne table today."

In the five months since their descent he'd hardly touched a drop of alcohol. Now, he sank a pint and half the refill before she'd managed a sip. They sat down side by side, their backs to the wall.

"I need something stronger," he decided, fetching himself a large Scotch.

He was drinking to destroy 'Tim', to throw him off the bridge he was building between himself and Moira and drown him in the blackness below.

"He's a bloody worm."

"That's right," soothed Carla. "You've got nothing to worry about."

"Who's worried... He's a seedless wonder."

"I don't know about that," she laughed. "He had children of his own before he met Moira."

This information created a hole just large enough for the first real doubt to slither into his mind. Perhaps 'Tim' was fertile after all. Perhaps his seed was just slow in germinating.

"What's the longest pregnancy you've ever heard of?"

"I don't know. Twelve months?"

"That would just about cover it."

"Oh, don't be so ridiculous. For a start, she stopped sleeping with him long before she disappeared. Then what about all the years before that when she couldn't conceive?"

He suddenly buried his face in her neck. She, mistaking his gesture for anguish, put her arm round him and emitted a compassionate hum from her diaphragm.

"Stay like this for a minute," he whispered. "Those two who've just come in. I know them."

This was an event he'd vaguely dreaded. Peering through Carla's hair, he saw the navigator and his wife sit down opposite, he with a half-pint mug, she with a minuscule sherry schooner.

"How well do you know them?"

"Too well. I used to play bridge with him. And I once played poker with her."

Having chuckled at his own joke, he peeked at the wife again and wondered how he could ever have fancied her. Her face was flaccid, her body stout, her aura stultifying. He couldn't remember their surname, or either of their Christian names.

"We can't stay like this until they leave," murmured Carla. "They're looking at the menu now."

"Fuck it," he said, sitting up straight and exposing his face. "Why the hell am I hiding? If they say anything I'll just deny who they think I am. I wouldn't even be lying, would I? The person I was isn't just officially dead."

"I see what you mean... Do you never have any regrets?"

"None. The only thing I miss is the jet-engine."

Tipsiness now expressed itself in a slight stumble when he went back to the bar, in an irresistible impulse for mischief. While waiting for the refills he'd ordered, he returned the astonished stare of the navigator's wife. She tentatively smiled at him. He grinned broadly back. She nudged her husband, who glanced up from the menu, shook his head and muttered something to her.

"I'm sorry for staring," she said, as he passed on his way back to Carla. "But you look the spitting image of someone we used to know."

Barg shrugged:

"Yth of vy bargos," (I am a buzzard.)

"Pardon?"

"Yth os ta eskelly-grehyn." (You are a bat.)

"Sorry. I still can't make out what you're saying."

"He doesn't speak much English," interjected Carla.

Barg turned towards her, opened his mouth wide to show his glee, then sat back down at her side.

"What language is he speaking?"

"Breton," said Carla, blithely. "He's just over here on holiday."

"Degol," nodded Barg. (Holy day.)

"Same with us. We love this part of the world."

The navigator kept his head down, drummed his fingers on the table, plainly longing for the embarrassment to end. Barg empathised with him: why should he have to acknowledge anyone he didn't want to acknowledge? No doubt his wife was always initiating acquaintanceships on pretexts just as flimsy as the vague resemblance between some scruffy Breton peasant and a dead pilot whose career had once intersected with his for a few months. Barg chuckled at this insight: not only did it strike him as hilarious; it also implied that his own safety was guaranteed.

Carla's bag began to bleep. She excavated her cell-phone:

"... He's with me... He's fine... At the pub... Alright... We'll be back soon."

'Tim' had gone for good.

They emptied their glasses and stood up.

"Bye," said Carla. "Enjoy your holiday."

Barg held out his hand to the navigator's wife. She took it and shook it. He delved hard into her eyes. When the handshake ended, he left a definite caress upon her palm.

"Muer ras a'n cof," he murmured, delighted to see her blush. (Thanks for the memory.)

Her husband was now compelled to accept Barg's hand, to make their first eye-contact.

"Un askel yw gwell ages askel vyth." (One wing is better than none.)

The navigator coughed; nodded; hitched up the corners of his mouth into an effigy of a smile. Following Carla to the door, Barg heard, or thought he heard:

"Bloody French. Always shaking hands. What's the matter with them?"

Outside, he caught up with her, squeezed her shoulders from behind and whooped.

* * *

Snow had just settled for the first time this winter. Moira had taken the baby out to acquaint him with *gwynder an bys* (worldly whiteness). Bargos had stayed behind to mind the fire. He was sitting in an armchair, in a stupor, in the middle of a Sunday afternoon. The logs kept spitting loudly, maliciously, yanking him back from dream. He would scan the carpet for embers before drifting away again, but when he also heard floorboards groaning above his head he became completely and anxiously alert: Rhiannon might be getting up.

She'd recently relapsed, clogging the cottage with oppressive vapours. For a couple of months they'd believed she was on the mend. She'd obeyed the rules Moira had imposed, rising early and staying awake all day, contributing unsullenly to the chores, participating unsceptically in the rituals. She'd begun to smell and look better. Then the other evening something someone said had sparked an astounding tantrum, during which her jealousy and hatred of Piran, her envy and hatred of Moira, were obscenely revealed. She'd retreated to her room and, without apparent sustenance, had been there ever since.

He heard the stairs being descended, the kitchen being entered, crockery being broken. Only when he felt a current of icy air around his ankles did he reluctantly get up to investigate. Wearing nothing more than a night-dress, she stood in the open doorway looking out. A plate lay disintegrated across the flagstone floor. He tiptoed around the shards and gently took hold of her.

"Ergh," she sobbed. (Snow)

"You'll catch your death," he predicted, pulling the back-door shut and ushering her through to the fire.

She actively clung to him now, pressing her pubic bone against his leg in a manner he found both inappropriate and unconvincing. He prised her away. She let out a little anguished squeal and scurried from the room. Hearing the back-door slam he returned to the kitchen, to see her footprints leading up the garden and her crawling through the hedge.

"Great," he muttered, pulling on his boots.

She was easy to track, difficult to catch up with. She'd fled across the adjoining field, climbed the stone wall and jumped onto the moor proper. He ran flat out for another few hundred yards, only slowing when the stitch in his left side became too painful to override. The trail was now also marked by pink stains in the snow. At first he thought she must have cut her feet on submerged edges of granite, but as he stumbled further the stains became darker, indicating heavier falls of blood. Believing she'd grabbed a knife on her way through the kitchen and was wantonly wounding herself, he accelerated, bellowing her name.

She lay face down in a drift. The blood was coming from her womb. He picked her up, staggered over to a jutting rock and crouched against it. She was definitely breathing, apparently unconscious. He removed her icy soaking night-dress, his own jumper, shirt and vest; wrapped her up as best he could; set off back.

"Na ge. Ny a'gan bues ethom ahanas yn bys ma," he implored, hardly knowing what he was saying. (Do not go. We need you in this world.)

Despite the oncoming dusk, he felt confident enough to take his own route, bypassing the thick tufts and deep snow which she'd led him through. Even when a fresh blizzard began he bounded on unhesitatingly, marvelling at the funds of stamina and surefootedness available. She seemed so light in his arms now. If she'd been his own infant daughter he couldn't have felt more concern.

The old story about travelling in a circle while imagining a straight line lurked threateningly in the back of his mind, yet here, far sooner than he'd expected, was the stone wall materialising through the blizzard; and there, not ten feet away, were the fast-disappearing tracks they'd made earlier. He marvelled at such accurate navigation without visibility or instruments, felt sure it must signify a good outcome. The steam rose from his bare shoulders. His breathing was quiet and slow. He laid her on top of the wall while he clambered over. Five minutes later, they were home.

Moira was on her knees, resuscitating the fire. Without a word, they immediately swapped roles: he deposited his burden on the settee and took over the bellows; she fetched blankets and towels, then stripped, rubbed and wrapped Rhiannon. Meanwhile, the logs were beginning to bluster. He pulled the settee towards the hearth. Moira reappeared with a cup. She cradled Rhiannon into a semi-sitting position and began spooning drops of warm honeyed water between her lips.

"Yth yw an kenso prys hy gos dhe dhevera aban gasa an wlasva," she murmured.. (This is the first time her blood has flowed since she left the settlement.)

"Ah."

A gurgle from the armchair told them Piran was awake. Barg picked him up and held him tight.

Printed in the United Kingdom
by Lightning Source UK Ltd.
117731UKS00001B/44